black heart

# Intersections in Communications and Culture

Global Approaches and Transdisciplinary Perspectives

Cameron McCarthy and Angharad N. Valdivia
*General Editors*

Vol. 12

PETER LANG
New York • Washington, D.C./Baltimore • Bern
Frankfurt am Main • Berlin • Brussels • Vienna • Oxford

*Phillip M. Richards*

# black heart

*the moral life of recent
african american letters*

PETER LANG
New York • Washington, D.C./Baltimore • Bern
Frankfurt am Main • Berlin • Brussels • Vienna • Oxford

**Library of Congress Cataloging-in-Publication Data**

Richards, Phillip M.
Black heart: the moral life of recent African American letters / Phillip M. Richards.
p. cm. — (Intersections in communications and culture; v. 12)
Includes bibliographical references and index.
1. American literature—African American authors—History and criticism—
Theory, etc. 2. African Americans—Intellectual life—20th century. 3. Criticism—
United States—History—20th century. 4. Literature and morals—History—
20th century. 5. African Americans in literature. 6. Moral conditions
in literature. 7. Ethics in literature. I. Title. II. Series.
PS153.N5R53   810.9'896073'0904—dc22   2005015548
ISBN 0-8204-7122-4
ISSN 1528-610X

Bibliographic information published by **Die Deutsche Bibliothek**.
**Die Deutsche Bibliothek** lists this publication in the "Deutsche
Nationalbibliografie"; detailed bibliographic data is available
on the Internet at http://dnb.ddb.de/.

Cover design by Sophie Boorsch Appel

The paper in this book meets the guidelines for permanence and durability
of the Committee on Production Guidelines for Book Longevity
of the Council of Library Resources.

© 2006 Peter Lang Publishing, Inc., New York
275 Seventh Avenue, 28th Floor, New York, NY 10001
www.peterlangusa.com

All rights reserved.
Reprint or reproduction, even partially, in all forms such as microfilm,
xerography, microfiche, microcard, and offset strictly prohibited.

Printed in the United States of America

Whoever has an ambition to be heard in a crowd must press, and squeeze, and thrust, and climb with indefatigable pains, till he has exalted himself to a certain degree of altitude above them. Now, in all assemblies, though you wedge them ever so close, we may observe this peculiar property, that over their heads there is room enough; but how to reach it is the difficult point, it being as hard to get quit of number as of hell.

"—Evadere ad auras, Hoc opus, hic labor est."

To this end the philosopher's way in all ages has been by erecting certain edifices in the air; but whatever practice and reputation these kind of structures have formerly possessed, or may still continue in, not excepting even that of Socrates when he was suspended in a basket to help contemplation, I think, with due submission, they seem to labour under two inconveniences. First, that the foundations being laid too high, they have been often out of sight and ever out of hearing. Secondly, that the materials being very transitory, have suffered much from inclemencies of air, especially in these north-west regions.

—Jonathan Swift*

---

* Jonathan Swift, "A Tale of a Tub: With Other Early Works: 1696–1707," in *The Prose Writings of Jonathan Swift*, ed. Herbert Davis (Oxford: Basil Blackwell, 1957), 2-3.

# Contents

*Acknowledgments* . . . . . . . . . . . . . . . . . . . . . . . . . . . . . . . . . . . . . ix
*Preface* . . . . . . . . . . . . . . . . . . . . . . . . . . . . . . . . . . . . . . . . . . . . . xi

Introduction: Through the Looking Glass . . . . . . . . . . . . . . . . . . 1

**Section One: Signifiers and Signifying** . . . . . . . . . . . . . . . . . . 23
Chapter One
    Gates' Cultural Synthesis: A Revived African-American
    Critical Practice. . . . . . . . . . . . . . . . . . . . . . . . . . . . . . . . . . 25
Chapter Two
    The Proof of the Pudding: Reading Gates; Reading
    Sterling Brown. . . . . . . . . . . . . . . . . . . . . . . . . . . . . . . . . . 57
Chapter Three
    Gates' Criticism and Middle-Class African-American
    Taste: A Tradition of Firsts . . . . . . . . . . . . . . . . . . . . . . . . . 71

**Section Two: Theory and Sensibility** . . . . . . . . . . . . . . . . . . . . 83
Chapter Four
    Signifying as Romantic Myth of Origins: An African-
    American Religion. . . . . . . . . . . . . . . . . . . . . . . . . . . . . . . . 85
Chapter Five
    Michael Eric Dyson's *I May Not Get There with You*:
    The True Martin Luther King, Jr. . . . . . . . . . . . . . . . . . . . . 105
Chapter Six
    Black Literary Criticism Meets Black Realities . . . . . . . . . . . 115

**Section Three: Signifying as Cultural Explanation** . . . . . . . . 127
Chapter Seven
    Moll Flanders in LA . . . . . . . . . . . . . . . . . . . . . . . . . . . . . . 129

Chapter Eight
  Toni Morrison and the Romance of Signifying ............ 135
Chapter Nine
  White Patrons, Black Clients, and Middle-Class
  Apocalypse............................................. 147

**Section Four: Older Exemplars** ........................ 155
Chapter Ten
  Theology and Black Literature: The Early Work of
  Benjamin Mays ........................................ 157
Chapter Eleven
  Robert Hayden: The Poet as Cosmopolitan Historian ...... 171
Chapter Twelve
  Earlier Integrated Worlds: Langston Hughes and
  Charles Chesnutt...................................... 183

**Section Five: A Marxist Humanism and Literacy** ........ 195
Chapter Thirteen
  Angela Davis as Cultural Critic ....................... 197
Chapter Fourteen
  Adolph Reed: Politics of Gesture...................... 205

Conclusion............................................. 209

*Notes* ............................................... 217
*Bibliography* ........................................ 233
*Index* ............................................... 243

# Acknowledgements

IT IS A PLEASURE TO ACKNOWLEDGE THE HELP and support of the following individuals and institutions in the writing of the essays which compose this book. I benefited greatly from a year at The National Humanities Center, particularly from the attentions of the then directors, W. Robert Connors and Kent Mullikan. I cannot thank either enough for their contribution to my work and my family's comfort during the Center year. I am not alone in my idebtedness to them. Glenn Loury of Boston University made me at home and stimulated my thinking at Boston University's Institute on Race and Social Division. I have also been guided by a series of remarkable editors. Cameron McCarthy and Damon Zucca at Peter Lang courageously took on the task of helping me write this book. Long before, I benefited from the advice of Michael Walzer at *Dissent*, Neil Kozodoy, and Gabriel Schoenfeld at *Commentary*, Jules Chametzky at *Massachusetts Review* and Curtis Conroy at *The Journal of Blacks in Higher Education*. I am deeply grateful to Charles Long, Kenneth Warren, and Linck Johnson for thoughtfully reading these essays at many stages and sharing their broad knowledge of American culture with me.

Finally, I would like to thank my wife Louisa Armstrong Richards who read drafts endlessly, encouraged, prodded, criticized, pursued a fruitful career, ran a household, raised children and created a home in Washington D.C., Arkansas, Central Africa, North Carolina, New York, and diverse other points along the way.

· · · · · · · · · · · · · · ·

I would like to acknowledge the following publications for permission to reprint *The Massachusetts Review*, *The American Scholar*, *The Times Literary Supplement*,

*Journal of Blacks in Higher Education*, and *Commentary*. "The Diver". Copyright © 1962, 1966 by Robert Hayden, "Electrical Storm", "Elegies for Paradise Valley". Copyright © 1978 by Robert Hayden from COLLECTED POEMS OF ROBERT HAYDEN by Robert Hayden, edited by Frederick Glaysher. Copyright © 1985 By Emma Hayden. Used by permission of Liveright Publishing Corporation; Journal of Blacks in Higher Education; "Robert Hayden (1913-1980); An Appreciation," by Phillip Richards. Reprinted by permission from The Massachusetts Review, Volume 40, Number 4; "The Conjure Man" September 2002 and "Signifying", June 1998. Reprinted from COMMENTARY, September 2002 and June 1998, by permission; all rights reserved; Times Literary Supplement; "Black Romantic: A Review, The American Scholar, Volume 72, No. 3, Summer 2003. Copyright © by Phillip M. Richards

# Preface

Arriving at Yale in the fall semester of 1968, I immediately encountered the newly segregated world of integrated life: dining room tables unofficially appropriated by black students, residential college entryways assigned by race, and informal gatherings limited to black students seemed to appear everywhere I turned. Words still fail to express my horror. I came to New Haven hoping to find a cosmopolitan intellectual world beyond the black bourgeois institutions I had known in Cleveland. Instead, the noisy emptiness of Antioch Baptist and Alexander Hamilton Junior High had followed me to the Ivy League. Wherever one went in academic black New Haven, the pulsing melodies of rhythm-and-blues and the suave cynicism of street slang were not far behind. During my sophomore year, it would become fashionable to bring black ghetto teenagers to one's residential college dining hall, where the inner-city young men took up plates and dined like Yalies. It was not clear, however, who was patronizing whom in this academic game of confused status. The slum youths eagerly moved through the line, making the most of a free meal, taking as much of whatever they pleased. As it turns out, however, they were setting the cultural standard to which their hosts would aspire. Their brashness raised the bar for African-American student effrontery at Yale. Whatever their cultural nationalist aspirations, black working- and middle-class Yale students had to work especially hard to keep up with their newly made friends from the Hillhouse ghetto. I was out of this competition before it began; and I held it in nearly speechless contempt. I quickly learned to avoid Black Studies classes, those all-black enclaves filled with leather jackets, black berets, and the oily smell of the ghetto. I despised the middle-class Negro appropriation of this pop-cultural nationalism, the ideological nexus that had fueled Cleveland's riots in 1964 and 1966, costing black, inner-city youth—like those in the dining halls—their lives, and getting many of my black classmates into Yale.

Let me admit now that I soon became isolated and lonely; the reminders of my black junior high world soon called me with an erotic force. For all that, I shunned them even more. I avoided the new African-American enclaves like the plague. I fled them as my parents had fled the encroaching ghetto in Glenville, Mt. Pleasant, Lee-Harvard, and finally Cleveland Heights. Indeed I remember seeing few, if any, black classmates in the series of literature and language courses that formed the core of my Yale education.

In hindsight, of course, I had it all wrong. The appeal of the black ethos I fled proved irresistible to nearly everyone else in New Haven. Gifted and charming to begin with, my cohort of black fellow students succeeded remarkably. Many were tapped for Yale's exclusive secret societies four years later, when the school's academic and social elite sifted my class's grain from its chaff. Their success would continue. Two of my black classmates would become Rhodes scholars and later successful lawyers. As they began to pursue success, an older talented group of black Yalies was already making its way. Armstead Robinson would become a distinguished historian at the University of Virginia. Glen De Chabert would take up law and enter the entertainment business. Many people I shunned (and who shunned me) would become successful attorneys, skilled physicians, and influential business people.

My contempt for Black Studies proved even more misguided. The work and scholarly example of Roy Bryce-La Porte, John Blassingame, and Houston Baker became the cutting edge of a new academic movement. Black Studies would thrive at Yale, attract Charles Davis as a director, and nourish the careers of Robert Stepto and Cornel West. Just two or three years later, I confronted their work as a graduate student, roaming the stacks of the University of Chicago's Regenstein Library on Friday and Saturday nights, my first and only course in African-American Studies.

I correctly disapproved, however, of the easy consensus that linked the Yale blacks' rhythm-and-blues nationalism to the upper-class liberalism of the school's white student elite. The two groups were engaged not in integration, but rather in *Realpolitik* segregation that acknowledged the possibility of a shared interracial political life but prohibited social and cultural exchange across the boundaries of race. The two groups combined as oil and water, rarely mixing fraternally or romantically, but functioning together as fingers on the hand in all things strategically vital. They observed and respected each other's political turf in ways that anticipated the *de facto* segregated society of today's multicultural university. African-American Studies—a product of this social movement—yielded its best scholars an important intellectual payoff in the form of new points of view that enriched historical and sociological interpretation. However, that academic movement— and the social phenomenon of which it was a part—also tended to reinforce and extend the culturally parochial aspect of black middle-class life that I came to Yale to escape. I was not the only loser in this. The academic and institutional initiatives of African-American Studies encouraged many black students and faculty to escape the diversity of viewpoints by which one interrogates oneself and achieves self-consciousness.

I am now a tenured English professor at a selective liberal arts college in what is called the diverse academy. I am, despite my intentions, part of the segregated apparatus of American academic life, the same one I feared and fled at Yale. In retrospect, I understand that the current academic apartheid of the humanities emerged from the interracial, cultural entente hammered out thirty years ago in New Haven. I have always agreed to teach African-American literature, implicitly passing as a black cultural nationalist whenever hired (at better and better posts) to teach early American culture. I review books and referee articles on African-American topics in my period specialty. Nevertheless, I observe the widening influence of the black sub-disciplines in the humanities with ambivalence. As I write these pages, I am teaching African-American literary texts in a French university, where black American writing has enormous appeal to remarkably literate French, African, Algerian, Chinese, and Dutch students. The spread of this racially segregated academic culture among Third World peoples in Europe and Asia is a matter of deep concern for me. This development does not bode well for the life of colored intellectuals beyond America.

Equally disturbing has been the stateside university career of the new black sensibility as it presently swallows African-American literary culture whole. The middle-class evangelical mores of sentimental novels by Hannah Crafts and Harriet Wilson are now considered appropriate matter for serious study, although they attracted no such attention when they were thought to have been either the entire or partial work of white authors.[1] Feeble literary productions of black women—such as the essays of Ann Plato and novels such as *Our Nig*—have become ur-texts of a new black canon. Only recently have I reread them, still surprised that anyone might consider them serious literature of any provenance. Having fallen into the profession of black letters, I found myself struggling to find an intellectual clearing. These essays, written over the last ten years, represent an attempt to land on my feet.

I

Many of this book's chapters began as essay-reviews written for *Dissent*, *Commentary*, *The Journal of Blacks in Higher Education*, *The American Scholar*, *The Times Literary Supplement*, and *The Massachusetts Review*. Some started life as talks, grew into papers, and later became essays—published or unpublished. As I began to take the measure of current African-American literary-critical work, I inquired into its dominant interpretive methods and style. Dissatisfied with the cultural production of my contemporaries, I sought intellectual exemplars among the earlier black writers I discovered in the stacks of Regenstein. My disappointment with the failures of present-day black literary criticism led me to a reconsideration of an older group of black artists and scholars—Robert Hayden, Benjamin Mays, Charles Chesnutt, and Langston Hughes—authors whom I have always admired. The intellectual norms I discerned in their work finally provided me with a fuller understanding of the contemporaries I valued most: Angela Davis and Adolph Reed.

I have organized this book around an inquiry, which began with a look at the strategies and methods of signifying, particularly those of Henry Louis Gates Jr. This examination accounts for my analysis of both Gates and his extended critical family—its distant cousins, the black theologians Will Coleman and Dwight Hopkins, as well as nearer kin such as cultural critics Karla Holloway and Michael Dyson. Reflections on these writers and their work helped shape my understanding of Toni Morrison novels *Sula* and *Paradise*—fictions that moved me quite differently—as well as of the film *Glory*. The last three works represent both the powers and limitations of the critical style and sensibility that expresses itself in signifying. This book's next section pays homage to the now largely abandoned ancestors of our present age—Robert Hayden, Benjamin Mays, Langston Hughes, and Charles Chesnutt—all of whom incisively addressed the issues that now preoccupy contemporary black critics. The following section finds reasons for honoring the work of Angela Davis and Adolph Reed according to my new literary-historical insight. The conclusion returns the reader to our present-day cultural circus.

As I began to see African-American literary tradition in a perspective extending beyond the segregated academic world of sixties Yale, I discovered a great deal. I learned that the black awakening at Yale was a representative moment in American literary culture; and that the ethos of self-invention deployed by my black academic colleagues was a recognizably American style. Finally, my complaints against these developments identified me as a by-now archaic form of 1950s liberal. My horror was a kind of innocence, itself a form of historical ignorance. The literary and academic political stands I took only echoed earlier black literary traditions, ending just before the brave new world in New Haven began. At the end, I discovered the error of my own exceptionalism. Like the black separatists, I had deceived myself into a sense of uniqueness. As I wrote these pieces, I not only recovered history but found my place in it.

There exist, nevertheless, good reasons to recount my cultural journey. The black American middle class rarely engages in sustained introspection. Consider how few letters and private papers have been collected from the most famous black writers or political figures. My friend, the late novelist, playwright, and actor Julian Mayfield, often recalled that W. E. B. Du Bois consistently complained about the paucity of writing by black men. We live now in an era in which relatively large numbers of black writers have flocked to the criticism of black texts. Whatever final judgment one makes of what recent black critics have written, their large body of textual commentary possesses a significance in and of itself. Few forms of writing reveal a writer so completely as literary interpretation. What one chooses to notice, explain, judge, or ignore in a work often tells the careful reader as much about the commentator as the fiction, poetry, or essay at hand. As black critics have asserted their cultural and political impulses, they have narrowed their intellectual scope. This examination of black writing about African-

American literature has allowed me to scrutinize a form of black middle-class life that evades its own self-consciousness.

## II

Explicitly autobiographical texts such as *Colored People*, *Parallel Lives*, and *Black Ice* have not given us full, nuanced accounts of this generation's passage to adulthood in the hitherto segregated enclaves of white American society. We still lack, that is, an adequate account of the importance of Gates' brief, albeit successful, academic stay at Exeter, his interracial dating in a segregated West Virginia world, and the full consequences of his intellectual orientation during a "coloured" childhood. Neither Brent Staples' *Parallel Lives* nor John Wideman's *Brothers and Keepers* attempts to assess the full width and breadth of youthful experience, extending beyond Staples' response to his advisor's insults or the put-downs experienced by Wideman at the University of Pennsylvania. These writers clearly encountered broad intellectual vistas during their educations. What difference did those experiences make to them as intellectuals? Indeed, what difference did their lives as intellectuals make to their lives in general? Like much of the black autobiography and fiction of this period, both works respond to the trauma of individual and social loss. (Even Gates' memoir addresses the passing of a "coloured" world.) Yet, these separations (Wideman's work is an important exception here) rarely evoke the depth of self-examination that one expects from a sensitive writer's confrontations with disaster. Given this evasiveness, this recent criticism of African-American literature may constitute authentic intellectual autobiography in an age when black writers do not write about their intellectual lives.

Predictably, the sentimentalist who evades autobiographical reflection often selects unsophisticated texts for criticism, exerting a ruthless will-to-power over them. This intellectual orientation is anomalous in the modernist and postmodernist era. Professional interpreters of literature in the late twentieth century have typically sought out allusive, self-reflexive, and hermetic works not only for academic self-display but to extend their reflections on culture and society. This impulse prompted the literary recoveries of important, but once undervalued, American writers such as F. O. Mathiessen writing on Melville or Philip Rahv and Lionel Trilling on Henry James. All the same, black critics now devote an extraordinary amount of print, paper, and time to writing which would have been considered sub-literary (in its simplicity) by conventional academic standards fifty years ago. The recent black feminist drift to aesthetically mediocre or deficient texts, such as the essays of Ann Plato, a nineteenth-century black evangelical, exemplifies this trend.

Plato's collection of essays would not have seemed exceptional to the author's nineteenth-century Protestant contemporaries: the work presents its audience with wholly typical biographies of pious women and discourses on religion. Nevertheless, this bland text has attracted aggressively expressed black feminist attention. In the last few years, this work has attracted commentary, and its stock has of late continued to rise.² Katherine Bassard, for instance, argues that Plato, like other early black women writers, addresses a hoped-for audience of future African-American female readers. Robert S. Levine finds her reading illuminating because it may signal the existence of a black literary origin near the start of American letters.³ Similarly, Farah Jasmine Griffith, another well-known student of early African-American literature, finds Bassard's work important for its extension of the vernacular paradigm beyond the realm of the folk into an early American discourse, untouched by Southern slave culture.⁴

For Levine and Griffith, Bassard's highly ideological readings of Wheatley and Plato become interesting because they make writers such as Plato symbolically "black." And this blackness may, through interpretive legerdemain, be used to find an African or African-American "element" in a "genealogical literary narrative"—which is to say, a myth of origins for American literature. If Plato's text is black, however, that blackness seems indistinguishable from the commonplaces of mid-nineteenth-century Protestant middle-class culture. In addition, Bassard's claims—and by extension those of Levine—attract notice because of the extremely naive character of Plato's account of her subject's piety:

> Julia Ann Pell was born at Montville, Connecticut, in the year 1813. She did not enjoy the privilege of living with her parents when a child. Her age did not exceed eight years, when she was sent to live with a family, where she served as an apprentice until she was eighteen. From thence she went to East Granby and lived some years in the family of the Pastor of that village, where she was much respected for her honesty, and stability of character.
> 
> In the year of 1836, she thought to benefit herself by coming to Hartford: she therefore was obliged to leave the family, who much regretted her loss. She remained in Hartford till the close of her life. She was esteemed for good behavior, and assistance in society; attending to the concerns of her own, and leaving alone those of others. She did not figure in the gay and more fashionable forms of society, nor had she any particular relish for those external attractions, which wear such an alluring aspect to the fashionist and votary of worldly pleasure.
> 
> While young she had not the advantages of a school education. Perhaps not attending school more than one or two days in a week. Yet, even then, it was her most eager desire to be a scholar, though fortune seemed to forbid it. She gained some of the rudiments of knowledge with great labor and difficulty; and Her perseverance was put to a most severe trial.
> 
> The years of her childhood being spent in the country, she had less advantages of education than many. There being but one school, the scholars were quite numerous; and those whose station was inferior to many in the school, were neglected; their rights trampled upon, and their time abused.
> 
> She had a permanent regard for the Sabbath, and for religious services; attending both the Sabbath School, and divine worship three times upon that day. The intervals of worship, she spent in reading the Holy Scriptures, or religious books. She was exceedingly strict in her improvement of time. By rising early, she secured the best part of the day for her domestic employments, and for the necessary duties devolving upon her station. Simplicity of living and industrious habits, she particularly regarded; ornaments seldom known, among the nobility of a republic.
> 
> She took good care of all that was entrusted to her. Order she had practiced from a child, and she took delight in it. "A place for every thing and every thing

in its place," was one of her characteristics. Said she, "a constant habit of putting the same things in the same places, and performing the same duties at the same times, will always enable us to find what we want, and to do what is to be done, readily, pleasantly, and without any annoyance to others."

In the year of 1838, she became a member of the Church of Christ. The society of religious persons was very pleasant and agreeable to her; and to the end of her days she was anxious to live in the fear of God, and to walk before him with a humble heart. Her last sickness, which terminated in death, was painful in the extreme. She bore it with Christian patience. When physicians and friends had hopes of her recovery, said she, "I shall never recover." Under all trying circumstances, she enjoyed the sweet peace of the believer, founded on the Christian hope. When she had the smallest prospect of life, she seemed far from being alarmed with the view of her dissolution. She expressed her willingness either to live or die, as it should please Divine Providence. "If," said she, "I had any hopes of recovery, it would be my soul's desire to bring glory to the name of the Lord, proportionable to all the dishonor I have done Him, in my whole life: and particularly by endeavors to convince others of the danger of their condition, if they continue impenitent; and by telling them how graciously God has dealt with me."

All the faculties of her mind were perfect until the last. It is thought that few people see death approach them, as she did. In short, her death was like her life; easy, unaffected, and pious.

The morning that she died, she came down stairs with little help, and appeared to be gaining health. But such appearances are often deceptive. She sat down awhile, when she was persuaded to return to her room; she seemed to be unwilling, and said that she would like to sit awhile. She had grown weaker by leaving her room, and required much help to get back. When she reached her room, she threw herself upon her bed and exclaimed, "Never again shall I see, what I have seen."

Between six and seven in the evening, a friend went to her room, and said that she was going to hear a lecture on that evening. She expressed her willingness, and wished to have her repeat to her what she heard when she returned. The friend had not been long seated before some one called for her. Said she, "Is Julia dead?" It was indeed true. She had ceased to breathe. Thus she peacefully died, in the 27th year of her age, March 17th, 1839.[5]

The current attraction of this work for black feminist critics lies in its vulnerability to ideological manipulation. The simplicity of Plato's essays makes them easy targets for commentators defining a canon of black female-authored works written for black women. Plato's neglect of the theological and moral complexities scanned by Jonathan Edwards, Thomas Shepard, and Cotton Mather presents feminist critics with an important advantage. They have nothing to gain from an intellectual Christianity suspicious of sentimental motivations for community, psychologically shrewd about ethical self-deception, and skeptical toward untested personal revelation. Lacking the particular cultural elements that might test the ethical limits of black American feminists, Plato's text—as does much of Phillis Wheatley's poetry—easily fits into a vaguely defined African-American women's canon.[6] The satisfactions of these easily bullied texts, however, are purchased at a dear moral and intellectual price. The continued practice of such textual wrenching can only harden into a habitual act of bad faith which values writing for its pliability, its naiveté, or its immediate political usefulness. This bad faith presents African-American intellectuals with a professional and ultimately moral difficulty. The wish-fulfilling interpretation of such childish texts reveals the black critics' unwillingness to scrutinize their own assumptions and beliefs—which would be thrown into relief by more intellectually and aesthetically challenging work. This unwillingness to engage serious thinking seriously is an evasion of the inwardness and reflection that transpires in all serious reading. No true political, social, or ethical self-consciousness is possible, given this escapism.

## III

My doubts about Black Studies grew as I became aware of the movement's increasing ascendancy in the late sixties and early seventies. Both Robert Stepto and the distinguished Whitman scholar Charles Davis would be hired at Yale in 1973, the year after my graduation. My sense of the movement's oncoming flood may explain my presence in Larry Neal's seminar on black fiction during the fall semester of my senior year. I knew vaguely of Neal's literary politics from his poetry and essays. I thought of him as a Black Arts advocate like Maulena Karenga. Neal's appearance at Yale was a sobering hint that the movement's radical fringe had already entered the mainstream of academic life. I was even more surprised to learn that the National Endowment for the Humanities had sponsored the seminar, an affiliation that explained the presence of the young white assistant professor beside me—up from the South—to observe the emerging field of African-American writing. I was surprised to see Neal too, elegantly dressed in a glen-plaid sport coat and black turtleneck, urbanely chatting with the class participants who had already arrived. He was even then far more a part of the profession's black Ivy League world than I would ever be.

Having introduced himself to his audience, Neal launched into a rambling lecture, ostensibly locating African-American literature in Anglo-American cultural tradition. The speech was especially bizarre for a Yale English major, who in English 25 would have intensively studied the major poems of the English literary canon in strict chronological order. Neal haphazardly skipped through this literary history, making shocking mistakes for which any student would have been reprimanded by his probably untenured junior professor. By the end of five minutes, Neal had (according to my memory) misplaced the historical provenance of Chaucer, Spenser, and Dryden, among others. Horrified at this display, I determined to leave in a few minutes. But Neal's ramblings left me paralyzed, and I delayed ten minutes, noting as many mistakes. I have if anything underestimated my response to this performance, which shocked me in another way: it was the appearance of black cultural nationalist cynicism in a Yale English Department classroom. Neal simply didn't care about the dates of the poetical careers and literary works he discussed, although he was clearly an educated man, and wrote stimulating interpretations of Hurston, Ellison, and others.[7] What I took to be the freewheeling intellectual corruption of the ghetto—also the name of a black student entryway—had now entered literary studies at Yale, through the back door of the university's justly famous Department of English.

The dutiful response of the young professor in the next seat surprised me as much as Neal's chutzpah. Calmly and diligently, he listened, pencil poised to take more notes. What, I wondered, could he possibly be writing, for Neal's speech was empty of the information that I associated with the Yale English Department classroom. Although my New Critic teachers often spoke of a literary text as an isolated aesthetic object, they inevitably parsed its language into generic categories, definitions, rhetoric, and philosophical ideas before beginning the work of interpretation. To be sure, the pedagogical function of this historical, literary, and philological world had become somewhat unclear. It had, as the Yale New Critical school ebbed in influence, been wholly subordinated to the primary activity of textual explication. Neal's confusions—and by extension those of Black Studies—often (it must be said) echoed the growing dislocations of the then-doddering New Criticism. However, even the most severe formalist interpreters, whether at Yale or Chicago, discussed texts within a sphere of institutional wisdom: a historical, philological, and linguistic background that—as an institutional social knowledge—went unmentioned because it was so taken for granted.

The absence of this institutional wisdom was the most disturbing aspect of Larry Neal's discussion of Barry Beckham's *My Main Mother* (1969), a conventional (albeit then recent) novel of teenage initiation. Beckham's book, in the course of Neal's talk, floated free of the conventional aesthetic boundaries within which such a book was interpreted. In Neal's sphere of hitherto unexplored black literary tradition and disciplinary knowledge, *My Main Mother* took on the look of significant art, and the talk itself began to glow with the excitement of discovery. This excitement in turn buoyed the session's sense of the scholarly and intellectual validity that Neal had been careful to advertise by fiat at the course's introduction. Finally, this display went uncontested by trained literary scholars who, although they had little reason to take him seriously, were clearly as charmed as I.

Neal's performance as well as his white audience's acquiescence was a frequent ritual during my Yale career. Around the same time, a group of black students had stepped onto a podium while Edward Kennedy was speaking, interrupted him, and made a set of political demands of the university. Kennedy genteelly fell quiet, moved aside, and let the blacks continue. A graduate school friend, an alumna of a Southern black women's college, on one of our evening walks, discussed this event with especial contempt. "You, black Yale students," she sneered, "certainly know how to manipulate the white centers of power." Her sarcasm was to the point. The triumph had clearly gone to Kennedy, who through his forbearance won more prestige as a sensitive and thoughtful liberal than the students, whatever political case they were making. Kennedy's genteel yielding was an upper-class display of politeness that only real power—such as that embodied by his family—could sustain. What the blacks won in this event was symbolic presence in a world over which they had no real control. This manifestation was only the emptiest chimera of power, and was itself validated by the eminence (the Kennedys) which let it have its noisy say. Powerful families such as the Kennedys, of course, the Mellons, and the Rockefellers largely run America and they have no parallel in black life. That power had built the buildings in which black entryways such as "the Ghetto" were housed. The black revolution at Yale was run only with the good-humored acquiescence of this supremely powerful, wealthy white entity.

By the late 1960s, the upper-class world of the elite American university had become impressively distinguished and, in the process, cosmopolitan. It was a world that honored excellent Jewish, black, as well as WASP intellectuals with distinguished chairs. At the University of Chicago, Bard College, and New York University, Ralph Ellison had been so honored, on the basis of splendid literary accomplishment and exceptional learning. Although Ellison was not formally trained as a scholar, he had written formidable critical essays now enshrined in American literary tradition. Those essays gained their authority through a hard-won and elegantly articulated knowledge of literary tradition and its canons of rhetoric, literary convention, and cultural history.[8]

However, Neal's authority in the classroom was that enjoyed by the ghetto youngsters in the cafeteria—the slum kids who tutored Yale blacks in those shows of verbal power cultivated in the street. This was the empty cathartic authority wielded by the black students on stage with Kennedy. The university had during the previous three centuries seen many dislocated provincials. Yale was, ironically, far more attuned to the dislocations of mobility than the dislocated blacks themselves. Yale thus decided to tolerate these displays from its newest cohort of unsettled arrivistes. As a charismatic figure, Neal was the beneficiary of a related good-humored patronage by a great institution too powerful and sophisticated to be bothered by such a nuisance. Moreover, as part of the black newcomers' literary elite, he could be accepted into other elites, like the black student organizers tapped by the senior societies, the founders of Black Studies courses, and eventually black members of Yale's boards of trustees. Like all elites, the black elite must have a literary heritage. And Neal was the representative of the black cultural tradition now demanded by the youngest, most dislocated members of the university's newest upwardly mobile, middle class.

The admission of the black middle class to Yale's pantheon of literary studies exacted, however, a high price. In return for entrance into this elite cultural enterprise, black literary intellectuals gave up academic or intellectual claims to legitimacy according to the generic standards of traditional literary studies. The new black separateness like all such separation could never yield equality. This implicit contract had important implications. Literary study relies on institutional structures: canons of texts, traditions of aesthetic inquiry, systems of demonstrable rhetoric, and understandings of bibliographic method. As such, the profession of English depends on verifiable methodologies, bodies of knowledge, and, finally, a heritage of accumulated skills. These elements—and the sustained reading and analysis they implied—were often lacking in Neal's work, as they were in that of his Yale successors, Houston Baker and Henry Louis Gates.

In the wake of Neal's example, an often-abbreviated set of New Critical, semiotic, or deconstructive close readings soon became the format for a recognizable kind of African-American literary study. These *explications de texte* often laid the basis for paradigmatic statements, and sweeping canonical claims. This strategy characterized *Long Black Song* and *Figures in Black*, essay collections with which Baker and Gates announced their careers. This writing could be intellectually fruitful when Baker or Gates bore down on those textual particulars that Yale New Criticism or structuralism illuminated so well. Gates could draw thoughtfully on formalist, semiotic, and deconstructive paradigms to provide metaphors with which to discuss Jean Toomer's *Cane* and his career as well as Sterling Brown's folk poetry in *Southern Road*. Houston Baker initiated an important line of inquiry in his discussion of animal imagery in Frederick Douglass' 1845 *Narrative*. Indeed, Baker's chief academic importance would continue to rest largely on a few shrewd readings such as his interpretation of the Trueblood incident in Ellison's *Invisible Man*, Booker T. Washington's use of minstrel "darky" jokes in *Up from Slavery*, and economic themes in Zora Neale Hurston's *Their Eyes Were Watching God*. However, Baker and Gates had higher aims: they sought to enumerate the elements of a literary tradition and establish disciplinary paradigms. These attempts were rarely sustained by adequate example. Indeed, this freewheeling construction of tradition often suppressed important voices, texts, and authors in black writing. In a gesture that would become commonplace in the new African-American literary criticism, these interpretive moments were more notable for the critic's aggressively displayed will-to-power over the tradition itself, a will displayed in the deployment of a sweeping, commanding style as notable for what it excluded as for what it revealed.

Early on in their careers the rapid construction of a black canon seems to have become a first order of business for these critics. Baker and Gates sought to call a black literary tradition into being, but they inevitably courted failure when they attempted to find textual motifs, literary figures, and *topoi* that could encompass African-American literary tradition as a whole.[9] I take a glaring example of such methodology here in a passage from Gates:

> Out of Brown's realism, further, came Richard Wright's naturalism; out of his lyricism came Hurston's *Their Eyes Were Watching God*; his implicit notion that "De eye dat sees/Is de I dat be's" forms the underlying structure of *Invisible Man*. In his poetry, several somehow black structures of meaning have converted to form a unified and complex structure of feeling, a poetry as black as it is Brown.[10]

Brown's poetry—and apparently only his folk poetry—here becomes the origin of modern black literary tradition. Despite its inclusion of unquestionably significant writers, this high modernist, black literary moment has conspicuously excluded Langston Hughes, Gwendolyn Brooks, Robert Hayden, and James Baldwin. Brown's use of genre, style, and metaphor comes to constitute a plenitude from which the texts of Skip's canon emerged.[11] In moments such as this, African-American literary tradition was being reduced to a convenient myth of origins that resisted—as Gates resisted the traditional lyrics of *Southern Road*—what could not be easily assimilated into a new racial ideology defined in semiotic terms. Less talented imitators of Gates' interpretive methods only increased the damage done by his and Baker's inadequate literary-historical technique, producing even more tendentious historical constructions such as Karla Holloway's mythic female language or Michael Awkward's sparsely populated genealogy of black women's writing. As semiotic and deconstructive practice was carried out by ever less deft hands, notions such as "trace," displacement, and difference were employed in less discriminating ways. Literary texts were not so much explicated for their linguistic dynamics as examined for certain rhetorical figures, motifs, and themes, heedless of those resistant semiotic powers, by which significant writing challenges the application of any literary "approach." Gates' early subtle essays on Johnson, Toomer, and Sterling Brown did not serve as the benchmark for future criticism; the Yale signifiers tended to imitate Gates' language and stylistic flourishes rather than the acute sensibility informing the best writing in *Figures in Black*. In the process, much of black literature lost—in the hands of these new black critics—the thorny particularity that had drawn a new black readership to works like *Cane* and *Southern Road* in the first place. Despite much of the then-current talk about the adversary, resistant aspects of black culture, African-American writing often passed through the tracts of English studies unexamined by seriously cultivated sensibility.

In the rush to create a black canon, the complex historical, biographical, and bibliographical relationships of these African-American texts to American literary tradition were often forgotten. The new generation of black literary commentators started a scholarly conversation in African-American Studies that often ignored the important, more historically established work done by literary critics such as Sterling Brown, Saunders Redding, and Arthur P. Davis. Black critical studies in the subfield lost the intellectual depth and rigor of Brown's work on black characterization in American fiction, Redding's narrative describing the tradition's cultural energies and historical constraints, and Davis' well-documented portrait of major twentieth-century figures.[12] The black newcomers' work rarely attained the excellence of contemporaries like George Kent, Charles Davis, and Nathan Scott, who often remained unappreciated by white and black critics alike. Their work consistently drew upon an understanding of cultural, institutional, and literary aspects of the Anglo-American canon that authorized both their close readings and cultural generalizations. Kent's conception of "blackness" in modern African-American literary tradition was informed by an intellectual framework, based upon a cogent understanding of "tradition" and "movement," as well as data, careful explication, and historical inquiry. Charles Davis' work drew on his erudite recall of poetic tradition from the romantic to the Modernist periods and—like Kent's—upon the dynamics of literary tastes, ideologies, and aesthetics. Nathan Scott's work—though rarely touching on black writers—was grounded in a broad grasp of modern continental philosophy and literary modernism as well as an ability to discern theological issues within particular literary texts or authorial careers. Facile paradigms and a sparse set of readings cannot make a discipline or subfield. Without the literary, historical, and sociological understandings of figures such as Davis, Kent, and Scott, no literary-critical discourse—and surely not one recently invented by untested young black scholars—could be a legitimate academic undertaking.

The intellectual presence of African-American Studies emerged from a number of important archival projects. And here the fundamental work of collection, indexing, and encyclopedic writing was often done by white fellow travelers of the movement. Those excellent textual and bibliographical scholars—including William L. Andrews, Randall Burkett, and the late Richard Newman—were the real heirs of Benjamin Brawley, Carter G. Woodson, Charles Wesley, and Dorothy Porter; whatever importance is enjoyed by African-American literary studies is largely a product of their work. They helped create the major bibliographical and textual productions on which all serious literary study depends. Furthermore, as shown by Brown's comprehensive studies of American literary tradition, and the impressive documentation of Redding's *To Make a Poet Black*, the intellectual cutting edge of the older generation's work emerged from an encyclopedic recall of literary texts, historical events, and cultural documents. Few recent black critics have aimed at anything like the erudition that the new disciplinary movement required not only for legitimacy but also for interpretive power. Even while sponsoring important archival projects, Gates assumed the symbolic status of a power broker, a role he himself knowingly flaunts when he styles himself a scholarly impresario in his introduction to *The Bondwoman's Narrative*.[13] There, the reader sees Gates receiving news from the scholarly front as major scholars call him with new discoveries about his topic of inquiry. Above the actual dirty work of fact-finding, Gates oversees a host of distinguished literary historians parsing the hard documentary evidence provided by the historical record. Such arrangements, no one can fail to notice, frequently exist in post-colonial Third World countries, whose dictators ostensibly manage nation-states which are in fact directed by highly skilled technical advisors and administrators from the ex-colonial power.

The collapse of serious philological and historical inquiry by the most influential new black literary scholars had serious intellectual consequences for the growing subdiscipline. Powerful counter-themes have emerged within African-American Studies beneath the apparent notice of Gates and his company of signifying scholars. Underneath their dicta runs a historical continuity from American Protestantism to romanticism, the continuity implicit in well-documented studies by Dickson Bruce, Wilson Moses, and Carla Peterson, to name only the most important authors.[14] This scholarship shows the existence of a genteel Victorian elite that self-consciously cultivated traditional letters, engaged in serious political reflection, and adapted a Protestant-Victorian social identity. This continued up into the Harlem Renaissance and constitutes the cultural backdrop against which that epoch's most visible literary radicals such as Langston Hughes, Zora Neale Hurston, and Wallace Thurman take their stands. The central bearers and transmitters of this tradition include the African-American intellectual stratum whose members first encountered and appropriated black folk tradition, under the cultural influence of white abolitionist intellectuals such as John Greenleaf Whittier, Thomas Higgenson, Lucy McKim, and others. This pattern of influence was by no means unique to cultural observers such as Charlotte Forten Grimke. Indeed, nineteenth-century black writers such as Charles Chesnutt seem to show little interest in representations of folk culture as racial wisdom until the epoch of white observers such as Higgenson, Lucy McKim, and later Joel Chandler Harris. The appropriation of the language of the folk by black writers cannot be dissociated from the cultural anthropology of postbellum literary transcendentalism and regionalist realism.

As an intellectual culture, the Protestant-romantic literary tradition drew heavily on various modes of evangelical piety and romantic discourse. It contributed language, outlook, and political strategies to the American nineteenth-century worlds of reform, domesticity, and bourgeois-Victorianism. An inadequate grasp of this evangelical-romantic culture has much to do with the misguided perspective of recent black feminist commentary on the women's sentimental novel. The influence of the signifiers appears in such a misinterpretation. The discourse of the new black critics demands that African-American literature represent an adversary response to mainstream American literary culture. Black feminist literary criticism in particular has been especially overdetermined by this interpretive imperative. This misguided perspective appears in the late Claudia Tate's arguments for the politically adversarial nature of black women's fiction such as *Iola Leroy*. To be sure, the black Protestant world was deeply concerned with the creation of bourgeois order and civic consciousness within the black community. However, it is not a foregone conclusion that a literary fiction constituted a *de facto* political intervention.

Hazel Carby, a politically sophisticated reader who has remained outside of the "signifiers" and the folk romantics, argues that a novel such as *Iola Leroy* may contest racist and class-defined hegemony on an ideological level. She thereby creates a nuanced account of the "limited" extent to which a black woman's novel may be political. Hers is an important qualification of the "adversary" nature of black women's writing especially in regard to the Protestant-romantic continuity I describe here. The domestic world of the family functioned as an important site for social reproduction and the maintenance of social knowledge in middle-class nineteenth-century American ideology. To the extent that nineteenth-century blacks existed in a sphere of stable bourgeois life, they contested a racist American society's conception of them as subhuman: this was a response to a hegemonic ideal. But again such an implicit ideological response is not necessarily "political" in the radical sense of action within a *polis*.

Tate's interpretations are badly skewed by an ideological impulse that Carby's arguments have tempered. Drawing on a language of "desire," Tate sets forth a view of the novel as nakedly political by virtue of its deployment of "desire." Here, the texts of the sentimental black female authors such as Frances Harper and Emma Kelly become explicit "protests," dramatizing through an "allegory" of domestic life an implicit "political" reality. In making this argument, Tate is forced to interpolate patterns of erotic and domestic desire into Harper's and Kelly's writing to argue for its political radicalism.[15] Despite Tate's interpretation of domesticity as political opposition, the conservative, private thrust of social reproduction as conceived by black sentimental women writers remains evident.[16] Tate's interpretive lockstep leads her to ignore Carby's subtle distinctions about the political dimension of literature. At each point in her discourse, Tate must translate the "private," "sexual," "domestic" world of Kelly's novel (for instance) into a public, politically adversary one. Thus, according to Tate, the conflict between oppression and liberation or equality is plotted in Hopkins' novels as part of the ideology of true love. And Tate must go on to explain, unconvincingly, "th[a]t civil conflict of social equality is narrated symbolically as a private sexual dispute among characters."[17] This interpretation is an ideological fiat that seeks to proclaim rather than convince. Real politics must be a matter of not only voluntary choice but also willed action in the material world. Serious politically oriented interpretations must understand the definition—and therefore the real-world limits—of the political.

Tate (and implicitly Carby) is correct in sensing political impulses or implications in the domestic "desires" of their sentimental women writers. However, that world of feeling must be placed at least partially within the Protestant-romantic continuity, which writers such as Hopkins and Kelly simply took for granted. The ideological, taken-for-granted quality of their spiritualized worldview had, as I argue throughout this book, cultural consequences that in some sense escaped their political origins. The middle-class Protestant imperative to establish a godly, ethically disciplined household immediately brought bourgeois blacks face-to-face with the economic and social limitations of a racist white-dominated American society. From such contradictions in black Victorian Protestantism grew romantic conceptions of self, society, and history. Within the context of Victorian black culture these represent a wish-fulfilling supplement to a Christian worldview which cannot be wholly realized on Earth. Black romanticism represents a displacement of certain crucial Christian literary and pietistic modes into secularized autobiographical, historical, and eschatological forms. These forms borrow freely from the emerging set of insights that would be fully articulated in Freud's cultural psychology in works such as *The Interpretation of Dreams* as well as in traditions of archetypal forms of American "character" elaborated by Richard Chase and Daniel Hoffman.[18]

Our political and cultural sense of those African recoveries of the late nineteenth- and early twentieth-century writers must be placed within a broader Euro-American romantic cultural context. These continuities have been discerned in the powerful synoptic literary histories of M. H. Abrams, F. O. Mathiessen, and others. Many of the texts I describe implicitly show the nexus between this evangelical culture and traditional Anglo-American romanticism: a nexus corresponding to a "Natural Supernaturalism" (to use Carlyle's phrase, echoed by Abrams). A romantic union with an idealized vision of the folk becomes an image of personal (and, eventually, world-historical) salvation for frustrated black saints whose full human development has been thwarted by racism. Without acknowledgement of this

Puritan-evangelical-romantic synthesis (as much American as African-American), we will never be able to place signifying in an authentic literary-historical context.

To be sure, Yale's creation of a program of black literary studies had immense advantages in the racial *Realpolitik* of the academic world. Yale at that moment, and other academic institutions, acquired an academic arrangement that might appease student and professional demands for the study of black literature. Significantly, these institutions never confronted the deep inadequacies of these *ad hoc* exceptionalist black literary traditions they promulgated as well as the consequences of giving quasi-academic legitimacy to black interlopers such as Neal. Let me suggest that an important opportunity was lost here—despite its threatening character for an increasingly segregated, white profession of English. Our implicit realization of a black offshoot of the Protestant-romantic continuity suggests the important perspective that interpreters—beginning with the African-American literary tradition—bring to American Studies. This point of view, neither one of assimilation nor one of subversion, could nevertheless reorient our vision of romanticism around questions of will, wish-fulfilling fantasy, deferred dreaming, and millennial expectation: issues that African-American literary tradition and politics shares with American "mainstream" ideology and romanticism in general.

Questions about the consensual or culturally disruptive orientation of American Protestantism seem irresolvable without recourse to the African-American encounter with the "mainstream" tradition described here. In the end, serious black critiques of the canonical texts of American and European literature would probably be deeply threatening politically and ideologically to the white literary establishment which at least sometimes wished—it must be said—to relegate African-American Studies to a literary, cultural, and social ghetto.

One such threat apparent in recent literary-historical work in African-American Studies is the possibility that black writing—either literature or criticism—may not exist as a cultural entity in and of itself. It may simply be a significant moment in the transition from American Protestantism to romanticism, a transition that has been observed—and is indeed simply taken for granted—many times in English and American literary studies. Black authors may have been writing American literature all the time, and African-American critics may have been engaged in a far more traditional philological project than they knew. The philological dimension of early African-American Studies (an approach which all academic literary studies require) may also have intimidated both white and black intellectuals. Black literary criticism may simply be a sometimes radical, sometimes conservative, sometimes inchoate response to modernity—clothed in the language of romanticism. Indeed, a true sense of what is left, center, and right may depend upon reorienting African-American literary studies around its authentic, Euro-American cultural ground. Such interpretations might find the volatility, incoherence, and revolutionary temper of black writing—as well as its philosophical powers—to be the results of an experience of Americanization. One suspects that this was the deepest threat posed by the black presence in the academy. A segregated Black Studies movement made sure that this development never took place.

## IV

Although I did not know it, Neal's glib presentation of himself and his critique of Barry Beckham's *My Main Mother* followed a rhetorical strategy, a plan to make way for the literary claims of Black Arts. Neal's presentation flaunted Black Arts as the aesthetic point of view by which black critics might interpret, evaluate, and canonically place African-American literary texts. Following the Black Power movement and the riots of the late sixties, the Black Arts movement sought to create an intellectual "high" academic black culture founded in the storytelling, religious, and musical forms of unlettered blacks in the rural South and Northern ghettos. Langston Hughes, Zora Neale Hurston, and Ralph Ellison had made such attempts variously in their poetry, fiction, anthology collections, and literary criticism. What distinguished Black Arts scholars such as Neal and the young Houston Baker was the appropriation of the street's effrontery and brashness in forwarding these claims to the center of the elite academic world. Neal and Baker presented their critical undertaking as a symbolic subversion of the intellectual's formal tradition-bearing function. In their raucous behavior, they *prima facie* rejected their status as professional intellectuals to claim the charismatic presence of the black folk masses. Having created an institutional style, the Black Arts mavericks began to extend their previous analyses of folk-based literature into wide-ranging cultural theory. The mixed results of the first generation's work appeared in scholarly systems such as Henry Louis Gates' "signifying" or the "Black Theology" of James Cone, Peter Paris, and others. The enterprise of the creation, promotion, and application of theory advanced Black Studies as an academic institution, a presence in the "diversified" field of the humanities, and an intellectual identity.

The process by which black literary critics or theologians created theory made them specialists in black subfields of the mainstream professional disciplines. To be sure, black studies humanists shared important subject matter and theoretical outlooks with their white counterparts. On the whole, however, the narrowly linguistic and semantic orientation of theory cut this new cadre of humanists off from vital intellectual conversations with black social scientists. Sociology is, in its intellectual orientation, engaged in an intellectual enterprise that questions day-to-day assumptions about social reality. As demystifying inquiry, it proceeds from the perspective of a well-established discipline, a far deeper and broader tradition than that of African-American literary studies. Sociology has always been strongly represented by black intellectuals, such as W. E. B. Du Bois, E. Franklin Frazier, and now William Julius Wilson, all of whom have written widely influential works in the field. Indeed, the breakdown of the kind of conversation that existed between Richard Wright, Louis Wirth, Horace Cayton, and St. Clair Drake is an important part of the intellectual decline I describe in this book. A major contribution to my understanding of Black Studies' early life at Yale occurred in the few conversations I had with Arna Bontemps, a fellow in my residential college during my senior year. He observed once that he had always felt extremely uncomfortable around the Yale campus. He identified formalists such as William Wimsatt and

Robert Penn Warren as descendents of the Southern literary agrarians who, led by Alan Tate, had snubbed Jean Toomer forty years earlier.[19] Bontemps had—as his now-published correspondence with Langston Hughes shows—long feared the consequences of the New Criticism and one of these fears was its parochialism: a narrowness that led to the breakdown of communication between sociologists and black literary critics.[20] For Henry Louis Gates the rejection of "sociological" approaches to interpretation permitted a new focus upon the literary and linguistic aspects of African literature.[21] However, this resolutely "literary" focus clearly resulted in the new black critic's imprudent rejection of historical and sociological understandings essential to not only the textual interpretation but also the construction of literary tradition. This sociological innocence created the intellectual vacuum in which the signifier's critically unrestrained theorizing and freewheeling institution building flourished. Whatever their claims, all critics place themselves in literary history's institutional life, traditions, and continuities of experience. That institutionalized cultural life is necessarily touched by social reality, as is every other institutional existence. The loss of perspective on African-American literature as a social institution may perhaps be the deepest fault of the black formalists. As the new black critics cleared a space for themselves, they forgot the academic continuity which might give perspective and coherence to their inquiry.

A gross oversimplification of the literary world's intellectual protocols and structures marked the professional style of the new black literary movement in the elite academy. By the eighties and nineties, the seeds of Black Arts had blossomed into visible subdisciplines, institutions, and academic initiatives. Drawing upon the language of semiotics and deconstruction, young African-American scholars had created what seemed to be unique ways of talking about themselves and their objects of study. However, this intellectual style largely functioned within an often-unexamined semiotic framework—one that suppressed institutional paradigms from which semiotics emerged and the literary historical contexts which might give it significance. Like the similarly freewheeling cathartic discourse of the street, the black arts strategies twisted the white enemy's language into a curse upon his culture. However, the new cohort of critics lacked the intellectual self-consciousness developed by critique and debate in professionalized academic discourse. They rarely read their texts against the grain of their own semiotic analyses. They rarely exercised their ironic inquiries upon themselves.

A strange lack of self-awareness therefore pervaded the sarcasm of the academic dozens. To be sure, the cynicism of the all-black dining room table echoed in Neal's voice as it filled the seminar room. This tone appears in Henry Louis Gates' sly signifying styles, Cornel West's mimicry, and Michael Dyson's rapping. This cynicism, however, addressed a rarely acknowledged but fiercely enforced side of the now fulfilled contract between this new black intelligentsia and the white academy. Despite their roles as "public intellectuals," the new African-American literati were excluded from the most serious considerations of public policy and the highest levels of intellectual journalism. Their plight was increasingly identifiable as a variant of a larger black middle-class predicament: the glass ceiling of the white professional world. The academic "perpetrator" walk of the black critic's self-consciously ghetto demeanor responded to the dislocation of a new black bourgeoisie now feeling an old constraint. The decision to cut themselves off from the codes and restraints of established intellectual disciplines only exacerbated this alienation.

To be sure, the new black criticism yielded—as do all interpretive grids—its own insights, its distinctively tuned sensibility. The ethos of signifying in critics such as Henry Louis Gates alerted a host of commentators to similar gestures in the conjure tales of Charles Chesnutt, in the literary styles that Zora Neale Hurston had culled from folk speech, and in the practice of modernist American poets such as John Berryman and Ezra Pound. They too had exploited black popular styles in fusing "high" literary tradition with the American vernaculars. Yet the freewheeling interpretive acts of the "dozens" could not serve as an intellectual basis for an institution of African-American literature. When applied indiscriminately to the whole of black tradition, these tactics produced an exceptionally vacuous literary-critical discourse.

In the main, the focus on "adversary" styles of rhetoric in black literary gesture obscured the breadth of genres and contexts in which blacks had actually written from the late eighteenth century to the late twentieth. A literary tradition founded on "oral" folk culture—and African-American culture could not be wholly oral in a long-established world of print—also had limited explanatory possibilities. An all-black tradition did not in and of itself provide a broad enough range of texts, authors, and literary innovation to explain either the most or the least sophisticated black writers. It was not adequately encyclopedic to justify a taxonomy of the various styles, conventions, and points-of-view of its writers, who are better understood under the more comprehensive rubrics of Anglo-American or Anglo-European literature. The emergence of such a phenomenon in the elite academy of the late sixties, the seventies, and the eighties is difficult to explain.

The rise of black literary movements paralleled the emergence of the new social history, comprehensive studies of Republican tradition in Anglo-American thought, and the revitalization of studies in Anglo-American romantic traditions.[22] Contemporary, sustained investigations of Puritanism, Congregationalism, and the transformations of American Protestant theology spoke directly to the issues faced by the signifiers, particularly as they entered the late eighteenth- and early nineteenth-century ground on which they often sought to stake canonical origins. The extent to which Phillis Wheatley is an adversarial voice at odds with a mainstream American Revolutionary society is clarified by historians such as J. G. A. Pocock, Bernard Bailyn, Edmund Morgan, and Gordon Wood, who consistently pondered the ideological dynamics of New England politics and religion in both the Revolutionary and early National periods. It is difficult to understand how a growing number of African-American literary critics can discuss the subversive nature of Phillis Wheatley's poetry without reference to related concepts of political "opposition" that were crucial to contemporary thinkers. There is also a debilitating parochialism in the general refusal of black critics, in their assessment of the black appropriation of the nineteenth-century intellectual world, to make sophisticated reference to romanticism or pragmatism.[23] Black literary tradition had lost touch with the most recent wellsprings of historical data necessary for its own self-understanding.

A narrow, often mechanical reasoning of recent black literary inquiry emerged from the Black Arts' inspired attempt to glean linguistic structures from the language of black culture. This narrowness has been accompanied by an ideological repressiveness that has not only strangled discussions between black critics concerning literature, but devalued the intellectual legitimacy of African-American literary studies. This has accompanied the establishment of Black Studies as a vehicle for disciplinary advancement (and recruitment) in the academy. One senses a link too between the suppression of recent social and intellectual history (with its emphasis on ideology) and the political impotence of present-day black humanists. Their thought lacks a political and social cutting edge as well as a critical self-consciousness. Having dropped out of intellectual competition with white scholars, black intellectuals no longer sharpen their polemical weapons in the same shops.

The increasingly residual intellectual role of black humanist scholars and pedagogues in the American university only reinforces this parochial element of African-American Studies. Interestingly enough, black literary intellectuals in Black Studies programs often find themselves in the caretaking functions of administrators, student advisors, and interracial go-betweens—vocations that the black middle class has traditionally filled in social work agencies, public schools, courts, and poverty programs. At a time when black students in high school and college can barely read, write, calculate, or display general liberal arts knowledge, they are pushed into African-American Studies as an appropriate formation for professional life. The most simplistic and romanticized notions of African-American culture now pass as the "black" element in the curricular mosaics of "multicultural" studies. In this respect African-American literary studies parallels similar developments in black psychology, many of whose exponents set forth Afrocentric theories of personality development, socialization, pathology, and education. This movement has, like African-American literary studies, produced both elite academic scholars like Reginald Jones and Linda Myers James, and intellectuals like Na'im Akbar who negotiate both elite and popular levels of discussion. A quick look at the Net reveals a plethora of course syllabi in African-American psychology as well as a growing number of academic research facilities committed to the subject. It is clear that black social workers, ministers, and teachers increasingly encounter Afrocentric theories of personality development and education which provide racially exceptionalist accounts of personality, group behavior, and even cognition. These often distinguish, for example, between uniquely black behaviors oriented toward community, and a desire for individual achievement.[24] In the context of these psychological approaches, the cultural myths of black studies function as compensatory ideologies for the guidance of a black middle-class cadre of social workers, ministers, and so on. The larger culture of popular self-help, child-rearing, marital, and wholistic-person consumerist psychology only further diffuses this therapeutic worldview throughout the media. In a white-dominated America, it is difficult to keep such middle-class ideologies from drifting into paradigms of internalized social control—a control traditionally maintained by the middle-class black social workers, educators, and therapists.

The new black intelligentsia's receptivity to these outlooks proceeds from its tenuous place in the academy, and from a pragmatic style endemic to twentieth-century African-American political life. An arriviste class of intellectuals has entered the university elite. Unsure of its academic authenticity and legitimacy, it has—within the context of newly integrated schools—assumed the traditional social managerial functions of the black bourgeoisie, while appropriating the cathartic gestures and personal styles of the African-American lumpen. This professional style embodies what Martin L. Kilson has described as the "black modernist paradox":

> The black modernist paradox—the seemingly contradictory pattern within the evolving twentieth-century African-American society whereby popular society among blacks exhibited cathartic interests in aspects of Black Nationalist leadership orientations on the one hand, but on the other hand overwhelmingly turned to the mainstream civil rights activist black professional class for operational-leadership functions . . . this black modernist paradox reflected a keen variant of pragmatism among both the civil rights activist sector of the black professional class and black popular society. The variant of pragmatism I have in mind can be called the activist-progressive pragmatism mode.[25]

The new black bourgeois intelligentsia has—for pragmatic advantage—appropriated what Kilson calls "cathartic styles" connected to "black nationalist leadership orientations." Deploying these strategies in the academy and the media, this arriviste class of intellectuals has made its way. This appropriation has in all likelihood also emerged out of the loss of black bourgeois cultural hegemony over black life. This hegemony has passed to another stratum of black society, the highly visible media figures in athletics, politics, and entertainment. These gestures have inevitably been co-opted by the commercial media, which has found them an endless source of fashion and ideas. The new black intellectual class—increasingly distant from the masses (whom it represents) in the integrated world—understandably appropriates these cathartic-symbolic gestures which are now taken-for-granted symbols of "blackness."

Access to the cultural forms of blackness gives African-American intellectuals legitimacy within their natural bourgeois roles as managers, advisors, and therapists. To be sure, the rewards for easing the adjustment of blacks into the integrated world only divert black intellectuals from serious scholarly life. However, the therapeutic cast of much recent black studies scholarship suggests this elite's implicit awareness of the explanatory ideological role which they now play. Media-staged performances of the new black intelligentsia are by now part of a therapeutic, socializing, and educational function suited for a racially volatile late twentieth-century American society. The televised antics of a Cornel West or Michael Dyson diffuse rather than inspire serious cultural and political reflection.

Through these rituals, the black middle-class intelligentsia negotiates and directs the internal pressures built up among lower, and middle-class blacks—especially youth—who rightly perceive their marginality in a high-tech, information economy which values symbolic-cognitive skills.

Addressing black bourgeois entrants into this social managerial class, African-American Studies supplies a worldview appropriate to various political and social functions. This undertaking is carried out through the media and schools under the aegis of a larger American capitalist system that dominates a now multiethnic Benetton youth culture. In addition, the new black middle class that bears this culture does so with the quasi-legitimacy bestowed by the newly arrived intelligentsia. This function also creates a politically and socially tendentious role for the new black intelligentsia who, craving legitimacy provided by any plausible social role, explain a progressive liberal worldview as an ideology of order in the volatile world of diversity. The black intelligentsia's complicity with this task of world maintenance, carried out in university lectures, political appearances, and other public events (often before college students), points to an internal crisis of social and political value within the African-American intellectual elite. Such a phenomenon has arisen elsewhere. Serious intellectuals in Eastern Europe, in the postcolonial world, and throughout Africa recognize the political stakes implicit in the manipulation of dislocated intellectuals and nervous bourgeoisies.

It is difficult to know where to begin in addressing this problem. However, it is largely cultural—a matter of how we see, interpret, and plan for action in society. As such a cultural phenomenon, literary criticism can help us better understand the cultural symbols, intellectual styles, and even leadership strategies now at work in the middle-class African-American worldview I describe. I want not only to criticize literary Black Studies but also to throw its rhetorical and political strategies into relief. In particular, I wish to examine the intellectual voices it represses. Despite my criticism of the therapeutic function of much of Black Studies, these essays necessarily rely upon an attempt to recreate the inner world of the new black intelligentsia and middle class. This recreation of an intelligentsia's inner world is, I think, a valid enterprise for literary criticism and literature.

This task has been necessary not only for my understanding of the African-American question, but for the clarification of my own goals as a critic and intellectual *vis-à-vis* the audience for which I write. It has not always been easy for black intellectuals to locate the importance of the canonical literary texts within their studies, their reflection, and their writing. This has never been so true as it is now. The corrosive skepticism now directed toward canonical tradition did not characterize the worldview of Charles Chesnutt, Richard Wright, and Ralph Ellison as it did that of the rebellious black students of the sixties. This breakdown in tradition diminishes the cultural resources that black intellectuals bring to political and moral thought. Considering the institutional dimensions of black intellectual life has helped me to reflect upon this problem.

# Introduction
## Through the Looking Glass

I

LITERARY CRITICISM HAS TAKEN VARIOUS FORMS at different times and places. The profession still remains, however, under the spell of the "linguistic turn" taken by the humanities over fifty years ago. The once innovative methods of grammatical, rhetorical, and semiotic analysis are now commonplace. Predictably, this development has come to shape African-American literary history and interpretation as much as any so-called mainstream field in the humanities. Academic literary tradition emerges from institutions that fulfill certain tasks. That institution is itself the sum of teachers, students, editors, and others who amass, organize, analyze, and transmit knowledge. Whether as a scholarly field, or a subdiscipline dissenting camp, this institution inevitably develops its distinctive rhetoric, canons, interpretive tradition, preferred commentaries, and protocols of reading. These, in turn, become the stock-in-trade of the entity's scholars and teachers, as well as of fellow travelers in publishing and the foundations. The work of this professionalized intellectual class finally appears in published monographs, scholarly articles, edited texts, dissertations, and theses.

The "linguistic turn" in the profession of letters has shaped all of these institutions decisively. Canons of interpretation have inevitably come to connect narrow linguistic structures with broadly cultural and political motifs, most recently those of race and gender. It is now futile to complain about this development, for it is a fact; it largely shapes the academic atmosphere in which we breathe and live our cultural lives. Academic as well as nonacademic readers now take for granted the legitimacy of interpretive methods that link meaning and form, structure and communication, and grammar and meaning with an extraliterary, often political issue. They accept these methods nearly without thinking. Interpretation has thus become not only a means of literary analysis but also an exercise in defining the immediate extrinsic significance of a text. Predictably, canonical traditions refined in the fire of literary politics have filled the intellectual landscape of the academy. They are the *de facto* constitutions relied upon by republics of print throughout the worlds of publishing and the academy. Their legitimacy, which is taken for granted, is the product of political force as well as ideology and traditional forms of reasoning.

The literary-political process I describe has appeared most nakedly in those fields that have emerged by fiat as opposed to the accretion of scholarly tradition. Exceptional even by these standards was the newly reconstituted field of African-American literary studies in the late sixties and early seventies. The play of forces, interpretations, interests, and personalities patently reveals the dislocations of the elite American university, the inner life of the new black middle class, the deep unchanging tides of literary experience itself, as well as the workings of interracial, intellectual patronage—a topic that has yet to receive sufficient attention in African-American literary history. I am primarily concerned, however, with the failure of African-American literary studies as the kind of institution I have described above. I conclude this book by questioning the institution's legitimacy and the interracial consensus that maintains it, as well as the workings of power that brought it into being. Let me state from the start that I claim allegiance to no systematic critical program. I am carrying out this inquiry in the terms of ordinary language, American literary-critical tradition, as well as the cultural commonplaces of Marx, Freud, and Max Weber—touchstones routinely evoked in our understandings of the arts. However, I have also frequently relied upon my own observations of literary practice as it appears in the various monographs and books that I read in my professional life. In doing so, I hope to bring this subject into a public arena where it may be freely discussed for its social policy as well as its cultural importance.

The institution of African-American literary studies has failed to provide an effective set of interpretive methods or a rhetoric that organizes the field's knowledge. Instead, African-American critics have drawn loosely on a theme-oriented formalism, semiotics post-structuralist method. The result of this strategy has been a set of interpretations that fulfills the critic's ideological fiat but often fails to recognize the text's important countervailing meanings. No positively defined superstructure of intellectual tradition has emerged. This intellectual reality provides the space in which the wish-fulfilling fantasies of black lumpen "toasts" echo in ivy-clad academic halls. The newly empowered bourgeoisie expounds the "oral," fantasy substitutes of the hopeless black masses. How has this happened? Instead of a school of semiotic literary history, critics such as Henry Louis Gates, Houston Baker, Karla Holloway, Michael Awkward, and Michael Dyson have fashioned a critical rhetoric to forward the institutional interests of a new black professorate's largely segregated enclave; and to negotiate a tenuous legitimacy for that cohort in the profession. The maintenance of this institution has required severe intellectual suppression not only of texts but also of the critic's intellectual self-consciousness. This repression on behalf of the interests of institutional power has been as freewheeling as the school's often vague critical language. Power cannot be a norm in and of itself. And in their worship of the will, the signifiers have in fact fashioned an intellectual version of the anomie that ravages black lumpen life. These are longstanding problems in African-American cultural tradition, but the signifiers have accepted the terms of their own critical enterprise.

I have chosen proponents of signifying to represent the widespread orientation that I here describe in black literary criticism. Important exceptions to this school—Kenneth Warren, Hazel Carby, Richard Yarborough, Robert Stepto, Carla Peterson, and others—continue to perform valuable work in important sites in the profession. However, the signifiers and their founder, Henry Louis Gates Jr., have been chosen here as a representative critical sample largely because they and their rhetoric make up the most visible and influential group of contemporary interpreters of African-American literature. The school's founding work, *The Signifying Monkey: A Theory of African-American Literature* (1987), remains, according to repeated polls, the most consulted academic text by a black humanist.[1] It has influenced a number of critics, black and white, including feminists such as Hortense Spillers, and traditional formalists such as Michael North. *The Signifying Monkey* furthermore played an important role in the black theology of Katie Cannon, Dwight Hopkins, Will Coleman, and Katherine Bassard.

Henry Louis Gates Jr. stands in a particular relationship to this school and its associated camps as founding father, leading entrepreneur, and major public intellectual. His latest essays in works of literary journalism such as *Thirteen Ways of Looking at a Black Man* bear little resemblance to early theoretical statements in *Figures in Black* and *The Signifying Monkey*. However, his recent literary career as a polite essayist is nevertheless deeply significant for my study. The theory and methodology developed in the early books, as well as their literary elaborations, represent a powerful explanation of African-American critical practice that sprang up in the sixties around formalism, structuralism, and deconstruction. The first two theoretical books in particular served successive waves of African-American critics as guides—and sometimes as interpretive templates—for actual practice. Gates' migration to the world of literary journalist, cultural critic, public intellectual, and impresario set a pattern for a similar turn in the careers of Michael Dyson, Karla Holloway, Cornel West, Wahneema Lubiano, and (whom one might not otherwise expect) writers such as Toni Morrison. Gates' later essayistic work remains powerfully driven by signifying and reveals both the powers as well as the limitations of that sensibility. Taken together, his literary theoretical as well as his later broadly cultural writing constitute a lens through which the African-American letters of the last thirty years may be viewed. This work gains its importance through its explanatory and exponential powers, its grasp of possibilities in the media, and its implicit understanding of the therapeutic-managerial function of black humanists in the university's public life. Gates' career is duplicated elsewhere in the professional lives of Dwight Hopkins in religion and Robin Kelley in history. To the extent that an institution is one man's length and shadow, the present black age of criticism is best measured by the breadth and depth of Henry Louis Gates Jr.'s life as a literary professional.

Let me say at the outset that Gates' monograph—whatever my strictures—has more than earned its pedagogical, scholarly, and intellectual keep. It has instructed at least two generations of black students in semiotics and deconstruction. And whatever one thinks of its interpretations, it has provided influential readings of *Their Eyes Were Watching God*, *Native Son*, *Black Boy*, *Invisible Man*, and *Mumbo Jumbo*. It is no small praise to say that *The Signifying Monkey* transformed our sense of modern and postmodern black literary tradition, as well as provided a forcefully stated theoretical explanation for existing literary strategies and critical practice. As a meditation on African-American literature, it continues to inform the thinking of current American writers. It is in these respects a valid source of Henry Louis Gates' reputation as an imaginative reader, excellent literary pedagogue, and what Nathan A. Scott Jr. would call a shrewd prophet of Tendenz. *The Signifying Monkey* is, I will not deny, a noisy, self-dramatizing, and provocative text. But those who wish to take Gates down will find themselves wrestling an angel. Let me thus preface this often severe criticism with heartfelt thanks for a text whose ideas and observations stimulated my thinking and finally brought it into focus. Whatever Gates' confusions, contradictions, and messiness, *The Signifying Monkey* continues to move its readers in the way we associate with all important books. Something similar might be said of the work of Dyson and Holloway. As these writers persisted, they inevitably encountered questions that went to the heart of both the signifying enterprise in particular and their generation's appropriation of black culture in general. That they may have foundered on the rocks of this largely unmapped intellectual shore is in one sense beside the point. Their work—whatever my faultfinding—inevitably maps the landscape of the inwardness experienced by the first black bourgeoisie to have time and money for sustained reflection on literature.

Any literary study of *The Signifying Monkey*, *Figures in Black*, *The Journey Back*, *Blues, Ideology, and Afro-American Literature: A Vernacular Theory* and their spawn must, however, first acknowledge their bankrupt intellectual procedures and finally arrive at the rank garden of interracial bad faith in which they flourish. Critical language and cultural advocacy of the sort set forth by these texts depend for their usefulness on the capacity to discover, through publicly defensible procedure, the meanings embedded in a work's words, figures, grammatical structures, borrowed conventions, and generic commitments. The exposition of such erudition in the middle and late twentieth century has led to some of the important work of a by-now distinguished line of twentieth-century European and American scholars. This endeavor has included the heroic undertakings that produced Erich Auerbach's *Mimesis*, Ernst Curtius' *European Literature and the Latin Middle Ages*, and Johan Huizinga's *Homo Ludens*. Reading these books, one encounters deeply learned scholarly voices transmitting antique cultures through the conduits of philology and hermeneutics from one age and place to another. For all their *prima facie* narrowness of traditional rhetoric and method, these critical texts ultimately, through their vast learning, become what political theorist John Pocock has called a "political language": the literary vehicle by which a society, its culture, and its cosmos are carried (or translated in the Latin sense) through "speech acts" from generation to generation.²

This formidable genre of literary-cultural history addresses a significant moment: the interval between the end of World War I and the aftermath of World War II. This period saw the world-shattering dislocation of European societies, the consequence of genocide, national collapse, and continental war. *Mimesis* and *Homo Ludens* are the response of a towering European intellectual tradition, conscious of its own approaching end, to the possible destruction of all Western civilization. At the heart of these works is an almost religious hope in the redemptive powers of literary history and philology to recover the spirit of past cultural tradition.

The capacity of immense learning to deliver a sacred hope amidst the cultural confusions of the late twentieth century now gives M. H. Abrams' *Natural Supernaturalism* its great power, and contributes other-worldly depth to similar commentary such as J. Hillis Miller's *The Linguistic Moment*. I mention these books because they draw upon the universally acknowledged plenitude of Judeo-Protestant religion, represented by the forms of historical, autobiographical, and world-redemptive narrative. Abrams and Miller read writers such as Wordsworth and Stevens with exceptional intellectual and experiential depth, relying on our age's romantic understanding of this earlier Christian vision. These readings gain their literary and spiritual power as they dramatize a secular redemption in a cultural world seemingly bereft of spiritual and psychological depth. The redemptive power of art—its power to project illusions whose powers demand demystification—returns many critical readers to works in the Anglo-American tradition despite the reductiveness of recent linguistic, historical, and gender interpretation. It is in such a seemingly dehumanized cultural sphere that mainstream critics continue, whatever their critical approach, to write about Emerson, Wordsworth, Stevens, and Whitman.

Literate African-Americans now contemplate the breakdown of the black social structure itself in urban ghettos plagued by crime, disease, and psychological dysfunction. The trauma suffered by the masses not only threatens their day-to-day capacity to cope in the world, but complicates the worldview of black literary intellectuals, who have inherited a romanticized vision of the folk from their immediate predecessors. Those present-day black literati in the academy have, in the last twenty years, felt compelled to articulate that vision of the folk in contemporary demystifying modes of semiotic criticism. Fueled by the orientation's success as a black middle-class style in the academy, this initiative has shaped African-American studies particularly in the humanities. The present crisis-laden moment in the African-American experience has undoubtedly led intellectuals and students to place more than ordinary stock in the literary canon as a symbol of hope, ethnic unity, and cultural wisdom. This tendency appears in the continued demand for African-American literary scholars in both traditional English and African-American Studies programs. Yet the black literary studies project, no matter how institutionally successful, has failed in a scholarly and intellectual way. The persistence of the black literary worldview which I study in this book has only exacerbated that failure.

The traditional texts of Curtius and Huizinga draw largely on literary rhetoric, as understood in classical or twentieth-century formalist or semiotic terms, to dramatize the linguistic continuities by which a sacred plenitude is translated from generation to generation and from age to age. This plenitude, understood in rhetorical terms, is the social world of antiquity as communicated by shared medieval literary, legal, and pedagogical traditions. These cultural conventions, in the case of Curtius' *European Literature*, represented the life-world of human experience itself, a universe of meaning that persisted from epoch to epoch through literature. The conception of an infinitely varied and graduated world of culture is nowhere better expressed than in Curtius' introduction:

> Just as European literature can only be seen as a whole, so the study of it can only proceed historically. Not in the form of literary history! A narrative and enumerative history never yields anything but a catalogue-like knowledge of facts. The material itself it leaves in whatever form it found it. But historical investigation has to unravel it and penetrate it. It has to develop analytical methods, that is, methods that will "decompose" the material (after the fashion of chemistry with its reagents) and make its structures visible. The necessary point of view can only be gained from a comparative perusal of literatures, that is, can only be discovered empirically. Only a literary discipline which proceeds historically and philologically can do justice to the task.[3]

Far from being dry, rhetorical, literary-critical, historical sourcebooks, the work of Curtius, Auerbach, and Huizinga dramatized the politically and socially restorative powers of human culture itself, particularly in times of crisis. And although Curtius stresses the nature of this plenitude's existence as a "timeless present," his conception of a sacred infinity is the measure against which any work of the present must be judged for a true literary self-consciousness. Indeed, this measure of the present against the wealth of a persistent past must always be forestalled against the future.

Part of the power of *The Signifying Monkey, Blues, Ideology, and Afro-American Literature: A Vernacular Theory*, and *Moorings and Metaphors: Figures of Culture and Gender in Black Women's Literature* is that they seek—whether explicitly or not—to summon such a cultural sphere with which to address the present-day collapse of black lower-class life in America (not to mention that of the Third World).[4] Henry Louis Gates Jr., who of all the signifiers is most conscious of the stakes in canonization, promises a plenitude already created and available for examination. The new African-American literary critics affect to deploy a canonical response to their culture's crisis similar to that of Curtius' *European Literature* as well as to its American predecessors and variants: F. O. Mathiessen's *American Renaissance: Art and Expression in the Age of Emerson and Whitman* and M. H. Abrams' *Natural Supernaturalism.*

> The black tradition exists only insofar as black artists enact it. Only because black writers have read and responded to other black writers with a sense of recognition and acknowledgement can we speak of a black literary inheritance, with all the burdens and ironies that has entailed. Race is a text (an array of discursive practices), not an essence. It must be read with painstaking care and suspicion, not imbibed.[5]

Gates insists not only on the tradition's distinctive idiom (or language) but also upon the need for distinctively black tools in its interpretation:

> This is the challenge of the critic of black literature in the 1980s: not to shy away from white power—that is, literary theory—but to translate it into the black idiom, renaming principles of criticism where appropriate, but especially naming indigenous black principles of criticism and applying them to our own texts. Any tool that enables the critic to explain the complex workings of the language of a text are appropriate here. For it is language, the black language of black texts, that expresses the distinctive quality of our literary tradition.[6]

This book, *Black Heart*, rejects the possibility of such an implicitly essential "indigenous" cultural plenitude constituted by an African-American literary language, cultural tradition, and institutionalized form of interpretation. An oppressed people and their oppressors necessarily meld the crucial elements of their worldviews into a creolized culture. The interface between the West and Africa and African America is too well established for either blacks or whites to move in separate authentically African-American or white American purities. In particular, it is too late in the day for African-American literary critics to distinguish themselves and their work essentially from the West.[7] On the contrary, Gates' distinction between identifiably African and African-American qualities in any work depends upon sustained essential differences between the literary work and language of white and black authors. The Gatesian critic, to the extent that he wants to establish a non-Western canon, must engage not only in Curtius' vast comparative literary task but in an even more comprehensive and universal undertaking. It will not do to say, as Gates does earlier in *Loose Canons*, that the black authors of the slave tradition—recipients of white abolitionist patronage for their authentic witness—wrote the slave narratives in response to Enlightenment European assertions of the absence of black literary tradition.[8] To make a claim for an exceptional black literary tradition, much more is required. One would have to determine the distinctiveness of the slave narratives and slave narrative fiction from the contemporary religious and secular popular literature of their day. And as recent work (such as David Reynolds' *Beneath the American Renaissance*) makes clear, the supposedly "subversive" tendencies of the slave narrative have become harder and harder to maintain.[9] The slave narrative, combining spiritual autobiography, antislavery fiction, captivity tale, seduction romance, and sermon, increasingly appears to be less a distinctive genre than an evolving generic fusion, resulting, as elsewhere in Anglo-American literary history, in the novel.[10] Without the institutionalization of an exceptionalist African-American literary tradition, race-related distinctions might wither away, leaving black critics with the more important task of analyzing the antebellum American cultural mélange absorbed by early nineteenth-century black writers and encoded in their work. Although Gates asserts the existence of a cultural plenitude and systematic philology, both must be the result of an accretion of culturally distinctive works of art. At present, such a tradition may only be summoned into existence by the wish-fulfilling fantasy so prevalent in the African-American literary criticism this book examines.

The literary plenitude claimed by Gates exists only to the extent that its conventions, hermeneutics, and institutional wisdom have been historically and repeatedly recognized. Gates' merely superficial use of the black tradition's critics—Sterling Brown, Arthur Davis, Charles Davis, George Kent, Larry Neal—all of whom he is clearly aware of, is particularly striking here. Any black tradition must surely establish a relationship to its antecedents; however, his work did not fulfill this necessary task through the elaboration of a historical narrative, the identification of shared critical standards, and a search for the canon's shared literary genres, conventions, or rhetoric. Without the identification of an accumulated body of historical wisdom and experience, no tradition can be said to exist. Gates' superficial evocation and mimicry of canonical rhetoric does not provide us with sufficient data with which to define the tradition. *Without* such an institutionalized literary tradition, it is not clear what it means to be "distinctively African-American."

The hyperbole of Gates' claims is telling. The black literary culture embodied in signifying emerges not from a confident African-American literary intelligentsia engaged in the patience-demanding task of philology, comparative literature, and rhetoric but from a besieged cadre of the black middle class, attempting to create a discipline amidst the storm and stress of newly integrated elite universities. Called into being during the days of black power, this group lacked the authentic intellectual traditions upon which any literary inquiry and practice must rest. Tradition cannot be ordered as one calls for a pizza; it is the product of innumerable past comings and goings. During the seventies, eighties, and nineties, the critical writers I describe brandished a flurry of cultural symbols as a means of institution building, professional advancement, and therapeutic-managerial activity. The particular limitations of their undertaking proceeded inevitably from this method. The historical and philological stories told by the signifying critics have not parsed their idealized tradition of African-American folk culture into a useful set of rhetorical, literary-critical generic categories. As a result, works such as *The Signifying Monkey* and *Moorings and Metaphors* have not been able to summon the supposed strengths of the black folk culture to the present-day debacle in African-American life. Indeed, these texts fail to put the literary works and "African-American culture" that they (and their critical progeny) survey in a politically, culturally, and socially useful perspective. Amidst social collapse under the pressures of epidemic crime and educational decay, the signifiers cannot articulate their culture's or community's ultimate concerns. At this moment, black critics and intellectuals badly need the literary knowledge and artistic vision that cultural history traditionally promises. Such knowledge is, of course, no guarantee of moral wisdom. However, signifying has produced nothing equivalent to the spiritual and intellectual depth that post–World War II European and American academic society expected and received from Auerbach, Curtius, Lionel Trilling, and M. H. Abrams. A literate society wants and needs this depth when its social and cultural supports begin to buckle. These criticisms of signifying as a theory, professional style, and ethos are harsh. However, this severity responds to the cultural stakes involved in African-American political self-consciousness in the present-day crisis.

## II

"Signifying" takes its name from a ritual contest of insult practiced in black lower-class life, a kind of verbal agon common in traditional oral cultures. As such a contest, the game embodies the adversarial ethos common to the world of orality. When African-American writers in the late nineteenth century began to recover folk tradition as a source of theme and stylistic method, signifying was appropriated to the written world of print. This appropriation deeply shaped the literary styles and strategies of Charles Chesnutt, Langston Hughes, Zora Neale Hurston, Ralph Ellison, and Ishmael Reed. In these literary contexts, signifying takes the form of irony, which, as Wayne Booth usefully observes, often serves as a means of communication.[11] This communication is, however, commonly self-referential, allusive, and metaphorical. Through the appropriation of signifying, black writers discovered what seemed to be a distinctively "black" register of literary devices, a register that complicated the "written" protocols of print with the affective nuance of face-to-face speech.

Signifying communicates through concrete, often material representations—rather than through abstractions such as other ideas. Like much communication in a traditional "oral world," signifying rarely employs abstract logical forms of reasoning such as induction and deduction, but tends to use analogies based upon objects and events taken from the speaker's daily world of experience.[12] Thus the signifier makes his argument in a dramatic but commonsense manner. Rhetorical improvisation and witty topical reference are the hallmarks of signifying communication. The prominence of the terms "to signify" and "to represent" in present-day African-American youth culture show that world's inclination to adopt the rhetoric of orality in their confrontations with educated speakers trained in the culture of print.

The signifier not only expounds conventional semantic meanings but effects a "representation" of the black point of view. "You are not," my son dryly remarks as I examine an advertised rapper T-shirt, "ready to represent." Represent what? By "represent" he refers to an assumed countercultural, quasi-nationalist, symbolically black stance in the public space. This term's force comes not only from its politics but from its historical context as well. "My students," laments a successful young Latino professor of philosophy at a Boston think tank, "expect me to represent." To represent is to project the meanings of a "signified" black culture, the lower-class ideological response to the post–Civil Rights era. In what way, the students are asking, has he acknowledged his connection to the political developments that have brought him to the elite American university? The signifiers, not surprisingly, seek to convert this rhetorical method, the culture it communicates, and the goal of representation into a literary institution embodying black culture. In the hands of the signifying critics, this oral style carries the symbolic weight of not only black folk culture, but the recent political consciousness of the late twentieth-century urban masses.

Given their emphasis on the adversarial oral character of black culture, the signifying critics' use of this rhetoric of representation becomes plausible. They too seek to shock—often through agonistic means—blacks and whites into an awareness of a newly evoked cultural plenitude. Nonetheless, the signifier's attempt to use the face-to-face rhetoric of signifying as a literary-critical language raises several problems. These only multiply as signifying is pressed into service as a means of canon-building. The signifier may import many of the affective elements of orality into the discursive world of print. This move provides him or her with some of his most powerful rhetorical and emotive effects. However, black folk orality cannot compete with written literary discourse as a language for the construction of an academic tradition. Signifying is not intended to amass, retain, manipulate, analyze, and store language in ways that a canon requires.

Moreover, the signifiers have not developed a distinctive critical language from black folk culture. They have not wrought the face-to-face rhetoric of orality into a comprehensive set of black tropes linking key literary images and figures. Instead, the signifiers' method is extremely vague and nearly impossible to distinguish from conventional rhetoric. Most frequently the new black critics draw upon the appearance of irony or upon an apparently ironic link between tropes or texts to declare a text black. An extremely open-ended form of interpretation, signifying allows a critic to claim an essentially black linguistic connection between any two words, semantic structures, grammatical forms, or literary works. The vagueness of this method has allowed signifiers to claim the whole of their literary-critical practice—as well as any black-authored text—as black. Works once thought to have been written by whites (such as *Our Nig*) can therefore display signifying links to other black texts, once an African-American author has been located or posited. Moreover, the ease with which signifying relations may be established sometimes obscures the necessity of gathering the infinitely various plenitude upon which any canon depends. Signifiers sometimes locate this plenitude in the past, and at other times in a future philological fulfillment. In an account of his understanding of African-American literary tradition, Gates states:

> And while we are at the earliest stages of organization, I can say that my own biases toward canon formation are to stress the formal relationships that obtain among texts in the black tradition—relations of revision, echo, call and response,

antiphony, what have you—and to stress the vernacular roots of the tradition. For the vernacular, or oral literature, in our tradition, has a canon of its own.[13]

This is the soft statement of a position which he makes more forcefully as he describes the signifying links existing between any set of black texts. In his introduction to the volumes in the *Schomburg Library Collection of Black Woman Writers*, Gates writes:

> Literary works configure into a tradition not because of some mystical collective unconscious determined by the biology of race or gender, but because writers read other writers and ground their representations of experience in models of language provided largely by other writers to whom they feel akin. It is through this mode of literary revision, amply evident in the texts themselves—in formal echoes, recast metaphors, even in parody—that a "tradition" emerges and defines itself. This is formal bonding, and it is only through formal bonding that we can know a literary tradition. The collective publication of these works by black women now for the first time makes it possible for scholars and critics, male and female to demonstrate that sexuality, race, and gender are both the condition and the basis of *tradition*—but tradition is found in discrete use of language acts.[14]

This essentialist character of the "relation" between reader and writer parallels a similar attribution of "essence" and "presence" to black voice. Within this parallel the process by which African Americans read and interpret black-authored books becomes in itself black. This move has a number of consequences for signifying that Gates—a suave and subtle exponent of his views—usually sidesteps, but which continue to hobble less-discriminating black commentators. One is that white critics may not experience the same literary encounter as that of a black reader perusing a black book.

Gates' rhetorical assumption carries important consequences in the newly integrated university world. Signifying only reinforces the racialist logic of English departments that limits blacks to narrowly defined and intellectually limited inquiries on African-American subjects. Furthermore, the need to provide a plenitude for this tradition—and the ease with which that plenitude may be textually established—creates a "scholarly" program for new members of the profession's black enclave. They may be put to work establishing links between black texts and tropes or converting white literary idioms and conventions to black. Any institution has a function that occupies its members and eventually fulfills a goal. And signifying is a source of endless work—whatever its intellectual worth—toward the creation of a culture-sustaining black literary plenitude. This of course leads to reductive, motif-hunting, text-manipulative literary intepretation—which, however, ultimately serves a compelling social policy well, given signifying's function as a black middle-class compensatory ideology.

If Gates' point of view has not directly influenced African-American commentators, it has at least caught the mood of the pragmatic, cultural nationalism that pervades present-day black criticism as well as the political style of the new black middle class. However, this success has exacted a high intellectual and cultural cost. With very few exceptions, signifiers tend to work with African-American literary tradition and a narrowly conceived idea of African-American vernacular. The self-evident quality of their logic exempts them from defining their aesthetic standards or defending any "African-American" literary approach as exceptional. Given this professionalized African-American perspective, everything a black critic does is black. He lives in what he assumes to be a black literary world parallel to a white one. He need not demonstrate the superiority (or even the relationship) of his literary methods to any aesthetic standard, whether African-American or Western—whatever "Western" means in this context: for it is certainly impossible to imagine that the whole range of Western practice has remained untouched by African influence (consider, for example, the American language). African-American "signifying" interpretations have thus predictably been the product of mechanical thought: the flip-flops of binary reasoning as well as naive romantic myth, most often appearing as a vaguely stated myth of origin. This is particularly true of the work of Gates and Karla Holloway.

One of the first, if unintentional, revelations of a signifying book such as *The Signifying Monkey* is how little it has to add to traditional Western philological and critical histories that, like *Homo Ludens* or *Mimesis*, catalogue conventional rhetorical forms, literary conventions, and *topoi*. The vague capaciousness of Gates' categories and the sparseness of his yield reveal not only a (characteristically American) dearth of inherited custom, tradition, and society, but also how much any African-American writer must rely on Western culture whenever he writes. This literary emptiness, which successive critics have done little to fill, extends also to the signifier's lack of a mature psychology and sociology by which he or she might describe or analyze the rhetorical settings in which signifying is deployed. For all their claims to interdisciplinary depth, the signifiers draw only superficially on the extensive work done by linguists, sociologists, and rhetoricians concerning the rhetorical worlds in which signifying takes place. The signifiers are constrained from doing so by a professional commitment to a narrow literary "linguistic" and "semiotic" method that reads itself and its black-authored predecessors as African-American—not to mention a disturbing lack of curiosity and reflection. Between Gates' witty moments of self-display, mimicry, and parody in *The Signifying Monkey* lay vast spaces of arid theory and even drier practice. These wastes abound also in the works of those who come after him, such as Holloway and Awkward.

Except for the glib ironic pieces penned by Gates in his early literary-critical essays and journalism, most signifying theorists have written a leaden prose, pervaded by a mechanical, perfunctory, and even estranged quality. This estrangement often appears in the naked in instrumental style that the signifiers associate with their work. Gates has spoken directly, and alarmingly, about the papers, articles, and books black critics write for promotion. Much of this literary production reveals a quality of intellectual alienation inherent in such an overtly goal-directed process. The signifier communicates to his audience through a carefully manipulated mask, held at a prudent distance from him. He persuades through the ethos of his persona, the character implicit in the mask so deftly tendered to his readers from afar. Emotionally protected by irony and disinterestedness, he uses the mask to evoke a variety of pathetic effects in his audience—anger, surprise, and at times sympathy. Defensive and reactive as it is, signifying is an appropriate strategy for those situations in which the weak confront powerful aggressors, curry support from patrons, and confuse their attackers. Signifying operates not as a strategy for political, social, or cultural change, but as a day-to-day tactic adapted to a shifting terrain of bad faith, political favor, limited resources, and red-lined possibilities. These are not conditions to instill the enthusiasm, motivation, or overflow of feeling and thought which drive significant writing. The absence of more than purely instrumental motivation hollows the signifier's manifestos throughout.

The signifier's instrumental task of professional gain and day-to-day institutional world maintenance can therefore never be a source of significant spiritual or humane value, absent some compelling political, religious, or social motivation—although it is not clear whether the imperatives of racial gender politics have made a difference in this regard. The signifier may project a charismatic image of endless creativity, energy, invention, and copiousness; however, he will never create the core of stable values on which any institution must permanently rest. Indeed, exponents of signifying assume the absence of such a secure black institution and thus an authentic politics in the academy, grounded in scholarship. Their cynicism rests on skepticism about the long-term intentions of the academy itself, toward themselves and their institutional goals. This condition goes far to explain the paucity of books and articles written by the signifiers on anything other than a few African-American literary texts.

Signifying, in the end, is one more product of American racial inequality, and where is such a cultural consequence of racism more likely to appear than in an academic endeavor requiring patient, leisurely reflection, sustained reading, slow steady accumulation of knowledge, careful analysis, and a motivation that transcends purely instrumental purposes? No one better manipulated the possibilities of black-white patronage relationships than Booker T. Washington, who in *Up from Slavery* described a young black teacher seeking a job in the Jim Crow South. Informed of a local debate over Earth's shape, the canny young man offered to expound on either a flat or a spherical Earth according to the community's preference.[15] I offer this anecdote less as a sample of Washington's cynical wit than as a parallel to the signifiers' tactics in the newly integrated elite academy, now the signifier's home. More tragic than the community's ignorance—horrible enough as it is—is the young teacher's repression of his knowledge and good sense. The corrosive effect of severe economic need upon intellectual integrity is the grimmest law of disadvantaged life. The first significant thinkers of the nineteenth-century capitalist world of Emerson, Hawthorne, Melville, and Thoreau are at great pains to stress the intellectual's reliance on commodity and patronage—what Melville called "time, strength, cash and patience." Houston Baker gives us some idea of the signifier's style in *Blues, Ideology, and Afro-American Literature: A Vernacular Theory*, where he explicitly proposes a theory of black expression as commodity exchange, developing a history that extends from Equiano's *Narrative* to Ellison's *Invisible Man*.[16] A more explicit signature of the signifier's desire for quick profit is the proliferation of fly-by-night cultural commentary that characterizes much of the writing I examine in Holloway and Dyson, not to mention the texts of Cornel West and Gates. The most characteristic literary signature of the signifier is the shoddily argued text, marred further by the grammatical and stylistic marks of haste. On the evidence of Holloway, Awkward, and Dyson, the signifier conceives of his literary production as a commodity estranged from himself as author. In the course of such estrangement, he or she devalues the leisurely reading, reflection, and revision required by all thoughtful writing. He or she ultimately devalues his or her own imagination.

To evoke Booker T. Washington's example is to remember another aspect of the signifier's condition: the great inequalities of power and authority between blacks and whites in the elite spheres of professional intellectual life. Signifying is a strategy well adapted to flourish in these conditions, which first appear in the world of the Gilded Age where Washington confronted rich white businessmen: the potential donors to whom his fable is directed. To this audience, Washington directs his many "darky" jokes as both plantation humor, a sign of deference, and evidence of his "inside" knowledge of black human character.[17] As critics of the black public intellectuals have noted, the new African-American cultural critic often assumes the stance of popular ethnographer for a white upper-class public distanced from urban life. In this case, signifying communicates said "inside" knowledge of a lower caste or subaltern world that may be of instrumental use to the powerful. Not surprisingly, black commentators have been drawn to the signifying-like strategies by which the poor black Uncle Julius of *The Conjure Woman Tales* addresses John, the frame story's naive wealthy white narrator. Gatesian signifying emerged in a rhetorical world defined by parallel inequities of wealth and power—the newly integrated world where black student intellectuals and political activists faced upper-middle-class and upper-class white students as well as faculty in the newly integrated elite colleges and graduate schools of the late sixties and afterwards.

The extreme black-white inequality that created the signifier's intellectual world was shaped by two important trends in the academy. The first was the extension of elite college admission to middle- and upper-middle-class white students from well-endowed suburban public schools.[18] Another was the racial integration of these schools by the black middle and stable lower classes—a cadre that had hitherto never appeared in such large numbers in these institutions. These trends brought together a white middle-class cohort giddy in their newly minted elite status in the upper-level American academy. This was, of course, an illusion. The transformation in white admissions merely exploited an expanded pool of intellectual talent now available as a result of the post–World War II economic boom. The new white public school cadre, however, bore a sense of academic belonging shaped not only by test scores but also by the class privilege of those ethnically segregated suburbs or urban communities in which they gained their academic advantage. They were—it must be emphasized—the indirect beneficiary of growing inequalities in black and white wealth, and the expansion of the upper white-collar levels of the American economy. Although the whites drew upon the traditional American ideology of success to define their merit and claim to elite status, both had been established only by the fiat of a much higher corporate and governmental elite working through the foundations and university administrations.

More needs to be said on this point. The superior academic preparation received by the new white cohort resulted from one more of a series of post–World War II government-enacted policies that benefited a new white ethnic bourgeoisie far more than blacks. These included the G.I. bill, bank loans, and federal housing assistance, as well as improved working conditions and benefits won by unions that often excluded blacks. The reverse side of the expansion of the white elite was the increasingly isolated—indeed, ghettoized—status of urban blacks. As white beneficiaries left the public schools and inner cities, largely urban communities often found themselves without the funds for buildings, material, and teachers needed for competitive schools. Indeed, the white fugitives to the suburbs took with them the tax bases required for many basic urban infrastructure needs and services, especially education. The competitive advantage of the new white academic elite was often built on the sustained deprivation of urban blacks, particularly those of the inner-city ghetto. Within the world of the university, this competitive advantage was framed by a white middle- and upper-middle-class sense of superiority, continuing earlier patterns linked to Jim Crow oppression in the rural South, the segregation of labor unions, and the geographical exclusion of urban blacks from the middle class in Northern cities and suburbs.[19]

The new resentment frequently expressed by middle- and upper-middle-class whites against their black confreres stemmed from related causes. Among other things, it continued the historically ingrained aversion of middle- and lower-class American whites to black competition. It expressed middle-class white fears for the prospects of their racial privilege, newly enhanced by the economic success of the post–World War II boom. Most importantly, the new white racist resentment displaced middle-class anger from the real source of this threat to a convenient substitute. The anger directed against blacks resembled the gesture of an older sister who hits her younger brother after she herself has been scolded. This redirected rage rarely touched the upper echelons of the established American elite in the foundations and most selective universities who promoted and administered the new racial diversity. Instead, the whites victimized blacks.

White hostility flourished with the newly fluid relationship between the white educational establishment and an upwardly mobile white middle-class cadre. Black students were far less able to defend themselves psychologically or socially than the Harvard Board of Overseers or the Ford Foundation. Scorn was thus often heaped upon African-American students in elite schools—often motivated individuals drawn from populations located (to a far greater extent than the whites) in black communities which, whatever their growth, had expanded less than their white counterparts. In the setting of the elite university, these blacks carried a further stigma of inferiority by virtue of lower test scores, grades less stimulated by competition, and a less rigorous preparation than the upper-class graduates of suburban schools. Such conditions are generally recognized throughout the Western European world as the inevitable determinants of academic performance. In the American university, this historical situation became the basis of the anger directed by a self-proclaimed class of self-made, middle-class whites towards supposedly privileged blacks.[20]

The new academic playing field—similarly inhabited by an increasingly middle-class and ethnic white-professorate—shaped the rhetorical ground on which signifying was deployed. It accounts for the sometimes muted, sometimes explicit contempt and hostility that often undermined interracial education in the elite university. This ethos persists in the educated professions, especially in the liberal white academy, where the new multiethnic white elite claims social legitimacy on the basis of meritocratic norms of intellectual excellence. Black responses to the earlier academic mismatch—and persistent middle-class white resentment—shape much recent African-American autobiographical writing and appear memorably in the criticism of Hortense Spillers and Michael Awkward.[21] In such vignettes, important literary elements of signifying appear, as can be seen in this example taken from a recent collection of essays by Michael Awkward:

> A black male cultural worker at the podium must be dedicated to producing discourse that seeks to cut through the calcified terms of signification attached to "black man anywhere," including "Buck," "Lazy, Shiftless Nigger," "Rapist," "Ghetto Blaster," and, more recently, "Affirmative Action Baby" and "Car Jacker."[22]

"Black male cultural worker" is, of course, Michael Awkward's partially ironic reference to himself. Fiftyish, black male academics will easily recognize the racial epithets he enumerates as abusive remarks overheard by Awkward while he lectures or participates in a panel discussion. Awkward's writing here displays far more passion than elsewhere in *Negotiating Differences*. The unexpected appearance of the ghetto's face-to-face world of violent orality in an academic setting accounts for this difference. Awkward employs the tactics of signifying both to create an ironic distance from his audience through the expressions "cultural worker," "producing discourse," and "calcified terms of signification," as well as to flaunt his "car jacker" persona who mocks the white audience and its fear of black men. These provocative-symbolic-cathartic gestures represent the book's most significant "border crossings." A traditionally literary exploration of the event Awkward describes here might have been more rewarding than his excursions into theory.

Long after "cultural worker," "discourse," and similarly calcified academic and ideological terms have passed the reader, a savage parody of white Negrophobia proceeds. The terms "buck," "carjacker," and "affirmative action baby" are directed at whites resentful of an alleged black racial privilege. Awkward's mask taunts an educated white audience with the ghetto slang of people for whom white professors talk like books. He can behave so aggressively towards his white audience largely because of the same fears that explain the murmuring, rather than direct statement, of their insults. For white resentment, if unmuffled, would risk itself politically in attacking the foundations and universities that patronize blacks. These institutions, from the white academic point of view, have sullied the arena with a black presence, yet remain invulnerable to mainstream middle-class recourse. Moreover, the white audience fears Awkward as a black man. If, as Awkward proclaims, the black academic is indeed a buck or a carjacker, then he will be perfectly willing to dismiss academic protocol and confront his white opponents without ceremony. Philadelphia, as Awkward has reminded his readers a few pages earlier, is his turf too. Aware of the city's geography and people, he knows his academic audience to be sheltered and soft. The white men who smirk at him are—from the perspective of his neighborhood—in over their heads. They tempt a fate for which the Bryn Mawr schools have poorly prepared them.

The black speaker's real message to his audience is his intention of bringing the anomic, freewheeling violence of Walnut Street into the secure world of academic privilege. There, despite his alleged inferiority, he will have his way with his enemies. Although his rhetorical distance grows out of the (wish-fulfilling) fantastic element of his imagery, his anger is wholly plausible amidst the face-to-face urban realities experienced by a white academic Philadelphian audience. At the heart of this confrontation is Awkward's vivid truth: inequities of intellectual and academic achievement mean nothing to him. Power may be negotiated by other means than an SAT or achievement score.

Awkard's fierce mockery of the soft, white suburban high-achiever repeats another parodic scene in which Henry Louis Gates states an important principle of the signifiers: black writing possesses the semantic, grammatical, and rhetorical features of African-American orality. Like Awkward, he throws his curse from an ironic distance, situated behind a mask of anger, bitter contempt, and sarcasm. However, Gates further protects himself by addressing his monograph's audience through a proxy, a Black Power radical free to use far more vulgar language than the author himself in his present setting. Gates quotes H. Rap Brown, who equates learning to read with learning to signify. The text significantly dramatizes this point as well as making it explicitly. Gates, and occasionally Brown himself, set forth their message from a distanced "written" academic posture, explicitly referring to the act of composition, learning to write, and the repetitive exercise by which one refines the skill. One is, both Gates and Brown readily accede, initiated into the world of print—and, like all initiates, one refers to the ritual with self-conscious respect. Thus we have the phrases "he writes," "reading Dick and Jane," and "exercised our minds." From this sober distance, however, Gates goes on to deliver a tirade of obscenities to not only the publisher's reader-referee (no doubt an accomplished professor) but also to Gates' presumed university audience. These obscenities make his point by denigrating the world of writing to an equivalence with the oral world of the ghetto.

"I learned to talk in the street," Brown writes, "not from reading Dick and Jane going to the Zoo and all that simple shit." Rather, Brown continues, "We exercised our minds," not by studying arithmetic, "but by playing the dozens." Both reading and signifying are means of exercising the mind, but reading (represented by a primer) is "silly shit" and "playing the dozens" is significant communication. More than this, Rap Brown asserts provocatively that his teachers sought to teach him "poetry" when he and his fellows were making poetry in his neighborhood. "If anybody needed to study poetry," he maintains, "my teacher needed to study mine."[23] Here again Gates—always through his reckless proxy, Hap Brown—equates the oral and written word with a vengeance. The black student—having mastered the word on the street—reverses roles with the teacher of writing, who is presumably less adept at oral folk poetry. "Who is master here?" Brown and by implication Gates ask their reader. At the heart of Gates' theory of signifying is the assumption that this question is to be settled in the ghetto realm, where street credibility confronts elite academic achievement as an equal. If superior academic status in the suburban high school, the Ivy League college, and the prestigious graduate school gives Gates' referee at Oxford University Press his intellectual authority, that reader must nevertheless recognize the pecking order of the ghetto.

By 1987, the publication date of *The Signifying Monkey*, this populist black power had brought Gates to a chair at Cornell, a major American institution which had been awakened nearly twenty years before to the potential danger of the ghetto masses in the streets. The use of Rap Brown's name to a middle-aged audience of white academics in a book from a prestigious university press signalled not "street smarts" but the newly emerged authority of the violent black lumpen. Here, the arrogance of a white elitist audience, assumed to be hostile, is met by the threatened hostility of the blacks; Gates' mimicry is playful intimidation, what Tom Wolfe has in another context called "Mau Mauing." However, such hostility common to the streets of the ghetto had turned in the late sixties to destructive, and politically effective, violence.[24]

This rhetorical strategy—the ethos of its personae, its intended pathetic affect on its audience, and its distanced authorial presence—appears elsewhere in African-American literary criticism. Autobiographical accounts of signifying often dramatize conflict between wily blacks pitted against their white would-be superiors. The language of force, pointedly directed to the white interlocutor at close range, is deployed with the aim of disarming the suburban professor's hostility. This exercise is, of course, essentially therapeutic, expressing a black humanity and potential denied by white racism. Signifying—while acknowledging the cultural and in some ways academic superiority of its white audience—emotionally hardens the black rhetorician against the contempt of a profession in which he has, after all, invested his life. As therapy, signifying not only leaves the university's material structures of power in place, but represents the black critics' compensatory adjustment to them. Whatever this symbolic-cathartic value, signifying keeps the racialized institutional worlds of the white professional mainstream intact; indeed, signifying draws the lines even more vividly than before. It is a means of shaming one's contemptuous superiors into grudging patronage. However, the client must give up his dignity.

In the profession of English, the signifier's acknowledgement of his academic, cultural, and political inequality to his white audience represents an influential development, not least in terms of its interracial politics. The politics of diversity bristle with markers of racial difference, which have become in fact coded signs of black intellectual and academic inferiority. Indeed, the term "difference" has—at least in relation to African Americans—come *de facto* to mean little else. In the elite university, administrators, professors, and students now equate racial and class inequalities with black cultural inferiority in a way that disturbs few. An important set of professional consequences have followed. As the black newcomers have entered the mainstream profession of English with their racially parochial monographs, methods, disciplinary claims, and academic agendas, they have inevitably distanced themselves from the standard professional procedures and institutional wisdom of the elite English department. They often enter an enclave of black students and academics who specialize in African-American literature. Black graduate students in particular often separate themselves from the profession's institutional knowledge and communication by a horizon of racial identity. This phenomenon ironically sets off standard professional knowledge as a form of racial and class identity, while undermining the intellectual legitimacy of the field's newcomers. The consistent demand that African-American students and faculty specialize in black literature only exacerbates this problem.

## III

Signifying nonetheless seems the source of freedom to the many black critics, students, and scholars who have drawn on its tactics. Whatever their weaknesses, Gates' rhetorical strategies appear to explain much of what black writers have written and felt since the time of Zora Neale Hurston and Richard Wright. The sensibility of signifying—perhaps because of its alienated, resentful ethos—corresponds to the ambivalence of many twentieth-century black writers entering a literary mainstream just opening to blacks. Furthermore, any critic imposing a methodological grid on a given text will probably discover a meaning, merely from the suggestiveness of most literary categories. At any rate, the proof of the pudding is in the eating. The fact that signifiers approach texts without real concern for the conceptual grounds of their method matters less than the fact that, as a rhetoric, signifying—whatever it really is—helps those critics produce a work of interpretation, however lackluster the text or commentary, however alienated the reader. Signifying and its strategies seem to promote the fluency with which black critics interpret African-American works of literature. The very flexibility and vagueness of the signifying categories allow critics to evade, defer, or co-opt resistant themes and linguistic structures—literary obstructions which nonetheless keep interpretation honest by setting the critic's limits. The signifying critic enjoys the illusion of unlimited authority over his text, thus reinforcing his original biases, and often obscuring what he does not wish to observe or know. The reduction of interpretive criteria to a few categories of rhetoric can (when not wholly vacuous) only suppress a text's complexities. In the absence of categories such as oral, black, and signifying itself, what is left for the critic's guidance but his day-to-day will to shape the text according to the most nakedly topical demands? Given the formalist narrowness of the signifying creed, however, this interpretation will be wholly barren of the psychology, social understanding, and cultural depth needed to define—in any reasonable way—his audience, his rhetorical situation, and ultimately the rhetorician himself. Signifying is built for the fling and not the long romance. The signifier soon finds himself dependent not only upon his faculty for invention but also upon the most conventional and easily assimilated understandings of his topics—which, whatever its ideological content, often passes into the critic's bag of tricks without careful inspection or scrutiny. His carelessness, however, permits an exercise of will that the signifier could not otherwise exert. This freedom is, however, illusory: the signifier runs roughshod upon not only the text at hand, but his own powers of perception and interpretation.

Signifying thus represses not only the signifier's analytical ability, but also his sensibility: that unity of heart, mind, and perception by which we make value judgments about texts, interpretations, and ourselves. Unlike the democratized sensibilities dramatized in Baudelaire's in "The Painter of Modern Life," in the prose essays of Addison and Steele, or in the literary journalism-history of Le Roi Jones in *Blues People*, the signifiers work within an extremely narrow cultural range, lacking the same historical, philosophical, and aesthetic awareness which informs those canonical texts. Racism is a predictable consequence of this self-limitation, which implicitly makes the critic's "blackness," rather than his range of knowledge, the criterion for interpretation. This essentialism accounts for the signifier's implicit tendency to see non-black critics as racially unqualified to attain a full understanding of black authors or black-authored texts. We find, therefore, Michael Awkward applauding Robert Hemenway's modest claim that he, as a white man, cannot engage the full extent of Zora Neale Hurston—as if black women writers, immersed in the now fashionable modes of black rhetoric, are inherently able to do so.[25] Awkward assumes, I take it, that the narrowly defined and broadly applied linguistic categories of signifying might produce an interpretation comparable in depth to Hemenway's, despite the white critic's evident breadth of knowledge of Hurston and her times. Hemenway's remarks may mean many things, and Awkward does not honor their possible range or subtlety—in an omission wholly typical of the signifiers. The overall effect of signifying sensibility is to narrow the breadth of feeling that allows for a full understanding of either Hurston's work or the remarks of a fellow critic. Awkward courts real political and social danger in assuming such a callow lack of sophistication in his professional and academic superiors.

In place of value judgment and ultimate concerns, the signifier deluges us with disconnected meanings and fashion. Black sensibility—if I may be allowed one unearned essentialist generalization—strikes nearly all observers with its copiousness: the culture's capacity to generate style after style, and taste after taste. The current modes of black feeling observed by signifying enact the enormous creativity of the black lumpen not only as invention but also as powerful authoritarian will. This lumpen sensibility has gained its influence not for its spiritual or emotional depth, but for its imaginative transformation of the fierce class, racial, and cultural resentments possessed by the black masses. Vaguely suggested though they are in the earlier passages by Awkward and Gates, these energies provide a populist aesthetic and legitimacy for the new fields of black literature and African-American Studies in general. The signifying critics draw their sense of a cosmic center not from a wealth of literary data, but from a critical plenitude assumed to inhere in a mass sensibility: the lumpen's capacity to produce a flood of signs taken for wonders. These signs, flying like sparks from the signifying forge, immediately become sacred, numinous evidence of a divinely black culture. The signifying sensibility repeatedly discerns this in the creative persons of Michael Jackson, Tupac Shakur, and more recently Marvin Gaye. They have become the charismatic centers of "meaning" in black culture. Similarly, the signifying canon gives hyperbolic praise to the tricksters of Ishmael Reed's slight fictional satires, the parodic side of Ralph Ellison's, the vernacular high jinks of the narrator Uncle Julius in Chesnutt's *The Conjure Woman*, and the crude humor of obscene rappers. It proclaims ideologue-outlaws such as H. Rap Brown to be important thinkers and writers who dramatize ultimate truths of black life.[26]

The numinous quality of signifying offers intellectual compensation to black literary academics in the fiercely competitive world of the American English Department. The social distinctions that disable blacks are held in place by unevenly distributed public wealth and the willful exercise of class and racial privilege. Yet the critical language of signifying only exacerbates this problem by narrowing the intellectual range within which black critics write, read, think, and feel. Nonetheless the signifier must still compete within the economic, political, and social dynamo of American society, as embodied in the university. Whatever the signifier thinks of present-day white-dominated America, it is a nation of enormous creativity and power. In the academic sphere, these advantages have made the top American graduate programs the high-water mark for the world's best students and researchers.

As upwardly mobile members of this world, the signifiers have drawn upon the resources of the signifying style to negotiate their way through the nexus of political, social, and economic power that the American university has become. Seeking his own *Realpolitik* leverage, the entrepreneurial signifier has appropriated the trickster strategies of the masses, recognizing the potential of black folk culture in a white American consumer economy that no longer discriminates between politics, academic speculation, and fashion. This new black elite, represented by figures such as Gates, Baker, Holloway, and Awkward (as well as a host of black theologians), has succeeded academically by reproducing the trend-setting, fashion-making creativity of the poor in the academy. These gestures inevitably seduce white middle-class academic audiences and the media that see the instability of black life from the distance of sedentary scholarly existence. Moreover, these postures make the new black academic an attractive commodity in the media—a source of wealth and power that in turn may pave his way in the university.

This has been the largest cultural and social success of signifying. However, this odd combination of academic entrepreneurship and black hustling style has fitted the new African-American intellectual elite poorly for the task of cultural leadership. Its empowering gestures stem from alienation and reproduce the dislocating violence of the urban poor in the university, thereby appealing to the worst aspects in the psychology of potential white patrons. Such gestures are the product of an ethically unregulated will and a resentment directed not only toward others but also toward certain aspects of oneself. In this respect, the strident orality of Gates' signifying strategies grimly anticipated the latest horror in black life: the rejection of traditional learning by poor and middle-class black children. The ultimately repressive definition of black written culture as "oral" now flourishes in the subculture of inner-city youth. In *The Signifying Monkey*, Gates unabashedly described a class in which a teacher allowed his black students to release their intellectual frustration after an achievement test by letting them design a counter-test aimed at ETS in Princeton. Appropriately enough, this test—as it was "rewritten by the disadvantaged students"—was called "The In Your Face Test of No Certain Skills."[27] The rewritten aptitude examination eerily foreshadowed the now widely discussed black student perception that he (or she) plays no part in the test-taking culture by which this nation sorts its elite. The teacher's use of academic protocols as symbolic targets for black rage prophesied the role that many African-American Studies courses and events would play as therapy, as relief from the inevitable conflicts of any culturally "diverse" society.

Black leaders who must confront the illiteracy of the black masses directly appear less amused by this phenomenon than Gates. Illiteracy, arithmetical incompetence, and a horrifying ignorance of liberal arts commonplaces now constitute a national crisis in black education, a crisis recognized by black politicians and the NAACP but by few black literary scholars at the nation's elite schools. The idealization of the folk and oral culture by the signifiers, as Adolph Reed and a number of others have begun to show, always leads to an extreme political and social dislocation. And this dislocation now takes the form of an intellectual impotence which leaves the signifying critics dumb before the self-destructive ignorance of the urban folk. Unable to locate themselves in the broader traditions of the West, the signifiers have predictably finished by relying upon the most clichéd and derivative accounts of blackness on which to forge a canon. They themselves now reiterate the cultural terms of the West's racist contempt for blacks.

# Section One

# Signifiers and Signifying

---

Henry Louis Gates Jr. has long occupied the center of the academic world as theorist, academic entrepreneur, social commentator, and belletristic essayist. Not only have his literary paradigms and cultural criticisms explained much of current black writing, but they have also set a template for much of the African-American literary work done in the academy. Gates managed to combine the sensibility of the newly integrated African-American academic elite with an awareness of the traditional roles of black critics. He adapted all of this in the field of English studies to the literary revolution in semiotics. The result was a highly fashionable but also on which the profession's new black cohort built an institution of critical commentary. This process—elaborated in the narrative of the following three chapters—shows Gates as he is often celebrated: institution-builder and black cultural spokesman. He is also an opponent of traditional American humanism. This aspect of his intellectual style also played a significant part in his successful career.

---

# Chapter One

## Gates' Cultural Synthesis
### A Revived African-American Critical Practice

Henry Louis Gates Jr. succeeded as an academic entrepreneur, cultivating the ground cleared by Larry Neal and the early Houston Baker. Beyond this, however, Gates' endeavors benefited from a historical perspective possessed by few of his contemporaries. He grasped the role that literary studies had played in middle-class African-American life during the previous sixty years. This understanding, plus his streetwise grasp of black culture, allowed him to fashion a canon that not only satisfied the academy but spoke to the needs of a new black bourgeoisie. He saw eventually that the rhythm-and-blues sensibility of signifying that spoke to African-American literary critics and students of semiotics could be marketed even more directly to a mass audience. The literary explication of texts, by his own account, never had more than a purely instrumental value for Gates. Seizing upon semiotics as a democratic critical method, Gates quickly saw how interpretive readings and literary knowledge provided raw material for fashion and the shaping of tastes. He was to take this insight and run with it. As an academic wheeler-dealer, he was nonpareil. Fewer than ten years after receiving his Ph.D., he occupied an extraordinarily visible and powerful place in the academic world of literary scholarship. Exploiting that role ruthlessly, he became a media mogul.

One imagines that Gates' connection with Charles Davis, the distinguished black scholar of nineteenth- and twentieth-century American poetry and culture, was exceptionally important in his literary and entrepreneurial education. Indeed, Gates' academic literary career may be said to have begun when he decided during the seventies to finish his Cambridge University doctorate in English, after returning to Yale. In New Haven, Davis arranged with the authorities at Cambridge to supervise Gates' dissertation. Davis had been educated at Dartmouth, the University of Chicago, and New York University. An internationally known scholar of the highest academic standards and now a chaired Yale professor, Davis was an entirely appropriate choice for this undertaking. Not surprisingly, Gates speaks of him as an ideal reader.

Davis enjoyed an intimate connection with the history of African-American literature and literary criticism. He was—as his cousin Arthur's filio-pietistic biography shows—the scion of a far-flung, multigenerational clan of black intellectuals that included many administrators at Hampton Institute, Arthur P. Davis at Howard, Chuck Stone at Chapel Hill, and *Village Voice* editor and writer Thulani Davis.[1] Davis' career and professional orientation emerged within an intellectual network already in place at the end of the twenties and thirties, and firmly entrenched by the beginning of the integrated epoch in the academy. He brought with him a clear conception of the literary scholar's role in black middle-class life as well as a sense of the possibilities of integration for elite university education.[2] This knowledge made him an exceptionally able and successful director of African-American Studies at Yale.

Gates' introductions to the works of Redding (*To Make a Poet Black*) and Charles Davis (*Black Is the Color of the Cosmos*) showed an ever-growing understanding of the pedagogical role that earlier black scholars (such as Arthur Davis and Sterling Brown) had played in introducing the New Criticism and basic literary history to an African-American academic audience. Such a role had been a part of black scholarly tradition in literature for some time. In the work of Sterling Brown, the scholar-author's teacherly role appears in extended anthology introductions, question-sets ending chapters, as well as many book reviews clearly intended to provide the black middle class with accounts of recent scholarly and literary work by and about blacks. Gates possessed nothing like the depth of Brown's literary knowledge, academic-intellectual energy, and vision, but he adopted Brown's, Saunders Redding's, and Arthur P. Davis' role as literary instructor to the black middle class.

From the start of his career, Gates' references to figures such as George Scarborough flaunted what seemed to be an impressive hold upon the African-American literary canon. Although Gates would refer to the founding figures only casually and superficially, he broke into the arena of Black Studies aware of the erudition already amassed by figures such as Dorothy Porter, Charles Wesley, and Benjamin Brawley. Reading Gates in the late seventies and the eighties, one immediately encountered his acquaintance with the late nineteenth- and earlier twentieth-century traditions of African-American literary criticism—an intellectual connection conspicuously missing in even Houston Baker, George Kent, and Larry Neal, who appropriated this background more substantially, but with less show. Indeed, Gates immediately recognized how this earlier tradition might be constructed to define himself historically in a setting where knowledge about African-American literary history was still undeveloped.

Finally, Gates also benefited from the immense intellectual-institutional savvy of his mentor. Davis was *au courant* of the contemporary academic scene in an extraordinary way. As a chaired professor in American Studies at Yale and a former professor at Princeton and Penn State, he had had time to take the measure of the intellectual explosions occurring in the literary worlds of not only ethnic studies but also criticism. As an important textual bibliographer of Walt Whitman, and exponent of early twentieth-century American poetry, Davis was not one to lock himself in an intellectual ghetto. He—and, I suspect, Michael Cooke—must have shown Gates the possibilities of the literary history being done by both New Critic formalists, as well as structuralists and post-structuralists at Yale. Within this critical world, Gates quickly saw how a black literary canon might become a symbol of African-American culture in the elite university world. At Yale his models would have included not only the early literary history of Harold Bloom and Geoffrey Hartman, but even more importantly that of their continental antecedents, René Wellek, Erich Auerbach, and Ernst Curtius, as well as American forefathers William Wimsatt and Cleanth Brooks. Gates' references also show an awareness of a revival of interest in traditional rhetoric by figures such as Richard Lanham and the early Stanley Fish.

As a Yale graduate student working with the erudite, Chicago-educated Davis, Gates would also have been aware of other initiatives in formalist literary history, like the impressive work of the neo-Aristotelian critics R. S. Crane, Wayne Booth, and Arthur Friedman. These critics, too, sought to define literary historical periods and shape their narratives through reference to convention, rhetorical strategies, and linguistic forms. It would have also been impossible for Gates—given the influence of Davis and the Yale English Department—to ignore M. H. Abrams' *The Mirror and The Lamp* and *Natural Supernaturalism* in the seventies and eighties. Gates must have scanned the possibilities of pluralist literary history.

Gates' early work synthesized these influences into an extraordinarily ambitious project: he sought to harness the tigers of Euro-American literary history to the horses of African-American literary instruction. This project clearly influenced his role in the Yale NEH seminar "Minority Literature: The Reconstruction of Instruction," which sought to acquaint young African-American critics with new semiotic methods and implicitly with new ways of doing literary history. This effort reflected both Gates' often avant-garde critical tastes and the early twentieth-century black sense of pedagogical urgency. These blended aims created a sometimes mixed intellectual bag in the seminar's printed proceedings and his introductory essays. From the beginning, Gates spoke—sometimes high-handedly—of black professional backwardness and displacement within the academy.[3] At the same time, Gates' early essays, in their explications of recently recovered African-American texts such as Frederick Douglass' *Narrative*, also demonstrated the possibilities of structuralism for black critics.[4] A similar combination of scholarly and instructional aims would continue to characterize much of Gates' later work. A familiar pedagogical purpose appears in *The Signifying Monkey*, which introduced post-structuralist forms of intertextual, psychoanalytical, and narrative criticism to a new audience of African-American critics. However, Gates shows a deep awareness of conducting his classroom in a post-seventies moment of black political self-consciousness, amidst the tensions of the newly integrated elitist university. Encouragement of theoretical sophistication and a deepened sense of African-

American literary tradition continued to embellish the expository sections of *The Signifying Monkey* and some early essays—which were, however, always aimed at the intellectual progress of the race. In an odd way, Gates is both an old fashioned "race man" and an avant-garde critical theorist.[5]

*The Signifying Monkey* outdid Brown's *The Negro in American Fiction* in ways that would be important for future African-American literary studies. Gates' monograph established an empirical basis for the black canon, implied a suggestive historical narrative, and set forth an aesthetic standard in its emphasis on the parodic and ironic elements of signifying. Sterling Brown had similarly sought empirically based categories for black characterization, set forth a historical narrative about the evolving realism of black fictional representation, and implied an aesthetic standard in an albeit vaguely defined realism. In retrospect, Brown covered much more textual ground than Gates, categorized many more texts, discovered fictional techniques shared by black and white writers, and laid the basis of a more ambitious career as a literary critic and folklorist.

Gates engaged in less implicit and explicit analysis, and heavily weighted his historical narrative to the conventions of postmodernist fiction of the sixties and seventies. Nonetheless his book quickly gained the attention of its black academic audience. *The Signifying Monkey* appropriated the literary strategies of earlier black twentieth-century writers to the demands of the present-day black academic experience. Within the energetically applied deconstructive analyses of this monograph, Gates dramatized an intellectual, critical, and—broadly speaking—literary sensibility that drew upon the work of Ralph Ellison, Richard Wright, Zora Neale Hurston, and Sterling Brown. They, too, had looked to rhetoric, anthropology, psychoanalysis, and formalist criticism to explore the language of the folk. However, Gates' book distinguished itself from other literary histories by its bold attempt to retroject definitions taken from these inquiries into the folk onto earlier writers. In doing so, he created a literary history that provocatively suggested the impact of Jean Toomer, James Weldon Johnson, W. E. B. Du Bois, and even Douglass upon their late twentieth-century black contemporaries.

This strategy displayed its deepest weaknesses in Gates' discussion of the late eighteenth-century texts of Olaudah Equiano, James Gronniosaw, and Ottabah Cugoano. Here his literary historical narrative was reduced to an unconvincing attempt to link these early texts through their imagery of gold chains. Gates did give an account—if perfunctory—of the religious, social, and political-intellectual background of these figures. However, his central problem in discussing them was their resistance to the idea of signifying itself. They believed in a divine presence that pervaded Christian selfhood, society, and history. They did not signify on central religious themes in their writing such as their participation in a divinely prescribed missionary work, their ordained progress toward Christian conversion and adaptation to the Western world, or the guidance they received from white Christian patrons. Far from standing as cultural adversaries to the West, these writers linked their intellectual and rhetorical authority to the cosmic centers of the Anglo-American Protestant worldview. Their necessary presence at the work's beginning, and Gates' expedient interpretation of the chains, exemplify the habitual text-wrenching by which Gates and other signifiers would confront black writing's seminal late eighteenth-century texts.

Gates' exposition on the golden chains points to the weakest element of his canon-building evidence, its reliance on tropes which link or revise images, rather than on a broad range of literary conventions, set pieces, and rhetorical strategies. From the beginning, *The Signifying Monkey* lacked the traditionally catalogued philological and literary evidence Gates needed to make his case. Gates' account of the early writers' revision of the gold chain might belong under the ghetto's oral practice of signifying—but Gates could not summon enough examples from his text to show the pervasiveness of this rhetorical practice in the first black works.

Gates' adaptation of the signifying strategy comes to life in his discussion of Richard Wright and Ralph Ellison. But here too there was the problem of persuasive data. The careful reader finds many echoes of Wright's *Black Boy* and *Native Son* in Ellison's *Invisible Man*. However, few explicit textual connections between Wright and Ellison are convincingly hammered out. Gates' decision to eschew the task of evidence-gathering is telling here. The author implicitly chooses to rely less on sustained presentation of evidence and careful argument than on broad interpretive strokes and his own adaptation of the signifying rhetorical style. And, interestingly enough, it was here that *The Signifying Monkey* succeeded best: as a critical text that dramatized the sensibility identified by the author in his objects of study. Despite its elaborate apparatus of post-structuralist technique, the work made its case most forcefully as a work of impressionistic criticism and an eager critic's self-display. The reader was guided to possible fields of inquiry in other texts by Gates' playful example: his frequent parodic manipulation of other critical systems, his mock-revolts against established scholarly authority, and his assumption of the ironic black lumpen mask to tweak an overwhelmingly superior white literary authority.

This method reaped a surprising institutional payoff within the world of African-American literary studies. Gates' work had a seductive force earned more by shrewd literary manipulation than by sequential argument. Gates' map of tropes became the source of an influential template for joining any two or three black-authored writings into a tradition, without regard to ideological or cultural difference. Ironically, this mirrored the symbolic gold chains linking the autobiographies of early black narrators. It provided future signifiers with not only a cookie cutter for future interpretation, but a professional style with which to communicate to a literary audience. Gates' example suggested, moreover, that in the newly integrated world of the academy, the interpreter's ethos, his ironic distance, and his manipulative rhetoric were more important critical styles than Brown's merely positivist undertaking.

The instrumental nature of Gates' professional style gained credibility from another more serious trend in the profession. Reading the work of figures such as Abrams (*Natural Supernaturalism*), Bloom (*The Visionary Company*, *The Ringers in the Tower*, *Yeats*, etc.), and F. O. Mathiessen (*American Renaissance*)—as any graduate student of his era did—Gates could not have ignored the canonical critic's power to direct institutional scholarly activity. He astutely saw the influence to be wielded in the formation of cultural tastes and academic life by charismatic tradition-builders such as Abrams and Bloom. Gates was clearly impressed by this power—not as an opportunity to maintain a humanistic vantage on black historical experience, but to guide the academic enterprise itself. Not only could he direct the rivers of study to the appropriate academic mills—but he might buy the forest with the profits. As Gates conceived the academic enterprise, it was purely instrumental. His interpretive project provided a new cadre of minority entrants into the profession with an entering wedge and leverage. Within the study of English, they might become prophetic black interpreters expounding the canonical wisdom. Gates' pragmatic professional politics took many shapes; however, it appeared most often as an antihumanist form of middle-class black careerism (a phenomenon to be discussed later).

Recent founders of canons have been concerned not only with aesthetics but also with an important allied concern: the canonical values by which the tradition assigns philosophical, political, and cultural value to its constituents. The canon-builders who provided Gates' models of literary-critical institution-building possessed profoundly humanistic outlooks. They brought these humanist visions to bear upon the historical situation of mid-century American society, culture, and politics. Comparing their work to Gates' throws a revealing light upon a traditionally black bourgeois cynicism that takes such a pragmatic form in Gates' professional style. F. O. Mathiessen's *The American Renaissance* is a case in point. A canon of mid-nineteenth-century American fiction and poetry, Mathiessen's book defined a "renaissance"—comparable to that of late sixteenth- and early seventeenth-century Europe—in mid-nineteenth-century American national literature. In addition, he justified this characterization of the era's cultural and philosophic depth by demonstrating its artists' flexible appropriation of German idealist aesthetics, the literature of the English Renaissance, and emerging techniques in sculpture, photography, and oratory. Drawing these elements together into a powerful intellectual synthesis, the American Renaissance writers, Mathiessen argued, projected a profound literary, cultural, and political vision. The power of Mathiessen's critical method grew from his store of erudition, particularized into literary conventions, *topoi*, stylistic modes, genres, and philosophical issues: a plenitude of methods and categories with which literature, both within and outside of the tradition, might be categorized.

In identifying and articulating the elements of the American Renaissance, Mathiessen furthermore identified the political significance that inhered in the aesthetics of Emerson, Hawthorne, and Melville.[6] In demonstrating this juncture between the symbolic world of culture and the material realm of society, Mathiessen depicted American literary nationalism at its mid-century moment of consolidation. Moreover, he convincingly identified this moment with a wealth of empirical literary data, a plethora of works taken from the contemporary sister arts, demonstrable aesthetic procedures, and a distinctively romantic-populist political orientation. Afterwards a new generation of white liberal middle-class entrants into the academy extended this critical perspective into the fifties and sixties.

*The American Renaissance* had an enormous impact upon the new academic literary class, who entered and democratized the expanding post–World War II universities. Mathiessen's canonical motifs invited his scholarly audience's ethical and cultural inquiry into the cultural assumptions underlying mid-twentieth-century America's technological, political, and military expansion. His program of inclusive reading—in Anglo-American, French, and classical literary traditions; philosophy; cultural history; and the burgeoning field of formalist interpretations—allowed the newcomers to situate American culture within an intellectually cosmopolitan context. And Mathiessen's book made profound suggestions about the political implications of an unchallenged American romantic literary aesthetic which emphasized the contrarian stance assumed by Melville and Thoreau against the liberal capitalist order of their day.

Mathiessen's tradition guided American Studies through the period of both McCarthyism and liberal anti-Stalinism in the mid-1950s, and implicitly defined the literary critic as an ethical and social judge. His inquiry spawned R. W. B. Lewis' *The American Adam*, which considered the ethical and cultural problems of New World innocence; Leo Marx's *The Machine and the Garden*, which engaged the issue of nineteenth-century technological transformation; and later Richard Poirier's *A World Elsewhere*, which examined the imagery of space set forth by nineteenth-century canonical authors.[7] These works, following Mathiessen's prodigious example, wielded wide literary erudition to go to the deepest political, social, and cultural meanings of American literature, as well as of the national experiment itself.

In the same way, Harold Bloom's early critical monographs—*Shelley's Mythmaking*, *Blake's Apocalypse*, *The Visionary Company*, and *The Ringers in the Tower*—created a similar canon grounded in a broad recall of the central imagery, rhetorical stances, literary conventions, and themes of English romantic poetry. In particular, this canon came to emphasize a tradition beginning with Spenser and culminating with Wallace Stevens and his literary progeny. Drawing upon this literary plenitude that sought to translate romanticism—as a spiritual, philosophical, and psychological language—to twentieth-century America, Bloom created his own post-Miltonic version of the canonical project of Curtius and Auerbach. Like Mathiessen's *American Renaissance*, Bloom's romantic canon bore an aesthetic standard, a narrative of Anglo-American literary history, and a host of touchstones by which his tradition evaluated itself in relation to early modern European culture. The canon's central motifs were the struggle of alienated post-Enlightenment man for imaginative redemption, and its cost. Bloom celebrated imagination as the faculty which might overcome this estranged self-consciousness which proceeded from an empirical and materialistic worldview. Focussed on this internalized psychological drama, Bloom illuminated the poetic careers and humanizing art of the writers he studied.[8]

All canons have their game-preserve of writers who best exemplify the tradition's values. And it is no accident that Bloom and Mathiessen focused their attention upon Emerson, much of whose literary career concerned the dialectic between the freedom of spirit and the limitations of matter. From Emerson's "Nature" and "Self Reliance" to "Fate" and the "Conduct of Life," the mid-nineteenth-century American writer struggled with both the will to imaginative self-creation and redemption, and the limitations imposed upon that will by Fate. Whether he succumbed to Fate, or only to another reductive self-consciousness, remains as important a question for his critics as it was for Emerson himself. The process of answering such queries, however, gave Emerson a vantage from which to consider the individual's conduct, the pursuit of self-fulfillment, the role of aesthetics in personal life, and his own encounters with human loss.

A similar dialectic existed in the work of Mathiessen and his successors. In *The American Adam*, Lewis was ultimately forced to ponder the conflict between moral reality of sin with the possibilities for self-fulfillment presented by the American experiment. A discussion of Cooper and Emerson ultimately ended Hawthorne's or Melville's questioning of Emersonian optimism. Educated during the early days of the New Criticism, both Mathiessen and Bloom engaged in close reading to create and order the erudition they deployed in their canon-related interpretation. The philosophical, theological, and psychological dimensions of Bloom's concerns—like those of Mathiessen and his followers—emerged from careful parsing of a text and ultimately a tradition's literary particulars.

Indeed, the broad cultural perspectives of Bloom and Mathiessen emerged naturally from the formalist critics' tendency to tease out the individual ideological elements in the semantics produced by form. The Yale new critical emphasis on paradox, irony, and tension stemmed *inter alia* from how these formal complexities complicated, undermined, or enhanced a poem's creation of meaning. The New Criticism, like other humanist critical languages examined in an essay by Paul de Man, led the commentator to confront his own internal intellectual conflicts as he engaged a work's literary tensions. These languages—even that of de Man—implied the existence of a critic who weighed alternative philosophical interpretations in a site where social and political values were formed. This was true whether the interpreter said so or not.[9] Thus the New Criticism was openly seen as a kind of ritualistic Anglican conservatism and Bloom's early romanticism was seen as humanism. These hierarchies of value—exposed by textual analysis and interpretation—made possible the setting of humanist priorities, whether enacted in the public world or in the local context of the classroom, department, or university faculty.

This humanist good could be co-opted for the consumer goals of late twentieth-century liberal capitalist American society. But that was unusual. One of the high points of fifties and early sixties American academic liberalism was its taste for meditative authors such as Henry James, Wordsworth, and Freud. This expressed itself at times in an orientation to the complexities of literary modernism—as an exercise in that reflection necessary to confront the ideological distortions of both

Stalinism and McCarthyism and also of consumer culture at large.[10] Close reading in liberal 1950s and 1960s America meant not only a consideration of moral complexities but also reflection on the nation's disturbing orientation towards merely recreational leisure, ideological simplicity, and ethical insensitivity in the postwar years. This balance is reflected earlier in the criticism of Lionel Trilling in *The Liberal Imagination* and *Beyond Culture*. Critics to his political left (such as Irving Howe and Philip Rahv) as well as those to his right (Norman Podhoretz and Saul Bellow) also sought to achieve it. And these figures too were, in their own way, behind Bloom, Hartman, and Poirier.[11] The liberal ethos persisted even into the seventies, when it turned into a neoconservative rejection of the cultural excesses of the student revolts at Columbia, Harvard, Yale, and Berkeley. The earlier liberalism was marked by openness to the intellectual, rhetorical, and philosophical resources of tradition as *technê* and not as a bag of interpretive tricks.

As Gates extended the enterprise of canon-formation begun in his early essays, he neglected his teachers' deep humanist commitment at the expense of a professionalization that emphasized narrow techniques of semiotic reading and various theoretical outlooks. To be sure, the late sixties and early seventies saw the popularization of much high academic culture into mere professionalized discourse. This may well have been the product of a historical moment in which the once politically and socially meaningful orientations of literary taste had themselves become book chat, displays of class-linked cultivation, and ultimately objects of consumption themselves. Gates was not interested in the moral, political, and sociological conversations by which earlier canonical critics such as Abrams and Mathiessen organized and interpreted literary knowledge around a series of aesthetic, psychological, and philosophical issues. Gates' primary interests concerned the possibilities that canon-formation held for black professionalization and interracial politics in the newly integrated university. He sought a literary method that established an institutional structure based on the cathartic, symbolic, and charismatic styles of protest at Yale. To be sure, Yale saw the creation of an immensely strong academic program in Black Studies, reflecting the learning of Charles Davis, Michael Cooke, Sidney Mintz, Roy Bryce La Porte, and John Blassingame. However, Gates' criticism found its impulses in styles of symbolic power—a power whose intellectual and spiritual force was largely cathartic. Far from encouraging political inquiry, such a stance would necessarily repress it in favor of self-gratifying intellectual and spiritual display.

Gates had already staked out a persona as a remarkable undergraduate student at Yale, Skip. He was himself the signifying black Yalie, a member of that upwardly mobile class who parlayed the folk ethos of the street into the social enclaves of academic New Haven. In his own writings about that time he is pictured amidst the Black Panthers, leaders in the black student organization, and the emerging world of Black Studies. Not only was he Phi Beta Kappa, but he studiously pursued the cultural politics of the period, even hiking through Africa and living in Tanzania for a year. As a young black cultural nationalist student, he attracted the attention not only of emerging black luminaries at Yale, but also important white intellectuals such as Sidney Mintz and John Morton Blum.

This experience gave him access to the feelings of black middle-class marginalization, which the ethos and instrumentality of signifying so incisively addressed. Indeed, autobiographical accounts of his alienation as a literature graduate student in Cambridge early formed an important aspect of his critical rhetoric. In one such essay, he describes his discovery of semiotic criticism as a response to an impasse in a tutorial. Interestingly enough, he speaks of his first graduate school essays as exercises in a prevalent mode of cultural nationalist discourse; he wrote of black literature in terms of historical analysis. This rhetoric—however persuasive in New Haven—got him nowhere in Cambridge, where he was forced to turn to structuralism as a formal academic language in which to conduct intellectual life. Such autobiographical fables describe experiences that gave Skip legitimacy not only as a literary pedagogue but as a psychological fellow traveler to a newly dislocated black middle-class entering the professional world.[12]

Skip's canon joined texts through tropes of echoing, hyperbole, and understatement—the figures by which black writers revise the rhetoric of previous black writers.[13] This rhetoric was identified with the insults of the dozens in particular and the expressive side of orality's agonistic world in general. In Skip's interpretive practice, the critic identified a later writer's antagonistic "signifying" against the work of an antecedent. Clearly influenced by Bloom's literary adaptation of Freud's Oedipus theory, Skip did not trouble himself with the broad humanism which shaped Bloom's far-reaching history. Indeed, the serious concerns underlying Bloom's rich narrative, literary psychology, and rhetorical systems all drop away in *The Signifying Monkey*. In place of an artist forging an original contribution to tradition, Gates's writer engages in a game of the dozens with his predecessors. This playfulness was quite clearly a response to alienation in the newly integrated university. As such, Gates' canon came to life most vividly as a gesture of cynical defiance directed toward what many African-American literary scholars took to be a contemptuous profession. The estrangement and defiance implicit in Gates' criticism has important affinities with the frustrations and adversarial styles of black university students studied by Jacqueline Fleming and Thomas Sowell. Their work not only elucidates this psychological dislocation but links it to differences in academic ability, ethnic culture, and achievement—differences central to the "diversity" created in the newly integrated elite institutions of the American academy.[14] In the context of Gates' canon-building enterprise, his adaptation of Bloom's romantic construction of tradition represents only the barest framework for intellectual inquiry. Like Bloom, Gates conceives of his canon as a means of defining a romantic selfhood. However, signifying is too barren a discipline for this task.

Such appropriations are still recognizable as part of the inherited ethos of African-American Studies, even in the academically legitimate Yale program. In a recent well-produced pamphlet celebrating the program's thirtieth anniversary,

Elizabeth Alexander, a recognized poet, still describes her acquired knowledge vaguely as a discovery of selfhood in community. Quoting the late poet June Jordan to illustrate this point, Alexander asserts:

> We, Black America, on the prospering white American university campus; we come together as students, Black students. How shall we humanly compose the knowledge that troubles the mind into ideas of life? How can we be who we are?[15]

Speaking for herself, Alexander restates this idea in personal terms. "For the first time in my life, at Yale, taking courses in African-American Studies and finding community there, I was trying to articulate myself as part of a 'we'."[16] Here, too, we have education as a quest for self—a self that is found not through individual inquiry and reflection but rather through an engagement with a communal "we." The bold interpretive moves of signifying, grounded in a seemingly unlimited will to power over the text, would make this affirmation of knowledge-as-recovered-selfhood available to future black students, readers, and teachers. However successful in monetary or institutional terms, this therapeutic strategy could never direct its proponents or students to a legitimate self-consciousness, grounded in real literary knowledge. Indeed, signifying would often lead to the vague, unfocussed interpretation of the past so vividly revealed in Alexander's memories of June Jordan's remarks.

Gates also linked tradition with a romantic conception of a primal black self and black community. From the essays in *Figures in Black* down to the glibly packaged *Colored People*, a seemingly naive but shrewdly presented myth of origins has shaped Gates' thinking and cultural self-presentation. From his beginnings, Gates emphasized a highly nostalgic view of black literary tradition that seemed grounded in the origin of a secure racial world, and this ethnic world of family and culture was embodied in a timeless origin in an ahistorical past. What Gates contributed to this well-established black nostalgia was a strategy of filiopietism strangely at odds with his status as a black newcomer to the white academy:

> Let me expand this idea a bit. For as long as I can remember, I have been fascinated with the inner workings of black culture, its linguistic and musical resources. My fascination with black language stems from my father's enjoyment of absolute control over its manipulation. My father has mastered black language rituals, certainly; he also has the ability to analyze them, to tell you what he is doing, why, and how. He is a very self-conscious language user. He is not atypical. It is amazing how much black people, in ritual settings such as barbershops and pool halls, street corners and family reunions, talk about talking. Why do they do this? I think they do it to pass these rituals along from one Generation to the next. They do it to preserve the traditions of "the race." Very few black people are not conscious, at some level, of peculiarly black texts, of being. These are our texts, to be delighted in, enjoyed, contemplated, explicated, and willed through repetition to our daughters and to our sons. I acknowledge my father's capacities not only to pay him homage but because I learned to read the tradition by thinking intensely about one of its most salient aspects. This is my father's book, even if cast in a language he does not use.[17]

This brief anecdotal version of Gates' paternal myth is—even more centrally than his tendentious application of the Yoruba and Ibo mythologies—the foundation of Gates' historical fable. Here is the juggling father, in the cloistered sense, ethnic security and comfort to be found around him by his children and descendents. Here is escape from the tensions of the integrated world of the academy and professional life to a safe, enclosed world of black play. The important values of this world are not matters of moral and intellectual judgment but rather an escapist, childish fantasy of pleasure, embodied by an all-powerful original father. Gates' literary history of the folk is one in which successive generations of increasingly mobile blacks return in their leisure to the kind of improvisation that goes on in the barbershops and beauty parlors of the black world. Gates' language conflates both the cosmopolitan attitudes of the academy and the down-home talk of the folk in this vision of playful retreat, a haven from the confusion of norms accompanying the cultural dislocations of the black bourgeoisie. In this vision, the contradictions of folk and cosmopolitan cultural conflict are seemingly ironed out. What Robert Redfield called "big and little traditions" consort strangely but seductively here. Gates' father is a master theorist of a chattering ethnic group of lesser scholar-talkers who talk about talking. The lower- and middle-class community itself, its rituals and gathering sites, is a kind of eternal literary seminar of black culture. However congenial and charismatic this father, he has no moral or indeed any intellectual presence. Thus, signifying—and the related motifs of "call and response"—are not a dialectic of alternative moral or intellectual choices leading to resolution or antinomy, but a leisurely diversion. Similarly, Gates' method aims not at a final philosophical or literary vision but at the pleasures of juggling texts.

The passage quoted above bears attention because it is as close to a statement of canonical value as Gates would ever get. However, its naive definition of play points to the method's uselessness as a catalogue of cultural categories, and to its tendency to be a source of intellectual repression. (There is a similarly vacuous quality in Jordan's catalogued events of Yale student experiences.) In connection with Gates, we are assured that the father will be a source of this catalogue, which the son has discerned in his language. But how can we know? Oral language is notorious for its focus upon the needs of the immediate situation and its tendency to dispense with that which falls from use. Oral performers may make changes and revisions in the primary text. But can genetic texts really be found in oral tradition? Moreover, many traditional guides, beginning with Aristotle's *Rhetoric*, catalogue tropes, oral convention, and expository knowledge as a way of retaining tradition.

The application of the paradigms of oral discourse to written tradition is an odd critical move, especially with respect to critical tradition; written traditions are capable of holding far more texts, textual variants, literary allusions, genres, and topics. Gates' reference to the juggling father might provide a touch of joking illustration in a serious moment. But on the page, Gates' reference to simply and naively described play, given the literary traditions of play and retired leisure, is inadequate for the book's presumably sophisticated audience. The signifying father—he appears throughout Gates' work—is reductive, and seems inadequate to the reality of a man who raised two remarkable sons in black West Virginia. Furthermore, the kind of retired play described by Gates here has been a literary subject explored in important canonical works by Theocritus and Virgil, Andrew Marvell and Alexander Pope, Benjamin Franklin, W. H. Auden, and Robert Lowell. It has been analyzed not as a simple retreat from the city, but as a preparation for urban life; as a site of artistic creation and a sphere where one enjoys a hiatus from the world of literary production; as an escape from the corruptions of luxury and a symbol of elitist literary refinement; as a shelter from battle and a training ground for the cultivation of the military virtues.

Earlier writers in this tradition, as well as contemporaries Saul Bellow and Tom Wolfe, have more effectively examined Gates' juggling signifying "father"— and his leisure—by means of informed literary observation. "I know a nigger his name is Seville / He never worked and he never will." No literary critic interested in the cultural significance of play can parse this saying (by one of my Harlem in-laws) without reference to the teeming cluster of political, cultural, and social meanings that leisure, luxury, and the oppression of blacks have acquired through the history of Western literature. To speak of "play" in Gates' context is to evoke a host of present-day literary texts concerning lower-class black life, of which Gates was no doubt aware, but refused to examine in this aspect of his work. I refer to Tom Wolfe's pictures of the "pimp" style in *Radical Chic and Mau-Mauing the Flak Catchers*, as well as in *The Bonfire of the Vanities*. The pimp and hustler turn up in Gates' own era, as Tom Wolfe is not afraid to say, in the court of law, the poverty program office, the ghetto high school halls, and the university.[18] In works such as Saul Bellow's *Mr. Sammler's Planet* or *Ravelstein*, we similarly encounter signifying black characters that evoke the dissemination of once aristocratic forms of leisure or literary expression. The romantic criminal (Jean Valjean) or the image of sumptuary excess now belongs to a *lingua franca* of consumption, which provides what remains of civic and cultural life. This democratic appropriation is writ large in the joking name of "Seville" itself, an allusion to the *luxus* now available on an installment plan. Within this joking context, as both Wolfe and Bellow show, the displays and celebration of "niggerhood" are not only obscenities but cultural gestures in which those who were once social outsiders now deploy symbols of high culture, while confronting established legal and intellectual authority. Among the "Sevilles" are the youth confronted by Chuck in *Ravelstein*'s Hyde Park, young black men who engage Bellow's autobiographical fictional subject in discussions of upper-class English tastes in male fashion; or the bejeweled thief on the bus who so entrances—and simultaneously disgusts—Mr. Sammler in the novel bearing his name.

On a political level, the references to the signifying play of the barbershop and hair salon can refer to the adversarial retreats described by James Scott in a far-reaching theory of resistance, or Victor Turner's liminal spaces for the release of social tensions.[19] Gates' illustration, considered in present-day literary terms, is far from an adequate account of everything retired play might mean in the urban barbershop (as opposed to the pastoral suburbs). What was the meaning of their play there? And how does the language and style of the pimp enter into the rhetoric of these writers? To engage in this explanation would be to write a book closer to the philological examinations of Huizinga that speak of "play" in some of the contexts that I have named above—law, government, consumer marketplace, and school. Such a book would be sensitive to a by-now long catalogue of literary references, both popular and serious. Anthropological, economic, and psychological accounts of the legal and educational worlds in which signifying takes place would be vital. There probably *is* a contemporary "philology" of word, rhetoric, and allusion that would illuminate the pimp's play, much as Huizinga's *Homo Ludens* illuminates the European upper-class conception of play. This philology does not reside, however, in signifying. Nor could signifying draw intelligently upon such philology, given the method's narrow linguistic categories and superficial protocols of interpretation.[20] In the absence of culturally, socially, and politically rich spheres of meaning, no full understanding of Gates' "playful" father or Jordan's "student community" may be had.

The paucity of interpretive categories brought by Gates to the readings in *The Signifying Monkey* becomes increasingly disturbing on repeated readings. We suspect in this passage a sensibility that has sacrificed its depth and breadth for the deceptive powers of a superficial literary "approach." Gates' account of the father reveals a critic who has lost the sense of the "plenitude" of meanings with which one may read a text. Indeed, Gates' literary-critical adaptation of his father's oral mode of discourse limits his thought to a face-to-face world—which, in *The Signifying Monkey* and *Figures in Black*, as in much of *Colored People*, sheds little light on what would seem promising material. The critic creates an illusion of originality by a willful forgetting of the old categories at the cost of ignoring the bases of comparison and contrast by which he can know the new. Gates is an immensely canny and perceptive man, but we don't get the full value of his observations of the world around him—least of all in an autobiographical work such as *Colored People*, where such wide-ranging observation might be expected. Throughout, *Colored People* paints a cheery portrait of segregated life, lived for the most part beyond the shadow of white oppression. It dramatizes Zora Neale Hurston's view that within this site, black life was lived with a lack of self-consciousness that allowed for the depiction of an African-American authenticity. Thus, the book significantly stops in late adolescence before Gates' entrance into Yale. But even as a picture of childhood, this book is inadequate. Our strongest memories of youth are often formed by character-determining traumas. Gates particularly encounters such an injury in the shape of an incompetent doctor. However, the book does not expand on this experience as it might—and as we expect. The relationship between an educated, ambitious mother and a straight-talking, lower-class father should provide Gates with a vantage from which to see his family and himself. Gates does not make good on the illumination that his subject matter promises. Also disturbing is the lack of commentary on his departure from Philips Exeter, which he mentions at the book's end but never fully develops. He has earlier been caught in the tensions of class and race before coming to Yale. He studied in a community college before entering a major university. Gates' youth was complicated by tensions of class, cosmopolitan educational provenance, and personal growth that he has suppressed from his autobiographical account—although they are clearly germane to his intellectual style.

I attribute these absences not only to the inevitable packaging of a trade publisher's book, but also to the intellectually limiting nature of the signifying sensibility itself. Gates cannot step outside of his ironic mask; indeed, the distance he adopts largely constitutes a defense against a more relentless examination of himself and his surrounding society. The greatest praise one can bestow on Gates, however, is the sensitivity that his ironic masking has given him to disingenuousness in others. He has shrewdly recognized and exploited the possibilities of masking, even the benefits that accrue to suppressing one's aims. Gates is thus at his best in the Sam Slade stories of *Loose Canons*, where he cunningly evokes pictures of major literary critics in their haunts and their intellectual pursuits.[21] Slade is the critic seeking to find their secret; the assumption that they have a hidden lust for power is the *sine qua non* of their ascent to fame. Here, Gates wittily reveals the personae of Yale, Harvard, and major publishing luminaries as signifiers, masking their success and ruthless ambition. This scrutiny—as Norman Podhoretz found to his sorrow upon the publication of *Making It*—inevitably exposes the concealed ambition of the upwardly mobile, an exposure for which victim and writer must be punished. Gates, ironically aloof from his prey, deftly flushes out his victims' egoism, concealing himself—sometimes to the neglect of what ought to be his principle intellectual concerns.

Gates' *New Yorker* pieces on Anatole Broyard and Colin Powell, and others in *Thirteen Ways of Looking at a Black Man*, amuse and provoke the reader as they cannily penetrate the public masks of some very famous blacks.[22] *Thirteen Ways* is particularly interesting for its use of the surfaces of a distinguished man's life—his world, his reputation, and even his dwelling—to provide a sense of how he "made it" to his high position of importance. Even here, however, the tone too often slips to that of "the success" trading notes with "the successful" (a problem also in Dyson's later books). We still lack an account of the meaning of the "surfaces" of American institutional and social life to its most successful black participants. We are unlikely to get it in this generation. The sensibility of signifying inevitably leads the would-be beginning theorist down the path of ever less rigorous cultural interpretation and description. In the end, even the associative methods of signifying and the special pleading of romanticized autobiographies come to impose excessive scrutiny, scrutiny that would ultimately come back to haunt the signifier.

Gates' *Thirteen Ways of Looking at a Black Man*, despite the appeal of its vivid descriptions, rarely goes after its real subject: the relation of the self to the various masks and protocols with which success in the integrated world is achieved. This kind of success is what the lower class calls "getting over." And the book, despite its teasing reference to Stevens' poem, never goes beyond an account of "how I got over" to the meaning of the ascent and its rewards. The poetic voice of Stevens' poem cannot choose between "the beauty of inflections and the beauty of innuendoes": the signifier chooses—to our loss—innuendo. In the end, the interviews become the in-group chatter of successful black professionals, implicitly trading self-congratulation. Gates is too casually linked to his subjects by notoriety and status to give their lives and work the reflective meditation they deserve. Thus, although he notes that Colin Powell is an "ordinary brother," he stresses at the same time Powell's close working connections with people who know absolutely nothing about the typical lives of black people—presumably including that "ordinary" aspect of Powell. How does Powell negotiate this day-to-day impasse within his psychological and social life? Similarly Gates, himself a literary critic, writes about Anatole Broyard, a highly ambitious man of letters who had to pass for white to write seriously about serious literature. What is the meaning of Broyard's example for Gates in a literary world in which these color restrictions arguably persist in much of the humanities? Gates' journalism cannot broach the most important questions of value raised by his interview—largely because he works within a literary scheme in which such central questions have become out of bounds for him, as they always were for the black bourgeoisie. Gates' writing in *Thirteen Ways of Looking at a Black Man* foreshadows the trap of *Ebony*-style feature-writing into which other signifiers will eventually fall.

Gates' masking contributes to the detachment with which he puts literature itself to instrumental use. This ironic stance, however, ultimately alienates the writer from his creative task, whatever his worldly task. Much of Gates' persona depends upon a sustained improvisation that would quickly become tiresome as the repertoire of a less spontaneous and resourceful writer. Elsewhere, Gates equates his creativity to the crafty, sometimes anti-intellectual evasions of the black folk trickster. Thus, Gates slyly finds an intellectual common ground among the barber, the father, and the scholar: a similitude that devalues learning while it inflates the wiliness of the unlettered. This strategy is an important intellectual weapon for Gates and those who come after him. It allows him to advance the institutional interests of Black Studies as an academic presence, while claiming to speak with the motherwit of the masses. He has, as a consequence, acquired entrance into the world of the university, which he claims (following Gramsci) legitimates knowledge. Gates has been socialized into power, and his authenticity has been tested. But in return, he pursues his vocation in a deeply estranged fashion. It is to the point of his alienation, however, that Gates makes no distinction between that social knowledge which grants our parents, teachers, and religious leaders their authority, and that professionalized knowledge of literary criticism, which is underwritten by the research, interpretation, and inquiry of trained scholars. Given that universities are composed of a faculty of intellectuals, do they recognize the legitimacy of the taken-for-granted knowledge of everyday life—or is their authority grounded in knowledge that is the property of professional specialists? Interestingly enough, Gates' definition of signifying explicitly and implicitly equates the two forms of knowledge and legitimacy; but, of course, they are different. In making this connection, he easily conflates scholarship with an affirmation of our taken-for-granted views of daily life. How much intellectual authority are we willing to give the rapper and his rap in our studies? How may he be defined as a bearer of tradition? Gates does not answer these questions—but they must be faced to avoid not only cynicism but worse. Given the freewheeling, intellectually repressive style of signifying, this is a license for illegitimate ideological and political authority in the profession: a power based upon the authenticity of the intellectual with his ear to the ground.

The signifier's alienation is always a threat to the quality of his writing. Gates' cynical wit in *Thirteen Ways of Looking at a Black Man* and *Colored People* is increasingly undermined by his glib superficial posture. The costs of alienation are much higher for successive writers such as Michael Awkward, Michael Dyson, and Karla Holloway. In these cases, the estranged intellectual reveals himself directly in carelessly edited published work, inadequate research, and (what is most tragic) suppressed curiosity: the absence of an alert consciousness within the text, aware of past assumptions, searching out new problems, and inventing fresh formulations. This alienation appears not only in clumsy (if revealing) expression but also in contempt for the discipline of clear writing itself. I quote a passage from Holloway, taken at random from her cultural commentary:

> As late as 1985, one of the patriarchs of African-American literary criticism, which was senior enough to have known Hurston, began a conference session dedicated to a critical discussion of Hurston as an author with an announcement that "Zora was a woman of many strange tastes." He drew out his pronunciation of "strange," lingering over the tone he knew it would suggest. Even though his comment was met with stinging rebuke from the audience, this intimation of his privately held opinion had already made its public impact. His comment put her on trial all over again as the conference session quickly lost its academic austerity and shifted into a passionate call and response between the distinguished panelists and the audience of (generally younger) scholars.[23]

Holloway's errors of logic, usage, and expression reveal more than her celebration of rudeness in a book entitled *Codes of Conduct*. The scholar's pronunciation of "strange" does not "suggest" a tone—it clearly *has* a tone to which "the audience" vehemently responds. Similarly, one may "linger" over words but not over a "tone." Finally, Hurston (who is dead) is not on trial—but either her reputation or the older scholar is. Rituals of "call and response" indeed provide rhetorical patterns for black life. However, is the audience's attack on the speaker really akin to a congregation's response to its minister in a sermon or to the musical answer made by one chorus to another? Is this brutal interruption by an academic audience acting as a repressive mob really equivalent to the gesture by which a congregation "amens" its preacher?

These serious mistakes in expression tell us much—however indirectly—about the author's attitude toward the significance of her printed communication with a literate reading audience. The imprecision of Holloway's language suggests both the author's disengagement from the task of writing, and her assumption that what she has to say to the reader in print is not very important—at least to the reader. The persona of this passage does not assume that she addresses an audience that either reads carefully or reflects upon the meanings and "tone" of her words. Indeed, it is assumed that the reader is as disengaged from the activity of reading as the writer is from serious communication with the reader. Neither is going to "linger" over this text. And why should they? The writer implies that her own response, and that of the audience, to the quoted statement were both immediately satisfactory.

The relevant parties already know about this event and further elaboration would only complicate matters for them. There is a reason for this suppression of ethical inquiry as well as for the misdirection of the reader. The speaker was not—as far as I can tell—allowed to explain himself before meeting with the audience's rebuke. Instead, the crowd delivered a summary judgment which mirror-like reflects the insult presumed (by the audience) to have been pronounced on Hurston. There is an important, compelling moral paradox in this passage: but it cannot be explored for the most serious professional and institutional reasons. These structural demands—common to signifying—underlie this (wholly typical) suppression of ethical inquiry, robbing this passage of its potential intellectual value.

Oddly enough, Holloway's literary sloppiness reflects a politically dangerous self-censorship. The carelessness of her prose thwarts her participation as a moral citizen within the professionalized intellectual world. It stems from a typical understanding occurring between blacks and whites in the elite levels of the profession. It is simply assumed that the world of the blacks is a self-enclosed, oral one with little need for communication beyond its own racial and political boundaries. The black critic's very task of representing blackness in the "oral" terms of African-American culture has left him with little analytical insight into some of the movement's deepest realities: generational conflicts of taste, varied attitudes toward gender roles, and a repressive stance toward intellectual outsiders. The university's institutional investment in the stability of its black population demands the resolution of such conflicts—best accomplished *in camera* by authoritarian tactics. These serious cultural, social, and ethical issues are subordinated to an event's immediate excitement, the crowd's summary judgment, and an unanalyzed, unreflective moral stance toward the event as a whole. The intellectual's reflection upon experience suffers, moreover, from the institutional imperatives in which African-American Studies must exist.

Of course the marginality of the black intellectual world gives it a cultural exoticism in some quarters. In its very hermetic quality, Holloway has acquired the quality of "inside gossip" about a taboo group, the kind of "racially privileged" information that attracts ethnic outsiders in and of itself. The retelling of this incident, in a book written by a noted scholar writing for a significant academic press, suggests that the university, as well as black intellectuals, has acquired a taste for the aggressive, menacing postures of lower-class life when they reappear in a neutral literary environment shorn of their larger social and political meanings.

All of this amounts to a trivialization of human life—an obscene simplification that looms over even as agile an ironist as Gates when he depicts the playful father in monograph, essay, or memoir. We expect literature and literary criticism to yield the tools with which to explore and categorize this human richness, not to belittle it. The appropriation of lower-class manners into the style of signifying brings this issue to the fore, especially when the signifier's own literary resources fail. One must suspect that beneath the signifier's ironies lies a deep ambivalence about the lower-class black masses whose mask he has borrowed to confront the professional world. Whatever the vitality, fecklessness, and invention of the popular folk culture, it is bereft of ultimate concerns—especially as gathered wisdom, transcending the ebb and flow of daily life. Indeed, the "natural" character of the folk that gives "exuberance" can also be the source of banality, ignorance, self-centeredness, and provincial prejudice. Furthermore, no alert intellectual can overlook the cynicism with which the folk masses necessarily confront the diminished prospects of their lives. This cynicism may afford the black post-structuralist critic an outlet for his will to power over the text. Yet whatever stance the critic adopts, he cannot help but be wary of the ironic detachment of desperate people.

The world of the folk must of necessity pose a special threat to the signifier who is willy-nilly an intellectual himself. The signifier reduces his subject matter to a few tropes to make sense of a complex, self-contradictory, sometimes irrational world—a world that an intellectual may mimic, but never wholly enter. Not surprisingly, this problem is brought to the fore by the promising young author of *Their Eyes Were Watching God*. These questions would become important to Zora Neale Hurston, a powerful rhetorician who shaped black folk speech into an insinuating, bewitching, metaphorical style. Hurston's literary technique, as well as her present-day popularity among the signifiers, makes her an important test case for Gates' method; and, to his credit, he has not neglected her in *The Signifying Monkey*. The results of this encounter are important. Gates' reading of *Their Eyes Were Watching God* shows the strengths of his critical language, but also uncovers severe conflicts and contradictions in this aesthetic style.

As a *soi disant* form of deconstruction, signifying immediately shows itself to be counterintuitive. The signifying critics, despite their demystifying claims, generally refuse to generate two or more contending semantic codes in their *explications de texte*. Such contradictions of meaning have usually marked the hermeneutic approaches influenced by the linguistic turn. They create those ironies, paradoxes, and ambiguities that give a text what New Critics liked to call a "richness of texture." In deconstructive readings, these contradictions reveal a work's most basic dynamics as "writing," indeed as literature. The pitting of two or more codes against each other discovers points of meaninglessness (*aporia*) and new patterns of meaning, and demands interpretive responses, made possible through repeated acts of reading (*diêgêsis*), to the competing semantic elements.

And these contradictions reveal the limitations of any given reading, thus thwarting overdetermined explanations. Once deconstructed, they make up an important safeguard against ideological overstatement. It is precisely these interpretive powers and safeguards which the signifiers have overthrown in their headlong rush to assimilate semiotics-deconstruction in their critical readings. They tend instead to reinstate the discipline's ideological assumptions, rarely sifting out challenging meanings or themes. The play of contending codes does not become a way into the rich self-contradictory context which is common to all deeply meaningful writing. Ambiguities, ironies, and paradoxes become instead a symbol of play, considered in the narrowest, linguistic way. And this play becomes, in the hands of the signifier, a symbol for the parodic, ironic side of African-American humor, which is presently denominated an essential blackness. We rarely return from the readings in Gates' *Figures in Black* and *The Signifying Monkey*, or in Holloway's book, with a heightened sense of a text's weave of meanings, its resistances to our interpretive attempts: its capacity to throw our own moral and cultural assumptions into relief. The deconstructive critical act has the potential to deepen the introspective, reflective aspect of the reading process. This creation of philosophical, spiritual, and cultural depth rarely appears in the work of the signifiers—indeed it is anathema to their ethos of escapist play. In the hands of the signifiers, African-American literature loses its capacity to challenge the historical, sociological, or philosophical assumptions that black readers—including the signifiers—conventionally bring to the text. And African-American Studies, as a process of inquiry, loses the possibility of intellectually testing, and therefore critically validating, itself.

One must honor the rule-proving exceptions here, and we find one in Robert Stepto's *From Behind the Veil*, a semiotic literary history of black autobiography, narrated persuasively through a consideration of its increasing complexity.[24] Analyzing the composition of bondsmen's stories and the authenticating narratives which typically preceded and concluded them—and which ultimately became the conventional literary introductions by which white intellectuals presented the work of black writers—Stepto found persuasive material evidence of semantic codes superimposed by white abolitionists upon these black-authored texts. His readings also suggest a great deal about the rhetorical situation that constrained the black writers' formulation of narrative and argument.

However, Stepto's canny analysis of the interaction of white patronage and black literary expression is not often duplicated in quality. And he might have read more narratives even more usefully, had he not resisted the opportunity to tease out further semiotic conflict by emphasizing the resistance offered to his strategies by his texts. The logistics of constructing a broad historical narrative imposed certain limits upon Stepto's already rich interpretations. I write under the same limitations here and therefore ask the reader's forbearance for my decision to explicate *Eyes* in strokes broad enough to identify its most visible contrary codes. I do not pretend to unravel fully the novel's densely woven carpet, but concentrate only on the text's most troubling semantic knots.

Gates' analysis of *Eyes* links Hurston's style with that of Jean Toomer and Sterling Brown, both of whom made literary language from the vernacular of the folk. Interestingly enough, he does not provide evidence of tropes joining the various texts of these authors. His argument—and *ad hoc* statements about sustained black tradition here—is weaker for this absence, although the point could have been maintained easily enough. Be that as it may, the crux of Gates' interpretation is in a relationship he discerns between the book's two narratives: Janie's quest for self-fulfillment and the education of the observing narrator, a whitened figure who speaks in standard English, but whose language eventually absorbs Janie's vernacular blackness. The narrative is for Gates not primarily about Janie but about the narrator's acquisition of a literary voice characterized by the racial double-consciousness as it is described in the first chapter of *The Souls of Black Folk*.[25]

In many ways, this reading represents an important extension of the theme which has predominated in critical commentary on the novel. Like other critics, Gates seeks the sources of the book's primary literary accomplishment—the haunting that greets the reader at the book's beginning and reappears as Janie wakes to self-consciousness (described by Barbara Johnson in the rhetorical language of inside-outside reversal—a semiotic interpretation that again gains its plausibility largely from conventional romantic ideology of discovered psychological depth).[26] On the face of it, however, this argument seems forced: the novel's narrator is not dramatized as either a voice or a character. I suspect that critics now overlook this textual difficulty as a consequence of the folk's current high stock as an emblem of authentic blackness. However, the present view of Hurston's interest in folk culture probably encourages literary historians to interpret her evolving capacity to make artistic use of the folk as the young woman writer's education into blackness. One suspects that these critics are reading that spiritual-ethnic education into the alleged intellectual development of the novel's narrator.

Hurston came to Harlem in the early twenties with a handful of tautly strung short stories such as "Spunk" and "Sweat," a promising body of fiction that showed her skill in the deployment of narrative, resonant metaphor, and the fictional exploration of love, marriage, and death. She did little serious work in the twenties, but nonetheless acquired a degree from Barnard and a patron. Later, as a Columbia graduate student researching in Florida, she clearly found a new depth of literary understanding in the stories, "lies," and songs that she recorded. The two novels show her evolving ability to use folklore, first in *Jonah's Gourd Vine* as a resource for character, setting, and plot; and later in *Their Eyes Were Watching God* for a varied narrative voice, storytelling technique, and character psychology.[27] Gates' interpretation of *Eyes* reflects the folk-oriented signifying critic's predictable tendency to see the high point of Hurston's career in her role as folk novelist. Her literary apex is based, in this view, upon her most effective literary appropriation of her highest achievement; the persuasiveness of this view is further strengthened by the fact that her later fiction rarely sustained the accomplishment of *Eyes* or fulfilled that novel's great promise. Indeed, the evidence for her later decline is only money in the bank for our inclination to concentrate—as Gates interestingly does—on her success as a novelist in *Eyes*, rather than on her accomplishments as a remarkably versatile woman of letters: folklorist, ethnographer, cultural critic, essayist, and collector.

This interpretation plays a large role in making the high valuation of *Eyes* far more than a gendered form of affirmative action for the Gates of *Figures in Black* and *The Signifying Monkey*, the Houston Baker of *Blues, Ideology, amd Afro-American Literature*, and Holloway in *Hurston: The Character of the Word*. Gates' reading of Hurston's career—implicit in his (and his contemporaries') enthusiastic esteem for *Eyes*—has important consequences for a recently emphasized tradition in black women's writing. His high valuation is a tactical move in another, perhaps more important strategic enterprise. Gates' literary biography gives us a self-consciously modernist author who, in the intuitive way of the folk, happens upon the artistic forms that will bear fruit in the future authors of feminist romances such as *Sula*, *The Color Purple*, and *Praisesong for the Widow*. She will not live to fulfill the promise of her literary discoveries; her literary daughters, however, will reap the benefits of her initial efforts. Hurston moreover becomes an important foremother in a female tradition heretofore dominated by female sentimentalists.

This reading, however, demands a suppression of important ambiguities in the tale of Janie's search for fulfillment and consequently the narrator's education. Her quest is for not only self-knowledge, but also a promised land of regular orgasms, compatible with what a lower-class black Southern farmer could only see as female shiftlessness. On the one hand, Janie appears to give up bourgeois life for the creative possibilities of an uncertain folk life. On the other, her willingness to take this mid-twentieth-century trip to a black Floridian Club Med on the muck is sustained by the wealth of a high-achieving second husband whom she symbolically kills shortly before he actually dies. In her third husband, Tea Cake, Janie clearly finds her fulfillment of sexual fantasy. She will consume him sexually as women at a party consume the dainty for which he is named. Janie is, in her own way, as morally problematic (and for the same reasons) as the materialist and sexually charged Sarah of "Long Black Song" in Richard Wright's collection, *Uncle Tom's Children*. Sarah's search for fulfillment through romantic relations is similarly mired in her desire for economic security, male protection and sexual stimulation. She also exploits the leisure and bourgeois comfort provided by a hardworking husband in the expectation of middle-class marital fidelity. If Janie teaches her white narrator by example, the lesson is ambiguous. And this is even truer in the case of Pheoby. Given the assumptions of Gates' reading, the supposedly instructed narrator's lack of ethical alertness and judgment to the ambiguities I describe is troubling. If this is a story of the literary speaker's moral education or uplift, then it is not altogether effectively crafted. What we have here is more likely to be a striking story that successfully, if intuitively, manipulates plot and motivations to tilt the reader toward sympathy with Janie's final declaration of imaginative fulfillment—a fulfillment that we now understand in ideal, almost redemptive, terms. Yet what are we to make of the obvious inconsistencies of plot, incident, and character that pockmark the novel with hints of Janie's self-centeredness, her economic caginess, and her calculating deployment of affection?

Other obvious imperfections of plot—poor motivation, implausible May-December marriage, and unearned self-discovery—raise a further question. Should canonical status be awarded to a literary work whose admitted success at psychological exploration, metaphorical diction, and romance strategies so bears the marks of uneven improvisation and a talented storyteller's luck? The commentary's silence on aesthetic matters is all the more bothersome for contradictory plotlines that seem partially a matter of artistic intention and partially a result of the text's free-floating semiotic play.

The fulcrum of this issue may well be located in Janie's remarks to Pheoby about the value of the tale and her role as a teacher. If, on the one hand, Janie appears to be an adventurer, she is also, as this growing strand of interpretation makes clear, a teacher. And a clear ambivalence in this role as an instructor appears in her attitude toward teaching Pheoby, whom Janie instructs with her autobiography. "You have to go there to know there," Janie asserts. Here she seems unsure—not only of her immediate possession of the means of instruction, but also of the site in which learning will occur. Is learning the fruit of wisdom conveyed by speech, a wisdom to be relayed to others? "My tongue is in my friend's mouth." Or is learning the consequence of an unrestrained immersion in experience? These contradictory patterns only reinforce the story's central opposition between Janie's ostensible rejection of bourgeois norms for a folk life, and the reality of her very bourgeois, managed relationships with men who, if they are not increasingly wealthier, occupy ascending places on the scale of erotic potency. The conflict between the novel's two major codes and associated strands comes to a head in an image that occurs in strategic points of the novel, the "high chair" in which Janie reflects upon the consequences of her marriages to ambitious, economically successful men. She reflects explicitly that Jody sits on the "rulin' chair."[28] The narrator reports that Joe is building her a "high chair" in his new town.[29] She speaks of Jody's desire that she sit in the special chair "idly with her hands folded."[30] And she speaks of her marriage to Joe as submission to her grandmother's command that she ascend the "high chair."[31] These references inevitably end with Janie's fierce claim that she rejects the high chair, finding it useless. To be sure, she has been placed in the elevated comfort foreseen by her grandmother and provided by Killicks and Starks. However, according to Janie, she despises her grandmother for her intentions and Starks for his plan to glorify himself by setting her above the folk. The high chair is a symbol of luxury, power, and leisure. Joe Starks aspires to it for himself not only as a symbol of authority but as a vantage from which he can know and manipulate the town's citizens. The use of the high chair is observation and reflection. However, as the narrator and Janie make clear, she is not an educated person who does what educated people do.[32] Janie, whatever her declared intention, clearly acquires a wealth and leisure that elevates her above not only the masses, but also the well-heeled black men who court her after Joe's death. Because of the wealth devolved upon her by Joe, she can—whatever her alleged suffering—make the choices on which freedom and a transcendence of black Southern material realities depend in the Jim Crow era. Janie, despite her complaints, ruthlessly seeks the chair not only as an ascendant freedom, but also for the broad perspective that will allow her to shape her final imaginative vision of her life with Tea Cake. This reality—deeply embedded in the text—quickly rises to any interpretive reading of her supposed rejections of elevated class leisure, wealth, and status. She wants all of these perquisites of upwardly mobile self-invention: In her words, she "wants to utilize mahself all over."[33] And she cares deeply about escaping that material and class-related humiliation suffered by the suddenly wealthy widow who is exploited and rejected by the appropriately named "Who Flung."

However, so much as she may complain of sitting in the chair the status it embodies propels her to either sexual gratification or a deeper wisdom, fit for her role as teacher. Her rejection of the chair hides her clear dependence upon everything that has put her upon it. And as the novel moves on, we confront it with an increasing skepticism. Whatever ambivalence she may have toward enacting the chair's possibilities, she clearly thrives on them throughout the novel. We read the image of the chair with more and more uncertainty as to its true meaning for Janie. Her deep ambivalence results from her difficulty in fully enacting either of the impulses it enables. The novel's ambiguities of articulated wisdom and lived experience, bourgeois privilege and its rejection, and male domination and submission to a beloved masculine figure (Tea Cake will beat her as does Joe) are worth noting in light of the parable-like quality of both this book, its predecessor *Jonah's Gourd Vine*, and Hurston's earlier stories. Here too a story's conveyed wisdom must be weighed in the balance of vital experience, possessing a power beyond moral categories. Stories like "Sweat" and "Spunk" may pass judgment upon exploitative males such as Sykes and Spunk himself. However, the central male and female characters all possess a vitality that, in the context, is good in and of itself. A similar moralizing strategy can be found in *Jonah's Gourd Vine*, in which a locomotive kills a philandering minister. However ready we may be to declare the onrushing train a vehicle of moral judgment, we must confront its significance as a metaphor for the preacher's unrestrained sexual powers. Sykes of "Sweat" is ultimately destroyed by the phallic rattlesnake that he unleashes in his wife's bed—but he himself at the novel's end has become the very embodiment of the male member whose potency repeatedly (with Sykes' explicit intention) attracts and holds women. Spunk (the essence of male reproductive power) may be killed in a judgment upon his predatory, seductive style. But the story ends in the vaginal perfumed cave in which the fable's most seductive woman plies her erotic wares. These stories preach a stern morality; however, they simultaneously suggest delight in the earthy eroticism of their villains or the villains' lovers. Hurston, the daughter of a town mayor and schoolteacher, was still close enough to the Victorian Puritan ethos to sense her role as moral teacher to the middle class. This sense of obligation, evident in both the early stories and (less directly) in the novels, coexisted with a worship of Eros. The forces that drive Hurston's villains to their ends are—like the sexual energies of the unfaithful minister of *Jonah's Gourd Vine*—powers to be worshipped in and of themselves. They are, despite the fictional strictures made upon them, a form of life that transcends good and evil. Their seductive power inevitably lingers in the reader's mind after the story's ethical lesson has been taught.

This ambivalence appears also in a narrative voice through which Hurston raises explicit questions about the nature of Janie's quest, however irrelevant these queries may seem at the book's beginning. The text itself teems with countervailing meanings that not only engender the code of emerging self-knowledge, but undermine it with a string of incidents that stress her prudential care. It begins to appear that Janie has it both ways, and the text raises the possibility that Janie protests too much, that she has pursued self-fulfillment and followed her grandmother's prescription for self-preservation. All of these goals have been accomplished by shrewd marriages, careful financial moves, and a final escapade down South. The story she tells to Pheoby in the book's frame tale may well be the sermon (in other words) that the grandmother wanted the granddaughter to preach from a higher ground. These two paths do not contradict so much as complement one another. Indeed, our celebration of Janie's feckless quest for experience only adds a plausible human complexity to her vigilance.

This ambiguity appears most tellingly in the text's reportage of Janie's thoughts and actions upon Joe's death—a moment for which Janie must have wished, whatever its impact as traumatic human separation. At issue in this consideration of the text's ambiguity is Janie's careless wayward reflection, which not only makes this text effective, but also dramatizes myths in which the text's contradictory codes of wisdom are enclosed. I begin with the narrator's report of Janie's reflections and emotions during this important moment:

> Listen, Jody, you ain't de Jody ah run off down the road wid. You'se whut's left after he died. Ah run off tuh keep house wid you in uh wonderful way. But you wasn't satisfied wid me de way Ah was. Naw! Mah own mind had tuh be squeezed and crowded out tuh make room for yours in me.[34]

At this moment in the text, the key words of the passage above have become rich with contradictory meaning. Chief among these motifs is that of the "road." The road is not only the route on which she escaped from Killicks but the road of married life; it is both a departure from an old enclosure and a new commitment to what seemed to be freedom but turned out to be another captivity. She will go down the road of married life with Tea Cake. He will give her pleasure; however, like all such roads in *Eyes*, this path will end when his fecklessness leads them to tragedy. She will swiftly dispatch him when he threatens her selfhood. And in exchange for the reality of their experienced relationship, she will accept vicarious imaginative fulfillment.

The road clearly signifies Janie's willingness to engage life fully, but also the inevitable limitations of freewheeling experience. The road may signify risk, but Janie never sets out on the highway of life without significant financial or male protection. The road may represent an acceptance of the bohemian's mobile life; however, it will inevitably lead back to middle-class sites of protection. Although

Janie may ostensibly eschew middle-class security, she enjoys a privileged life that guards her in her course of dangerous experimentation.

It is therefore no surprise that Janie, at this section's end, awakens to her long-restricted sexuality by not only releasing her hair but also binding it up again in order to manipulate the crowd, even as Joe might. Hurston devotes the opening third of a paragraph to Janie's finally emerging pity for the dead Joe. However, this report rapidly gives way to one—in pointed Standard English—of Janie's calculating assessment of her possibilities:

> Years ago, she had told her girl self to wait for her in the looking glass. It had been a long time since she had remembered. Perhaps she'd better look. She went over to the dresser and looked hard at her skin and features. The young girl was gone, but a handsome woman had taken her place. She tore off the kerchief from her head and let down her plentiful hair. The weight, the length, the glory was there. She took careful stock of herself, then combed her hair and tied it back up again. Then she starched and ironed her face, forming it into just what people wanted to see, and opened up the window and cried, "Come heah people! Jody is dead. Mah husband is gone from me."[35]

These ambiguities are nevertheless a deeply plausible representation of an ambivalent wife's response to the death of a spouse. Janie's feelings for the death of a longtime, if bothersome, companion are mixed. She celebrates the aesthetic beauty of her hair, but at the same time "takes stock" of its value, its worth on the market of heterosexual life. Although Janie has only recently complained to the dying Joe about his emotional distance, she now surveys herself, concocts her facial expression, and addresses the crowd from the same detached stance. These ambiguities—which speak to the heart of Janie's true nature—are also evidence of what George Kent described as the nonideological, extra-rational character of the folk.[36] This quality appears in many of the folk fables—describing fantastic myths of creation, destruction, death, and regeneration—that Hurston herself notes are wish-fulfilling. The ambiguities described by these "lies" are a central element in folklore narration, at least that which is described in *Mules and Men*. In this kind of storytelling, the speaker relies on the listener's sense of each related incident in the tale as a momentary presence that will never be recovered, much less placed in the story's preceding history. This feature, so easily taken for granted, assumes the reader's as well as Janie's lack of concern for what she has said before or its textual record. Within this plot structure, an associative logic obtains in inferences drawn by the reader from a face-to-face world of experience. Part of the oral world of the folk is the acceptance of the unpremeditated, disorderly, spontaneous character of life lived moment-by-moment in a face-to-face world, free of the interpretive order of the printed story.

This wayward, freewheeling mode of apprehending the world appears most strikingly in the folk's understanding of race. Janie, like many of the men attracted to her, finds beauty in her long, clearly Caucasian hair. Her image of beauty is that of the whiteness that makes her such a valuable acquisition for Joe Starks, and also makes her attractive to Tea Cake, who loves to comb and untangle this erotic mane. Although Hurston will—as author—speechify against Mrs. Turner's praise of whiteness, it is clear that what Janie displays to herself in the mirror is an image of Caucasian beauty and sexual experience, much like that which we associate with Hawthorne's Hester Prynne. Tea Cake's beating of Janie in front of Mrs. Turner reflects his "symbolic" mastery of his white-tinged wife. The assumed attraction of ambitious black men to light-skinned or white women remains a commonplace throughout American society, especially its least educated, its most "folk" elements. This topic is at present socially unpalatable and undoubtedly raised taboo issues in Hurston's time. But Hurston is nevertheless willing to show Tea Cake and Janie in a deeply erotic celebration of the long hair and Caucasian features so worshipped by Mrs. Turner. All three are drawn to its powers, which have the same vitalizing and self-destructive cast as other erotic forces in Hurston's fiction.

Janie, with the ideological waywardness of the folk, thus affirms conventional lower-class black standards based on white beauty. Furthermore, this element of the text openly caters to those elements of black representation which are based upon the assumption of white supremacy. It shamelessly offers its white audience the narcissist satisfactions that it desired from blacks as mammies and now as stage minstrels. One wonders what the "whitened" narrative voice makes of this racist primitivism as he or she takes in the racial delusions of the vernacular. Signifying interpretations work without the Freudian understanding of the psychological ambivalence inevitably incited by taboo objects.[37] However, if the narrator's education by Janie is at this book's moral center, then that ambivalence must be confronted. Here, again, the narrator's silence is noteworthy.

Janie's gestures are writ large in a folk language that bluntly identifies whiteness with wealth, power, and knowledge, the dark underside of the persona's journey to self-awareness. The text's intellectual waywardness also shows the semiotic price demanded for Hurston's journey to supposed imaginative selfhood. This underlying code of adulation has to be suppressed by the signifying interpretation. However, much of the power and character of Hurston's text comes from its willingness to flaunt these racial attitudes toward the taboo.

*Eyes* does not constitute the narrator's encounter with racial diversity but rather (whether intentionally or not) a striking representation of folk life in its ephemeral, uncharted complexity. It may, given the racial ideologies of the period, be better for its loosely construed and spontaneously improvised attitudes toward the black Protestant-Victorian, primitivist bohemian, and experimental artistic point of view. The hastiness and sketchiness of the novel's composition are a large part of its charm. The text's seductive freedom, however, undermines a serious commitment to the ideologically-tilted folk representations that the signifiers crave. Such thoughtfulness would require a technical mastery, which the still inexperienced novelist of *Eyes* lacked and even later rarely (to my mind) achieved. Is Janie's life truly a rejection of bourgeois norms and a quest for fulfillment through the folk? More importantly, has Hurston told a subtly ironic tale (albeit slightly tarnished), or has she blundered into a complex vision about fulfillment, which the novel itself cannot sustain? These are questions of philosophical, thematic, and aesthetic value, and any argument seeking to establish the importance of *Eyes* in the American or African-American literary canon must take them into account.

I harp on the book's contradictions because the significance of Janie's self-discovery does depend on the authenticity of her quest, contested from the book's very beginning by the porch-sitting women who watch Janie return. However, it is affirmed more by Janie's unpremeditated reflections on love than in straightforward inquiry. The novel is filled with moments in which Janie, sometimes movingly, wonders about the nature of true love, its mysterious collapse under the pressures of her marriage with Joe Starks, as well as its miraculous rebirth. *Eyes* is at its best when the grandmother, the wayward mother and ex-slave, her wayward granddaughter, Joe Starks, and Tea Cake act from spontaneous feeling: I refer here to the grandmother's initial threat to beat Killicks, whom she erringly suspects has mistreated Janie, when Joe Starks improvises a funeral sermon for a mule, or when Tea Cake tells the tale of his meandering into a macaroni-and-fried-fish dinner. In these moments, the characters become less the objects of their individual agendas and more lifelike in their imitation of the unpredictable character of play. The book is at its best when Janie's reflection about love is inseparable from autoerotic experience, as the two actions are during her observation of the bee entering the blossom. Janie emerges most plausibly when she lives unconcerned about the quest to which she finally concludes that she committed herself. She is most alive when, despite the deep contradictions in her life, she is least self-conscious.

Some of the characters in *Eyes*, such as Tea Cake and Motor Boat, seem deeply aware of the casual attitude they have taken toward life. Others, such as the grandmother and Joe Starks, live and die by a plan for future fulfillment. However, the sum total of our reflections upon their lives forces us to ponder the nature of a good life—a large question that emerges even in the seemingly trivial context of an erotic romance. The question of the authentically good love-life is very real for women who, despite their intelligence and ambitions, will not have intellectually fulfilling careers or acquire power. In the romantic novel of the nineteenth and twentieth century, this issue was the basis for a women's self-consciousness that ultimately became political with the emergence of feminism. *Eyes* appears among the first African-American novels to pursue this theme of evolving romantic self-consciousness with respectable intellect and passion. The novel is filled with characters who seek good lives, like Janie; who preach about good lives, like Janie's grandmother and Joe Starks and Janie; or who simply live so that others wish to follow, as does Tea Cake.

These questions of love and marriage inevitably concern the construction of black middle-class life, a central theme in American and African-American writing since the early twentieth century. As scholars begin to examine a long tradition of nineteenth-century black women's writing, we see in the novels of Pauline Hopkins, Frances Harper, or Emma Kelly, in the oratory of Maria Stewart, or in the essays of Ann Plato, a sustained interest in the maintenance of courtship, marriage, and the integrity of domestic life as a central social duty of middle-class black men and women. These authors wrote amidst the formation of new black urban communities, the Jim Crow era, or the Great Migration—a time when the creation of domestic order was imperative for the middle-class progress of the race. As opposed to a novel like *Iola Leroy*, where marriage becomes a matter of commitment to uplift, Hurston depicts romance and marriage as a site for self-invention and experience made possible by leisure. The sexual act, once valued solely for reproduction and the creation of domestic units (to furnish citizens in a black community), takes on a different cast as marriage becomes a matter for the exercise of the will.

It is significant that Hurston, herself the daughter of a middle-class mayor-preacher and his schoolteacher wife, reflects the predicament of the middle-class individual freed to create a meaningful life for himself. In *Their Eyes Were Watching God*, Hurston reveals *inter alia* ambivalence about the reflection that this situation imposes, especially on the individual of the twentieth-century Jim Crow South. In this sense, she is like Du Bois and Booker T. Washington, who muse upon similar choices of immediate and delayed gratification for the newly freed inhabitants of the Black Belt, who may now buy commodities such as organs and sewing machines on credit. Hurston forcibly brings these issues to the attention of Janie who, like it or not, has been placed on the "high chair" where such matters are pondered. The reader is thus sympathetically forced to ponder these questions. Janie's strength as a character ironically emerges out of her willingness to live above the anxieties produced by the questions of meaningful choice and existence in her situation. And in a stroke of luck, this formula produces for Hurston a text that exerts—despite its flaws—an identifiable aesthetic power and an attractive resistance to ideological reduction—often taking the form of Janie's anti-intellectual spontaneity. To be sure, a more serious book would have entailed an ethical and political reflection that, as Hurston knew, a black woman intellectual in the thirties and forties could not afford to show. However, Janie's beckoning carelessness often transcends the novel's most characteristic ethical and aesthetic faults.

A true aesthetic judgment of the book may well depend on a comparison between it and its most sophisticated American literary competitors. Hurston's story links not only Janie with Hawthorne's Hester Prynne, another dark-haired representative of sexual experience, but also with the reflective Lady Chatterly of Lawrence and in particular Brett of *The Sun Also Rises*. Hurston's aesthetic and moral limitations are, to her credit, visible only through contrasts between *Eyes* and superior works, a level maintained by Hemingway's novel, which shares many of her concerns. Brett is another woman moving from one well-placed man to the next in search of sexual pleasure. As in *Eyes*, another unreliable narrator, Jake Barnes, tells Brett's fable. Jake, however, is dramatized in a way that makes him far more intellectually and morally alert than the supposedly Standard English-speaking narrator of Hurston's novel. Pushing the reader beyond the moral limits of Jake's perspective, Hemingway, like Hurston, presents the reader with an attractive, passionate woman engaged in a dubious life. Unlike Hurston, he exposes the reality principle that the Janies of this world encounter—the volatile consequences of promiscuity among friends, disregard for the principles of others, the destruction of a community, and bitter estrangement from those psychological supports so necessary in an increasingly alienating world. Hemingway's ambivalence over the moral and social lives of the Lost Generation is dramatized not only in the coldness with which Jake answers Brett's question at the book's end, but also by the reader's enforced consideration of its title and its meaning. However, where Hurston's conclusion in *Eyes* leaves its implicit philosophical strands untied, Hemingway's work creates an aesthetic order, drawn from the conflicts of his major characters. This balance is implicit in the title itself: *The Sun Also Rises* may signify the passing of the night's erotic satisfactions, or the recognition that life goes on after the losses of self-delusion. It is, of course, impossible to distinguish one's fruitful from one's unfortunate endings in a world drained of meaning, as Jake's life has been. Unlike *Eyes*, however Hemingway succeeds in making his book's ambivalent presentation of meanings into an incisive representation of his generation's paradoxical moral perspective.

To be sure, *The Sun Also Rises* is a realistic novel that necessarily criticizes the wish-fulfilling themes of romance through its emphasis on the central motivations of sex, money, and society. However, Hemingway achieves a moral, psychological, and spiritual insight—again articulated in aesthetic order—that *Eyes* pursues but does not acquire, at least not to the depth of *Sun*. But *Their Eyes Were Watching God* is ultimately disappointing in its depiction of wish-fulfillment, identity quests, and moral evasions, because Hurston cannot create an ordered perspective in which to depict and weigh these issues. Without this vantage, Janie's spontaneous gestures often seem to reflect merely the author's whims, and not the serious issues they raise. Her story lacks the background of social and cultural meanings against which Janie's dream of satisfaction may be usefully contested. Although the text approaches a lifelike complexity in its warp and woof of codes, it cannot meaningfully frame that life's intertwined meanings in a compelling interpretation. *Their Eyes Were Watching God*, in contrast to *The Sun Also Rises*, reveals a still tentative moral perspective and aesthetic technique on Hurston's part (although the book is an important advance over *Jonah's Gourd Vine*). The network of meanings constituting Hurston's text remain less powerfully articulated than the contrary myths of Jake Barnes' thwarted spiritual quest, Brett's free-floating erotic desire, and Robert Cohen's attempts at sexual possession. Hurston does not approach the aesthetic balance by which Hemingway assesses Brett's sympathetic spontaneity at the service of a questionable decadence; Jake's moral seriousness, which he will drop for his friends' tenuous pleasure; and Cohen's seemingly innocent ambition, which masks a self-destructive drive for erotic power.

Tea Cake's sexual attractiveness to Janie is never tested, as she grows older and presumably less motivated, sexually speaking. Janie's final wish-fulfilling identity is never tried in further social life. Above all, Janie evades the most important problem posed by the book: How will she frame a meaningful life in a world in which material survival is no longer a primary concern? Much of the power of Hemingway's art emerges from Jake's willingness to engage in the self-consciousness which reveals the book's powerful aesthetic design to the reader. Janie seems unwilling, whatever her feelings deep inside, to engage in the reflection that might yield a similar aesthetic conclusion, balance, or antinomy. Prior to dismantling the text of *Eyes*, then, the critic must ask whether the text's illusion is powerful and persuasive enough to warrant deconstructive examination. Does this text communicate effectively enough to establish the significance of different interpretations? Is the text worth reading carefully as a source of the various kinds of moral, social, and political knowledge that reading can give? This inquiry, largely made by contrast with acknowledged masterpieces, may offer a better set of canonical questions to ask. Recent deconstruction in the romantic and postromantic tradition occupied by Hurston includes, for example, the work of Wordsworth, James, Melville, and Stevens, all texts that suggest that only the richest and most profound texts are worth deconstructing. In this connection, it is not surprising that analytically shrewd advocates of the realistic novel, such as Richard Wright and Alain Locke, quickly dismissed Hurston's book; its fictional setting, its historical background, and the presentation of Janie's psychological development and her final fulfillment all are just too vague.[38] They cannot provide the nuts and bolts on which not only realism but even romance depends. *Their Eyes Were Watching God* never moves beyond the flimsiest construction of plot in its articulation of Janie's various wish-fulfillments.

Such weak foundations notwithstanding, *Eyes* does succeed remarkably well as a wish-fulfilling fantasy. And the book's contemporary status in African-American Studies raises issues that demand some reflection. Part of the book's attraction may reside in an unspoken African-American critical perception that Hurston has touched upon powerful ambiguities and ambivalence in black life that have not yet been weighed completely in the balance of black American fictional or sociological commentary. A new cadre of black middle-class critics may be observing a mirror image of their own confusions about the leisure, the instrumental uses of reflection, and the pursuit of desire. Yet despite this contemporary resonance, *Eyes* has been too quickly raised to canonical status. Even more disturbing is the will to power that establishes this text as a canonical black or American text without full consideration of its artistic depth. Granted such fiat, the canonical critic's power is potentially unlimited.

# Chapter Two

# The Proof of the Pudding
## Reading Gates; Reading Sterling Brown

GATES' CRITICAL PRACTICE IS AN ANOMALY. Literary criticism operates on an economy of scale. Those with canonical ambition tend to rely on a wealth of knowledge and a breadth of reading, even if they focus on a narrow tradition. Copiousness of information, examples, and counterexamples is important to establish the canon's claims to encyclopedic authority, legitimacy, and invention—the plenitude constituting the sacred center upon which any canon rests.[1] As bearers of knowledge and expertise, intellectuals generally prefer more rather than less of both in the hands of author and critic. A critical practice that limits itself to an inadequate tradition of texts is itself dysfunctional and demands investigation on that ground. Intellectuals are of use to men who wield power, a group's cultural hegemony, or a society's contact with the sacred. Such contact often resides in powerful institutions, such as the church, or in those ascetic modes of life found in bohemia or other forms of otherworldly existence. Indeed, such styles in our day have been taken up by late twentieth-century high capitalism into the fashions of consumer culture. Given the power that Gates' critical discourse seeks to yield, what does one make of these limitations implicit in the signifiers' critical project? What is the source of the charisma and legitimacy by which his authority as a canon-making critic is grounded?

The lack of erudition, in terms of both canonical recall and literary-critical comparisons, is a telling fault in a book that self-consciously invites comparison between itself, *The Anxiety of Influence*, and various essays by Paul de Man. The intellectual enterprise of signifying is far less serious than the Derridean deconstruction, which builds upon Saussure's linguistics, the philosophical tradition extending from Plato to Nietzsche, the psychology of Freud, and the anthropology of Levi-Strauss. Despite some antihumanist tendencies, deconstruction emerges from a certain moment of intellectual self-consciousness in the humanist continuities of the West, specifically those of Freud, Marx, and Nietzsche, among others. The "deconstructions" performed by these writers have centered upon the texts of dreams, economic schemes of production, and Christian belief. These readings, even in attacking tradition, have relied on vast, highly systematized, historical, poetic, and theological knowledge—a kind of knowledge that is no longer available in the learning of a single scholar. These writers themselves were polymaths (of a now nearly vanished kind) whose reading comprehended (unlike that of most humanists today) an enormous range of languages, literature, philosophers, and art.[2]

The tragedy of the culture of signifying is that it cuts itself off from even the relatively meager resources of American literary tradition, a tradition containing much that is relevant to black life. Important literary resources for an understanding of African-American irony and romance may be found from Charles Brockden Brown to James, the literary philosophies of Emerson and William James, and the theological critiques of figures such as Nathan Scott. The reflections of Scott, a black existentialist theologian, are strangely absent in an African-American school of literary criticism so concerned with sometimes nihilistic interpretive methods and reflection. The absence of the critiques of black cultural anomie and nihilism in the work of W. E. B. Du Bois, E. Franklin Frazier, and St. Clair Drake is also especially troubling in the prophets of signifying.

This disturbing lack of contextual knowledge and humanist intent sets Gates free to move to the most materialistic and alienating aspects of pop culture, academic fashion, and the commercial media. In the end, *The Signifying Monkey* was less an intellectual statement than a vehicle for academic alliances and the definition of a disciplinary field. In these ways, however, the book—consistently quoted in the scholarship of African-American scholarship—has been profoundly influential. Gates' cynical use of Derridean deconstruction as a metaphor for the "play" of folk culture legitimized the sometimes cynical, sometimes pragmatic ethos by which the new black middle class pursued professionalism in integrated America. The ethos of literature as a hustling attempt to "get over" legitimized an improvisatory career in culture that quickly moved beyond literary interpretation to journalism and entrepreneurial activity. Gates himself was too serious about power-mongering to remain a literary commentator. However, there are serious cultural limitations to the ethos of "getting over," and these explain the emptiness of much of Gates' later journalism and of his autobiography, *Colored People*.

*The Signifying Monkey* was more important for its establishment of Gates as a paradigmatic guide and explainer in African-American culture than as academic inquiry. He created, however, a critical style that was available to exploitation by "diverse" academic institutions and the media. In this connection, he was shrewd about the coming synthesis of entertainment and scholarship just over the horizon. He was, like most entrepreneurs, a capitalist (committed to the very kind of professional specialization that Max Weber lamented in *The Protestant Ethic and the Spirit of Capitalism*). Indeed, it is here that he runs against the African-American and American humanism that extends from Puritanism through transcendentalism into a Victorian and pragmatist aftermath. His antihumanist style (and its critique) is not new in African-American culture. Literature for Gates, like piano music for the anonymous narrator of the *Autobiography of an Ex-Coloured Man*, is a vehicle to a higher life of capitalist enterprise that leaves liberal humanist cultural concerns behind, except as entertainment and as a vehicle for seduction. Gates has made the movement from scholarly commitment to literary tricksterism possible for a black middle class alienated from the institutional centers of cultural tradition. Within this context, the black therapeutic withdrawal from white-dominated intellectual life may be understandable. As a scholarly, cultural, and political strategy, however, it is unacceptable. Whatever instrumental value such careerism might have in the estranged black bourgeois academic world, the productions of "signifying" cannot be taken seriously in existential terms. It is a product of his social isolation, his alienation from both a black and a white world that would willingly draw upon his reflection. The result has been the black critics' devaluation of reflection itself. Since the early twentieth century, serious black students of African-American culture have feared, in books as different as *The Souls of Black Folk*, *Up from Slavery*, and *The Autobiography of an Ex-Coloured Man*, the ruthless entrepreneur determined to live by his wits.

Significantly, Gates shows no compunction in describing both the instrumental quality of his performance as a critic and the masklike persona that the young black academic assumes in order to get tenure:

> This is an exciting time for critics of Afro-American literature. More critical essays and books are being produced than ever before, and there have never been more jobs available teaching Afro-American literature in white colleges and universities. In a few years, we shall at last have our very own Norton anthology, a sure sign that the teaching of Afro-American literature is being institutionalized. Our pressing question now becomes this. In what languages shall we choose to speak, and write, our own criticisms? What are we now to do with the enabling masks of empowerment that we have donned as we have practiced one mode of formal criticism or the other?[3]

The black critic here works, at the beginning of his career, behind a mask, attempting to fulfill an ethnically inauthentic set of cultural criteria. Afterwards, Gates claims in this passage, these demands wither away, and he enjoys the freedom to choose a "language" in which to write his criticism. It is not clear, however, how this "choice" of a critical language consorts with the clear needs of the university, institutionalized before the critic began to write. Given that he has his origin and being in the university, to what extent can the critic operate outside of its goals and roles? To what extent is he always acting behind a "mask" of theory? Indeed, how can anyone write about any literary work without a body of conceptions, no matter how incoherent? What is the relation of the values of that "mask" to the traditions of criticism that have provided a long continuity of critics with their personae? The burden of answering these questions must clearly be great for the critic who, given Gates' schema, must maintain and reproduce his separate institution, its wisdom, and its social knowledge—all within the context of the elite American university.

Significantly, however, something more is at stake when Gates advises his African-American audience to don the empowering mask of theory and to discover the "universe" of black discourse that—he assures us—awaits us sight unseen. Without such an authentically racial mask, the black critic will seem inauthentic, implausible, indeed ridiculous to his colleagues. "We must redefine theory itself from within our own black culture, refusing to grant the premise that theory is something that white people do, so that we are doomed to imitate our white colleagues."[4] Gates' fear is precisely that the black critic will become a minstrel, an absurd clown donning white face to please an academic audience. This fear is wholly understandable, not only from Gates' perspective, but also from that of Houston Baker who, significantly for this discussion, discusses the great rhetorical achievement of Booker T. Washington as the adaptation of the mask of minstrelsy to a more sophisticated black mode of irony. This stance, according to Baker, allowed Booker T. Washington "to earn a national reputation and its corollary benefits for the Afro American audience."[5] This style, as the careful reader of *Up from Slavery* can attest, often opens up into ludicrous nonsense: the black farmer amazed that Washington desires to have a hen house cleaned out during the day; the white farmer who points out to Washington that he will have to address *en masse* at the Atlanta Exposition the very people that he courted separately on other occasions; and the joke about "passing" in a dining room car. These remarkable references to minstrelsy by two accomplished black intellectuals lie on the surface of their discourse. Without visible prompting, both Gates and Baker, in the course of their critical performance, slide into a disquisition that reveals what must be the signifier's deepest fear: that he and his existence are absurd to all who watch him; that his intellectual undertaking lacks the most basic social legitimacy; and that he himself will lose his identity in the ironic role that he presents to the public. At the heart of signifying is the signifier's profound anxiety that his shifting hall of mirrors ends in a shimmering cul-de-sac. This fear is in the end shame for the exposed vulnerability that engendered the signifier's rhetoric from the beginning.[6]

The nature of Gates' signifying is clarified by a consideration of earlier African-American critics, more firmly and confidently grounded in their social worlds, which looked to them for moral and intellectual guidance. Sterling Brown grew up and pursued his career in black middle-class Washington, D.C., during the age of segregation. These facts, and much of Brown's writing, suggest an important link between socially secure status, the capacity to become a bearer of intellectual tradition, and the psychological distance needed for black middle-class thinkers to reflect successfully on folk life.[7] This intellectual distance is also the product of historical and cultural experience from which the thinker draws wisdom. As Brown's work shows, such a tradition and its wisdom cannot merely be called into being. Seen in this light, the rapid establishment of Black Studies programs in the seventies and the sixties was often an exercise in futility.

. . . . . . . . . . . . . . . .

Sterling Brown's criticism centered around two foci. One was a concept of realism, which he carefully elaborated in his early study of black characterization in American and African-American fiction. The second was a concept of black folk culture that persisted from the pre-capitalist agrarian world of the antebellum South through the Great Migration to the disorganized social world of the Northern ghetto. As he circumscribed these realities, Brown defined an African-American literary culture within which he discerned a nexus of moral and intellectual value from which he drew a critical system. To be sure, Brown employed this as a measure of the black humanity that the plantation tradition had trivialized. In attacking such stereotypes, he carefully considered the ethical and aesthetic limitations of ideological art, measuring the racist conceptions of plantation tradition against increasingly realistic forms of black characterization. Similarly, in his consideration of the evolving life of African-American folk culture, he stressed the folk's capacity to choose among moral alternatives with the guidance of tradition.

Brown found the power of African-American culture in its capacity to make normative choices on the basis of accumulated wisdom. Such choices allowed the folk to affirm (or reject) past values as they confronted the rigors of new conditions, such as those in the Northern ghetto of the twentieth century. And however mechanical his conception, Brown exhorted his black middle-class audience to a literary self-consciousness of great import. Not only do his reviews in *Crisis*, *Phylon*, and *Opportunity* identify the moral dialectics of African-American literature itself, but his literary journalism often invited his audience to reflect on the different perspectives that they might bring to folk culture in order to value it properly. Most importantly, his sense of himself as a critic was grounded in the imperative to guide the black public. He saw his writing as a means of educating the black bourgeoisie into cultural, and thus political, self-consciousness. He sought to create an equivalent of what Lionel Trilling would later—in another context—call "our educated classes."

Many of Brown's important ideas and literary touchstones remain tactfully just under the surface of his elegant, ironic, often aphoristic prose, which frequently suggests interpretive approaches rather than blatantly imposing them. His key concepts often come clothed in the ironic language of the folk, teasing out the implications of a story or event, rather than developing an *explication de texte* full dress. As a critic, he is more concerned with bringing his reader into contact with folk tradition as a mode of reflection and choice than as a "scholarly" system. At bottom, however, his conception is founded in a romantic notion of organic historical process, his notions of character in a broad definition of realistic description. It is a traditional folk life whose creative energy persists from generation to generation, even through the tragedy of his historical moment—the formation of the Northern ghetto in the wake of the Great Migration. Like all traditions it ebbs and flows. The following passage details its most recent twentieth-century transformations:

> The migration of the folk Negro to the cities, started by the hope for better living and schooling, and greater self-respect, quickened by the industrial demands of two world wars is sure to be increased by the new cotton picker and other man-displacing machines. In the city the folk become a submerged proletariat.

Leisurely yarn-spinning, slow-paced aphoristic conversation becomes lost arts; jazzed-up gospel hymns provide a different sort of release from the old spirituals; the blues reflect the distortions of the new way of life. Folk arts are no longer by the folk for the folk; smart businessmen now put them up for sale. Gospel songs often become showpieces for radio slumbers, and the blues become the double-talk of the dives. And yet, in spite of the commercializing, the folk roots often show a stubborn vitality. Just as the transplanted folk may show the old credulity, though the sophisticated impulse sends them to an American Indian for nostrums, or for fortune-telling to an East Indian "Madame" with a turban around her head rather than to a mammy with a bandanna around hers; so the folk for all their disorganization may keep something of the fine quality of their old tales and songs. Assuredly even in the new gospel songs and blues much is retained of the phrasing and the distinctive musical manner. Finally, it should be pointed out that even in the transplanting, a certain kind of isolation—class and racial—remains. What may come of it, if anything is unpredictable, but so far the vigor of the creative impulse has not been snapped, even in the slums.[8]

An older world of hope, leisurely conversation, aphorisms, spiritual renewal, and ironic blues is lost here. Commercial creations of less human range and depth replace an authentic world of tragedy and fulfillment, aspiration and trauma, celebration and mourning. Gospel music becomes a "showpiece" and blues devolve into signifying and mere catharsis. Framed in aphoristic language dramatizing the passing of the folk, this poignant passage laments the estrangement of the modern world, the breakdown of those human fulfillments of hunting in the morning and thinking in the afternoon. Yet if the passage reflects the loss of past sensuous unities, it also anticipates the revival of other values. Some of these persist in debased form: blues is signifying, gospel is a showpiece, its emotion mere catharsis. And there also endures the aesthetics of "the fine quality of their old tales and songs," of "the phrasing and the distinctive musical manner," and of ethnic identity "a certain kind of isolation—class and racial."

To be sure, Brown has projected many of his own humanist impulses upon the folk in his romantic critique of a dehumanizing ghetto culture. But he has done so to dramatize a folk's capacity to choose between an older human wholeness and the new emptiness experienced so vividly in city life. This mode of criticism, as eloquent as Jacob Lawrence's vividly colored prints depicting the Great Migration, insists on the existence of folk conceptions of moral, political, and aesthetic values central to all human life—white *and* black. Implicit in this reflection, available even to the unlettered black masses, is the assumption that their lives, as well as those of their scholarly observers, may acquire value. This sense, clearly lacking in Gates' model, is at the heart of the moral problem that signifying represents as a cultural point of view for the middle class to whom Gates addresses himself.

The romantic element in Sterling Brown's criticism resides in his concept of black writing as an expression of an organic black spirit. Brown draws upon what M. H. Abrams has comprehensively studied as "expressive" forms of poetic discourse and criticism in order to define African-American poetic tradition. Later critics such as Gates and Holloway will—despite their pretensions to semiotic critical method—essentially draw upon the same metaphors of "organic" and "expressive" forms to describe black literary discourse. Brown's excellence as a critic stems largely from his realization that seemingly "natural," "authentic" modes of literary expression are intentional artistic constructions, works that must be articulated —whether by the writer or the critic—in traditional literary terms. Which is to say that "folk" poetry and criticism draw directly—whether well or badly—upon literary tradition. The chief vice of recent black criticism has been the tendency to jettison the broad world of literary tradition in which the "authentic" expressions of the folk become art—if that is what they are meant to be.[9]

Sterling Brown's realism also participates in his dialectical humanism. Part of what was weighed in his criticism was the ideological distortions of racism against what he called "realistic" representation.[10] This dialectic opposes merely ideological outlines to fuller depictions of life's variety: that is, pictures brimming with those particulars, perspectives, and tones by which we distinguish the real world from its imitations. Such full representations resist simple ideological reduction, exactly like day-to-day life experience. It might, given Brown's definition, be found in unexpected sites: the literary and painterly modes of impressionism, pointillism, and cubism. It exists in black literature as well as in plastic representation. Furthermore, it can inhabit various forms of romantic, postromantic, and modernist literature. Just as painters create realistic description by capturing the textures of skin, or the emotional depth of a person in the course of his social life, so realistic imitation (in Brown's sense) reproduces the textures of the quotidian. In narrative art, this requires details, events, and imitations that create plausibility through the adjustment, fulfillment, reversal, enhancement, or undermining of mechanical expectations. Realistic art draws upon the surprise and freshness of everyday experience as well as its conventionality. Brown advocated such realism for its political thrust, its means of demystifying the stereotypes of the plantation tradition. Brown's perspective helps the reader discover and value subtleties that he might not otherwise notice in Hurston or Hughes. Taken as a whole, however, the critic's concept has an aesthetic potential that is still not fully explored.

Brown's commitment to romantic-realism as a means for the moral education of the black bourgeoisie explains the excitement with which he reviewed works such as Langston Hughes' *Not Without Laughter* and Richard Wright's *Uncle Tom's Children*.[11] Hughes' novel possessed the lively complexity that Brown valued, a verisimilitude especially important for political reasons. His account of the book as a portrait of viable family life is deeply suggestive in its argument that Hughes contradicts notions of childbearing, courtship, and socialization central to late nineteenth- and early twentieth-century black Victorian life. In works such as Frances Harper's *Iola Leroy* and Pauline Hopkins' *Contending Forces*, formal courtship and stable middle-class marriage emerge as the *sine qua non* of black culture. In his novel *Not Without Laughter*, Hughes questions the notion of the family's central social function in deadly earnest. Can the strengths of black tradition be transmitted without the structures of stable family life? In doing so, Hughes asks how black society is passed from generation to generation. And, as Brown suggests, Hughes portrays a young folk character, Sandy, choosing those aspects of tradition that will sustain him in the future. Hughes' conception of the folk affirms this hope in the face of the desperate early twentieth-century worlds of the Jim Crow South and the Northern ghetto. This understanding of folk possibilities emerges from the novel's careful parsing of the central characters' virtues as opposed to their limitations. The characters examined include the narrator's father, the wanderer Jim-Boy; his mother, Angie, the unmarried day-worker in the homes of wealthy people; Sandy's cousin, a young blues singer and ex-prostitute; and his grandmother, the traditional Southern mammy. To be sure, the novel subjects all of these characters to the criticism of humor—and thus the book's title. However, Hughes affirms the father's wandering, Angie's persistent attachment to the boy's father, the grandmother's acceptance of antebellum paternalism, and the cousin's capacity for self-sacrifice to others and to the art of the blues. Significantly, Sandy-Hughes recognizes these possibilities within examples of selfhood provided by the black folk whose culture the author has chosen to celebrate. From the chaff of irresponsibility, lack of ambition, sentimentality, and aimless materialism, Sandy-Hughes separates the moral grain of openness, tragic acceptance, sincerity, and a capacity for simple pleasure that will sustain him.

All of these qualities show the human possibilities of the black folk undergoing the oppressive experience of the Great Migration and the formation of the Northern black ghetto. These strengths, as they are celebrated by Hughes, allow us to project a heroic future for Sandy as their inheritor. As narrator, Sandy is a clear autobiographical stand-in for the young Hughes contemplating the possibilities offered by life as a bohemian black artist on the cusp of the Depression, loss of patronage, and personal upheaval. Brown's critique forces the middle-class reader to reflect upon the potential social strengths of lower-class black life. While affirming the need for choice, however, Brown also warns against the dangers of unbalanced judgment. The critic, like many of the age's cohort of black intellectuals, deeply condemned bourgeois snobbery toward the folk. However, he knew that Sandy's survival would depend upon identifying the excesses and irrationality of the folk world that he inherited from his parents. Brown thus not only shows Sandy celebrating his entire world as a "band of dancers" from whom he must learn, but also clearly indicates the suffering that Sandy's blues-singing aunt and his mother undergo as a result of the recklessness of folk life. And in the image of band we find an image of a balanced and comprehensive vision that imposes an important closure upon the novel. Sandy has not so much learned a way of life as a way of viewing and interpreting it.

Although Brown agrees with Hughes' critique of Aunt Tempy's snobbery, he argues that Hughes' judgment against her is excessive. The author's depiction at some points maligns the full humanity of all blacks who engage in the self-criticism on which true self-consciousness depends. Brown faults Hughes for stereotyping the book's most conspicuous black bourgeois and, in doing so, weakening a potentially useful self-awareness:

> Of all of his characters, Mr. Hughes obviously has least sympathy with Tempy. She is the arriviste, the worshipper of white folks' ways, the striver. "They don't

'sociate no mo' with none but de high toned colored folks." The type deserves contempt looked at in one way, certainly look at in another it might deserve pity. But the point of the reviewer is this: that Mr. Hughes does not make Tempy quite convincing. It is hard to believe that Tempy would be as blatantly crass as she is to her mother on Christmas Day, when she says of her church "Father Hill is so dignified, and the services are absolutely refined. There's never anything niggerish about them—so you know, mother, they suit me."[12]

This is a critique not only of black bourgeois like Tempy, but also of black intellectuals who, while criticizing the race, can often forget their own psychological complexity. It is right to say that Tempy would be more sympathetic of her mother on this tragic Christmas morning. Similarly, black intellectuals who criticize the African-American middle class do so because they maintain emotional ties to that group which complicate their thought in many ways. This strange intimacy was behind Langston Hughes' use of painful autobiographical detail as well as his (admittedly caricatured) depiction of a middle-class household in "The Negro Artist and the Racial Mountain." It appears too in his critique of black college administrators and faculties in "Cowards in the Colleges."[13] The disappointment that Brown, E. Franklin Frazier, and Hurston often expressed in a black middle class that would rather play cards than read was ultimately tempered with affection.[14]

In analyzing Tempy, Brown predictably criticizes the black bourgeoisie in a way that was nevertheless predicated upon their humanity. The deepest flaw of Hughes' novel appears in its oversimplification of Tempy's character: the failure to exploit what must be her internal psychological conflict between her familial past and social aspirations. This is a conflict that can destroy Sandy if he is unwary. In accepting Tempy and her pretentious government-worker husband, the narrator accepts himself and the complexity of his own aspirations beyond his family. He consequently represents the mature self-consciousness which Brown wished the black middle class to have. This quality, Brown wants to suggest, is not in and of itself corrosive of all humanity. In a similar reading of Richard Wright's *Uncle Tom's Children*, Brown affirms the realism of the author's portrait of a subtly brewed folk wisdom, suggesting that Wright's characters, which might seem stereotyped portraits of black doggedness, recklessness, and crude individualism, actually complicate conventional assumptions. Characters such as Man in "Down by the Riverside," Silas in "Long Black Song," and Big Boy in "Big Boy Leaves Home" make existential choices (Brown argues) in a Jim Crow world rendered meaningless for blacks by white supremacy. From that perspective, these characters' choices, which otherwise appear to be hardheaded, reckless, and desperate, emerge as forms of heroism. Moreover, characters who seem to be driven unreflectively by ingrained traits now appear as reflective agents of intelligent will. Their decisions depend, as an inspection of the stories shows, upon the careful observation, thought, and will that give the collection's heroes a rich humanity that readers often sense but cannot easily name. Silas' canny construction of Sarah's infidelity from a quick inspection of the room; Man's knowledge of the city that allows him to navigate its flood-covered major obstacles; Big Boy's humanizing series of regrets while hiding from a lynch mob—all illustrate a Southern black community whose depth of character makes its oppression more tragic. Brown's appreciation suggests a literary-critical refusal to understand Wright's stories through the narrow grid of proletarian aesthetics, or to caricature him as James Baldwin, Ralph Ellison, and Gates do.

Brown is willing to sit on the high chair of moral, political, social, and aesthetic engagement in a way that Hurston is not—the fruit of a complicated moral acceptance of the responsibilities that come with the leisure devolved upon a society's cultural elites. In subtle ways, moreover, he is an acute observer of the aesthetic aspiration in Wright, an aspiration that Hurston does not fulfill. His advocacy of the literary artfulness of Hughes and Wright suggests a persistence of the didactic Protestant Victorian culture through the era of the Harlem Renaissance and into the thirties and forties. Like Jean Toomer, Hughes, and Hurston, Brown is in his own way engaged in a kind of moral education akin to the earlier religious humanist tradition of uplift. The virtues of folk irony and motherwit expounded by *Cane's* Kabnis, the (not fully articulated) wisdom of Janie and her grandmother in *Their Eyes Were Watching God*, and the common sense of *Simple Takes a Wife* by Hughes all teach complex moral lessons directed at a new middle class attempting to make sense of its life in the urban black North—what E. Franklin Frazier called the "cities of destruction." Brown's critical voice self-consciously continues the nineteenth-century tradition of moral instruction borne by his father, the minister Nelson Brown. Sterling Brown differed from his predecessors only in his search for a richer, more subtle form of moral uplift than had been pursued by the late nineteenth-century Victorians.

Brown taught lessons about the complexities of moral and aesthetic judgment that were ultimately important for black political life. His irony prodded the reader into reflection. He himself understood that "folk style" could be not only ornament but a sly motivation to moral recognition, and choice, as well as parody. He combined these folk elements and earlier Protestant tradition into a larger continuity of black humanism. The last point bears some explanation. Brown's aesthetic and philosophical manipulation of black values was made possible not by an immersion in the folk world, but by a clarifying distance from it which stemmed from identification with larger traditions of American and Western literature as well as sociology. This was facilitated by his stable place in the upper-class black intellectual elite whose values blended with those cultural worlds that he would encounter at Williams, Harvard, Chapel Hill, Vassar, the WPA, and the Gunnar Myrdal's American Dilemma project. Whatever psychological difficulties Brown encountered (and he was to have emotional troubles), his work does not reveal the profound dislocation—the severance from much intellectual tradition itself—that figures so largely in Gates' antihumanism. On the contrary, Brown took naturally to the role of intellectual as bearer of tradition, a role that would make sense of his future connections with the white world. Brown's ascension to a post at Vassar, where he was offered a permanent tenured professorship, was the result not only of sustained scholarly publication at the highest level of excellence, but also a wholly typical professional mobility from generation to generation in American academic and intellectual families of all ethnic groups. He was part of an earlier segregated black elite pattern of intergenerational mobility that characterized the families of Horace Mann Bond and the Devises. The offer of a position at Vassar was moreover part of the opening up of high-level posts in the fifties: John Davis at the City University of New York, Kenneth Clark at Columbia, as well as Allison Davis and John Hope Franklin at the University of Chicago.

I do not wish to romanticize this era in which many deserving black scholars were kept from the high cosmopolitan academic positions, which they not only deserved but also needed for the furthering of crucial scholarly work. One thinks here of Leo Hansberry, E. Franklin Frazier, and, of course, W. E. B. Du Bois. What is to the point is that their intellectual balance as scholars was often aided by a solid sense of social status grounded in family, orderly social mobility, as well as stable black-white patronage relationships. This position made possible the attainment of elite scholarly status as well as identification with institutions which were rigorously selective—both academically and socially. Brown's distance from the folk and the new black middle class of his day allowed him to differentiate the two objectively, to distinguish between their orientations and needs, while calmly establishing his relationship to both.

From this point of view, Gates' representation of black literary tradition quickly falls into place. Not surprisingly, much black bourgeois society has little patience with the most blatantly violent ritualistic aspects of the signifying monkey. Upon being challenged to defend the honor of one's mother, the polite African-American responds, "I do not play the dozens." There is a reason for this. The competition that surrounds the dozens often leads to fights, knifings, and worse. Playing the dozens in the wrong ghetto neighborhood is a good way to get killed. This is a social reality that Gates is at pains to avoid in his monograph. From this point of view, Gates' representation of black literary tradition as signifying quickly falls into play as what Brown called the dislocations of the materialistic culture of the North. Brown saw the signifying play of drunken folk in the dives as a partial collapse of an earlier folk tradition. More precisely, the reduction of language to a few rhetorical figures and signs in signifying is an estrangement from human wholeness, an alienation familiar to romantics as a pathology of modern life. This decline of folk speech to equivocal counters had further dangers. Brown repeatedly warned against the appropriation of such hollowed-out images of mankind that might be used by racist ideologues (largely in the media) beyond the reach of demystifying critics such as himself. Signifying was the sophistry of those whose rhetorical powers were on sale. They were the enemies not only of philosophers but of all people without the power to purchase intellectual hired guns for their battles in the forums of public life.

Signifying represented not only a confusion of class identities but also a failure to choose lasting alliances and accept their necessary consequences. Gates' sophist is caught in the fluid travails of class mobility: When conflicts of interest arise, how does he choose between the university he serves and the black lower and middle class from which he springs? He cannot make those moral choices or discern realistic subtleties of complex human character, which for Brown are at the heart of a book such as *Their Eyes Were Watching God*. A large abyss in contemporary African-American cultural criticism is the absence of a serious discussion of this phenomenon in the interpretation of black middle-class life. This lack of discrimination appears in Gates' poorly considered comparison of the Renaissance prince to the jobless leisure of the modern black lumpen.[15] This glib comparison marks a deep confusion about class, social structure, leisure, power, and human value as a whole. To be sure, the Renaissance prince practices in an orderly form some tropes that Gates implicitly includes in his broad definition of signifying. Brown would have smirked at this upscale attempt to dignify the double-talk of the dive. He would have frowned at attempts to compare the brokering of power in the early modern court to the cathartic play of powerless black men in the ghetto. Gates' intention to shock aside, his adoption of the cynical lower-class signifying rhetoric is an uncritical appropriation of the moral confusion and political dysfunctions of the black poor. The Renaissance prince knew his place in the nation-state's network of power, but the unemployed signifying youth acting out fantasies of male aggression does not know his function or place in an even more complicated global world. In some sense the anxiety surrounding his alienation has been taken on voluntarily by the signifying intellectual.

There are many problems in Gates' critical position, but this ill-defined social and political self-consciousness may be the greatest, a self-consciousness most necessary for ethical judgment. Gates has made the estranged pleasures of the urban poor into postmodernist black primitivism. He has done so under the aegis of a debased consumer culture, an American conception of leisure as mere recreation. However, the free play of postmodernism is the activity of an elite with the leisure, patiently acquired knowledge, and surplus wealth to study and dismantle mandarin philosophical texts, constructing and reconstructing them against the grain of obvious codes of meaning. This activity assumes not only a profound acquaintance with Western tradition, but also the highest degree of social security, protection, and economic freedom. Such wealth comes from membership in an affluent social class with a clear sense of its economic and political interests. However long the rich may engage in this practice, it can only provide wisdom for an aspiring middle class, deeply reflective about the tenuous nature of its social, cultural, and political position. Whereas the dominant powerful class may appear to function without sociology of knowledge, no middle-class outsider ever survived unless he understood his interests within the larger social system in which he lived. Seen from this vantage, Gates' promotion of the ethos of signifying points to a confusion of class and the social position of the new black bourgeoisie.

This alienation is not only apparent in the intellectual mechanics of Gates' critical writing but also in his literary tastes. Seen from the perspective of Brown's practice, Gates' theories lead to problematic critical and aesthetic valuations, particularly in the case of a complex modernist work such as *Invisible Man*. In particular, Gates' programmatic elevation of the Rinehart section above the "realism" of Richard Wright leads to a gross simplification of Ellison's allusions to Wright's fiction. This oversimplified praise of Ellison is at the heart of Gates' rarely critical approach to Ishmael Reed, whose reputation has deeply benefited from Gates' academic boost. To overemphasize the importance of play as an aesthetic standard (simple delight and ironic pleasure sometimes seem to be the only norms associated with signifying) and to ignore its multitude of social purposes and meanings allows not only for knee-jerk approval of Reed's satires but also for an "appreciation" of work by Trey Ellis—work that in other contexts would be dismissed for its lack of reflective depth, even if considered as satire or playful wit. I submit a sample of Gates' "reading" of Ellison's "realism" here:

> By explicitly repeating and reversing key features of Wright's fictions, and by defining implicitly in the process of narration a sophistication more akin to Zora Neale Hurston's *Their Eyes Were Watching God*, Ellison exposed naturalism as merely a hardened convention of representation of "the Negro problem" and perhaps part of "the Negro problem" itself. I cannot emphasize enough the major import of this narrative gesture to the subsequent development of black narrative forms. Ellison recorded a new "way of seeing" and defended both a new manner of representation and its relation to the concept of presence.[16]

By Gates' lights, Ellison has emptied Wright's fiction of the moral, political, historical, and psychological depth upon which his complex human portraits depended. The invisible man's cartoon-like grandfather (taken from Wright's depiction of a stodgy elder in *Black Boy*) or the comic chase between the communist recruiters and Jack-the-Bear represent more than parody. These images reproduce historical memories that would haunt black writing during the eras of Jim Crow in the South and McCarthyism in the North. These dreamlike presences invoke and release profound anxieties of suppressed anger and fear that were still unspeakable in the political atmosphere in which Ellison wrote. The words "repeating and reversing" wholly oversimplify the many ways in which Ellison has not just "reversed" Wright's meanings but often elaborated, interpreted, and translated them into images of black intellectual victimization at the hands of "comrades," delusions of paranoia, and persistent, slow-burning but contained rage. Ellison's strategy is that of complex cultural commentary intended to stimulate a varied number of reflections, not just on literary genre but on African-American intellectual history itself.

Certainly, few will be able to read the central texts of Richard Wright, Ralph Ellison, and Ishmael Reed as they did before Gates' interpretation (and this is saying a great deal for *The Signifying Monkey*). However, Gates' reading necessarily must ignore or repress not only the form but also the rich substance of Ellison's dialectical moral judgment—particularly his criticism of the signifying style, which Gates values so highly. I refer here to Ellison's character Rinehart, whose name not only designates the great jazz artist but the moral emptiness of signifying allusion itself. To the extent that the novel's narrator adopts Rinehart's style, he fails as a black leader. Jack-the-Bear's final retreat to the underground world of the book's ending only further embodies the ethically and politically problematic aspects of Rinehart's strategies. The narrator's adoption of Rinehart as a model only leads him to an existence closer to that of Dostoevsky's Underground Man than to the engaging potential leader and teacher of the *Invisible Man*'s first section. Rinehart is clearly the precursor of the black, postmodern artist. As such, the Harlem pimp exemplifies the rhetorical, political, and ethical styles of the ghetto. His artistic progeny include the literary personae not only of Charles Wright and Ishmael Reed, but also of Black Arts writers such as Don L. Lee, Larry Neal, and Imamu Amiri Baraka—some of whom would ultimately prove among Ellison's fiercest enemies. Rinehart's protean maneuvers ramble at large in the writing of black fiction and the novel. Gates' criticism is in many ways a follower of these movements. As a literary discourse, Rinehart's artistic rhetoric of dress and manner has made a predictable alliance with the mainstream adaptations of postmodernist culture. Not surprisingly, this movement has largely ignored the profound social, political, and philosophical realities of African-American life (except in the most symbolic and cathartic ways). Here, too, Gates has been part of this tradition.

Furthermore, whatever Rinehart's symbolism as the figure of the artist or of Ellison himself, he represents a moral fraudulence that is a highly problematic element of Ellison's text. There is a moral perspective in *Invisible Man*, from which Ellison judges the cynical patronage of wealthy whites and the even more cynical manipulation of that patronage by blacks. There is a side of the book in which an authorial presence displays the ideological constraints of communism as another oppression of the dislocated black intellectuals whom it inevitably approaches. There is a perspective of the book from which Ellison—through the text's various personae, scenes, and rhetoric—condemns Rinehart as manipulator. And to some extent, the dialectic between the book's two sides anticipates the struggle between Ellison and his Black Arts enemies, and possibly a struggle within the author himself. It is not clear that Gates fully understands what is at stake—ethically, politically, and socially—in this conflict. He wears the colors of signifying but is unwilling to consider its moral consequences. He is not a politically or even culturally conscious player in the critical arena that he has so boldly entered.

However, serious moral and political reflection is not Gates' aim; indeed, it would be a danger for him. Gates speaks to a disoriented middle class, seeking to exist within the bounds of an invisible color line while still competing in an increasingly complex American society. He clearly offers himself as a teacher of literary method on the order of Sterling Brown or Robert Scholes. Gates—as a thinker—lacks the self-conscious, philosophical perspective that this undertaking (from whatever political perspective) requires. At the heart of Brown's humanism was skepticism about the materialistic capitalist culture into which Gates has so easily moved. This opposition to emerging consumer society appears also in Du Bois, partially in Booker T. Washington, but primarily in the Protestant-romantic American literary culture that goes back from Emerson (for example) to the Puritans. Like his romantic precursors and their descendents, Brown opposed the alienated conceptions of human leisure, political choice, and pleasure which join the smart businessmen and the disorganized folk in a dehumanized society. In gutting the liberal critical historians of their moral content, Gates has left his middle class defenseless against an even more alienating present-day materialism, which humanly debases not only the poor but also, ultimately, their conception of themselves.

# Chapter Three

## Gates' Criticism and Middle-Class African-American Taste
### A Tradition of Firsts

GATES' AUTHORITY RESTS ON THE CANON of texts juggled by the sacred father and his literary children. This is a problem for two reasons: (1) the first significant African-American writers appear to have been women, and (2) their writing partook of an American Puritanism that was far closer to Renaissance humanism or early modern Protestantism than to Gates' antihumanist poststructuralism. Chief among these writers is Phillis Wheatley, whose work is now generally recognized as a product of provincial, New England neoclassical literary tradition; post-Great Awakening, evangelical culture; and Whig ideological thought.

Wheatley's refashioning of Horatian odes, Ovidian *epyllia*, Popean essays, and Miltonic paired verse make her a typical late eighteenth-century New England poet, a topical versifier like Mather Byles. Furthermore, her intellectual and aesthetic orientation is religious. Like many popular American evangelical poets, she saw herself as a moral teacher. She intended her simple poems to edify a religious audience who valued the unadorned Puritan plain style in its poetry as well as in its hymns or psalm-singing. Not surprisingly, she won a following that included the Anglo-American circle of evangelicals around the Countess of Huntington. Also in this group were the preacher George Whitefield and other black writers such as James Gronniosaw.

Wheatley succeeded as an occasional poet because of her simple democratic language, the taut singing quality of her verse, and a personal signature that made her ditties immediately recognizable. However, as many of her poems show, she self-consciously imitated certain homiletic styles. She often describes ministers and their power to move an audience through meter, gesture, and figures of speech, and in her early verse imitates their styles—from the open-ended revival preaching of "To a Deist" and "To An Atheist," to the genteel sermons in her elegies for Samuel Marshall and George Whitefield, as well as her address to Harvard students. She did not by any stretch of the imagination see herself as juggling literary counters in deconstructive play. She believed passionately in a divine presence that might be conveyed through not only God's word but also her own. To give her pride of place in the signifying canon requires a wrenching of facts and texts. This wrenching has tested even the will to power of our present-day black middle class.

After the efforts of a number of earlier Black Arts critics to make Phillis Wheatley into an Afrocentric poet, Gates hit upon a formula that seems not only to have persisted but also to have thrived. This version, repeated in a recent address at PMLA by Nellie McKay, had its start in *Figures in Black*.[1] In his essay, he suggested that Wheatley had been examined by a group of white male guarantors who wrote the note of attestation that preceded her 1773 collection of verse published in England. Although Gates himself cites no explicit evidence, his account of Wheatley's "oral examination" persists as a central theme in his literary criticism and personal essays. Thus in her PMLA address, McKay treats the alleged event as a matter of fact.[2] I have heard a similar affirmation by the historian and critic Paula Giddings in a talk at the National Humanities Center.

Clearly the ideological point of this scenario is now more important than any empirical evidence that Gates could adduce as support. Myth is gossip made old, and carries truths that often transcend facts, although scholarly repetition of myth as fact is disturbing for many reasons. From the vantage of myth, however, the young black female facing examination by white male intellectuals was immediately recognizable as a recasting of the unequal academic and cultural ground—the rhetorical context—from which signifying emerged. This signifying, academic Wheatley is made into a timeless point of origin, much like the earlier juggling father of *The Signifying Monkey*. The frequent retellings of this myth—with its final enshrinement in the NEH Jefferson lectures—places this reading within the American scholarly canon. More importantly, in the age of multiculturalism, Wheatley's signifying voice provides a black "integer" to which a white tradition can be joined.

This scenario generalizes Wheatley's role as a literary signifier to similar parts enacted by the black middle class in professionalized academic worlds still marked by inequality. Wheatley comes to embody black resistance to both subtle and overtly racist denigration of African-American intelligence, staging resistance through her writing and displays of knowledge, which are frequently repeated. Slyly, the tale refers not only to the historical confrontation between poet and white guarantor-patrons, but to the confrontation between the story's author, its skeptical white readers, and amused black onlookers perusing the text. In this wish-fulfilling academic fantasy, Wheatley and her bourgeois black audience are rewarded with the cathartic (but by no means the political, social, or cultural) defeat of the white male intellectual enemy.

This myth now influences much of the writing by African Americans about early black figures. After this story of initiation, Gates finds Wheatley signifying everywhere she makes the slightest allusion to Milton or Homer. Inevitably, a less tenuous link between Wheatley and African religious practices has been constructed by translating the concept of the "vernacular"—once the voice of unlettered rural and urban black folk—into a "subject" position.[3] One critic has now announced that the young Wheatley's sincere pietistic language is double-voiced.[4] And tricksterism similarly appears in the sermons of Jupiter Hammon, a barely literate eighteenth-century preacher who apparently deconstructs the religious rhetoric of his time.[5]

Such extreme measures are absolutely necessary to preserve the legitimacy of Skip's canon. There is, in fact, no evidence that the earliest black writers in America were influenced by an African-derived folk culture, nor did it play any significant role in the main line of African-American literature for most of the nineteenth century. Published African-American literature begins in Protestant poetry, spiritual autobiography, adventure stories, political writing, and the many popular forms of the late eighteenth and early nineteenth centuries. Not only did most black writers keep a careful intellectual distance from the folk; they tended, if anything, to adhere to a genteel bourgeois ideal of assimilation into middle-class Victorian culture. This was true of many (there were few separatist) black nationalists. Even the recently recovered body of black women's writing shows the persistence of middle-class Protestant attitudes deep into the Harlem Renaissance of the 1920s.[6] Moreover, writers such as Langston Hughes, Zora Neale Hurston, and Sterling Brown were continually in dialogue with black Victorian evangelical culture—largely because that culture, whatever its restraints, provided valuable political unity in the resistance against Jim Crow, and in the formation of Southern black churches and the socialization of black youth. Whatever its parochial limitations, this movement—which spiritually linked a black intelligentsia to its patrons, defined black citizenship in America, and set forth a stable social order—could not be lightly put aside. It addressed the most fundamental values of black society, politics, and community.

The folk style in black literature made its first appearance in the late nineteenth century. But even then, it subsisted alongside more powerful genteel tendencies before finally—and only partially—overtaking them. This posed a particular problem in the first edition of the *Norton Anthology of African-American Literature*, whose opening section on the vernacular sought to present the collection as representative of the signifying canons.[7] *The Norton Anthology* is, of course, a momentous literary monument for the post-structuralists—indeed, for the whole generation of new black scholars in the academy—and it often fulfills one's anticipation. It includes the writings of acknowledged authors like the poet Phillis Wheatley, the ex-slave Frederick Douglass, and the novelist Richard Wright, and it is arranged in sections approximating the traditional chronological divisions of American literary history. Competent introductions by period specialists—William L. Andrews (eighteenth- and nineteenth-century literature),

Richard Yarborough (nineteenth- and early twentieth-century literature), Arnold Rampersad (twentieth-century literature), and Barbara T. Christian (twentieth-century and women's literature)—present familiar materials of African-American literature in now commonplace ways.

The anthology also shows the literary importance of many newly recovered black women evangelical Victorians, such as Maria Stewart, Pauline E. Hopkins, and Angelina Weld Grimke, as well as more recent black middle-class literary figures like William Stanley Braithwaite. Reprinted in full, for example, are texts that have been absorbed into the signifying canon: Frederick Douglass' *Narrative*, Jean Toomer's *Cane*, James Weldon Johnson's *Autobiography of an Ex-Colored Man*, and W. E. B Du Bois' *The Souls of Black Folk*. But a careful reading of the collection may do more damage to the signifying discourse than any polemic mounted in the present book. Although the proof texts of folk culture are here, the efforts of recent black feminist scholars have contributed to the heavy presence of black women's writing of the Victorian Puritan school. This school has clear alliances with the discourse of uplift and a conservative antebellum black nationalism. In light of the heavily Protestant evangelical character of late eighteenth century, the *Norton* consolidates what has been an undercurrent in African-American literary scholarship for some time: the existence of a conservative humanist tradition for over the first century and a half of African-American literature. Moreover, a careful reading of the *Norton* as a whole sustains the existence of a Puritan, broadly Protestant, Victorian continuity throughout black culture, exerting its pressure even in the inverted or rewrought forms of the Harlem Renaissance radicals. Read against recent work on evangelical culture, republican thought, and figures such as the Grimkes and the Fortens, the *Norton* reveals a trend that recent commentators have usually given short shrift, but a tradition of which Hughes, Hurston, and Brown were deeply aware. They had to be, for that earlier cultural hegemony weighed most heavily upon them.

It is in this respect that the introduction to the book's opening historical selection on the vernacular is particularly important. In his introduction, Gates had gone to exceptional lengths to stress that he did not ground black literary tradition (at least chronologically) in the vernacular. This caution is understandable, given the persistent lack of evidence for vernacular culture in these early writers. Every tradition must have its sacred origin, however, and in the chapter from which I extract the following excerpt, it is clear that the the language of the folk and African culture plays such a role. Not only a source of creativity, it is—although this point is hedged—timeless in a way that subtly undermines Gates' earlier chronological care:

> Indeed the vernacular is not a body of quaint folksy items. It is not a male province. Nor is it associated with a particular level of society or with a particular historical era. It is neither long or far away nor fading. Instead the vernacular encompasses vigorous dynamic processes of expression, past and present. It makes up a rich storehouse of materials wherein the values, styles, and character types of black American life are reflected in language that is highly energized and often marvelously eloquent.[8]

Like all sacred centers of cosmic meaning, the vernacular transcends the entire temporal existence of its culture's "vigorous dynamic processes of expression, past and present." This is discreetly suggested in the claim that the vernacular is not limited to "a particular level of society or with a particular historical era." Thus, as Katherine Bassard will show in *Spiritual Interrogations*, it underlies the evangelical expression of Phillis Wheatley and Ann Plato, writers who on the surface seem wholly influenced by the ethos style or discourse of folk language.

The vernacular is not only timeless. It embodies a wholly Western conception of romantic expression. And the writer pointedly makes use of Wordsworthian terms to describe it as an "overflowing" entity:[9]

> Black vernacular forms are works in progress, experiments in a still new country. They have not survived because they are perfect, polished jewels, that are sonnetlike in finish but because they are vigorous fountains of expression. Not only are they influential for writers, they are wonderful creations on their own. In the black tradition, no forms are more quick or overflowing with black power and black meaning.[10]

Despite the clear links to Western conceptions of the holy and expressive romantic form, the author insists upon the ethnic exceptionality of his thought.[11] This, too, represents a repression in which the underlying concept of the tradition itself must be violently wrenched from its obvious origin.

Significantly, Gates has often introduced members of this tradition as "first" novelists and poets without considering the implication of their Protestant conservatism for African-American literature as a whole. *Our Nig* is such a work that quickly came to prominence as a black-authored text. (It was earlier identified as the work of a white man.) In his introduction, Gates brought this typically evangelical text into the canon of signifying by demonstrating its subversion of the traditional sentimental novel. Gates' most recent find is Hannah Crafts' *The Bondwoman's Narrative*, a hitherto unpublished, apparently mid-nineteenth-century manuscript that the eminent black bibliographer Dorothy Porter—relying on internal evidence—quite correctly identified as black-authored. Porter's remarkable find has been overtaken by Gates' flashily advertised rediscovery of the manuscript in Porter's papers.[12]

Crafts' book was significantly left unpublished by Porter. However, the discovery of such an early black fiction manuscript virtually guaranteed a publisher's attention, especially when Gates himself forwarded the project. Promoting the work as black literature, untouched by white editorial hands, Gates produced *The Bondwoman's Narrative*. In turn, the book received enormous critical attention as a free-standing novel, and an untainted access to the black mind.

The forces which present such a derivative book—so obviously part of a racially integrated evangelical culture—as serious literary art are legion. They obscure not only critical judgment of the text but the reader's judgment of his or her own tastes. Bad books not only lack the power to put their own subjects into perspective, they also fail to give the reader a vantage from which to understand himself. Widespread publication, distribution, and praise for this clumsy writing have threatened to have such an effect on not only an unsophisticated black reading public but also its teachers. Hannah Crafts' expensively produced but mediocre slave narrative-cum-sentimental romance came to market when a new black bourgeoisie was again in love with popular fiction. Sterling Brown and E. Franklin Frazier had criticized the parents, grandparents, aunts, and uncles of this new audience for playing cards and otherwise trifling their time away. Langston Hughes intimated quite correctly that the cultural predecessors of today's middle-class Negro audience of *O*—Oprah's magazine—had little use for anything black that had not yet been approved by the white commercial world.[13] Their warnings have acquired new significance as retrograde black middle-class taste reasserts itself—to an unheard-of extent—with the recognition of Gates' book. *The Bondwoman's Narrative* now sees the light of day because of its mainstream imprimatur and a nineteenth-century parochial sentimentality, which resonates with present tastes. Why has this book passed muster by such eminent black critics?

The "bankability" of *The Bondwoman's Narrative* rests on cultural standards, that have sifted down from the black academic elite in Cambridge, New Haven, and Ithaca to the subway readers of *Essence*, *Quality Book Review*, and *Ebony*. The sensibility that combines female resistance against an aggressive male patriarchy, the celebration of female empowerment, and a conception of social reproduction as political activity is now a commonplace in both black feminist academic discourse and the audience of *O*. Present in literary texts ranging from Toni Morrison's *Sula* to the popular fiction of Bebe Moore Campbell, this taste not only appeals to a varied African-American audience but to a growing number of white readers. They have often become acquainted with it in Black Studies classes or the paperback books they read on the Number Six subway while going to midtown. More a style of reading and feeling than a critical system, this mode of "Reading Black; Reading Feminist"—to appropriate a Gates title from a wholly different context—is not only a means of cultural celebration but also, and more darkly, a stern form of cultural repression. This appears in the attempt to impose gestures of feminist political resistance onto these texts, as well as a variety of critical and popular encounters. In these readings, the intense cultural conservatism of texts such as Harriet Jacobs' *Incidents in the Life of a Slave Girl* and Harriet Wilson's *Our Nig* is blatantly repressed in the name of a nakedly political desire. Ideological "re-readings" of such typically sentimental texts dramatize the subversive victory of the African-American writer rather than the thwarting of the black female will. Indeed, as more and more of these middle-class black women's texts are recovered, this mode of cultural reeducation has become a cottage industry.

*The Bondwoman's Narrative* will easily be appropriated into the black canon in the present feminist dispensation. Like *Incidents in the Life of a Slave Girl*, the novel is narrated by a genteel slave woman, taught to read and exposed to polite middle-class values by her grandmother and her polite Quaker patron. And, although the narrator does not become a significant actor until the end of the novel, she witnesses two women who assert their autonomy and in the process win, albeit in an unexpected form, a victory over evil (however unearned in terms of plot). The narrative itself consists of three linked stories. The first story presents the blackmail of a young mulatto woman affianced to a rich white man, her escape with the narrator's help, and finally her suicide to avoid submission to the evil lawyer who has attempted to blackmail her. She dies, however, only after he has expressed his love for her and she has forgiven him. In the novel's second tale, the narrator observes the marriage of a highborn Englishwoman to an American slaveholder who keeps his black paramours in an isolated home. Upon riding out to find this concealed harem, the English woman falls from her horse and eventually dies. But not before she has converted to Christianity, assumed a new mantle of religious humility, and—like the blackmailed mulatto of the first episode—forgiven her husband. The narrative's concluding story repeats the first two in the experience of the mulatto narrator who rejects a forced marriage to an abusive black man. At the novel's end, she returns to a nearly infantile security in the genteel world from which she came, teaching school and forwarding the work of racial uplift. This conclusion, however, both repeats and elaborates the narrative's central fable: the middle-class world created through a marriage between a mulatto and a white man inevitably fails to reproduce itself in the lives of the female offspring.

Significantly, however, Henry Louis Gates' introduction is silent on many of the most conventional aspects of *The Bondwoman's Narrative*. Crafts' fiction is obviously an entertainment novel, intended to titillate and reassure its audience, even as it protests slavery. The evil lawyer's pursuit of his mulatto quarry is a tale of interracial lust, as is the Englishwoman's expedition to discover her husband's coven of black paramours. The final attempt to force a marriage upon the highminded narrator is equally sensationalistic. Her career is less a tale of a developing personality than a regression to childhood gratification without the trials of adolescent and adult experience.

Even compared with such simplistic work as Jacobs' *Incidents in the Life of a Slave Girl* and Wilson's *Our Nig*, Crafts' storytelling is distressingly naive. Unlike Jacobs' heroine, who must confront impotence as she recognizes her inability to win a home for her family, Crafts' protagonist lacks basic human concern for companionship, marriage, and social reproduction. Craft, restores the heroine-narrator to her paradise-like home, again through another set of implausible coincidence. *The Bondwoman's Narrative* does not convincingly explain—or even satisfactorily narrate—the growth of its heroine into an agent of uplift. Indeed the book seems to suggest, fantastically, that this role can be assumed without acquiring serious political consciousness—this in the age of the Fugitive Slave Act. In light of the deepening political crisis in the 1850s, this is a wish-fulfilling story of political commitment, acted out by a sheltered free black from an atypically comfortable haven.

The poor quality of Crafts' narrative is not only a literary-critical problem but also a political one. In its desire for commitment, the heroine's wished-for moral stature is unearned, lacking the drama of internal moral choice. There is, indeed, an important issue in the novel: its suggestion that moral stature is in and of itself the fruit of desire. Despite the book's ending, the novel represents a flight away from politics. This casts important light upon Gates' implicit claim that the novel is an authentic expression of the black mind, an uncensored account of slavery by an African American in the world of African-American bondage. If Rudolph Byrd (whom Gates cites approvingly) is correct about this authenticity, then the "black mind" is—as the romantic racialists would have it—a creature of fantasy and desire.[14] Indeed, the derivative quality of Crafts' work would even suggest that the "authentic" black mind is, as Thomas Jefferson said of Wheatley, capable of little more than feeble imitation.

Crafts' failure as a fictional observer appears most vividly in her appropriation of the period's prevailing literary models, which is naive even by the standards of early black fiction. Gates has trumpeted near plagiarism as a subtle appropriation of Western tradition, taking Crafts' reworking of an extract from Dickens' *Bleak House* as proof of literary sophistication.[15] Whatever words she may have adopted from Dickens, Crafts never equaled that author's grasp of the modern social world—an understanding that is found not only in scenes of eternal legal proceedings, the dust heap, and the circumlocution office, but in equally vivid representations of human psychology, by the powerful plots that detail Pip's social ascent through that world. To be sure, America—as its first serious writers such as Irving, Hawthorne, and James asserted—lacked the strata from which cultural history might be gathered, assembled, and interpreted. Yet even this is beside the point. Crafts is severely deficient by the standards of her fellow black authors' appropriation of their favorite models. It is her maladroit borrowing from Stowe's *Uncle Tom's Cabin*, the novel most usefully imitated by Crafts' contemporaries, that most clearly shows her inadequacies. Drawing upon the slave narratives, sentimental fiction, traveler's accounts, and journalism, Stowe set forth characters such as Uncle Tom, the Shelbys, Rachel Halliday, little Eva, and Simon Legree—all of whom became stand-ins for African-American authors almost in spite of themselves. Stowe's novel provided a host of devices and characters that the white public found not only convincing but also moving. Crafts, however, borrows only the most easily imitated features of Stowe's novel, and does that superficially. Thus *The Bondwoman's Narrative* features the cultivated mulatto slave displaced from kind patrons into dehumanizing slaveholding households. There are journeys of escape and rescue by kindly whites, by Quaker women who echo Rachel Halliday. In her portrait of the savage black male to whom the narrator is to be married, Crafts evokes the gothic horror of Stowe's Sambo and Quimbo.

Crafts, however, lacked the literary acumen to appropriate Stowe's most powerful contribution to late nineteenth- and early twentieth-century black writing: her exploration—albeit sentimental—of the psychology of the interracial household. Much of the dramatic force of Stowe's novel stems from relationships between virtuous masters like Mrs. Shelby and favored slaves like Eliza Shelby, humane cynics like Augustus St. Claire and manipulative bondsmen such as Adolphe, as well as between the pathological Simon Legree and the human monsters Quimbo and Sambo. Within Stowe's simple but influential psychology, the white superiors, who exerted a special power over their favorites, forged the moral character of the household slaves. At the same time, however, these favored mulatto bondsmen had to establish their independence to form autonomous families and communities. Privileged slaves who came to adulthood under incompetent or cynical masters learned to manipulate white heads of households, creating the chaos that exists in the household of Augustus St. Clair.

In her depictions of the Shelbys, Augustus St. Claire, and even Simon Legree, Stowe opened up the patriarchal world of the white master and the favored slave for literary exploration by black authors. *Uncle Tom's Cabin* alerted black writers (like Crafts) who wanted to mine the psychology of the slave household with more penetration than *The Bondwoman's Narrative* could muster. It provided searching pictures of the paternalistic master, the self-divided slave, and the precarious middle-class black life in which the autobiographical heroes of Jacobs' *Incidents in the Life of a Slave Girl*, Douglass' 1845 *Narrative*, or Brown's *Clotel, Or, The President's Daughter* were inculcated. Jacobs was obviously influenced not only by the conventional scenes of escape and female collaboration but also by Stowe's hints about the dilemma of the mulatto who cannot reproduce her grandmother's bourgeois world two generations later. Much of the interest of Jacobs' *Incidents in the Life of a Slave Girl*—which was published under the name of Linda Brent—comes from the protagonist's depiction of a woman who owes her sexual autonomy to an illicit relationship with a white lover. In contrast to Crafts' heroine, Brent's concern for black uplift and the promotion of good works lead to curiously self-denying actions, as when she advises her true lover, a young black carpenter, to leave for a better life elsewhere.

We have tantalizing hints of Jacobs' literary acumen in Linda herself, a heroine who approaches psychological territory that Jacobs can survey but not enter. Linda's violation of middle-class norms entails not only feminist empowerment but also the possibilities of complicated attachments, betrayals, and self-understandings. How does she feel toward Mr. Sands when she wakes up pregnant and realizes that she no longer has to submit to her master? How can her sexual victories over the doctor fail to yield a sadomasochistic satisfaction over the manipulation of his sexual jealousy? How far would Linda expect Mr. Sands to go in saving her life and that of her children? Would they ever talk about it? What would be Mr. Sand's response? Moreover, how does Linda reconcile her joy in sending Mr. Sands on a wild goose chase with the fact that she must do so from a cramped garret in which she cannot comfortably sit or stand?

Linda's deepest potential human triumphs are at times denied the fulfillment that her aggressive character would seem to demand. This theme of the thwarted will finds its ultimate expression in Linda's final discovery that she cannot gain full freedom without the help of her white patron. To treat these questions fully would be to write a different book—the book that Crafts promises yet does not deliver. Drawing upon the tensions of privileged, cultivated mulatto characters that must seek autonomy, Jacobs is—as a beginning writer—nevertheless underway to suggestive paths of inquiry.

The divided self of the cultivated favored slave who must break with the conventional world around him to assert an ultimately limited autonomy is also an important theme in Douglass' 1845 *Narrative*. Yet Douglass was blocked from a full exploration of these psychological tensions. Garrison's strictures against the notion of permissive slaveholding inevitably prevented Douglass from fully describing his ambivalent interracial friendship with Auld, the impact of the Aulds' wealth upon him, and his relationship with the young Auld women.

The literary example of *Uncle Tom's Cabin* clearly helped free Douglass to mine his own psychology, both in its relation to his own black relatives and to other black authority figures on the plantation and in Baltimore. As it turns out, the subtlest interpretations of the African-American world of the 1850s emerged from the best black readers and—probably an inevitable consequence—the most artistically adept writers. This fact leads to the saddest reality of the new crop of nineteenth-century black female scribblers: the narrowness of their provincial world. Read against even other women's writing of the period, the fiction and memoirs of these young blacks show a narrow range of cultural reference, little knowledge of the day's current thinking on society, religion, and politics, and an interesting unwillingness to experiment with the consequences of their ideas. The ideology of domesticity quite easily and understandably led more sophisticated writers like Stowe to consider its implications. What was the relationship between the female world of, say, Mrs. Bird, and the male world of economics and politics in which the money to create the household sphere was won? Stowe, of course, thinks about this issue cogently in *Uncle Tom's Cabin* when Mr. Shelby's mismanagement necessitates the sale of slaves in a household crisis. Augustus St. Claire's own incompetence leads to a similar collapse after his death, sending sheltered young females out into the cruel slave market, and plunging his wife into insecurity.

Many of Stowe's character insights come from her Calvinist understanding of human personality and society. However, beyond this doctrinal knowledge was a broader intellectual cultivation and a sense of the transformations that would accompany Calvinist religion in mid-nineteenth-century America. This underlies her creation of Augustus St. Claire, who is in many ways the novel's most complex and compelling figure. St. Claire is a moral skeptic, whose benevolence to his slaves is not tempered by the moral authority, which for Stowe is the *sine qua non* in the socialization of virtuous blacks by paternalistic masters. St. Claire's religious skepticism as well as his moral cynicism are clearly the product of political and religious trends of the age: the secularization of society during the French Revolution, the erosion of literal understandings of the gospels, the liberalization of Protestant theology, as well as the loosening of providential views of biblical history. They are, moreover, the inevitable response to twenty previous years of American intellectual life in which many biblical meanings had lost their stable moorings in the flurry of antithetical antislavery and proslavery stands that had been argued from biblical texts.

At the same, time, St. Claire—who appears to have achieved salvation shortly before his death—is only worth saving (in fictional terms) because of his very secular human goodness. St. Claire's seemingly ironic decision to pair Topsy with Aunt Ophelia is only one instance of a humanity that is not at all Calvinistic. Topsy, an extreme version of the anomic character created by slavery, significantly wins the appreciation of St. Claire. Significantly, St. Claire's decision to place Topsy with Ophelia displays a largely pragmatic sense of the civilizing and ordering force of religion. It also displays a philosophical insight into the human benevolence that Ophelia's Calvinism must acquire to be godly. That is, St. Claire intuits the limits of Aunt Ophelia's Christian benevolence, its abstraction, and its lack of grounding in moral realities. In the book's greatest insight, St. Claire realizes that Aunt Ophelia's so-called spiritual love is really displaced vanity. He knows intuitively, however, that she can only grow ethically by acknowledging the disorderly human world beyond her city of God.

*Uncle Tom's Cabin* is marred by an extreme moral sentimentality; however, the novel has its own psychological shrewdness. Stowe's ability to think about her native Calvinism in a detached psychological and sociological way comes from the ability to assume another intellectual standpoint—a perspective antithetical to strict Protestant faith, a standpoint from which she could gain a dialectical understanding of her own beliefs. It is this self-consciousness of their Victorian bourgeois culture that the first black women novelists of the 1850s lack. This absence results from a provincial, intellectually thin culture which shows up in the merely perfunctory settings, landscapes with little or no symbolic depth, and characters without intellectual or emotional complexity.

The failure to read black women's novels for their aesthetic worth has led to a ham-fisted evaluation of them as cultural, social, political—or practically any serious—intellectual endeavor. These novels simply lack the erudition and intellectual deftness to understand the full human implications of slavery—a failure writ large in Harriet Jacobs' *Incidents in the Life of a Slave Girl*. However, these simplistic—and, as I have argued, escapist—visions of black life will never receive the stern appraisal they deserve in today's multicultural classroom, given the climate of black feminist thought. A rude comeuppance is nevertheless somewhere around the corner. *The Bondwoman's Narrative* and Wilson's *Our Nig* are increasingly taught alongside canonical American texts of the 1840s and 1850s. There is, and will be, much temptation for the acute literary student—who will always read to discover the rich new worlds yielded by the best books—to ask why "The Custom House" section of *The Scarlet Letter* is so much better written than Jacobs' *Incidents in the Life of a Slave Girl*. Whatever initial attempts might be made to answer the student in the politically correct way, he or she, black or white, will inevitably ask—in the angry way of teenagers onto an adult con game—whether this text is only being read because the author is a black woman. He or she will want to know just what this choice means.

Gates' inflated praise for this wholly inadequate book is to be criticized for its inattention not only to such students. All serious readers will inevitably inquire into the art and thought of what they read. Although these questions are suppressed by the kind of public literary culture extant in much of African-American Studies today, they will soon reemerge in other contexts. The most perceptive students will, moreover, catch the whiff of disingenuousness in otherwise intelligent and cultivated people who profess such books, for they will be agonized about a pedagogy that represses the aesthetic and formal inadequacies of our current crop of black women's texts. It is, of course, bad enough that politically correct black professors of African-American literature—under the pressure of literary fashion—submit to these pressures. Even worse is the evasion of such discussion by the intellectual black public itself. Outside the richer, more psychologically incisive texts by Hawthorne, Melville, Thoreau, and James, a literary ghetto has emerged in which works such as *The Bondwoman's Narrative* can—and, to a certain extent, must—be indiscriminately praised.

Of course, this problem is not new. In the late 1950s, E. Franklin Frazier pointed to the tendency of the black middle class (then segregated) to cut itself off in a social or intellectual play-world and create fictions of great Negro business or important black institutions.[16] Black literature—in particular, nineteenth-century women's writing—has become such a play-world of African-American cultural achievement. This sentimental celebration of black life, from the most romantic wish-fulfilling perspective, is now an even larger phenomenon, given the proliferation of black romance writers who cater, ironically, to the same audience as Henry Louis Gates' new edition of Hannah Crafts' novel.

Black academic culture and the African-American educated classes, such as they are, will sustain the deepest harm done by the uncritical celebration. It is wrong to give this book—so easily read for the most trivial sentimental thrills—to black students, whose reading abilities usually fall below those of their white peers at whatever academic level. They, more than anyone else, need the analytic skills required for the literary and moral distinctions I discuss here. Just as disturbing is the glorification of texts that competent African-American teachers and scholars of literature know to be intellectually second-rate. The excuse of providing this text as an encouragement for poor black student readers simply will not do. It was clearly Crafts' object to reward her audience by suppressing the cultural, social, and political complexities that shaped the black world of the 1850s and that press upon us now. The success of today's black literary romance reveals a large middle-class black readership all too ready for such an evasion. This market niche will do quite nicely for itself without newcomers. Henry Louis Gates' edition of Hannah Crafts' *The Bondwoman's Narrative* reproduces the provincial limitations of nineteenth-century middle-class, African-American literary life in the consumer culture of a twenty-first-century black bourgeoisie. Frazier, Hughes, and Brown had the courage to criticize the failings of their middle class, and the analytical prowess to map out the fault lines of its psychology.

# Section Two

# Theory and Sensibility

---

Gates' importance increased as a cadre of new black literary critics and theologians grasped the significance of his theory for their work. It provided a suggestive model not only for literary inquiry, but for cultural criticism and understanding the public postures assumed by later writers. These followers were rarely as deft as Gates in their exploitation of signifying as an ironic, essentially belletristic, literary style. As a result, neither Dyson nor Holloway has achieved Gates' stature as clever, sometimes engaging, essayists. His stance may have kept Gates from seriously partisan cultural, social, or political engagements, but it freed him to explore and exploit the consumer world of CD-ROM encyclopedias and PBS documentaries. Gates clearly understood the emerging nexus of educational products and media entertainment. Commentators like Michael Dyson and Karla Holloway have followed in his footsteps in their work on black popular culture (particularly Dyson's books on black musical performers). Unlike Gates, however, his followers, although often more politically direct,

---

have not been able to develop their cultural projects into a distinctive voice or enjoy the same influence.

An examination of these critics and their misunderstandings is nevertheless extremely valuable. Their naive confusion renders them vulnerable to fuller inspection than Gates invites. In their innocent formulations, they reveal the contradictions of signifying and signifiers in a way that Gates often deftly avoids. Given signifying's nature as a rhetorical disguise, this self-revelation, however unintentional, is valuable in and of itself. In both their early theoretical work and their later descent into a congenial popular nonfiction, they draw out the consequences of the professional literary style initiated by Gates in *Figures in Black, The Signifying Monkey, Loose Canons, Colored People*, and *Thirteen Ways of Looking at a Black Man*. Like Gates, they fall into a Johnson publication-style of in-group chatter. They too end by producing consumer media for black popular culture. Instead of assuming a critical stance towards the African-American consumer world, they have engaged in its eager exploitation. This may be their deepest inheritance from the example of Gates. These writers' willingness to align themselves with the popular-consumer side of American culture has much to tell us about present-day black intellectuals and the emerging African-American consumer middle class.

# Chapter Four

## Signifying as Romantic Myth of Origins
### An American, African-American Religion

I HESITATED TO REVIEW THESE FOUR BOOKS until I recognized their link to the Protestant-Romantic-Victorian continuity so central to the development of African-American literature.[1] My initial anxiety thus proved unnecessary. Read closely, Katherine Bassard's *Spiritual Interrogations*, Olmos and Paravisini-Gebert's *Healing Cultures*, Wil Coleman's *Tribal Talk*, and Jon Cruz's *Culture on the Margins*—whatever their official disciplinary home—are immediately recognizable as American romantic texts. Deeply influenced by the signifying theories and sensibility of Gates, their authority depends on a typically American voice: an autobiographical persona who assumes variously the stances of prophet, cultural critic, historian, and meditative saint. However much Coleman, Bassard, Olmos, Paravisini-Gebert, and the many contributors to *Healing Cultures* may invoke a diasporan spirituality, their literary provenance is unequivocal. Willy-nilly, they express themselves in literary voices, rhetorical strategies, and imaginative visions made available by Wordsworth, Coleridge, and Carlyle, and later by Emerson, Whitman, and Thoreau. Like "Nature" or *Walden*, these books draw their literary being and shape from a well-established myth of origins—the autobiographical journey of an alienated modern who recovers his or her personal or national origin through imaginative vision. Beneath their signifying language, Coleman's *Tribal Talk* and Bassard's *Spiritual Interrogations* seek recognizably American selves who have fed themselves from estrangements described nearly a century and a half earlier in "Man the Reformer" or the *1844 Economic Philosophical Manuscripts*. As expositors and subjects of this myth, Coleman and Bassard not only are akin to Emerson, but suggest his importance for an extended interracial family which includes James Weldon Johnson, James Cone, Larry Neal, Robert Stepto, and Shamoon Zamir, as well as R. W. B. Lewis and Eric Sundquist. We can pick our friends but, as Jimmy Carter once said about his brother Billy, we cannot pick our relatives. We can only live with ourselves, it might be added, when we live sincerely with our family—whoever they may be. Will Coleman and Katherine Bassard would, perhaps, be surprised to learn that their chief intellectual flaw lies not in mimicking American romanticism, but in refusing to take it seriously enough.

The conventional Afrocentric understanding of a communal, countercultural, cyclical African world is at bottom a romantic illusion, the primitivist, cross-cultural hand-me-down of a deeply Euro-American tradition. Whether in Bassard or Wordsworth, this myth raises questions that all must confront who wish to translate the spiritual virtues of infancy, childhood, or pre-capitalist society into utopian goals. How should the realities of our present social, political, and economic world shape our recovery of the good in the past? How have we idealized the good unnecessarily? How will our recovery of that good affect others with whom we live? The ideological programs by which the past becomes an outline for the future are thus very much to the heart of the recovery of the past, whether in the form of the juggling father or signifying mother. These questions are deeply pertinent as the Afrocentric ideologies are formulated into programs for black education, social work, and even health care.

A truly valuable black self-consciousness may emerge only after black writers have secularized their evangelical conceptions of spiritual life and salvation into romantic images of imaginative aspiration and fulfillment, transforming the heavenly recovery of Eden into a millennial achievement of man's unity with nature. This romantic discourse, which facilitated sophisticated studies by Lawrence Levine and Eugene Genovese, had a hundred years earlier allowed figures such as the Douglass of the 1855 *My Bondage and My Freedom*, or the Charlotte Forten of her *Journals*, to conceive of black music as more than noise and of black religion as an expression of spirit. The pervasive influence of this discourse, which runs from the transcendentalists, through early students of black folklore, *fin-de-siècle* black writers, the radicals of the Harlem Renaissance, and finally to the young Turks of Black Arts, has yet to be fully studied. Such an undertaking would also—perhaps paradoxically—have much to tell us about the present-day culture of the literary black middle class.

Such reflection would allow us to interrogate, for example, those frequent expressions of desire and its fulfillment that lie at the heart of black American religious thought, not to mention fiction and poetry. A mature romanticism demands that one distinguish narcissism from the mature ego's stability, that one take the best of childhood memories while rejecting infantilism in adulthood. Political and literary equivalents of this understanding exist in the utopias of Marx and the imaginative romantic therapies of Wordsworth, Emerson, and Thoreau. Although these projects may seek to resurrect a past spiritual union with nature, they must take up considerations of economy, discipline, and artistic rigor to do so meaningfully. Intellectually competent romanticism must be fully aware of the dynamics of idealized selfhood and of the authoritarian impulses lurking beyond the promise of freedom. A regressive authoritarian impulse can appear in the recoveries of the past to which romanticism exhorts us. Those who endorse and appropriate versions of romantic discourse must negotiate this danger.

Will Coleman's *Tribal Talk*, Katherine Bassard's *Spiritual Interrogations*, and many of the essays in *Healing Culture* evade, ignore, and outright repress these psychological, cultural, and political discriminations that must lie at the heart of any serious romantic vision. They neglect the complexities of self-consciousness acquired and engaged by serious romantic thinkers. The flight from the central texts of romanticism, endemic to black literary and religious traditions, here exacts a particularly high price. This freewheeling black romanticism is especially disturbing when it appears in the therapeutic discourse so prevalent in black theologians, for example. At stake are the socialization of young blacks, the professional careers of African-American humanists, and the pedagogy of multicultural studies. If the black middle class increasingly seeks to reclaim its authority over the black masses by means of a kente-cloth identity of African origins, then we should weigh that identity in the balance of actual religious and political life—two activities rarely separate in African-American history.

As African-American Studies becomes institutionalized, these questions will eventually come to the fore. It is no secret that many white administrators in selective colleges treat such programs as agencies to socialize, and provide therapeutic adjustment for, young blacks in the turbulent interracial academic world. For these schools—when integrated—are sites of enormous cultural and economic inequality, as well as social conflict (whether administrators will admit the fact or not). The ensuing tensions often scar the most sensitive. My experience suggests that black youth flock to compelling teachers of black theology and African-American religious studies. One suspects, in turn, that the charismatic and therapeutic style of the field has been shaped largely by its instrumental use for administrative purposes. I have often seen a religious sensibility which links personal redemption to an African past. Its character is not overtly political, but deeply tinged with escapism from life at a selective school. This, of course, is not the conventional wisdom about the (disturbing) variety of Afrocentric religious experience discussed by Bassard, Coleman, and many of the contributors to the Olmos–Paravasini–Gebert collection. And yet religious experience—as many of these writers will quickly admit—often does play an important part in political thinking. This makes black theology an appropriate object for the present interrogation of African-American intellectual culture.

• • • • • • • • • • • • • • •

The early generation of black theologians included Peter Paris of *The Spirituality of African Peoples: The Search for a Common Moral Discourse*, Dwight Hopkins of *Shoes That Fit Our Feet*, and Katie Cannon of *Katie's Canon*. These figures self-consciously addressed what they perceived as the racism of the white academy.[2] Like the "vernacular" critics emerging in the just-integrated white universities of the sixties and seventies, they experienced severe anxieties as professional intellectuals, haunted by a sense of illegitimacy in the presence of their well-schooled colleagues. "Without a faith context and the interest of the majority, we can often seem like a new form of intellectual minstrel performing before white folk's voyeurism in the academy," remarked Dwight Hopkins in a deeply ambivalent mood, approaching the end of his populist account of black folk religion.[3] Gates and Baker often assumed the role of trickster-theorists in an attempt to ground their academic authority in a black populism. The black theologians who have appropriated "a vernacular" discourse have pursued this strategy with even more vigor. Sometimes identifying themselves with Gramsci's organic intellectual, they spoke from the standpoint of the masses.[4]

The formation of the institutional and disciplinary structures of Black Theology followed a similar route. Like the proponents of the Black Arts movement, Cone and his protégés insisted that that black folk culture carried its own theology, which bore an adversarial relationship to Western religious thought.[5] The equation of folk religion and formal theological discourse—whether historical, philosophical, or sociological—was a new development, but paralleled the connection made by Gates between oral and written black expression. This was further reinforced by linking, as Gates and Baker had, the freewheeling rhetoric of the black vernacular to the prestigious literary-critical method of deconstruction. With this strategy, black theologians spoke not only with an authority grounded in the oral wisdom of the folk but also in the fashionable languages of post-structuralism. The antagonism of Jacques Derrida's critical theories to notions of a human (or divine) presence embodied in voice was overlooked, although the black theologians' willingness to racialize the issue of presence created innumerable intellectual confusions.

Not surprisingly, these maneuvers did not entirely resolve the problem of legitimacy. Some thinkers like Stephen Reid and Hopkins claimed the moral and spiritual authority of African-American theology as the West's cultural adversary.[6] Other black theologians claimed the guidance of Derrida, although they rarely read their own texts in a deconstructive way or backtracked across their previous interpretations, reading them against the grain.[7] Like many black post-structuralist critics, they seemed unwilling to apply to themselves the astringent readings they directed against the West. Indeed, for these thinkers, "blackness" itself assumed the role of the very presence and voice that deconstruction would seem to deny.

In reality, black theologians like Hopkins were far closer to Gates' signifying than to more critical post-structuralist methods of reading. Although they casually assumed the instability of Western thought, their formulations enjoyed the privilege of all essences. At heart they were ideologues, interested in deconstruction as a welding iron, not a blowtorch. Signifying quickly established itself as both an interpretive and a constructive jack-of-all-trades, which allowed African-American theologians to form canons and fields of knowledge simply by showing that any given text contained either a verbal repetition or a figure of speech from another. The technique also allowed the black critic to move quickly between the stance of ironic trickster and that of elite academic professor. This ambiguous and protean identity, moreover, carried subtly concealed institutional authority. Gates' method gave black theologians sovereign power to appropriate and distribute academic prestige as they chose, whether to fellow black intellectuals whose adolescent high school slang was transformed into theology, or to illiterate rural informants who now purveyed ethical thought. It did not seem to matter that the theologians own authority as professional intellectuals was threatened as they granted the same distinction to just about every articulate black person.

This generous distribution of intellectual authority created a wide spectrum of allies, including sympathetic, radical white theologians and the black masses whose vernacular allowed them to be immediately (if tacitly) pressed into service. The black theologians had quickly gained a potent political alliance with which to fight the ethnic turf wars of the multicultural university. *Tribal Talk*, *Spiritual Interrogations*, and many essays in Olmos–Paravasini–Gebert make full use of this alliance, its variants of popular sovereignty, its democratic ethos, its cynically populist style, as well as its elitist pretensions. The rhetoric of these literary critiques and case studies—which depend on the authority of this entente—is not so much intellectual inquiry as it is an adversarial political strategy, trading upon the institutional prestige of the academy.

• • • • • • • • • • • • • • •

These works draw upon a simplified romantic mythology to define academic authority and gather this coalition. Coleman and Bassard not only seek to appropriate the black folk culture as an intellectual system, but crave the authority that folk authenticity wields in multicultural discourse. Their academic expositions enact rather than intellectually defend their authority. They preach to the already converted rather than evangelize the skeptical. Only Coleman is willing to confront his political enemies in the academy, and his tactics here are telling. Coleman identifies himself as a postmodern, post-structuralist griot conjurer. His book—we find at the conclusion—is not a coherent narrative but a discontinuous discourse, marked by postmodern ellipses and African rhythms. These fiats of authority and rhetorical self-definition do not (nor are they intended to) justify his long, disorganized accounts of Dahomeyan religious myths, slave religious experiences excerpted from WPA narratives, and recent critical theory. Indeed, Coleman classifies his work in accord with debased notions of so-called primitive thought. To be sure, semiotic principles could be adduced to support Coleman's rejection of noncontradiction in his own thinking; however, his conception of the primitive as incoherent threatens the very logic on which he wants to build an Afrocentric theology.

From the beginning, however, he has told us that he is more interested in the authority of the griot conjurer than in the post-structuralist literary critic or theologian considered as a rigorous anthropological observer. Despite the disorganization of the narrative that will come, Coleman introduces his study as inquiry with a curative purpose: he wishes to find the key to the slaves' survival. Thus it is important for "the survival and ingenuity of slaves [to give] testament that the 'haint' of white supremacy can be deconstructed and exorcised. It is a stubborn Demon, but it can be overcome." Constant exposure (the naming and sending away) of its false powers is the key to its exorcism. Coleman goes on to assert that "the book is an experiment in retrieving ancestral stories as a foundation for doing theology." Significantly, the payoff of recovering the slave's "deconstructive" and "critical" critique of the "haint" will be the defeat of the white devil, a new black autonomy, and an undefined black American freedom:

> Once this "handkerchief head" demon is removed, we can go about initiating instead of responding to someone else's "whatever." Through the discovery of how slaves survived under extremely oppressive circumstances, new insights are gained on how to go about the business of being a really free African-American.[8]

Coleman addresses himself to the liberation of the black bourgeoisie and he intends, paradoxically, to find it in the culture of the enslaved. This idea is not entirely surprising in black Christian thinking, for something like it has appeared elsewhere in Anglo-American Protestantism. Coleman's assertion that the slave possessed autonomy strangely resembles sixteenth- and seventeenth-century Protestant notions of spiritual freedom in writers such as Sidney, Milton, and John Winthrop, which they defined as an autonomous moral ability. This freedom could be the source of both revolution against illegitimate authority, and the repression of those who—like Anne Hutchinson—subverted Protestant doctrine. It was an impetus both for revolution and for the imposition of social authority. They explicitly asserted, as did William Bradford in *Of Plymouth Plantation*, that spiritual freedom might exist under the conditions of oppression.[9]

Important political questions, however, immediately emerge from Coleman's discussion. If the slave's freedom is to be a model for that of future African Americans, who is to decide its limits, its difference from mere license, and the nature of the authority that withholds as well as distributes liberty? Once the "haint" of white demonology has been exorcised, how will the new free state be run? These were the very questions confronted by religious reformers like Milton and John Winthrop in their experience of actual revolutions and emerging polities. Significantly, Coleman emphasizes from the beginning that he is not thinking about the politics of the real world. Not only does he understand white oppression as an immaterial spirit—as opposed to political, social, or economic subordination—but he understands revolution as a similarly abstract notion: the world of conjure in which his griots and "haints" abide. This posturing dramatizes a striking and disturbing intention; Coleman's griot-conjurer voice claims the magical authority of the priest or voodoo man—a traditional authority on whose ethnic authenticity Coleman based a claim for the superiority of African spirituality. This spirituality, as he implies in the passage quoted earlier, bears a power that white supremacy cannot resist. It exceeds that of the modern white rationality whose claims for scientific knowledge are (unbeknownst to itself) incomplete and mistaken. Coleman's arrogant style trades on the assumption of the primitive's authority as a primitive. And it is clearly aimed at an audience whose romantic sensibility links authenticity and purity of intention with the premodern lives of primitives.

Coleman never reveals who will order his free society. Indeed, he conceives of authority in only the most fanciful and immaterial terms. One can only conclude that his postures as a conjurer are unrelated to serious political consideration, and are nothing more than a wish-fulfilling fantasy—a world in which his "haints" and "griots" prevail. This reliance on wish-fulfillment fantasy is legion in black theologians such as Hopkins, Coleman, and Cannon. For these writers, the alienated black intellectual, questing for his origins, seeks not only the spiritual wholeness of the masses but also their alleged freewheeling ability to realize their desires.[10] Imitating the fantastic powers of the folk, these theologians assume an extraordinary exegetical license, a will to power over the text whereby the object of study itself is subsumed into the scholarly reader's desire, as Coleman subsumes primitive African religion into his own fantasy. Indeed, in Dwight Hopkins' first—and deeply influential—theological work, desire itself becomes nearly indistinguishable from that ultimate concern and sacredness normally associated with God:

> The ultimate power in African-American folk culture is the Way Maker, a being so infinite in abilities that anything is possible. Similarly, the ultimate destination of these folk's aspirations is the Way Made, a Place or condition fulfilling the basic desires of life…. Likewise, the Way Made, in the minds of the folk in their culture, stands as the reality in which poor blacks can name themselves in a place they have claimed. The Way Made means finally accepting the self and being accepted by others.[11]

This celebration of the Way Maker may be the most politically telling aspect of the new romantic vision of the folk. The endless capacity to have one's own way can be only a dream. And the fraudulent fiction of this omnipotence can be arranged and maintained only by a superior political power whose actions are guided solely by his own will and in his own interests. An oppressed caste will be indulged in this fiction only for purposes of their own repression and political diversion.

Coleman's fantasies of powerful conjure are the hallmarks of a political style. This style flaunts prestigious scholarly modes while seeking the authenticity of the romanticized primitive. Coleman's political posturing—which often takes the form of the presentation of evidence—is the most disturbing aspect of his book. Uncle Rias, an ex-bondsman who appears in Coleman's excerpted WPA slave narratives, clearly represents one such romantic-political image. However, Rias ends up less a case of African religious continuity (as the structure of Coleman's book implies he would be) than as a stand-in for wish-fulfilling fantasy. Rias is quite predictably a creature of the Way Maker, who allows him to improvise his own ethical and religious norms in a hypocritical white world—a "theologian" who reasons from his indirect "oral" access to the Bible:

> Sin, according to Uncle Rias, is anything and everything one does and says "not in the name of the Master." The holy command, "Whatever ye do, do it in my

> name," is subjected to a very elastic interpretation by this aged Negro and by others in his community. For instance, he firmly maintained, "two clean sheets can't smut"—which means that a devout man and woman may indulge in the primal passions without being guilty of sin.[12]

Rias is for Coleman an exemplary figure of the folk's powers of fantasy in the same way that H. Rap Brown is a better student of poetry than his teacher and, presumably, other scholars of "print" culture. Indeed, Rias himself takes on a theological role as biblical interpreter, functioning without an exegetical tradition, coherent morality, or normative limits of any kind:

> Before passing judgment on Rias and his community, we must bear in mind that the African-American slaves' interpretation of both personal and communal ethics is based on "hearing" the word with common sense rather than on reading either the biblical narrative itself or "scholarly" commentaries on the Bible. In fact, their masters intentionally withheld the latter from them. Consequently, they had to improvise from their own sense of appropriate and inappropriate behavior in light of the hypocrisy of Euro-American Christianity. Ultimately, therefore, their experience of miscegenation had taught them how to engage in a critical reading of the morally ambiguous text (behavior) of their "Christian" masters with respect to the issues of sexuality, adultery, and fornication.[13]

Like Rias' freewheeling interpretation of oral language and behavior as written text (a key strategy of the signifiers), Coleman's account of Rias' sexual behavior cannot be distinguished from the anomie that commentators from Du Bois onward feared as the ex-slaves and their descendents carried Southern folk religion into the emerging Northern ghetto. To be sure, Du Bois in his own way agrees with Coleman's implicit representation of Rias as one aspect of the bawdy improvisatory ethos of slave religion—although Du Bois himself would refer to this aspect as sensualist and fatalistic, as well as ultimately self-destructive:

> It is difficult to explain clearly the present critical stage of Negro religion. First, we must remember that living as the blacks do in close contact with a great modern nation, and sharing, although imperfectly, the soul-life of that nation, they must necessarily be affected more or less directly by all the religious and ethical forces that are to-day moving the United States. These questions and movements are, however, overshadowed and dwarfed by the (to them) all-important question of their civil, political, and economic status. They must perpetually discuss the "Negro Problem,"—must live, move, and have their being in it, and interpret all else in its light or darkness. With this come, too, peculiar problems of their inner life,—of the status of women, the maintenance of Home, the training of children, the accumulation of wealth, and the prevention of crime. All this must mean a time of intense ethical ferment, of religious heart-searching and intellectual unrest. From the double life every American Negro must live, as a Negro and as an American, as swept on by the current of the nineteenth while yet struggling in the eddies of the fifteenth century,—from this must arise a painful self-consciousness, an almost morbid sense of personality and a moral hesitancy which is fatal to self-confidence. The worlds within and without the Veil of Color are changing, and changing rapidly, but not at the same rate, not in the same way; and this must

produce a peculiar wrenching of the soul, a peculiar sense of doubt and bewilderment. Such a double life, with double thoughts, double duties, and double social classes, must give rise to double words and double ideals, and tempt the mind to pretence or to revolt, to hypocrisy or to radicalism.

In some such doubtful words and phrases can one perhaps most clearly picture the peculiar ethical paradox that faces the Negro of to-day and is tingeing and changing his religious life? Feeling that his rights and his dearest ideals are being trampled upon, that the public conscience is ever more deaf to his righteous appeal, and that all the reactionary forces of prejudice, greed, and revenge are daily gaining new strength and fresh allies, the Negro faces no enviable dilemma. Conscious of his impotence, and pessimistic, he often becomes bitter and vindictive; and his religion, instead of worship, is a complaint and a curse, a wail rather than a hope, a sneer rather than a faith. On the other hand, another type of mind, shrewder and keener and more tortuous too, sees in the very strength of the anti-Negro movement its patent weaknesses, and with Jesuitic casuistry is deterred by no ethical considerations in the endeavor to turn this weakness to the black man's strength. Thus we have two great and hardly reconcilable streams of thought and ethical strivings; the danger of the one lies in anarchy, that of the other in hypocrisy. The one type of Negro stands almost ready to curse God and die, and the other is too often found a traitor to right and a coward before force; the one is wedded to ideals remote, whimsical, perhaps impossible of realization; the other forgets that life is more than meat and the body more than raiment. But, after all, is not this simply the writhing of the age translated into black,—the triumph of the Lie which to-day, with its false culture, faces the hideousness of the anarchist assassin?

To-day the two groups of Negroes, the one in the North, the other in the South, represent these divergent ethical tendencies, the first tending toward radicalism, the other toward hypocritical compromise. It is no idle regret with which the white South mourns the loss of the old-time Negro.[14]

This sociological wariness, by now a commonplace for informed commentators on black religion (of all periods), is disturbingly absent in Coleman's work. Mechal Sobel explores the possibility that, in the eighteenth-century black South, the inherited African frame of reference would not wholly explain the reality of American society or sustain social order and personality.[15] The theme of anomie persists in Benjamin Mays' *The Negro's God as Reflected in His Literature*,[16] which organizes different stages of African-American literature around eras of norm-contesting trauma. And a fear of anomie is deeply implied in E. Franklin Frazier's studies of black middle-class life.[17] The swaggering presence of the Way Maker often, one suspects, hides a profound fear that, without fantasy, black life might have no meaning at all.

Katherine Bassard's *Spiritual Interrogations* is another recent African-American literary history dominated by the language of desire. Bassard argues that Phillis Wheatley, Ann Plato, and Jarena Lee sought a future audience of black women gathered in community to recover the ethnic communal unity lost during the slaves' removal from Africa and their exclusion from the New World. Like Coleman, Bassard seeks to identify with her subjects as a displaced black person caught between Africa and America.

The original scene of traumatic separation pointedly appears in Bassard's own autobiographical account of her trip to Africa. Encountering Africa, she too senses the impossibility of a true return to the Dark Continent, and an ensuing alienation. She self-consciously projects her own attempt to create a community of female writers and readers upon each of her objects of study. Like Bassard herself, they too find themselves neither American nor African, and therefore seek a new black American homeland to replace their African home:

> I was struck by the irony of my own position as an African-American woman intellectual whose possible return to the African continent had already been both foreseen and prohibited. Indeed, my return could scarcely be called a return at all given at least ten generations of genealogy on American soil, and the irretrievability of any certainty as to the spot on the massive continent from which I might construct a history of origins. And yet there had been something compelling about the view of the Atlantic from "the other side" that challenged many of my assumptions about the theorizing of African-American subjectivity and discourse before Emancipation. While I had no inclination to return to a positivistic search for "roots," I found my scholarly positionality had shifted somewhat off the mainland of North America, only to remain in a kind of suspension over the Atlantic.[18]

Like Coleman's critical work, Bassard tellingly invokes the problem of origins in this romantic autobiographical passage. The payoff of such a quest will be the scholarly authority to create a canon. Phillis Wheatley, not surprisingly, becomes an original figure whose desire to create a home and female community anticipates future black women's writing. As with Coleman and Gates, this reinterpretation of Wheatley demands a fierce wrenching of texts and facts. However, Bassard's interpretive work in extending a folk "vernacular" canon to include "positionality" allows critics to apply the same critical terms to both neoclassical poetry and oral folk expression. At the same time, Bassard's extension of a signifying deconstructive ethos to Wheatley gives the slave an autonomy and political agency that she would not—in Bassard's view—otherwise have. However, such deconstructive ability and institution-building intentions must be seen as a wish-fulfilling power that Wheatley might never enjoy in real life. As a reader of Wheatley's poetry, Bassard consequently becomes another beneficiary/victim of the Way Maker's illusory freedom from or triumph over history. The imagined community of longing that she envisions in her subject's work is clearly a place in which she (the author) would be at ease. The homecomings she celebrates in her authors are her own.

Bassard continually reads Wheatley's poetry as a deconstructive writing—essentially a kind of signifying—that subverts the conventional assumptions of late eighteenth-century American evangelical Protestantism and political ideology. In an important close reading, Bassard considers the poem "On Being Brought to America," a short verse which apparently reveals the seamless nature of Wheatley's providential deliverance from Africa to America. This reading assumes that Wheatley moved easily from the Dark Continent to the New World. Moving against the code of a providential will that guides Wheatley to "America,"

Bassard discerns a break in the middle of the poem—a break implying a code of movement from one separate world to another. A more rigorous reading would demand other points of slippage in Wheatley's ostensible meaning, slippages that would more thoroughly undermine the primary code. This, Bassard does not provide—although its results might be interesting.

Bassard's failure to provide sustained resistance to the code of providential mission in Wheatley is worth noting because so many of the poet's near contemporaries deploy the same providential code to describe their passage from Africa to America. Autobiographical texts by Venture Smith and James Gronniosaw, as well as a poem by Jupiter Hammon, flaunt the existence of a divine providence that has brought Africans to British North America. Indeed, their blithe manner in this respect accounts for the dullness of many of these works as literature. Attempts at the "deconstruction" of these texts becomes less an assertion of textual resistance to hegemonic (and all necessarily imposed) meanings in Wheatley's poetry than a naive assertion of the poet's supposedly exceptional rhetorical powers that allow her to undermine her society's racial norms with conventional language. Far from finding breakdowns in textual meanings, Bassard's "deconstructions" are crude allegories asserting Wheatley's subversion of conventional Puritan notions of God's providential permission of evil. Yet debate about such ideas was rife in late eighteenth-century New England. Wheatley's manipulation would by no means be "subversion," but participation in a central contemporary discussion. In a republican and Puritan culture that cultivated oppositional discourse, Wheatley's "subversions" of racism were not rebellions but the enactment of an important mode of late eighteenth-century American theological and political writing. Jonathan Edwards III, Samuel Hopkins, Lemuel Haynes, and many others all rejected slavery on conventionally republican, liberal, Puritan and evangelical terms.[19]

Far from demystifying grand aesthetic, political, or social illusions, Wheatley's alleged subversions of Western discourse—assumed to be inherently racist—ultimately link her poetry to the spirit of the Revolutionary Age. Indeed, Bassard's linkage of "vernacular" forms (of resistance) to the folk paradigms of Gates and Baker suggests how deeply the supposedly oppositional styles of the black folk are grounded in Anglo-American religious discourse and the language of late eighteenth-century republicanism. If Wheatley's oppositional style makes her authentically black, her blackness—as she herself often argued—made her the authentically late eighteenth-century evangelical political poet that she was. Like Coleman, Bassard ruthlessly represses the institutional wisdom of the Americanist scholarship relevant to Wheatley's rhetoric, and she does so to create the illusion of Wheatley's poetry as an authentic origin of African-American literature.[20] Identifying paradigms of resistance and displaced community in Wheatley's writing, moreover, not only establishes the critic's power to pick a literary origin (that puts the poet in her vernacular place) but authorizes a bold set of methods and outlooks with which to overcome Protestant humanism's resistance to signifying. Bassard's ideological ruthlessness is of a piece with the black theologians' willingness to run roughshod over canonical American and African-American literary and critical texts. This ideological forcefulness is especially strong in the black theologian's repression of the historical provenance of literature.

Exercising this repression, Dwight Hopkins and Stephen Reid overlay upon literature a naive transcript of crude romantic images now concretized into historical realities. Although Dwight Hopkins adduces works like Toni Morrison's *Sula* as supporting evidence for the health-giving powers of black woman's funk, he rarely if ever sees how Morrison explores the central contradiction within black theology, the tension between way-making willfulness and organic community.[21] (A more rigorous reflection would find a severe limitation here. Qualification, however, is anathema to the Way Maker, whose importance lies in his boundlessness, his ability to transcend all limits.) Similarly the Afrocentric community, idealized by figures such as Peter Paris, turns out in *Sula* to be not only a source of social order but also a ruthless agency of female vindictiveness. Hopkins' childlike notion of black women's "funk" often sets characters such as Zora Neale Hurston's Janie and Morrison's Sula far apart from those "sisters."

It is therefore not surprising that Hopkins' *Shoes That Fit Our Feet* and Coleman's *Tribal Talk* steer clear of Charles Chesnutt, although he, of all black novelists, scrutinizes conjure most searchingly in those short stories collected in *The Conjure Woman*. Unlike Hopkins and Coleman, Chesnutt recognized that the symbolic victories won by conjure's exponents, such as the narrator Uncle Julius, are ultimately limited by the historical reality of Southern white supremacy. Although Chesnutt's work predates that of figures such as Lawrence Levine, it is important that the first major black writer of fiction had the literary acumen to weigh conjure in the balance of a stern psychological realism. Po' Sandy cannot escape early death and dismemberment despite the wiles of his conjuring wife. In the "Conjurer's Revenge," the ultimate beneficiary of the conjure woman's potions is the master who wins back the sexual willingness of his girlfriend. Chesnutt knows, too, that the folk world of the Southern past, recovered by cultivated blacks in the twentieth-century past, is marked off by racial boundaries. If the Way Maker carries the desire of the folk, he also experiences—and some of the best black writers have never forgotten this—the limitation of their oppression.

To study the interpretive and academic politics of *Tribal Talk* and *Spiritual Interrogations* inevitably illuminates *Healing Cultures* by Olmos and Paravasini-Gebert as well as Jon Cruz's *Culture from the Margins*. In their account of healing powers—considered in the broadest political, therapeutic, psychological, and social senses—most of the essays in *Healing Cultures* enact the cosmopolitan Hispanic's reconciliation with the African-Hispanic culture of his past. In many ways, the cultural reality they present is much more tangible and plausible than the construction of black culture that runs through recent work in African-American Studies. And this is only enhanced by the ordering of this Latin American romantic myth of origins into three connected units. The first exhaustively and convincingly documents the existence of a creative plenitude in Hispanic folk culture, linking man with nature in a sensuous unity. This plenitude is constituted by the large body of folk cures that have emerged from the intersection of Hispanic, African, French, and Native American culture in the Caribbean. The second powerfully enacts recovery from estrangement in its dramatization of cure: how these folk remedies have been articulated into treatments used by healers throughout the American-Caribbean diaspora. Finally, a series of essays and interviews traces the literary theme of alienated intellectuals and Caribbean emigrants healed through a return to their origins. At the heart of these accounts, however, is another rewritten version of a romantic myth of return.

The articles in the first section are most successful in demonstrating how the powerful Caribbean folk religions can effect real earthly cures. Olmos' "La Botanica Cultural: Ars Medica, Ars Poetica," Brian M. Du Toit's "Ethnomedical (Folk) Healing in the Caribbean," and Karen McCarthy's "Afro-Caribbean Healing: A Haitian Case Study" create a plenitude—of natural organisms, processes of healing, dynamics of growth, and possibilities of immersion—that is truly numinous. Here, the notion of union with nature as a basis for not only psychic but even physical health is deeply plausible: it explains the existence of a powerful Hispanic subculture bound not only by language but by ritualistic health practices.

However, one must distinguish the various contexts of these acts. Romantic return is the literary conceit of a cultivated middle-class intellectual with broad enough historical vision to see encroaching modernity against the precapitalist, prescientific past. Romanticism is essentially the property of the reader, who recognizes in the traditional patterns of romance a way of expressing secular redemptions from the estrangements and alienation of the present. The romanticist is a bourgeois intellectual whose leisure, education, and surplus wealth permit free personal experimentation (with body and soul). He differs from the urban Caribbean diaspora poor who are deeply in need of medical, psychological, and social care that is best provided by health care professionals—at least as a first resort. This is the most troubling aspect of the interview "Dolls and Healing in a Santeria House," conducted by Anna Wexler. The description, by a middle-class bourgeois intellectual author, of a faith healer in Boston who treats working-class Hispanic women facing serious psychological, physical, and familial problems, tells volumes about America's attitudes to the well-being of its poorest members. Romantic literary myth too readily turns into a template with which to understand the social, political, and economic levels of culture. As with Black Studies, advocacy of *Healing Cultures* lends naive but pernicious support to second-class health care for some of America's least advantaged citizens.

*Healing Cultures* represents the kind of therapeutic culture of "healing" at which many black writers aim in this country. They, too, would like to serve up literary versions of a tangibly grounded agency of "black health" for their middle class which would address the powerful disabilities—high blood pressure, obesity, diabetes, heart trouble, depression, alcoholism, and drug abuse—making deep inroads into even the middle-aged comfort of the black bourgeoisie. The literary payoff would be not so much a learned, reflective vantage on the complexities of public and private life, as a response to the still incomplete adaptation of the black middle class and lumpen to modernity. Both high and low black cultures seem to be filling this need right now. However, it is not clear that this is adequate for moral, political and social, pressures of the late capitalist era. Indeed, this compensatory black culture rewards a withdrawal from those very complexities.

Of all of the books under review here, *Culture on the Margins* offers the best hope of escape from the therapeutic horror show that pervades much of African-American and Hispanic Studies. Although repetitious and obsessed with documenting commonplace notions, as well as fearful of the literary texts whose evidence is at the heart of his argument, Cruz does an excellent job in tracing the intellectual line from the transcendentalists and their post–Civil War descendents down to the first folklorists. He does not delve deeply enough into Thomas Wentworth Higgenson's account of life in his colored regiment, or the journals of Charlotte Forten, for a full appreciation of the romantic malady he describes. But his cautious procedure is understandable; the terrain he explores is densely mined. He succeeds in showing how romanticism helped white intellectuals and folklorists synthesize the notion of an authentic black interiority. Yet his more important contribution is an observation which remains only tactfully implied. Underlying his argument is an observation that he clearly has made but refuses to voice. Black writers began to make literary use of folk culture at the same time as their white colleagues in the mid-nineteenth century. The shift from David Walker's and Frederick Douglass' perception of the folk masses as ignorant, bestial illiterates clearly owes much to the European literary discourse that redefined nature, and therefore "primitives," in powerfully suggestive ways. This insight lies at the bottom of Cruz's monograph like a shimmering gold coin in a deep well. Although he has useful things to say about the issue of authenticity, Cruz is far too shy in his discussion of the black intellectual's self-conscious folk appropriation—an issue that lies at the heart of James Weldon Johnson's *Autobiography of an Ex-Coloured Man*, *Cane*, *Their Eyes Were Watching God*, and even Richard Wright's *Twelve Million Black Voices*—to bring the sources of his glittering perception to the argument's surface where they might be fully examined.

It is hard to conceive how black literary representation of the folk might have found another language or plot than the transplanted biblical themes so prominent in Protestantism and later romanticism. Why has more than a generation of black theologians turned to the most simplistic views of folk religion, while repressing the modern world's most profound accounts of its spiritual life? And why does the naive account of black culture embodied in Bassard's notion of "performance" or Coleman's "conjure" come to satisfy our need for symbols of an original blackness that permeates American literature? Le me suggest that the immature romantic imagery cultivated by Bassard and Coleman does not represent resistance to the hegemonies of established academic discourse, but a capitulation. A conception of blackness which ignores the historical consciousness acquired by blacks in America is more easily absorbed and manipulated in the marketplace and the media than the rigorously dialectic notions of African-American self-awareness in Sterling Brown's essays. Brown believed in an African-American self-consciousness capable of an autonomous understanding of its historical, political, and economic condition. Bassard's and Coleman's naive romanticism tends to reproduce the most simplistic versions of racist American racial stereotypes—playful darkies or sly, sensual tricksters. This is minstrelsy. An earlier generation of blacks knew that oppression could never be resisted by fulfilling the oppressors' narcissistic desires.

The most important academic contribution of Bassard, Coleman, and Cruz is to alert us to the historical period in which folk romanticism emerged. One important early example of our modern psychology of the folk appears in *The Journals of Charlotte Forten Grimke*, a work spanning the mid-nineteenth and early twentieth centuries. Forten's journal, a record of complex relationships with intellectuals, friends, a lover, writers, and cultural heroes (white and black), presents the paradoxes, ironies, and metaphorical representations of contemporary black life as lived by politically, socially, and culturally conscious African Americans. The folk consciousness displayed by Forten in mid-nineteenth-century Port Royal pointedly corresponds to that of her nervous black contemporaries. The cultivated narrator, deeply self-conscious of his literacy, his problematic place in America, and his ambivalence toward white society and the black masses, appears also in Frederick Douglass' 1845 *Narrative* and David Walker's 1829 *Appeal*. These earlier writers, however, view the condition of the masses through the lens of their own sometimes thwarted aspirations. Douglass' awareness of being a self-made man clearly shapes his 1845 vision of fellow black slaves as politically and socially inept. Similarly, the "wretchedness" described by David Walker reflects the conflicts and tensions of his own desire for high literacy.

On the face of it, Walker's *Appeal* examines the black masses from the vantage of those forces—ignorance, religion, and the colonization movement—that hold it in place. The text is marked significantly by contempt not only for the white oppressors who impose the conditions of wretchedness but also for the black masses who, according to Walker, are in complicity with their ideological oppression. However, much of this contempt reflects his partial success in acquiring the analytic literacy with which he wants the folk to overcome their wretched condition, caused by their lack of verbal and numerical mastery. Walker's narrator parodies these maladjusted folk to shock them out of their misery, simultaneously revealing the author's own equivocal adjustment to the rigors of literacy. In many ways Charlotte Forten, granddaughter of the shipbuilder James Forten, represents the contradictions embodied in this passage of Walker's *Appeal*:

> I promiscuously fell in conversation once, with an elderly coloured man on the Topics of education, and of the real prevalency of ignorance among us: Said he, I know that our people are very ignorant but my son has a good education: I spent a great deal of money on his education: he can write as well as any white man, and I assure you that no one can fool him, &c Said I, what else can your son do, besides Writing a good hand? Can he post a set of books in a mercantile manner? Can he write a neat piece of composition in prose or in verse? To these interrogations He answered in the negative. Said I, did your son learn, while he was at

school, the width and depth of English Grammar? To which he also replied in the negative, telling me that his son did not learn those things. Your son, said I, then has hardly any learning at all—he is almost as ignorant, and more so, than many of those who never went to school one day in all their lives. My friend got a little put out, and so walking off, said that his son could write as well as any white man. Most of the coloured people, when they speak of the education of one among us who can write a neat hand, and who perhaps knows nothing but to scribble and puff pretty fair on a small scrap of paper, immaterial whether his words are grammatical, or spelt correctly, or not; if it only looks beautiful, they say he has as good an education as any white man and he can write as well as any white man, &c. The poor, ignorant creature, hearing this, he is ashamed, forever after, to let any person See him humbling himself to another for knowledge but going about trying to Deceive those who are more ignorant than himself, he at last falls an ignorant victim To death in wretchedness. I pray that the Lord may undeceive my ignorant brethren, and Permit them to throw away pretensions, and seek after the substance of learning. I would Crawl on my hands and knees through mud and mire, to the feet of a learned man, where Would sit and humbly supplicate him to instill into me, that which neither devils nor Tyrants could remove, only with my life—for coloured people to acquire learning in this Country makes tyrants quake and tremble on their sandy foundation.[22]

Celebrating literacy, Walker hopes for a religious awakening that will lead the wretched to seek true intellectual mastery. His derision, however, only alerts us to the fact that the narrator-speaker still inhabits the world of the unlettered. Walker's expression is marked by central characteristics of orality: repetition, an agonistic stance towards his audience, and continual reference to quotidian experience as opposed to the abstraction that one seeks of print. He makes a fetish out of literacy in a way typical of oral cultures, expressing his willingness to submit himself totally to a truly learned man. Such subjection represents the very intellectual helplessness that literacy lets the educated man or woman avoid.

Forten's *Journal* echoes Walker's anxious ambivalence and that of nineteenth-century free black writers such as Maria Stewart and William Hamilton, who also sought to exhort their fellows to greater cultivation. Forten was a member of a black intellectual elite, educated and cultivated among white abolitionist patrons. The daughter of Philadelphia activists, Charlotte Forten was raised in Salem, Massachusetts, among black abolitionists such as the Remonds, white transcendentalists, and literary figures including Whittier. As her diary indicates, her cultural interests were broad, extending from painting to oratory. She studied French and German, eventually translating a French novel. In her early twenties she went as a schoolteacher to the experimental community in Port Royal, South Carolina, where black ex-slaves were educated, given military training, and prepared for freedom.

Forten experiences the tension of belief in a Protestantism that can abet slavery and at the same time be used to protest it. She suffers frustration in her attempt to reach a high level of culture. This deepens when she encounters distinguished literary figures like Emerson and Whittier. The reverse anxiety appears in her worries, similar to those of Walker and Douglass, about the accomplishments of her "race." She regrets that there are not more blacks of literary cultivation, sniffs at the demeanor and discourse of William Wells Brown, and is embarrassed by an incompetent black speaker. Significantly, she seeks also to escape what she clearly sees as the world of black subordination—to associate with an English world sympathetic to black Americans, to achieve artistic and scholarly merit, and to overcome her present limitations through the personal cultivation of the imagination.[23]

A serious diary reflects the energies that shape the writer's future life. The tensions and contradictions of Grimke's early experience are heightened in the Port Royal section near the end of the journal. Significantly, it is here that Forten posits a myth of black aesthetic consciousness to compensate for her own sense of cultural and social inadequacy, so clearly and movingly described. As Carla Peterson observes in *Doers of the Word*,[24] Forten fails to identify completely with either the transplanted white Northern community or the Southern rural blacks. Indeed the limbo that she inhabits explains much of her distance—at times she almost seems an amateur ethnographer—from the black community that she observes. However, her accounts of its religious life constitute a romantic myth that serves another purpose than ethnographic observation. Forten has, under Whittier's wise advice, come south not to lift up the folk but to confront her own self-consciousness. Like a host of black authors afterward, she does so by finding that her anxiety's antidote is in the shrewd knowingness of the folk.

In the slave world that Forten describes, religion in the form of music—spirituals, shouts, and other songs—interpenetrates the fabric of daily life. Most of the songs concern the hope of salvation, the moral and psychological support offered by Christ. Forten records a world that is ordered by religious rituals which mark the major passages of human life: birth, baptism, education, marriage, and death. These rites are characterized by images of order and dignity, in marked contrast to the oppression from which the slaves have escaped. Significantly, this religious worldview of an orderly regulated life, lived with the ultimate hope of salvation, sustains the community's deepest values. Forten describes the eagerness of her old and young students to learn, as well as the ex-slaves' love of freedom and stoic acceptance of death. Forten observes a self-sustaining energy and power that contrasts markedly with her own insecurities. She envies the folk, whom she often describes as childlike, for what is indeed a childish narcissism. Adults, as Freud noted in his essay *On Narcissism: An Introduction*, covet the independence and self-possession of the naive youngster. And in such independence, Forten finds an imaginative resolution of her own not-quite-adult tensions.

An important element of Forten's idealized folk world is the aesthetic enjoyment it yields her. She gets the same sentimental pleasure from the religious music of the slaves that she does from the fiction of Dickens or the anti-slavery writer Mattie Griffiths.[25] Within Forten's deeply religious community—she recounts little tension or conflict on the part of the inhabitants—black aspiration to learning and other human fulfillment is equally simplified, past plausibility, and without the tension that Forten herself experiences.[26] Furthermore, Forten clearly identifies with the openness of the slaves who, unlike herself, are not hindered by a sense of personal inadequacy.

Thus the slaves' musical art is for Forten a wish-fulfilling expression of her own thwarted artistic and imaginative drives. Finally, her spiritual and intellectual transport represents a religious transcendence of the racial limitations that have scarred her deeply. At the heart of the myth of the folk is the insight that there is no black origin of a black culture or a black religion any more than there is an all-white origin of white American culture and the white literary canon. Folk consciousness is, and always must be, an imaginative projection at least partially shaped by an entrenched critique of our lives in a capitalist, technologically sophisticated society. Forten's black folk world can only be considered as an origin in the context of the cultural and social worlds that produced her vision. And we are far better prepared by our own experience to understand her anxieties than we are the idealized social perfection of the folk.

Bassard's and Coleman's scholarship is important for the way it makes us rethink the psychology of figures Douglass, Walker, and Forten, who are perhaps the true predecessors of today's crop of nervous black intellectuals. The nineteenth-century figures offer nobody a path to freedom and autonomy, only an unsettling measure of the distance that remains between blacks and their full and rightful inclusion in American society. In the beginning was, I must assume, an Age of Anxiety over origins—small consolation for those who want the political authority that beginnings give. Whether any cultural origin can exist outside a nexus of intellectual and political power is another question. I do not see how our present-day exponents of black theology and black literature can avoid or confront it.

One cure for fantasy is serious political and social debate in which the participants discover the material issues truly at stake in their lives. Black Studies departments and classes have often created an atmosphere in which such debates take place in a segregated world untested by the realities of contemporary scholarship. Yet integration with this scholarship is probably the only cure for the vagaries of the Way Maker, whose wish-fulfillment emerges in the academically segregated lives of many blacks in selective white institutions. Without confronting the serious questions that have consistently engaged Western observers of nineteenth- and twentieth-century romanticism, black scholars cannot fully illuminate the intellectual discourse, lying beneath their cultural concerns. At the heart of the Bassard and Coleman essays, as well as in many of those in the Olmos and Paravasini-Genert collection, is an attempt to install a fantasy-substitute for this. Bassard and Coleman in particular openly evade forty years of mainstream scholarship on early American literature and black religion from the period of slavery onwards. Their fantasies sustain an intellectual ghetto that keeps black thinkers from resolving how to attain full black citizenship in what remain white-dominated universities. No serious scholarship can be had apart from the competitive arenas, institutional wisdom, and traditions of sacredness implicit in those bodies of knowledge.

Literary Black Studies can be only an ersatz substitute for real participation in the intellectual *polis* of the university. Yet such a politics is needed, not only to produce viable black scholarship, but to address the current needs of black students in white institutions: financial support, serious academic remediation, health care, and competent professional therapy. The exercise of academic will-to-power in black theology and literature distracts the black professorate from the basic difficulties that the black middle class now faces in reproducing itself in the next generation. The fantasies of Coleman and Bassard hide the realities created by black powerlessness in the white universities and in American society. Within the academic *Realpolitik* of black romanticism, a very real political realism and literacy has been lost.

# Chapter Five

## Michael Eric Dyson's *I May Not Get There with You*
### The True Martin Luther King, Jr.

PART OF THE POWER OF ANY ACADEMIC MOVEMENT resides in its ability to institutionalize and thus extend the charismatic vision of the founding father. Michael Dyson embodies the second-generation success of Gates' rhetorical model.[1] High school dropout, gang member, hustler, Divinity School graduate, jackleg preacher, and finally holder of a doctorate in American Studies from Princeton, Dyson (as he represents himself on his curriculum vitae) self-consciously became the rapper-scholar envisioned in Gates' *The Signifying Monkey*. He displays—whatever internal conflicts in his work—the confidence of those born to the manor. In him, Gates' ironic play on the page is replaced by a visibly genial comfort in the public arena, an ease that suggests the assimilation and legitimacy of the signifying scholar to the highest level of the university as well as to the media. He simply assumes and shrewdly exploits the now taken-for-granted status of the "double talk of the dives" as an acceptable political, cultural, and social discourse. Within this world, the black inhabitant receives the vagaries of the Way Maker in return for bearing the stigma of black inferiority.

The new prominence of black double-talk has another cultural source in contemporary American life. In the last forty years, the legitimacy of the high professional and social institutions to which the white elite aspires has sharply fallen. The courts, political administrations, medical practice, and the military have been weighed in the balance of public scrutiny and found wanting. At the same time, membership in these professions has become fiercely competitive as the academic elite hardens into an upper-class stratum. Also important has been the admission to elite educational institutions of minority groups such as Chinese, Japanese, and Korean who bring—in high measure—those cultural orientations required for membership in the new cognitive elite. These two developments can only produce anxiety within this class, and within its white student aspirants in particular.

Within the context of exceptional Asian achievement, the academic fallibility of blacks looks perhaps less heinous to whites. As Asians begin to overwhelm whites in the upper echelons of the California university system, the latter must confront a racially tilted academic inequality of their own.

All of this may well give the signifier's cynical contempt for superior academic performance a new cachet among whites. The bantering jive and now legitimate double-talk of the signifying intelligentsia not only entertain but also provide cathartic relief for whites. As students scrutinize the languages of law and other learned professions by means of deconstruction, the former institutional foundation of public authority reveal themselves as interest and privilege. In this arena, the signifier's ironic ethos does seem to manifest a distinctively racial knowledge of the once invisible underside of white life. It is a new kind of data—at least about communication and its institutions—for an intellectual elite that, like all others, thrives on information. The rhetorical world in which the signifiers now operate—a world conditioned to what Walter Ong would call the secondary orality of television—corresponds to the signifier's ethnic turf. Indeed, it is clear that many signifiers have read or absorbed McLuhan's prediction of the media possibilities for marginal ethnic groups (presumably including blacks) in the coming global village—and taken it to heart.[2] It is from this rhetorical arena that Dyson's ethos of the congenial scholar-rapper takes its force.

Dyson's career began with the study *Making Malcolm*, which—whatever its faults—was an intelligent account of the transformation of Malcolm X into a public figure. (At his worst, Dyson's business sense and his nose for the news have pushed him to exploit the insecurity of his audience with pornographic diversion. I refer here to Dyson's titillating account of the interracial sex lives of his students at the beginning of *Making Malcolm* and an erotic encounter with a church member,[3] and his adoption of a rapper's voice and stance on the Charlie Rose show.) His paean to the African female in *Why I Love Black Women* is rife with poorly considered references to women's bodies—accompanied by the women's names.[4] Dyson's easy adaptation of down-home black, male-to-male talk is a development wholly consistent with signifying. If the lumpen may be intellectual, then the intellectual may easily gravitate to the social crudity of the lumpen. The intellectual lumpen is accorded the alarming privilege of claiming not only the disinterested posture of an academic, but also the raw sexism of the black urban poor. There is an unforeseen slippery slope here, however: one of the functions of signifying is to repress awareness of its dangers in order to extol its freedoms. These dangers inevitably attract the reader's attention as he considers the signifiers' most freewheeling celebrations of the folk. At its best, Dyson's street-smart intellectual guise allows him to harp upon his white audience's latent sense of its own creeping anomie to account for the appeal of Michael Jackson—his sacredness, his apparent charisma, and as a potential moral prophet.

It is no accident that Dyson has a Ph.D. In *Making Malcolm*, one finds well-schooled observations about American image making as well as the signifier's promise in this arena. His biographies and journalism show a capacity to explicate this aspect of many successful black entertainers. He has seen in hip-hop much of the rhetoric and ethos of the signifying style he has exploited. He perhaps comes closest to emulating Zora Neale Hurston with his cataloguing of black folk forms.[5] And in some of his best early work, such as *Making Malcolm*, he is underway to finding a material basis for black communication. Indications of success in this quest appear from time to time, even in *Why I Love Black Women*, which begins with an extremely suggestive account of the "vernacular" physical gestures of black women.[6] Among a host of academic signifiers all seeking the same motherlode in theory, he is an ironic exemplar: the male embodiment of Zora Neale Hurston's dictum that "to know there you have to go there."

However, in most of his later books, Dyson's method of culturally informed social observation soon falls into pedestrian accounts of social life. I quote a sample here:

> The pride so many blacks feel in Cochran's performance has a lot to do with an ancient injury to black self-esteem that not even Joe Lewis could relieve: the white challenge to black intelligence and its skillful defense in eloquent black speech. Among his many racial functions, the black orator lends credence to claims of black rationality. When black folk in barbershops and beauty salons say of Cochran that "The brother can talk," what they mean in part is that the brother can think. Thinking and speaking are linked in many black communities. And neither are abstract reasoning and passionate discourse often diametrically opposed to such circles. Like all great black rhetoricians, Cochran makes style a vehicle for substance.[7]

This passage is itself a cheerleading celebration of the late Johnnie Cochran. It is more of a chauvinistic appeal to a middle-class black audience and its pride in Cochran's oratory than a defense of their views of rhetoric. Rhetorical tradition includes argumentation in court. And a careful analysis of Cochran's appeals to black juries might reveal much about reasoning and eloquence in African American life. However, Dyson's reasoning here follows more from cultural assumptions than from evidence. In particular, Dyson relies on the Black Arts notion that black speech carries within it explicit aesthetic and rhetorical norms, norms that may be set forth in formal theory. But that theory and those norms are never really elaborated, even in the ordinary language of everyday conversation. We do not have a clear rhetorical guide to black lower-class behavior in criminal court. Some of the scenes in Tom Wolfe's *The Bonfire of the Vanities* reveal far more about the rhetoric of black and white self-presentation in court than Dyson does here.[8]

Indeed, the most interesting part of the passage is what Dyson admits is the therapeutic effect of Cochran's speech. Cochran's demonstration of black intellectual competence touches upon a now commonplace assumption of intellectual inferiority and dysfunction among young black males, routinely consigned to resource rooms, remedial classes, or special education.[9] Dyson's analysis of Cochran's speech provides—again—a cathartic remedy for this feeling of oppression, without making any demands upon the viewer beyond his attention to the television screen. (Cochran himself, of course, clearly did not envision a "therapeutic" stance *vis-à-vis* his television viewers.)

However, Dyson rarely moves beyond cheerleading to consider how the black middle class itself might be manipulated by the passionate rhetoric it prizes. What are the middle-class values that make Cochran's and Dyson's appeals so seductive? Dyson's blandly offered, unexamined accounts of "black culture" and the so-called black point of view pervade *Between God and Gangsta Rap*, with its celebrations of Michael Jordan, Ann Deveare, and black slang; *Race Rules* with its descriptions of black public intellectuals, sexuality, leadership, and pop culture; and *Why I Love Black Women*. As Dyson expounds these manifestations of black culture, he bears one more self-gratifying fantasy to the black bourgeoisie. Implicitly, he shows his middle class its potential power as source and arbiter of fashion and its many modes. And, the oral vernacular at the heart of black culture turns out to be an erotic, speechifying, song-writing, and media-savvy world. These elements, for Dyson, become signs of power, elaborated not by faraway book-readers but by the chattering masses themselves. Their thinking is mediated by the intellectual sessions that Dyson, like Gates, finds in "barber shops and beauty salons" and not, curiously, by the sustained cultural analyses of intellectuals like himself. Indeed, Dyson becomes little more than an evangelist, bringing the good news of the black lumpen to Charlie Rose. This celebratory discourse belongs to the genre of fantasy life that E. Franklin Frazier described in *The Black Bourgeoisie*. Dyson's vision of a powerful black culture purveyed by figures like Cochran is parallel to what Frazier described as the myth of black business. Figures like Dyson retail the fantasy of "culture" to create the perception of a specifically "black" political, social, and economic point of view, a fantasy that carries the imprimatur of African-American "intellectuals."[10] Like the older *Ebony* and *Jet* fantasies, this "authentically" black perspective is curiously full of old sexual stereotypes and the images of black "successes" in the music world. These, while amusing his black folk audience, probably do not harm him with his white audience either. Whites as well as blacks have long been familiar with the "sacrality" African Americans have invested in figures like "Father Divine," who seems to reappear—this time with Dyson's earnest approval—in the figure of Michael Jackson.

Like Gates, however, Dyson's point of view and life experience do yield him real insights on an important aspect of black culture—in Dyson's case, a major political, social, and cultural figure. In *I May Not Get There with You: The True Martin Luther King, Jr.*, Dyson has perhaps found his ideal subject. King was a middle-class minister who quickly found a way, through oratory, to reach the black masses, bourgeois, and a large liberal white audience. His "plagiarism" of other texts is, in the context of the American tradition of journal-keeping, not unlike the practice of Henry David Thoreau and another charismatic minister, Ralph Waldo Emerson. Like the transcendentalist worthies, King was not wholly at ease with the academic world and its procedures. Like them, he saw the university's wisdom as the source of sensibility, not a highly refined philosophical system. He was involved in his own translation of black culture to the West. Despite a personal distaste for rap as a vehicle for intellectual reflection, I too find a link between the commonplace book and the various musical plagiarisms of hip-hop ("dubbing" and "sampling"). There is a long tradition in American literature—black and white—of "making it new," especially in the sanctuary of the private sensibility, whether artistic or religious. And the archival use of past meaningful sounds as background to the rapper's chant probably does convey the source of the sensibility underlying a song's dominant voice or message.

Dyson's book occupies an interesting place in recent American popular literature. Although the influence of black theology on his thought is clear, Dyson's analysis of King does not get bogged down in abstract intellectual discourse. Instead, he uses the recent paradigms of the signifiers and other students of black culture to present a King that reflects the African-American culture around him. In an odd way, Dyson's book supplements straightforward historical and journalistic accounts like Marshall Frady's *Martin Luther King, Jr.* and David Garrow's *The FBI and Martin Luther King, Jr.* Given the terms of an African-American Studies which sees the project of Gates, Dyson, and King as valid cultural commentary, then Dyson's book—like anything else he writes—represents an African-American perspective on King. Given the marketability of black perspectives—defined in the now conventional way—Dyson's book has the validity of a saleable point of view, an orientation toward King to be consumed by a mass market. Part of the book's success hinges on the suggestiveness that these categories provide for Dyson's reading of King.

Like Martin Luther King, Dyson has an (admittedly revealed) erotic life at odds with the official morality of the black bourgeoisie. He too employs theology pragmatically, as a rhetoric more than a vehicle for moral or philosophical reflection. And like King, Dyson must confront its limitations for solving the deepest spiritual and intellectual problems. Dyson, like the King of the exhortatory sermons and books, finally represses this problem. However, Dyson is sufficiently smart to make his reader recognize this dilemma, which neither he nor his intellectual perspective can address satisfactorily. The ironies of signifying cannot provide consistent resolution of the struggle with our ultimate concerns. And the question of ultimate concerns very quickly emerges in a socially chaotic black life dominated by mask-making rhetorical posturing.

All of these issues give Michael Dyson's work on King a perhaps unexpected depth, an importance belied by his frequently casual, colloquial, and seemingly unpremeditated style. Dyson is exceptionally shrewd in his account of the image-making that now surrounds the figure of Martin Luther King, and the various manipulations by the King family, the corporate world, and the American state. Dyson argues for what might be called a blacker King, linking the dark side of King's life with the late twentieth-century icon. As Dyson weighs King's value in the American marketplace of ideas, he assays the ideological demands of our high capitalist society as well as the extent to which King resists them. In the process, Dyson casts a telling light not only on King but also on the society that has made King over in its image. Dyson reveals to us not only a politically ambiguous early

King but also a white-dominated society's tendency to exploit the image of black intellectuals and artists for its own political needs. This analysis throws into relief the strategies by which American democracy represses its deepest tendencies to political and religious innovation—even though innovations like King's have often strengthened American life. At the core of these reflections is an important question: How can a leader's inspirational greatness be insitutionalized? For King was too powerful and charismatic *not* to be assimilated into American tradition. Whatever his mask-making, he may be the closest to a real prophet that America can get. Yet his world-changing power must—to maintain the current social order—be made to serve the interests of America's dominant social, political, and cultural groups.

Dyson's first section shows how the politically mature King advanced a radical response to American foreign and domestic policy in the mid-sixties, becoming ever less popular than in the earlier stages of his career. Translated by proponents of a color-blind society, the language of the early integrationist King has been used to propound a social vision that neglects black America's tragic history. However, the rhetoric of this earlier King has little to do with the disturbing potential of a prophetic King, who became ever more convinced of the inherent racism of American society as he attempted to expand the Civil Rights movement into the North. It was this King who, having always been dubious about the war in Vietnam, began in the late sixties to speak out and organize against America's involvement in southeast Asia. More and more aware of economic and social inequality in the North, the radicalized King gradually espoused what amounted to democratic socialism. And he was influenced by the calls for black manhood made by the black power advocates of the mid-sixties. In commemorating the color-blind language of the earlier King, commentators such as Tamar Jacoby and Michael Tomasky—as well as American society at large—repress, in Dyson's view, the full prophetic stature and potential of the disruptive later figure who was ultimately drawn to a language of black pride. To reflect upon the later King is to question the legitimacy of America's military policy, increasingly stratified society, and racist practice.

Dyson also considers the question of identity. King, according to the author, belonged to the radical remnant of the black church, a tradition extending back to Bishop Henry McNeal Turner and Rev. Reverdy S. Ransom, and reflected in King's fusion of prophetic religion and politics, making sacred speech a vehicle for civic action. Similarly, King used religion as a means of addressing economic inequality. To hold up the prophetic image is ironically to summon the memory of King's human frailty: the plagiarist and philanderer. Significantly, however, these elements of King's prophetic identity were, for Dyson, shaped by his experience as an African American. His plagiarism may have resulted (Dyson argues) from enormous academic pressures at the predominantly white Boston University. Seen from the traditions of the black church, King was—as a Ph.D. student in theology—not engaged in institutionalized scholarly inquiry but seeking to enter a prestigious black pulpit in the South. His appropriation of other texts might be similarly understood in light of the black church's oral traditions. This King was—like most young preachers and orators—searching for his voice by trying on the voices of others. The theological outlooks from which he borrowed should be seen as sources in this search.

In a similar vein, Dyson attempts to deal with King's sexual promiscuity in terms of the erotic traditions of the black church. To be sure, King had always sought the attention and company of attractive women. In the Civil Rights movement, King found himself surrounded by available females, a situation he exploited. Illicit private sex, according to Dyson, brought release from the tensions of leadership and exemplary action, and the pressures of his prophetic role. This selfish, therapeutic dimension of King's sexuality was inevitably related to a deeply patriarchal attitude. Despite important black female Civil Rights predecessors like Mary McCloud Bethune, King was insensitive to the SCLC contributions of women participants, organizers, and leaders. Indeed, Ella Baker, an organizer in SCLA, sounded an important note of resistance to King's highly masculine, prophetic, top-down leadership. The sexism of his style also appeared in the patriarchal ethos of the King household. King, abdicating much domestic responsibility, expected Coretta Scott to limit herself to the maintenance of her home.

In this respect, King was a creature of the contemporary black theologian's Way Maker, a follower of wish-fulfilling desire that subordinated others to his own needs. This tendency could only be destructive in a way that King's family is wholly correct to repress. However, Dyson's emphasis on the recently uncovered dark side of this prophetic, highly masculine image is very suggestive. One of the book's deepest implications—and I do not expect Dyson to concur with this conclusion—is that King necessarily shared in the disorientation that we see today in black life. His importance as a leader comes from the fact that he, too, experienced the confusing social dislocation of black life and the taboos of American racism. King's preference for light-skinned women, his promiscuity, and his sampling of various sources in his oral art all link him—however paradoxically—to the world of hip-hop. Rappers frequently flaunt their preference for light-skinned blacks—not to mention white and Asian women—as sexual objects and not full human beings. The rappers, like Dyson (on the evidence of his writing), seek to enjoy a world of sexual freedom, although they do so more openly than did Martin Luther King.

A moral critique resides in Dyson's reading of King, although Dyson—quite consistently—does not make it. It is hard to dissociate the demands of what Dyson calls communal orality from cynicism about the public intellectual life of contemporary America. It is equally difficult to dissociate King's promiscuity from a deepening cynicism about conventional moral arrangements. Dyson's prophetic, oral King is a King who experiences both the pressures and disorder of a marginal black world, where rhetorical mastery and sexual conquest are a surrogate for the deeper gratification of a forbidden social and political experience. What might be seen as King's moral entrapment may well have had ethically regenerative consequences. As Dyson himself notes, King's acquiescence to the tragic limitations of African-American life may have inflamed his opposition to segregation. He too was caught in the social trap he hoped would disappear in a coming transformation of America. In this respect, Dyson's comparison of King to hip-hop rappers has its force—common entrapment in an often tragic African-American erotic experience. King's sexual adventures recall the alienation and sense of limitation of many lower-class blacks. Most suggestive in Dyson's analyses is the hint that such entrapment might generate political energy, that it motivated King to strike at its institutional and ideological sources. For Brown, the folk had an idealized creative force that carried with it its own aesthetics, morality, and politics. For Dyson, the very negativity of their condition engenders the desire and energy for human assertion that can foment political change.

Implicit in Dyson's text is a grim version of the black church as a world that neglects the rigor of intellectual life for rhetoric and prophet-like inspiration. Indeed, Dyson himself does not seem to understand how much King's tragic flaws, as he depicts them, reflect stereotypes about the black church and the Civil Rights movement at a crucial time. Those sites of black experience become a world of philandering and patriarchal exploitation of women. Dyson's reading of King's life unintentionally gives us another stereotypical image, the raucous Southern black folk preacher. Here again, King may have suffered revulsion from his own habits. And, given his own intellectual assumptions, he may have examined his own behavior in the kind of interior debate to which he called his white and black readers in works like "Letter from a Birmingham Jail." It is hard to believe that such an ethically sensitive man did not engage in such introspective moments. From our arguments with others, we make rhetoric; from those with ourselves, we make poetry. When the great sermonizer was alone, he may have translated his agony into higher moral reflection than ever his public oratory revealed. One of the greatest limitations of black middle-class culture is its lack of space for such meditation. Moral conflict, however, creates redemptive possibilities for black middle-class life, as it did for King. These are worth consideration.

Dyson's final section depicts the struggle of various interest groups to control King's reputation for themselves. First are the allegations of King's and his staff's communist connections. Against right-wing spokesmen, Dyson insists that King's associates had little or no contact with the party. Indeed, for King, civil disobedience was a high exercise of patriotism. He also dissociates King's moral politics from Ralph Reed's right-wing Christianity and from the antiabortionists, arguing that King always considered the immense inequities of African Americans and never sought to deny a woman's constitutional right to control of her body. Dyson goes on to detail what he describes as the King family's attempt to monitor his legacy—to control the appropriation of video and tape recordings of King's speeches, the maintenance of King's papers, and the upkeep of his home by the National Park Service. For Dyson, their efforts have crossed the line into a desire to profit from every aspect of his memory, in marked contrast to King's simple, selfless, nearly ascetic life.

Dyson does not make nearly as much of these deeply suggestive facts as he might. However, the right wing's red-baiting and the King family's control suggest another area of volatility in King's image. The leader was, as Dyson himself shows, a radical force in American life. Although King claimed patriotism, his social democratic views were deeply subversive of capitalism. Moreover, any group, such as the antiabortionists, could easily appropriate King's advocacy of civil disobedience, which claims to act in the name of conscience and higher law. And King's example was one of economic selflessness: he repeatedly gave away his earnings to the movement and to Morehouse College. Although King is commonly made an image of social consensus, the truth is that he resisted the tendencies toward social inequality and materialism which are deeply ingrained in American life. His truly radical nature made him vulnerable to those who sought to attack him, but resists the King family's attempt to commercialize his legacy.

Not surprisingly, the book's subtitle is "The True Martin Luther King, Jr." Dyson's King is blacker and more radical than the figure currently commemorated in America. Dyson intends to reclaim the King of the late sixties for an African-American middle-class audience, whom he familiarly addresses as a black preacher himself. Dyson's book, I suggest, creates a thorny, problematical King—as many prophets are—to be pondered by the new black middle class now entering integrated American life. This invitation to reflection is important given the deep ambivalence of the black middle class over the disorder and dislocation of their lower-class fellows—whose culture has nevertheless assumed hegemony over African-American communication as a whole. Dyson seeks a radical King who shares the moral contradictions of African-American life. Dyson is right to suggest the impossibility that a ready-made image of King, available for social use, can also be authentic. A true memorial of King is only possible if one can institutionalize an awareness of black life's instability and a questioning of American values—a process inevitably fraught with political misunderstandings, the baggage of self-interests, and the economic forces of early twenty-first-century capitalism. The true memorial is an activity of mind and spirit, and criticism of what society has made of the prophet. In his book, Dyson is clearly underway to such an authentic commemoration.

# Chapter Six

# Black Literary Criticism Meets Black Realities

BEM KARIN HOLLOWAY, A BLACK TWENTY-ONE-year-old male, was shot as he tried to escape with two comrades from a work farm where he awaited trial on two counts of first-degree murder.[1] He had already been convicted of attempted murder, rape, and robbery, as well as breaking and entering. If the new accusations were sustained, he would almost certainly receive the death penalty. His case is not exceptional in North Carolina. Nor, unfortunately, are such cases rare in America as a whole, where it is estimated that a third of lower-class black men between the ages of eighteen and twenty-five are in some way under the supervision of the justice system.[2] To die thus is not only par for the course in black lower-class life, but fulfillment of the now ubiquitous African-American myths of male violence and out-of-control masculinity which are celebrated in rap, MTV, and even beer commercials.

The case of Bem attracts our attention because he is the son of Karla Holloway, a distinguished African-American literary critic who has made her academic reputation in the interpretation of black women's writing. Her intellectual link to Bem's life bears serious examination. Bem's experience represents the violent and disorganized side of urban male black life, repressed by many of Holloway's models of black literary culture and tradition. In the early books *Hurston: The Character of the Word* and *Moorings and Metaphors*, Holloway established herself—despite appeals to the rhetoric of semiotics—by drawing suggestively on the language of romantic return. Her critical viewpoint is extremely important both as an extension of Hortense Spillers' work, and as a synthetic tool for the recoveries of the past enacted in Bassard's *Spiritual Interrogations*. In her systematic study of the black women's canon, she conceived of an African and African-American tradition grounded in a charismatic female spirit and a coherent spiritual community. This canon requires one to read women's texts by engaging with several historical layers, each of which articulates a myth of return to female origins. One finally confronts the embodiment of a founding creative female spirit. The voice of a text is the sum total of past textual voices embedded in it, along with a timeless, essential feminine voice. To read thus is to recover the original memory of the founding female spirit, and observe it passing through various historical expressions. The value of a text depends on the enactment or suppression of its various historical voices, with the most successful joining many distinct expressions into a multitimbered female voice.

In *Moorings and Metaphors*, Holloway elaborates this idea, formulating a complicated model for textual construction and the reading process. Let me reproduce here her assertion of that model's uniqueness and what I take to be its links to American romantic tradition:

> My use of revision as a gender-specific instance foregrounds gendered spheres of knowledge—women's ways of framing and keeping that knowledge in the place of the representation of the "speaking black voice."
>
> The second perspective that organizes this book is (re) membrance. It focuses on the way that memory is culturally inscribed. Generally, this kind of inscription is assigned to the genre of myth. The mythic dimensions within these works stress the intimacy between myth and cultural memory. In them, the spoken text retains a figurative intimacy to the spoken text. Memory is a tactile path toward cultural recovery. When we complicate this value with the de-stabilizing activities of traditional historiography, we are forced to acknowledge the distinct versions of memory that myth, as an a priori oral text, recovers.[3]

Despite Holloway's claim for the exceptional character of this reading process, it greatly resembles the central diegetic feature of Emerson's "Nature": the reader's repeated encounter with strategically placed metaphors symbolizing modern man's reunion with the Eden from which he has been estranged. These recurring images of human fullness foreshadow Emerson's concluding vision of spiritual ascent, a redemptive oneness with an idealized nature. In a characteristic maneuver, Holloway has taken over this romantic strategy—defining it as a black feminist protocol of reading. Here one finds feminized versions of the romantic's imagery, experiencing the text as an immersion in individual phases of a generalized feminine creativity. Holloway's return to human fullness is defined in terms of race and gender, a state preceding the original alienation of black women in a white man's world. The union of historically distinct women's voices is another facet of the feminine wholeness finally experienced by the reader. The text itself thus becomes a metaphor for the black female reader's transcendent union with a recovered feminine nature.

In this reading of the female text and, implicitly, the process of feminist reading generally, Holloway adopts what will be her characteristic approach. She takes a literary, philosophical, or linguistic proposition assumed to be universal—as the romantics conceived the return to origins—and applies it to a distinctively black female experience, faculty, or psychology. This strategy appears again in her appropriation of Noam Chomsky's generative theory of language, borrowing the rhetoric of his universally human "linguistic deep structure" to describe an inner faculty that produces a distinctive black female language. She claims a separate linguistic system and "deep structure" for black feminist literary discourse, distinct from that of white men. In Holloway's revision of Chomsky we find another interpolation of romantic myth, for here a woman's encounter with her deep linguistic structure engenders transcendent feminine literary creativity.

These related strategies provide a framework for Holloway's version of the signifier's central proposition: the equivalence of black written and oral forms. For Holloway, orality—in an extension of the Gatesian view—takes on many features associated with writing, such as the comprehensive retention of data and recording of speech. Holloway's view of oral expression as layers of speech—retaining particular historical experience—makes speech into a metaphorical palimpsest. This conception of cumulative oral wisdom differs remarkably from the usual understanding of oral retention in proverbs, wisdom lore, and fables, according to which infrequently used information and rhetoric often disappear. Holloway's theory requires a sustained retention of data, like information stored on a hard drive; from this unity of female speech, the listener can extract a voice constituting an exact historical record of what has been said. This retention gives black women's oral expression a depth—the presence of an original spirit—which, significantly, white and black male speech—and writing—do not have.

Holloway's model is distinctive for erasing the male component of human creativity, not unlike Emerson's repression of female generativity in "Nature." For Holloway, the feminine is largely responsible for the reproduction of culture, and she elaborates the gender implications of this proposition in a ruthlessly mechanical way—an obsessive discourse echoed in the feminist theorizing of Houston Baker and Michael Awkward. Whereas a woman's voice or text is characterized by "depth" produced by cumulative historical expression, male voices tend to embody no more than a man's encounter with the contemporary surface of his world. This deductive process yields a male psychology characterized by the absence of creativity, insight, and inwardness. Culture and society emerge from the eternal feminine, from the masculine spirit only the chaos and violence of "expressive behavior."[4]

Even by the standards of signifying, Holloway's Way-Making Feminine Will moves in an exceptionally dehumanized way. Signifying always held out the danger of making black culture into stereotypical white bourgeois life turned upside down and inside out. This tendency may be abated, as it is in Hurston and to some extent Dyson, by careful on-the-ground observation of everyday black life and culture. In Holloway, the inversive style of signifying runs wild. It is not only repressive, but obsessively totalizing, ruthlessly bifurcating black experience into female presence and male absence.

Not surprisingly, Holloway's intepretations of feminine and masculine experience move along parallel, mirror-imaged grooves. The mother-daughter relationship is particularly significant for the tradition of black women's literature, which is deemed to bear a gendered black universality alongside the creation of male authors. The two traditions exist side by side as—to compare small things to great—parallel galactic worlds. In Holloway's early books, black masculinity existed in its own shadowy, self-destructive realm. As she moved from the literary criticism of *Moorings and Metaphors* to the broader cultural observation of *Codes of Conduct* and *Passed On*, she had to confront the stern reality of African-American ghetto life, where the repressed masculine returns with remarkable force. The violent, self-destructive missing man of Holloway's earlier theorizing turns out to be far more central to her critical enterprise than Emerson's missing woman was to his.

Holloway established this romantic myth through a series of close readings in Zora Neale Hurston's *The Character of the Word*, as well as in *Moorings and Metaphors*. She moved from a monograph on a single problem first to a broader interpretive project, then to cultural criticism, and finally autobiography. This pattern paralleled the literary production of Henry Louis Gates, Michael Dyson, and Michael Awkward—as well as several highly visible Duke celebrities in the mainstream profession. As with Gates, the theoretical template set forth in Holloway's early work would have important implications for her wider-ranging social observations. *Codes of Conduct*, Holloway's first work of cultural criticism, takes on many topics already commonplace in the informal culture of African-American intellectuals—the treatment of blacks in white universities, the status of the black body as a literary icon, the mistreatment of young speakers of black English, and the black generation gap in the profession. The rambling energies of this collection eventually find their focus in observations on youth, morality, and crime. There suddenly appear chapters—linked by an intensifying emotional urgency—on the moral lives of children, the representation of African-American youth in recent fiction, and finally the criminal predicament of her son Bem—then convicted of attempted murder. A critical moment for Holloway, who suddenly found herself faced with the inescapable importance of male ghetto violence to the social dynamics of African-American life. Whatever her formal explanation, these chapters and the whole of her next book emerged from her confrontation with the gendered limits of her earlier theorizing.

*Passed On* is a study of black Southern funeral practices; Holloway's father and grandfather were both morticians. Her long, discursive account of past custom is deeply shadowed by the world of violent male death in the Jim Crow South—the reality to which Bem's death symbolically leads within the structure of the text. Holloway's ostensible thesis is that an earlier generation of black undertakers addressed the needs of blacks far more effectively than their white counterparts in the current integrated world. And her horror in the aftermath of Bem's death is offered as implicit support.

Underlying Holloway's argument, however, is an intellectual problem which Bem's death—and her thwarted grief—pose for her theoretical worldview. In *Codes of Conduct*, Holloway's female-centered paradigms fail to sustain her during Bem's conviction and imprisonment. Mourning death—and meaningful writing on the subject—depends on powerful explanations of day-to-day reality when trauma undermines our normal routines and assumptions. An account of the world-disrupting phenomenon of black male violence is now demanded. Holloway's book is, quite significantly, unable to address this problem and find resolution of the trauma of death. Instead her book provides a cathartic display of the practices by which an earlier generation of Southern black emotionally relieved itself. To the contemporary quest of the reflective mourner for existential meaning in the face of death, Holloway has nothing to give. And this failure is also endemic to the emptiness of signifying. Holloway begins her reflections at the end of *Codes* by acknowledging her inability to give Bem, when alive, the same nurture that she reserved for her daughter, that she could not find a "ritual" with which to tend his hair lovingly—as she tended that of the female child.[5] She is equally unable to find a ritual and a rationale with which to confront his death.

In Bem Holloway's execution and the writing of his mother's book, the chickens of black feminism come home to roost. The "authentic" vision of oral black folk traditions, promoted by coddled intellectuals, proves an inadequate substitute for those humanist conventions of literature and culture associated with mourning. The mother's incoherence and vague description of a son—never evoked physically, emotionally, or intellectually as a full human being—emerges as the traumatic result of what we all know to be our present-day black reality: male violence, social dislocation, and, ultimately, dehumanization. Holloway finds in a presumably life-sustaining folk culture no definitions of masculinity with which to make Bem a human being or to explain the trauma of his death. She vainly seeks to escape this dilemma by turning to an era in which such trauma was (it is supposed) resolvable, when funeral preparations took place in the comforting domain of bourgeois black men.

Holloway's romantic gendered—and repressive—treatment of the folk is now ubiquitous; it (or its variants) is the host upon which two generations of African-American literary critics have battened. In December the most successful of these well-bred black middle-class students sit in the elegant suites of luxury hotels vying for jobs at Amherst and Swarthmore, talking the talk of illiterate people whose sexual mores have generated AIDS, whose violence promotes wanton shootings, whose ignorance of Western civilization keeps its children unlettered, and whose music drives the boom boom boom I hear from my living room as my white upper-class students cruise by in their $80,000 Range Rovers. The intellectuals of the *Village Voice* have celebrated the emergence of rap music as an object of study at Harvard—all of which is to say that Karla Holloway and a new generation of black post-structuralist critics have become what the first signifiers beheld in the ghetto: intellectuals who are nevertheless *au courant* of the comings and goings of his or her homeboys and homegirls, past and present. But if the poor black men facing death on the streets are heirs of motherwit, the African-American folk tradition is facing and failing its acid test in the 'hood—whatever the judgment of Madison Avenue. That failure raises the question of just what our folk intellectuals do for black society, and what any intellectual does for any society. This question may be profitably explored by returning to Holloway and her most recent book.

*Passed On* claims to be a collection of mourning stories. But the book is structured more by the author's introductory assertion that a more humane practice of mourning and death preparation existed in the past. The well-used romantic myth gives the book its form: the black return to a comforting premodern existence. As a history and illustration of black funeral practices, however, the book lacks order and logic, as does its claim to celebrate a uniquely black form of death. *Passed On* is a disorganized, flashy account of burial services, funeral rituals, and the exotic related displays in the South. The book's most compelling aspect resides in pictures that only elaborate the escapist tendencies of Holloway's prose and the voyeuristic aspect of its appeal to readers. Its real rationalizing—reality explaining intention—is visible only in Holloway's expressed wish to memorialize the death of an only vaguely evoked foster son. Nor does Maurice Wallace, an expert on images of black masculinity, give such a description in what he quite honestly refuses to call a eulogy, although it is clearly a sermon confronting Bem's death. Such repression is probably the only hope this book can give its black audience for a future in which young African Americans like Bem will certainly play an important part.

I do not raise the issue of hope gratuitously: at stake in this book is the African-American's confrontation with what must be its most horrifying trauma. Holloway fails to bring her learning successfully to the task of addressing a crisis in the black community. This point requires further explanation. Karla Holloway is, as well known in the profession of English, a distinguished scholar at a major university in a central intellectual nexus of the South. She has been a director of African-American Studies and dean of the school of Humanities and Sciences at Duke University. This position is one of eminence not only in the American professorate and the mainstream academic culture of North Carolina's Research Triangle but also, and perhaps more importantly, in the traditional black middle-class world of central North Carolina. This region has habitually been the site of a black middle-class intelligentsia that, in the pre-desegregation world, taught in the black colleges between Raleigh and Greensboro, and now in the age of integration contributes its members to North Carolina State, the University of North Carolina at Chapel Hill, and Duke University, to name only a few.

The often distinguished members of this group have traditionally been an important part of the black bourgeoisie about which the sociologist E. Franklin Frazier wrote as early as the 1920s. Its most eminent academic citizen may be John Hope Franklin, who as a young man taught at Durham's North Carolina College for Negroes before moving—in an ironic circle—to Howard University, Brooklyn College, a chaired professorship at the University of Chicago, and finally, returning to Durham, to Duke. There he is now a chaired emeritus professor. Black academics—both Northern newcomers and members of the traditional Southern black middle class—tend to know each other. And this is certainly true of the relatively large group of black English faculty at Duke, Chapel Hill, and North Carolina State. As the acknowledgments and prefatory notes of Holloway's book make clear, she experienced her tragedy amidst colleagues (many of them at the elite schools named above) who clearly knew her as a friend, encouraged her writing, and helped promote the publication of the book—which significantly was part of the John Hope Franklin Series of African-American publications at Duke University Press, an imprimatur that suggests not only the influence of her black colleagues but the institutional support of the university.

In this world, the death of Holloway's adopted son Bem has special significance. To be sure, Bem's earlier experiences in an abusive family and inadequate foster homes, his pattern of adolescent criminal activity, and his final imprisonment for kidnapping and attempted murder are clearly anomalies in Holloway's middle-class realm. However, these experiences are wholly typical of black male experience in the pathological realm of the ghetto. Bem's life and death are, bluntly put, anathema to this black middle-class community, which distances itself from these breakdowns in the disintegrating communities and schools of inner-city Durham and the black lower-class community of Chapel Hill, as well as Raleigh. Increasing numbers of this community send their children to country day or boarding schools, or facilitate their way into the better suburban high schools in Durham. In mourning Bem's death, Holloway is joined by her black bourgeois academic community in facing fundamental social and psychological questions of its relationship to the neighboring black lumpen. This task demands confrontation of that ambivalence of affection and anger, attraction and revulsion, illicit joy and public sorrow that are at the heart of traditional elegy. Her literary failure reflects, therefore, a cultural breakdown that has, I want to argue here, its roots in the intellectual world of signifying.

Holloway's book cannot speak to this crisis because it ignores the traditional and modern literary approaches to the trauma she faces. The emptiness of Holloway's straightforward descriptive account of death practices is remarkable at a time when literary and critical treatments of trauma abound in both African and African-American Studies, and beyond the academic world. Mourning and loss are central subjects in our late twentieth-century African-American literary revival. The books studied by scholars in Holloway's academic field overflow with it, from the post–Jim Crow worlds of rural Southern peonage to the Northern inner-city ghetto. To be sure, *Passed On* draws on lurid funeral scenes from black literature. But Holloway's essay is—strangely enough for a literary critic interested in mourning—rarely incisive in its analyses of Jean Toomer's *Cane*, Langston Hughes' *The Ways of White Folks*, Richard Wright's *Uncle Tom's Children*, Zora Neale Hurston's *Their Eyes Were Watching God*, Ralph Ellison's *Flying Home*, and the early poetry of Gwendolyn Brooks (to name only some of the most celebrated works and figures). She ignores important treatments of mourning in Alice Walker's *The Color Purple*, Toni Morrison's *Sula*, and John Beatty's *Tuff*. Even more ironic is Holloway's seeming ignorance that her case—a middle-class black intellectual's confrontation with the loss of kin caught by the pathologies of ghetto life—is by now an established literary subject. For her own representation of Bem's death and its consequences was anticipated by the bourgeois-artist narrative voices of Kenneth McClane's *Walls*, Brent Staples' *Parallel Lives*, and John Wideman's *Brothers and Keepers*.

Holloway overlooks not only African-American accounts of mourning, but the most distinguished treatments in modernity itself. Holloway never makes sustained reference to the important discussions of death in the post-Renaissance Western world by Phillippe Aries, David Stannard, and others.[6] One would think the comparison necessary to show the ethnic distinctiveness—or lack thereof—of what she calls "black death."[7] Such contextualization would have humanized both her experience and Bem's death. The violent fall of maladjusted young men is a worldwide phenomenon, which has been confronted throughout history. Bem's tragedy is not what the Duke publicists call "Black Death," but a universal experience. His death connects Holloway and a traumatized black middle class to humanity in a way that her gendered signifying does not allow. The effect of her oversight is to further intensify the reader's sense of unexplained disaster. The lack of humanizing erudition explains the book's failure to give her educated but fearful black middle-class audience the renewed intellectual and psychological coherence provided by elegies and other rituals of mourning. Holloway does not see "black death" as a human tragedy—for which a literary wisdom exists—but a sensational, exotic phenomenon, easily brought to market. Her book reproduces—for consumption—the garish, flamboyant, clearly disoriented ceremonies she describes. The prize won by this book is entirely to the point of this argument. Its triumph is based on the voyeuristic appeal offered white onlookers by the dislocated Southern black masses moving from rural traditional life to the horrors of the Northern ghetto. In contrast with illustrated books like Richard Wright's *Ten Million Black Voices* or Langston Hughes and Ray Caravera's *The Sweet Flypaper of Life*, this portrait of early twentieth-century black life lacks the wisdom and perception upon which intelligent consideration of Holloway's funeral practices must depend.

In the end, Holloway's account of "black death" suppresses literary knowledge itself, comprehension of genre, mode, and expression. Artistic forms have traditionally offered a framework and rhetoric for writers to explain mourning and death; those crises we now grasp through psychoanalytic means.[8] One reason for the persistence of these genres and rituals outside of the parochial world of African-American Studies is that they address fundamental human needs in times of separation and loss. Not surprisingly, the ideologically driven tendency of many black critics to affirm a uniquely black culture has cut them off from those wellsprings of tradition that address their own deepest pain. Although Holloway is engaged in what amounts to an elegy for her son, she shows little awareness of what the genre, or indeed what mourning itself, might entail. Thus, Holloway seeks to reinvent—as African-American Studies necessarily reinvents the wheel—the elegy: a literary expression which confronts the loss, anger, sorrow, joy, passion, and calm that take place in the process of mourning. In ignoring elegiac forms, Holloway—quite intentionally—gives up her power as a bearer of that tradition. She sacrifices her opportunity to address an emotional crisis increasingly suffered even by middle-class blacks for a symbolic cathartic display of violent images that do nothing to relieve deeper pains.

The paradigms neglected by Holloway are not only those of Western literary tradition but those of a psychoanalytic tradition which in our postmodern high capitalist society has itself become a literary form practiced by humanists. Karl Abraham, Melanie Klein, and John Bowlby have variously formulated the nature and dynamics of mourning in a tradition of works that include Freud's essay, "Mourning and Melancholia." Nothing threatens the meaningfulness of life as much as separation from a beloved object. In Freud's view, the mourning ego redirects anger at the lost object from the object to the ego itself, producing deep feelings of worthlessness and rage. This is only exacerbated by the mourner's deepening sense of the world's meaninglessness without the beloved. In working through these feelings, the ego is gradually—and this is crucial for Freud—able to separate itself from the lost object. Thus the ego can accept the reality of loss, and can understand it.

The mourner's sense of meaninglessness has, however, an intellectual cutting edge. His anger directs his scrutiny not only to self-worth but also to the very social and cultural values upon which that worth is founded. Why live a morally sensitive, politically responsible, and professionally significant life, if one will finally face the nothingness of death in which these values will mean nothing? This questioning must, of course, be particularly intense for the black middle class; the values of the institutions for which they work often support the very social order that oppresses their communities. And, of course, it is especially volatile for a black middle class that not only precariously sustains families and churches, but must also confront a popular culture that violently attacks bourgeois norms.

In the absence of a viable humanistic approach to her grief, Holloway's claim to control over her subject may be a compensatory psychological defense. The book's mechanical interpretations are thus projected into a Way-Making will-to-power over the text. I quote her here in the midst of a statement describing that power and its scope, appropriately made on the first page of the book's introduction:

> Although the text of this book spans the twentieth century, it certainly could not cover the century, since there were, of course, more stories of death and dying in African America than could be recovered here. For that reason, the critical process of this book has been to make certain that the stories I do tell sufficiently echo others already familiar to the reader or shadow those that might not get fully recalled to voice or text but that nevertheless continue to haunt our cultural imaginary.[9]

This language is characteristic of the work's stylistic and intellectual sloppiness. In this undisciplined passage a text "spans" or alternatively "covers" a century. This disclaimer—like many of the other rhetorical statements in the book, which calls itself it a collection of mourning stories (there are hardly any here)—turns out to be false. Imprecise writing predictably appears. The stories here are comprehensive in that they echo ones that the reader has heard and that "shadow" (another meaningless expression) the cultural imaginary. This, of course, is vague and metaphorical—a sign both of intellectual carelessness and also, as elsewhere in Holloway, of an ordering authoritarian will. At the heart of this passage is a comprehensive metaphor of black culture as a psyche. And in extending the Freudian language she has introduced, Holloway claims to possess that psyche—and even its unconscious. Her superficial use of Freudian psyche, dreams, and traces is as ideological, repressive, and single-minded as her reading of other "texts."

The difference that serious intellectual and literary erudition might have made for Holloway may be seen by contrasting her book to Du Bois' elegy in *The Souls of Black Folk*. Predictably, Holloway's work refers to "The Death of the First Born," but in her desire to establish his and her work as a "black" response to death, she does not notice that Du Bois' essay follows the form of the pastoral elegy, a genre that dates back to Theocritus. Holloway's glib, self-serving appropriation of Du Bois to her own ideological purposes is especially significant, not only because she must be aware of Arnold Rampersad's discussion of Du Bois' generic choice, but also because Du Bois' situation as a black intellectual so closely parallels her own.[10] Although Holloway's memorializing account of black funeral practices clearly reflects deep emotional trauma caused by the death of her son, she never specifically names the individual fears and questions that Bem's death raises for her and middle-class black academics like herself. Although she imagines her preparations for his execution, she only foresees this event as a moment of eternal peace for the now dead boy.

In defining the nature of his attachment to his son, his fears, and his own late adult anxieties, Du Bois' use of the elegy forced him into rigorous introspection of a kind Holloway pointedly evades. In doing so, he located the psychological nature of the crisis faced by Holloway with far more incisiveness and emotional power in ten pages than Holloway can muster in two hundred. The questions of meaning raised by the death of a son—traditionally a family's hope for its financial, political, and social future—are deeply threatening for the black middle class because its status is so precarious. Indeed, so precarious is dignity for the middle-class black that Du Bois is momentarily glad that his son has died before experiencing the humiliations of black life:

> All that day and all that night there sat an awful gladness in my heart,—nay, blame me not if I see the world thus darkly through the Veil,—and my soul whispers ever to me, saying, "Not dead, not dead, but escaped; not bond, but free." No bitter meanness now shall sicken his baby heart till it die a living death, no taunt shall madden his happy boyhood. Fool that I was to think or wish that this little soul should grow choked and deformed within the Veil! I might have known that yonder deep unworldly look that ever and anon floated past his eyes was peering far beyond this narrow Now. In the poise of his little curl-crowned head did there not sit all that wild pride of being which his father had hardly crushed in his own heart? For what, forsooth, shall a Negro want with pride amid the studied humiliations of fifty million fellows? Well sped, my boy, before the world had dubbed your ambition insolence, had held your ideals unattainable, and taught you to cringe and bow. Better far this nameless void that stops my life than a sea of sorrow for you.[11]

From this shocking recognition, Du Bois is able to move to an introspective insight that reveals this joy as a breakdown of his positive hopes for the future:

> Idle words; he might have borne his burden more bravely than we,—aye, and found it lighter too, some day; for surely, surely this is not the end. Surely there shall yet dawn some mighty morning to lift the Veil and set the prisoned free. Not for me,—I shall die in my bonds,—but for fresh young souls who have not known the night and waken to the morning; a morning when men ask of the workman, not "Is he white?" but "Can he work?" When men ask artists, not "Are they black?" but "Do they know?" Some morning this may be, long, long years to come. But now there wails, on that dark shore within the Veil, the same deep voice, Thou shalt forego![12]

This hard-won insight could only have been achieved, as Du Bois well knew, through the well-established rituals of literature. Only through the elegy's power to order the feelings and thoughts associated with mourning into a dramatic whole can a victory over the emotional limitations of grief be achieved.

The ordering of thought and feeling dramatized by the elegiac pattern here, as well as the transparency of the lifted veil and the color-blindness of future "men," are romantic metaphors whose plausibility has been gained in conventional literary terms. Du Bois' moment of transcendent understanding is the result of inner self-examination that would have been familiar to Jonathan Edwards, Emerson, and Freud. Without this inward contest of opposed feelings, Du Bois might never overcome a profound ambivalence not only to his son's death but to himself and, ultimately, to the condition of his race. It is Du Bois' willingness to put his deepest feelings on the line that allows him to submit his emotions in "The Death" to the disciplines of rhetorical structure and earned insight. His sense of futility, he realizes, is a desire to evade not only his political life of leadership but also life itself. It is Du Bois' frankness that allows us to see the full extent of Holloway's unwillingness to face similar feelings, which her book powerfully suggests but resolutely evades. Early in the preface, Holloway—in maudlin language—speaks of her own anticipation of Bem's scheduled death by execution. She imagines her attempts to prepare herself and him emotionally for death by injection. No one, after reading Holloway's account, can imagine that there were not moments in which Bem's death must have come as the relief that Du Bois experiences: the relief of freedom from an unbearable burden. However, Du Bois' stern commitment to the demands of the elegy forces him to do precisely what Holloway cannot do: explain the meaning of Bem's loss and the fears that it evokes in her. Unlike Du Bois, the speaker of Holloway's text has no way of overcoming her profound ambivalence to herself, her condition, and her race.

Holloway must repress the answers to the deaths and self-destructive lives of Bem-like figures that have been given by central twentieth-century black poets like Langston Hughes and Gwendolyn Brooks. They too have encountered the horror of violent death of black inner-city males. They have drawn many times on the elegiac form to evoke the deep irony of an evanescent beauty that is only intensified by its short life. This is certainly the stance of a number of Hughes' poems, such as "Dead in There." One considers Hughes what Arthur P. Davis once called "the cool poet."[13] How "the cool" deal with the prospective trauma of death or the historical fact of loss is an important question for poems like this. The speaker of this work concludes that his prematurely dead friend has demeaned his own life through the acceptance of a "cool" posture. Significantly, however, the persona moves on to judge him for valuing the "cool" moral vision of his "ace boy." This is, of course, a question of mourning. If one is cool—if the cool are one's friends, one's best friend, one's "ace boy"—then how does one confront their loss? Moreover, how does one confront one's complicity with their values? The answer that Hughes implicitly returns here is a grim one. Condemnation of the "ace boy's" cool ultimately leads to a criticism of the poetic voice itself. Mourning requires disciplined self-examination, the heroism and elegant submission to traditional cultural obligations that make Du Bois and Hughes significant writers. It is this kind of moral introspection that is lacking in Holloway's book. Holloway's black middle class needs a heroic discipline now more than ever. *Passed On* does not deliver.

# Section Three

# Signifying as Cultural Explanation

Perhaps the most important achievement of Gates' program, whatever faults I have described, was to catch a certain mood in recent African-American literary life. Signifying not only guided a new group of critics, but cast a suggestive light on black women writers who came into prominence during the last third of the twentieth century—romance writers like Bebe Moore Campbell of *Singing in the Comeback Choir*, and more ambitious authors such as Toni Morrison of *Sula* and *Paradise*. Finally, as a rhetoric that emerged in the confrontation between white and black students and intellectuals, signifying had much to tell its followers about the workings of patronage relationships. Gates' critical orientation helps us understand not only the characterization and plot of a movie like *Glory*, but why it assumed such high visibility.

# Chapter Seven

# Moll Flanders in LA

THE LITERARY MOMENT I DESCRIBE IN THIS BOOK is a commonplace in English and American cultural history. It is an era of uncertainty about social norms, a culturally influential middle and lower class, as well as a nervous intellectual elite. Such rapid social mobility created the Grub Street critics satirized by Swift. The fierce graphomanic careerism of Gates and Dyson was mockingly anticipated two centuries ago in the bibliography introducing *A Tale of a Tub*. This is not surprising in itself. One of the first insights shared by writers in the early modern world of print was the power of rhetoric to take on an influential life of its own, for a fury of words to generate seductive enthusiasm, and for literary convention to legitimize itself with its own charisma. The moral critiques offered in Pope's "Epistles" and Swift's *A Tale of a Tub* are still incisive. Prophets made of print haunt the literary life of emerging modernity, whose dislocations are a seedbed for prophesy's emergence and growth. Amidst the chaos of present-day black America, these prophets and their tales have a peculiar force. They continue to exert misleading powers, distract imaginative vision, and impose intellectual constraints where they promise delusory freedom. For all the criticisms of this book, a real vigor is projected by the personae of Gates' *The Signifying Monkey*, Holloway's *Passed On*, and certainly Michael Dyson's work. These texts create imaginative presences that cannot be denied. They contain a literary sensibility that compels the reader by the brute erotic, violent, and visceral force of lower-class black life. This sensibility, it must be said, is now having its way with America. An important aspect of postmodernism was its tendency to erase the lines between high-, low-, and middle-brow culture, the distinction between literary and non-literary texts, between popular and scholarly. From the prestigious heights of the elite academy, the new black critics have reached deep into the ghetto, tapped its violent, erotic forces, recreated its seductions, and lured an unwary host of readers.

The eighteenth-century anglophone world not only saw the emergence of a fly-by-night intelligentsia but also stimulated a host of conduct books. The new class of public intellectuals found itself giving advice about the human rituals of courtship and marriage. These guidebooks, however, could not but generate new kinds of that venerable literary genre of romance. It is guidebooks that generate the epistolary style of Richardson's *Pamela*, underlie Pamerla's virtuous behavior, encourage equivocal responses to Mr. B's love, and win a domestic conquest that is as much hers as his. These guidebooks appear at a similar period of social fluidity in early postrevolutionary America. Here, too, conduct books provide an important model for seduction novels, such as *Coquette*, and perhaps for a slave-narrative fiction such as Harriet Jacobs' *Incidents in the Life of a Slave Girl*.

The literary influence of such guidebooks can also be detected in popular magazines and women's fiction since World War II. Not surprisingly, the new black cultural presence embodied in Gates' world finds a home in the writing of advice columns and the fiction it generates. Conduct material is now particularly notable in both black women's magazines and popular nonfiction. Increasing numbers of single black women seek mates, maintain careers, raise children, and cultivate a social life all at once. These women have higher expectations for personal comfort and luxury than earlier generations. They live—and this differentiates them from many of their white professional counterparts—only one or two generations away from the world of the ghetto or Southern rural poverty. They negotiate the rapid climb of social mobility that traditionally disorients bourgeoisie and their intellectuals. Although the black middle class continues to be an exceptionally religious segment of the population, many black women work in areas like finance, media, and information—sites of secular values considered by many to be deeply corrosive to traditional black religious values.

As the conduct books of the eighteenth-century anglophone world gave birth to novels, so did the many black romances. Both genres often confront the problems of courtship, failed marriages, single-parent child rearing, and life after divorce. Increasingly, they look at the dark side of lower-class ghetto life as manifested in the behavior of even the African-American middle class. Furthermore, it is not an accident that our signifiers have written books bearing on the rules and codes of race relations in the newly resegregated world of integration: books such as Karla Holloway's *Codes of Conduct*.

The tone of these texts is often upbeat. Like all romance novels, they trade heavily on the reader's desire that the sympathetic protagonist resolve his or her trials of the heart. However, these authors cannot create either a male or a female character of the intellectual stature of Eliza Bennett, Pamela, or the autobiographical subject of Benjamin Franklin's memoir. The black heroes and heroines of Bebe Moore Campbell's books lack introspective depth, the cultural-intellectual resources for full reflection, and the sharpened sense of class awareness needed to come to a true self-knowledge. Indeed, these books sometimes seem to seek to divert readers from reflection rather than to engage them in those questions so basic to present-day black life. Despite their undeniable alertness to life in the black community, Campbell does not stimulate the reader's self-consciousness or encourages his or her inventory of the forces that shape that world. Unlike the women of Austen's books, neither these authors nor their protagonists are underway to an intellectual consciousness that transcends their local condition.

Part of the charm of the slick signifying characters of these books is a fantasized capacity to walk on the thin ice of early twenty-first-century consumer culture, above the black water of dislocation, poverty, and personal chaos. These books tend to mystify, simply finesse, or sentimentalize the conditions of the black women they describe. To the extent that they reflect seriously on black women's lives, they reflect the ethical dilemmas that signifying poses for its black proponents. Bebe Moore Campbell's romance *Singing in the Comeback Choir* portrays Maxine, a black producer of a successful talk show. She lives in an affluent suburb in Los Angeles where she is married to an even more prosperous ex-lawyer named Satchel. In the novel, we see Campbell's heroine confronting the trials of marriage, career, mid-life, and her elderly blues-singing grandmother Lindy, who lives in the North Philadelphia ghetto. By the end of the book, Maxine has reclaimed her temporarily philandering Satchel, boosted the floundering ratings of her TV talk show, restored the career of her childhood guardian, recovered her psychological capacity for conjugal orgasms, initiated a new life for a teenage drug dealer, and found homes for five Hispanic orphans. In the banal language of the author and her black female middle-class audience, Maxine is a superwoman. This is not a gratuitous observation; Campbell's plot, characters, and scenes, her stuccoed comfortable LA home on a hill, her azalea garden, her tai-chi-practicing black lawyer husband, and her extra-large shower stall are the confections of middle-class black consumer magazines such as *Essence*.

The novel's broadly painted characterizations do not so much define individuals as expound the status anxieties of the new black middle class. Inviting her largely female readership to identify with this fantasy movement from wealthy Los Angeles to an earlier Philadelphia ghetto home and back again, Campbell invokes the recent disorienting rise of the black bourgeoisie. This rise, for all of its material glory, has not allowed blacks to escape a disintegrating black society whose pressures have been reinforced by links of kinship and available transportation. It is these underground social disturbances and not a two-person shower stall that Maxine shares with the presumed audience of this book. That audience, too, has poor relatives—or relatives unable to adapt to the rigors of professional or middle-class life—whom they must support. They, too, confront a black male population for whom the role of the "player" represents a sexual option amidst a world of unmarried and unattached black women looking for affection. They, too, have a powerful romantic nostalgia for an earlier ghetto home, which in retrospect appears to have been warm and comfortable compared to the upper-class white professional world. This collapse has bred trauma, which the novelists evoke but cannot painstakingly describe, analyze, and address in the manner of earlier intellectuals like Du Bois.

*Singing in the Comeback Choir* exploits this trauma as a site for wish-fulfilling fantasies of a future consumer life—the secular salvation of a fallen disoriented black world. An opening scene in which the pregnant heroine and her husband cuddle is a fantasy celebration of upwardly mobile, marital bliss in a world emptied of men by high incarceration rates, unemployment, and violence. Indeed, Maxine's union to a black man who is even more successful than she, is particularly remarkable in light of the well-known superior achievement of African-American women in the academy and workplace. It is to the point here that the author has written a black conduct book entitled *Successful Women, Angry Men: Backlash in the Two-Career Family*. Campbell's audience reads Satchel's "supportive" manner, relatively good humor, and presence—however interrupted—as signs of a stable relationship in an era of high divorce rates, rampant single motherhood among blacks, and the allegation that bourgeois black men exploit these conditions ruthlessly.

The most serious trauma exploited by Campbell's book is a question that, however philosophical, must haunt the minds of the mobile. At the heart of the suburban and ghetto worlds with which the author invites her audience to identify is a question: why has she (and, to some extent, they) been invited into America's material paradise when so many black peers have been left behind? The answer to this question expresses the book's most fervently projected wish. The author, somewhat like the ecstatic Baptist preacher, develops her audience's deepest fantasies and fears into a providential framework of belief. The novel's heroine often speaks of herself as a "miracle," her experience of past suffering and present well-being as a work of divine intervention, and her gifts as the sign of chosenness—a language that Campbell's largely churchgoing black middle-class readership knows well. And her novel is a world in which the redeemed—the jazz-singing guardian who returns to music and the drug runner who turns out to be a good back-up singer—are saved by their gifts. To sing in the comeback choir means not only to be saved but also to join the band of the elect. Campbell's heroine was saved because she was chosen. How did the heroine rise to *haute* bourgeois life? It happened by grace—an answer that Defoe, Richardson, and their American cousin, Benjamin Franklin, would certainly recognize and endorse in their own fables of success. And this chosenness has—like that of the Biblical Joseph—placed her in a position to help her family.

This answer, however, signals an important difference between Bebe Campbell's sentimental rags-to-riches story and that of other authors. There is a tragic and even fatalistic note in Campbell. Unlike *Moll Flanders* and Benjamin Franklin's *Autobiography*, *Singing in the Comeback Choir* does not elaborate an economic or political view of the world, the *ad hoc* sociology of success that we expect from those who have "made it" in America. Although Maxine is clearly competent, she does not associate her providential gifts with mobility in a coherent social world. Underneath her talent, good works, and consumption of her society's goodies is a cynical vision of the meaninglessness of the marketplace in which she has succeeded. "Miracles," as some eighteenth-century empiricists well knew, is also another word for something that we can't explain. And—seen in secular terms—Maxine's repeated dipping into providential religious language spells out the code of her inability to make sense not only of her own mobility but also of her world.

Part of the power of the Protestant world that Campbell evokes—like Defoe, Richardson, and Franklin—lies in its capacity to yield coherent patterns of meaning and experience in the saint's life. The regenerate saint continually takes moral stock of himself and his relationship to the world. The American romantics would translate this inward reflection into a secular, metaphorical version of the earlier spiritual experience. In doing so they created literary embodiments of autonomous intelligence and sensibility which range beyond the literary domains of American Protestant culture. Although Franklin, for instance, is underway to an account of his evolving consciousness, he cannot mine it as did Emerson or Thoreau, who work the same ground with sharper analytic tools. Franklin traces his inward path to knowledge in his aphoristic fables and the moral bookkeeping that will be imaginatively transformed in the allusive prose of Thoreau's *Walden*. Pamela, who goes to her closet and writes letters, is engaged in a moral ratiocination similar to Franklin's. Henry James' heroine will far exceed the psychological and intellectual breadth of her reflections. Campbell not only disdains the inward reflection that could create serious consciousness, but implicitly trades on an American anti-intellectualism that encourages this lack of thoughtfulness in blacks. Campbell's fame flows from a black and white consensus that celebrates Maxine's success as a Civil Rights miracle and a beneficiary of America's material paradise. Her failure to take political, philosophical, or personal stock of her situation can only make her more palatable to more than a black audience of readers. Our understanding of the political significance of Campbell's tale and her literary method lies in the psychological fault lines that course through the plot.

Few good storytellers will fail to initiate contrary patterns in their texts, deepening their art by implicitly testing its truths. Such patterns exist in *Singing in the Comeback Choir*, but Campbell—whom I believe to be a gifted storyteller—chooses not to let them emerge full-blown. As Maxine compulsively reaches forward for the pleasures of money and benevolence, she also reaches, as Freud of *Beyond the Pleasure Principle* would predict, back to the ghetto for death. People with high blood pressure who smoke, young black men who tempt death selling drugs, and women who return to philandering husbands while attempting to rescue Hispanic orphans are all courting self-destruction, whether intentionally or not. Maxine's success is not only a fantasy but also a diversion from an important truth about her own character. Maxine's attempt to save all her relatives is in and of itself self-destructive. This would, in a more realistic plot, raise genuine questions about her own sense of self-worth. A more searching author would let Maxine fail and suffer as such people do in real life. Such suffering would engender reflection, inward search, or further destruction, as it does for people of her energy and perspicuity. This novel might or might not end happily and reward the reader with all of Campbell's wisdom about the limitations of superwomen in general, the black variant of this persona in particular, and Maxine herself. The wish-fulfilling

Way Maker sensibility that demands folk success and victory thus obscures an important truth about middle-class black female life. Maxine has adopted a black middle-class view of the world that will not let her take a full measure of herself, although Campbell explicitly—and sensationally—trades on the emotional depths that give her heroine's life its chill of horror.

In Campbell's book, the *deus ex machina* triumphs of the Way Maker define a clear code: the obsessive need of the superwoman to cope with the meaninglessness of black life through self-destructive action. In Maxine's life, this meaninglessness becomes apparent in the fact that she can only establish her worth *vis-à-vis* her relationships with other people. Her self-destructive attempts to save everyone around her gain their plausibility through an unspoken assumption that she would not have a meaningful existence without the good she does her relatives and lovers. The last person that Maxine would ever think of saving is herself. This is not surprising, for behind the rhetorical ethos of the superwoman there is no one at home. In some ways, Maxine has ceased to exist as a person—at least in terms of any self-consciousness. Her sense of her own meaninglessness and that of her world indeed promotes her reckless attitude toward life.

Part of the war against those inflated printed images savaged by Swift turned not only on moral contempt but on envy for their seductions, their luminous attractions, and their very real psychological impact. These were literary powers unmediated by human reason. The chaos of the early modern world, like the chaos of the ghetto, was created by self-destructive human energies that first compelled but finally deadened consciousness. Bringing the world of the ghetto into the marketplace, a number of black writers have engendered these powers again. Yet in the end they are empty, large gaseous forces that evaporate. This emptiness is a cruel joke, for in their expanded state these powers—like gas and sensationalistic print—can appear at night to the oppressed as pillars of fire.

# Chapter Eight

# Toni Morrison and the Romance of Signifying

## Part One

GATES' APPROPRIATION OF HIS FATHER as the original figure of his canon embodies another important strategy of late nineteenth- and early twentieth-century black literature, as does his influential reading of *Their Eyes Were Watching God*—the pairing of a middle-class intellectual with a figure of the folk. The publication of Toni Morrison's *Sula* anticipates *The Signifying Monkey* by about five years. Whether or not Morrison encountered semiotics is less important than her shrewd understanding of the use of such cultivated/folk pairings, especially as a means of exploring black middle-class life and the folk in African-American fiction. These pairings begin to appear in African-American literature in the writing of Charlotte Forten Grimke and Charles Chesnutt, particularly those stories in *The Conjure Woman*. They are to be sure the staple of certain kinds of vignettes in American regional writing. However, this strategy provided an important model for the genealogical creations and self-inventions of critics such as Bassard, Holloway, and Hopkins. These literary tactics flourish in African-American romanticism, which emerged from the tensions and moral insights of an earlier Victorian Protestantism, reflected in the conflicts of Douglass, Walker, and Forten.

Like the earlier nineteenth-century American writers Hawthorne and James, Charles Chesnutt dramatized the cultivated bourgeois individual's initiation into experience and mental growth through a psychological double. In this development, the middle-class naif confronts cultural contradictions that thwart his own passage into full selfhood. His folk-double—who sometimes overshadows him—becomes the bourgeois character's fantasy of freedom from either the contradictions of middle-class life or its ethical limits. The naif is the product of the black experience in modern economic, cultural, and social life in the West. He enjoys the reflective experience made possible by the surplus wealth which underlies bourgeois life, when individuals have the security and leisure to read, write, and think. They are linked to cosmopolitan centers of culture through their manners and literacy, which give them aspirations to independence and full social citizenship that are necessarily frustrated in a segregated white American society. The cultivated black is often hindered by ties to patrons or middle-class American norms, which thwart his enjoyment of the freedoms represented by a wish-fulfilling folk-double. This double provides the equivalent of the romantic transcendence that Emerson, Whitman, and Thoreau often sought in nature. The black middle-class figure lives vicariously through the double; in doing so, the bourgeois naif provides the reader with an insight into his psychology of frustrated aspiration. This dilemma places the black bourgeois and his middle-class worldview squarely in what the late George Kent has movingly and profoundly called the "Adventure of Western Culture."[1]

In these fictional forms—which present far more rigorous depictions of desire than those provided by our current black critics and theologians—the naif is never able to give himself wholly to the fantasy freedom of his liberated brother or sister of soul, no matter how seductive the opportunity. Tea Cake in *Their Eyes Were Watching God*, Jubban in *Banana Bottom*, and Sula herself represent possible fulfillment desired by their counterparts. However, all of these novelists struggle to create sustained relationships between the folk and cultivated characters. Tea Cake must perish—for what kind of husband would he make in the long run? Sula sickens and dies, as do most people who commit themselves to lives of wholehearted sexual promiscuity. Jubban and Bita marry and have a child; yet late at night, when Jubban is done with work and Bita has read her Pascal, what do these two have to discuss? Moreover, the middle-class character's repressed fears of abandonment often return with a psychologically predictable violence. The concern of Janie's grandmother for her charge's security returns vehemently when Janie shoots Tea Cake. Nel must abandon both her husband and Sula, in order to raise her children alone—without the solace of a male lover or a woman friend. Inevitably, Nel returns to the isolation of her mother, Helene. The dream-work of freedom represented by the folk can never satisfy the naif's need for security. Finally, few of the folk characters can stand on their own as satisfying human beings worthy of the investment of the cultivated partner's commitment. Sula and Tea Cake have hardly any interest as characters outside of the more complicated psychologies of Nel and Janie. The same, of course, must be said for Jubban. Of all of these folk characters, only Jubban has anything like the conception of human dignity so central to the development of Nel and Janie.

The cultivated/folk pairing appears in major turn-of-the-century works like Du Bois, *The Souls of Black Folk*, Washington's *Up from Slavery*, and *The Autobiography of an Ex-Coloured Man*. The Ex-Coloured Man's swindling conductor companion, Washington's wily black informants, and Du Bois' Josie all show not only the possibilities but the tragic costs of the intellectual's investment in the folk world of experience. Characters in *Ex-Coloured Man* and *Up from Slavery* will in their own ways prey upon naive blacks, generous white patrons, and politicians. Writing from a different vantage, Du Bois in "The Meaning of Progress" gives us the most thoughtful version of this myth in his account of his response to the death of Josie. To pin one's hopes on the folk is to know that they will often die horrifying deaths in the dark Southern backwoods and the Northern urban ghetto. The middle-class naif's investment in his folk-double only makes him vulnerable to the worst kinds of trauma and separation. The South was never the lush paradise it seemed and the devil has built his city in the North.

These texts clearly alerted the early twentieth-century writers Jean Toomer, Fenton Johnson, and Langston Hughes to new ways of exploring the psychology of the black bourgeois. The Harlem Renaissance and its immediate aftermath in the thirties saw important developments of the cultivated/folk pairing in Hughes' *Not Without Laughter*, Zora Neale Hurston's *Their Eyes Were Watching God*, and Claude McKay's *Banana Bottom*. This psychologized discourse of the folk remained influential in the work of Ralph Ellison, and it plays an important role as a model for Toni Morrison's *Sula*.[2]

By the time she wrote *Sula*, Morrison had absorbed the literary tradition of Hurston, McKay, and Hughes and was prepared to employ and test its limits. As a symbol of wish-fulfillment, Sula temporarily provides therapeutic relief to Nel's deepest blocked self-fulfillment. On the one hand, the novel details a bourgeois continuity of households stemming from Helene to Nel and Nel's children. On the other hand, the same lineage is traced from Eva Peace to Sula. Nel and Sula's broken friendship is simply one more proof of the bourgeois individual's inability to achieve the vision of profound fulfillment embodied in the folk. On the other hand, the Peaces do not struggle to reproduce domestic order but rather live life to the fullest. To see the character Sula from that perspective is to see her as the product of folk life without the middle-class theodicy of providence and progress. The self's moment-by-moment experience becomes paramount. Self in the world of Sula and the Peaces is established through continuities of experience shared by Eva, Hannah, and Sula. Life is not lived for the achievement of delayed gratifications, but the enjoyment of the moments that have shaped other lives. And this vision, I suggest, represents a way of reading Sula and Nel's disrupted friendship as Nel's failure of empathy, her misunderstanding of those rich momentary meanings available in black life.

*Sula* turns upon the theme of thwarted middle-class selfhood. Like Bita and Janie, Nel seeks a fulfillment from which she is blocked by the contradiction of bourgeois life. However, here as in other books in this tradition, the quest for fulfillment demands the labors by which Helene and her grandmother attain middle-class life—as surely as fantasy emerges out of Nel's deepest self, to be nourished and blocked by middle-class life. It is a world of order, economic stability, filial relationships, and the relative leisure required for the development of inner reflection. Helene's grandmother has taken her north to establish a solid bourgeois life, in much the same way that Janie's grandmother sought stability for her charge. In Morrison's text, this stable social order is consolidated by Helene's marriage to

Wily Wright and Nel's marriage to Jude Greene, and the families so created. This social world allows for the daydreaming on the train and at home by which Nel discerns herself as unique, and repeats and reinterprets her past experience.

The Peaces, much like Angie and Jim Boy, do not struggle to reproduce domestic order but embody that vitality without which domestic life is sterile. All the same, it is only after the humiliations of her mother and herself in the South that Nel can establish a relationship with Sula. The trip's world, of contemptuous conductors, an obsequious Helene, physical insult, and repressed curiosity, introduces Nel to the spiritually thwarted life of the black bourgeoisie. Only now does Sula's value become clear to Nel. Nel plans to leave her home, a desire that comes to be embodied in her friendship with Sula:

> [T]o faraway places. Contemplating them was delicious. Leaving Medallion would be her goal. But that was before she met Sula, the girl she had seen for five years at Garfield Primary but never played with, never knew, because her mother said that Sula's mother was sooty. The trip, perhaps, or her new found me-ness, gave her the strength to cultivate a friend in spite of her mother.[3]

However, Morrison is careful to show that Nel's growing self-consciousness can only take place in Helene's bourgeois realm—that world of order, economic stability, relative leisure, and emotional equilibrium in which reflection is possible. This world first appears on the return trip home when the daydreaming Nel writes "me" on the train window. It persists in those moments when Nel and Sula are together in a home that Sula quite significantly seeks out, for needs that are similar to Nel's. Whatever self-consciousness Sula acquires would be impossible without the relative "peace" of Helene's dearly bought homestead.

Nevertheless, Sula's energies make possible the entrance into the world of extra-bourgeois experience that Nel craves. Indeed, Sula embodies the freedom that Nel hopes to achieve by leaving home. Sula will engage in the traveling sexual experiences and education that Nel's middle-class marriage forbids. In particular, Sula represents freedom from the bourgeois self's contradictions. Unconcerned with the self's boundaries, Sula sometimes appears, as many critics have noticed, to have no ego. As a young girl, Sula risks herself to defend Nel's selfhood in a way that Nel herself cannot. Although it paradoxically represents an act of self-defense (and castration of the male), Sula's public removal of her fingertip anticipates a self-destructiveness that ultimately comes to suggest the absence of the personality's power to unify its diverse elements into identity.

As a wish-fulfilling figure, Sula will subvert even as she fulfills Nel's aspirations for selfhood through marriage. However, Nel's vicarious fulfillment eventually signals the advent of Sula's destruction. She becomes a pariah among the women of Nel's neighborhood on account of her promiscuity. Sula is consequently condemned from the point of view of the middle-class world that helped to give her birth. Within this outrageous vision, Sula's self-destructive selfhood is too unstable for viability. Her loss of ego makes it impossible to extend her sexual experiences with Ajax into full relationships. She has only moments of sublime fulfillment followed by equal moments of dissolution—a dialectic that reflects the ebb and flow of selfhood in Emerson's "Self-Reliance," without the early Emerson's final assertion of self.

This dialectic of fulfillment and loss appears movingly and evocatively in the alternating ebb and flow of Sula's sooty self in lovemaking:

> Lovemaking seemed to her, at first, the creation of a special kind of joy. She thought she liked the sootiness of sex and its comedy; she laughed a great deal during the raucous beginnings, and rejected those lovers who regarded sex as healthy or beautiful. Sexual aesthetics bored her. Although she did not regard sex as ugly (ugliness was boring also), she liked to think of it as wicked. But as her experiences multiplied she realized that not only was it not wicked, it was not necessary for her to conjure up the idea of wickedness in order to participate fully. During the lovemaking she found and needed to find the cutting edge. When she left off cooperating with her body and began to assert herself in the act, particles of strength gathered in her like steel shavings drawn to a spacious magnetic center, forming a tight cluster that nothing, it seemed, could break. And there was utmost irony and outrage in lying under someone, in a position of surrender, feeling her own abiding strength and limitless power. But the cluster did break, fall apart, and in her panic to hold it together she leaped from the edge into soundlessness and went down howling, howling, in a stinging awareness of the endings of things: an eye of sorrow in the midst of all that hurricane rage of joy. There, in the center of that silence was not eternity but the death of time and loneliness so profound the word itself had no meaning. For loneliness assumed the absence of other people and the solitude she found in that desperate terrain had never admitted the possibility of other people. She wept then. Tears for the deaths of the littlest things: the castaway shoes of children; broken storms of marsh grass battered and drowned by the sea; prom photographs of dead women she never knew; wedding rings in pawnshop windows; the tidy bodies of Cornish hens in a nest of rice.[4]

The Cornish hens, rings, and prom photographs return to mock Sula in the inevitable postcoital depression just after she seems to have transcended the limits of domestic female life. Morrison's allusiveness draws out the further literary implications of this return to repressed daily existence. The self, as Emerson and Whitman well knew, not only broke with society in its most expansive mode but upon its contraction identified with the most negligible detritus of that world. The Emersonian moments of the self's fulfillment, marked by the loss of temporal sense and profound loneliness, are taken from the central sublime movement of "Circles," even as the imagery of the self's gradual dissolution becomes the erosion of self in Whitman's "As I Ebbed with the Ocean of Life."[5]

Sula's energies are a literary gesture, and Sula herself represents a literary energy that might help sustain, but never completely fulfill, creativity. The value of Sula's anti-middle-class experience is in its appreciation by a sensitive, educated audience. However, Morrison is able to treat Sula's transcendent if fleshly sexual experience with a psychological rigor lacking in Holloway's accounts of female psychology. Morrison records not only Sula's moments of sublimity, but also her moments of post-transcendent decline. It is an unlimited Way-Making freedom of sex that grants Sula her vision. After coitus, however, all animals are sad. And

Morrison does not neglect to make Sula pay her debt—at least in this case—to nature.

Sula's stories are appreciated by Nel in the same way that Morrison's novel will be appreciated by her audience. Like other folk figures, the bohemian Sula is not very interesting apart from her double, Nel. Indeed, Sula's own discovery of the nothingness—the final exhaustion of death—only becomes significant to her as new knowledge to be offered to the anxious, middle-class Nel:

> While in this state of weary anticipation, she noticed that she was not breathing, that her heart had stopped completely. A crease of fear touched her breast, for any second there was sure to be a violent explosion in her brain, a gasping for breath. Then she realized, or rather she sensed, that there was not going to be any pain. She was not breathing because she didn't have to. Her body did not need oxygen. She was dead.
> 
> Sula felt her face smiling. "Well, I'll be damned," she thought, "it didn't even hurt. Wait'll I tell Nel."[6]

This, of course, is Morrison's final ironic twist to Sula as a literary gesture (and a dislocated consciousness) that allows Nel to live vicariously beyond the limits of middle-class experience. Even in Sula's final moment of deathly transcendence of life, her significance depends upon Nel's middle-class point of view—thus consolidating the principle underlying Morrison's use of folk discourse. Sula's ultimate recognition of her role as an extension of Nel's consciousness implicitly celebrates the powers and sexuality of the middle-class world that gives that consciousness birth. *Sula* gains power from Morrison's vision of a creativity that emanates from a stable domestic self. Her novel succeeds no less because of her willingness to put those powers to a grim realistic test.

The notion of the folk as a romantic projection also implies an actual existence which the imagination can transform, a reality based in the world's economies of wealth, work, and human suffering. The folk are a nonentity without the spiritualizing energy of the bourgeois naif. Their emptiness and barren physicality are vividly represented by Morrison's black folk men, both in *Sula* and elsewhere, who persistently occupy a low level of existence: they live purely on what Emerson might call the level of commodity. This central proposition is powerfully developed in Morrison's fictional world of necessary matriarchies where few men work—a world that reproduces E. Franklin Frazier's "cities of destruction" that swallowed the Southern transplants during the Great Migration.[7] Men rarely function in the book's world as workers who sustain the home through wages; the ones who do, such as Wily Wright and Jude, are associated with Helene and Nel, the novel's marginal bourgeoises. And even these male figures are peripheral. Wily Wright is symbolically absent from home most of the time. The majority of adult men in the folk world of the Peaces are, like Ajax, Tar Baby, and Jude, engaged in menial labor. No young man treated in the novel grows up to be a physically or mentally full-fledged man. The bland, nearly subhuman identical Deweys are, of course, the book's most important case in point.

Aware of the utter insignificance of men in their world, the women of the Peace family symbolically flaunt their perception of men as nonentities except for sexual enjoyment. Sula will accidentally kill Chicken Little in an incident that echoes Eva's murder of her son Plum. Indeed, Eva must kill her son so that he will not enter her womb as a vestigial fetus—and not insignificantly—as a man. There is no sign that this death permanently traumatizes Eva or anyone in the family, although she does eventually see her daughter's death-by-burning as a judgment. This lack of normal human response is, however, wholly plausible in Morrison's fictional world. Men are mere appendages, to be shucked off when they are no longer needed, like Eva's own (rather phallic) leg.

Although Jude impregnates Nel and gives her children, he cannot give her a vision of life beyond her social limitations, the vision and experience that she sought as a young girl. These are embodied in Sula, who not only goes to college but returns to lead an energetic sexual life. Sula forces the destruction of Nel and Jude's marriage, leading Nel ultimately to acknowledge the importance of their girlhood friendship. Sula is—to draw ironically on Gates' language—a seminal imaginative figure. Not surprisingly, she displaces Nel's man. Nel's imaginative force lives symbolically through Sula's upsurges of sexual creativity, transcending the conventionally understood gender limitations of women. And Nel is also a stand-in for both writer and reader, the bystander and amanuensis who takes the story down. Nel and Sula don't require men in their relationship because their identity—in a strangely androgynous way—includes male powers.

Sula's dynamism, embodied in the expanding circles of energetic orgasms or powerful literary expression, is at the book's end translated into Nel's circling cries of "We was girls together." Here Sula is both the masculine stone and the feminine circling water. This embodies not only the story's deepest truth, but the process by which the fable has disseminated itself first to Nel and later its audience. In calling attention to the production of Sula's story itself, Morrison anticipates Gates' view of tradition as a juggling of signs. She does, in fact, take the tradition of the folk, reduce it to counters, and work them into complicated fugues and variations. No matter how much Morrison has borrowed from methods of structuralism, she is at pains to show that this text did not produce itself. It is the fruit of deeply human economies of money, sex, and pain. Such grounding does not appear in Gates' criticism. Nor did Morrison's future texts always reach the fullness and moral standard of *Sula*.

## Part Two

Ironically, the middle-class discourse of the folk in works like *Sula* reinstates the distance that literacy and cultivation create between acculturated and dispossessed blacks. The romance of the folk repeats and at times seems to celebrate the central truth of black Americanization. The energies of cultivated blacks are directed toward ultimately frustrated marriages and affairs. This dramatic structure, while articulating a powerful psychology, nevertheless leaves us with hollowed-out or reduced notions of the bourgeois and folk, both as social conditions and as models for characterization. Even a novel as rich as *Sula* sometimes threatens to collapse into the juggling of themes and counter-themes.

Significantly, this reductionism has been the weakest aspect of Morrison's work, particularly in books building upon the folk-double, such as *Paradise*. Toni Morrison, it is frequently observed, owes much of her lush literary style to Jean Toomer's *Cane*. However, she is also the beneficiary of his reductive middle-class grotesques like Rhobert, Dan, and Avey. Morrison's caricatures in *Sula*—for instance the Deweys and the Dewey-like clerks in the integrated stories—alert us to how her vital myths may harden into ideological markers. Once the play of binaries has started, the possibility of complex moral reasoning is lost in Morrison's novels. What remains is the up and down melodrama of middle-class characters who make fulfilling or unfulfilling choices *vis-à-vis* the novel's primitive folk.

Morrison's powerful female psychology of Sula gives the book a substance which is lacking in *Paradise*. Here the cultivated/folk pairing becomes merely a play of shallow counters that blunts Sula's character and prevents the moral discriminations needed in her world. On the other hand, the reduction of the world to a set of codes gives the fiction a fashionable postmodern, post-structuralist aura. However, the book as a whole is intellectually and ethically barren. In *Paradise*, the attack of the bourgeois citizens upon a group of runaway bohemian women is not given the psychological depth of a serious moral inquiry. The enigma of the novel's simultaneous highbrow and lowbrow success may be explained by its appeal both to devotees of literary abstraction and to more melodramatically inclined appetites. One suspects Morrison aims this literary mélange more at the marketplace than at the reflective reader.

This broad appeal is the result of an oddly mixed method. Like Faulkner of *The Sound and the Fury*, Morrison's work evokes the passage from traditional rural life to modernity with its dislocation, loss of perspective, and the derangement of vestigial male roles and eroding social structures. However, these myths are inevitably shaped into melodramatic conflicts, emotional appeals, and lyrical expostulation. Although Morrison is a child of Virginia Woolf, she is also, in some sense, the daughter of Harriet Beecher Stowe. *Paradise* is attractive not only for its portraits of the strains of migration and cultural transformation, but also for its seductive flow of prose, stock images of twentieth-century black life, and sentimental affirmation. This blend of high and low literary rhetoric accounts for the nearly iconic status of her writing as an accessible mirror for the nation's racial life. Yet even as Morrison creates a postmodernist myth of African-American history, sentimentality and sensationalism undermine her moral authority. The novel *Paradise* is indeed weakened throughout by such contradictions.

In its epic scope, *Paradise* revives Morrison's well-established fable of an African-American life shaped by mass movement. Braving the frontier, lawless white settlers, and unreceptive black communities, a close-knit network of families, which included Morgans, Fleetwoods, DuPres, Jurys, and Blackhorses, first settled in 1910 in Haven and next in 1950 in Ruby, Oklahoma. After rejection by black settlers in surrounding communities, the inhabitants of Haven and Ruby founded prosperous farming towns. The society created by the migrant Louisianans and their descendents is a material, religious, and communal haven founded on values symbolized by banks, churches, and a ceremonial oven that lie at the center of Ruby. The founding fathers' utopian impulse is embodied by the Morgan twins—allegorically named Deacon and Stewart—who run a bank that ultimately hires Deacon's wayward son, K. D. Both serve the Christian goal of establishing a city of God in Oklahoma.

One immediately recognizes this world, drawn from the symbolic psychologies of Morrison's corpus. Here, the Oklahoman posterity of transient Louisianans face the inevitable aftermath of migration: dislocation and reverie, trauma and idealization. *Paradise* thus resonates with the complicated memories of the Great Migration that underlie the Breedloves' urban world in *The Bluest Eye*, Helene Wright's bourgeois Ohio enclave in *Sula*, and the Northern city of *Song of Solomon*. Like the Breedloves, the Wrights, and Macon Dead, the townspeople of Ruby remember an earlier Southern world from which they have been displaced. However, confrontation with the past is particularly intense in Ruby, where the elders must pass their utopian values and fierce resentments on to a new generation.

Tension mounts as Ruby's youths, inspired by the values of the late sixties and early seventies, defy their parents, deface the ceremonial oven, and mimic the gestures of the period's Black Power movement. The older generation of men finds release in their hatred of a group of marginal women who have created their own counter-bourgeois paradise in a convent outside of town. These women are also displaced victims with tragic histories: Consolata, raised by the convent's original nuns; Pallas, a teenage runaway; Seneca, whose boyfriend has recently entered prison; and Mavis, a mother who has accidentally killed two of her children. Experiencing the traumas of abusive men, they have escaped to a safe refuge and sexualized conflict with each other—a world of feminist bohemian play. Inevitably, the women come to represent the deviancy that the townspeople fear in their young people, and the convent is destroyed.

The conflict between the townspeople and the marginal women spills over into a melodramatic scene, motivated as much by the logic of sexual jealousy as by the traditions of Ruby. In this climax, situated at the book's beginning and near its end, men from the town's leading families invade the convent and shoot a number of the women. The two paradises, situated so uneasily next to each other, are destroyed in a vindication of the townspeople's values. But more to the point is the symbolic rape: a fierce male entry into a feminine enclave. In the postcoital aftermath, the luridly phallic guns droop, and eventually the proud utopian spirit and macho swagger of Ruby's leading men erode. This explosive crisis ends in a downturn that stems from not only moral reflection but also the scene's sexual rhythms. Finally, in the book's conclusion, the convent women who escape are vindicated as empowered autonomous individuals, now free to begin significant lives.

This melodrama is motivated by a set of myths that frequently receive sensationalistic treatment in Morrison's fiction. Like Nel and Sula, and Geraldine and the black community in *The Bluest Eye*, the male elders of Ruby are engaged in a black bourgeois striving that leads them to reject and envy a more marginal life whose freedoms they will never enjoy. Mimicking the values of a white society to which they will never gain entrance, Deacon Morgan—like Nel and Helene Wright in *Sula*, and Macon Dead in *Song of Solomon*—finds himself in a problematic relationship to a blackness that both attracts and repels him as a middle-class observer. The harassment of the convent's Sula-like women, with their short skirts, tight tops, and garish makeup, recalls the black community's hostility toward Sula herself, or Pecola Breedlove in *The Bluest Eye*. The final triumph of Gigi, Pallas, and Mavis only asserts that of marginal vitality over the restrictions of a utopian bourgeois "paradise."

This nexus of mythic and sentimental justification, however, obscures more serious issues which the novel does not engage. One hears the eerie echoes of Richard Wright's *Native Son* in the book's first sentence: "They shoot the white girl first." Has Ruby's history of rejection and displacement dehumanized the elders in such a way as to motivate the shockingly brutal killings of the climax? Has it robbed them of the autonomy necessary for moral action? The characterization of Mavis and Gigi implicitly asks whether a history of traumatic relationships and wayward drifting can be redeemed as the autonomous female personhood celebrated in the novel's final pages. Do they finally come to possess a true utopian impulse that will eventually create an authentic paradise? The novel's melodramatic logic also evades other problems of morality and sympathy. Take, for example, the relationship between Deacon Morgan and Consolata. Should this dalliance win our sympathy for Morgan's experiments beyond the community's Puritan morality? Or was the affair only an example of patriarchal manipulation? Despite the poetry of Morrison's account of this love, the questions raised by the plot remain unanswered. There is a similar moral and psychological incoherence in Mavis, whose exploits are lyrically narrated at the book's beginning and sentimentally affirmed at the book's end. In Morrison's poetic account of a woman who has abandoned her family after the accidental death of two babies, we see the creation of a tough independence. How, we still ask, has this woman made peace with her separation from the rest of her children? What has been the cost of her self-sufficiency? In the trauma of her loss, does her humanity require explanations beyond her narrowly personal world?

Not surprisingly, reviewers have seemed forced to choose between the book's spectacular lyricality and sentimentality, its mechanical myths and its moral evasions. One may note the lush language and seemingly schematic structure, its moral complexities and its florid style. Morrison's magical word poetry, which attracts some, clearly mystifies important issues of plot and character for others. To be sure, *Paradise* is a combination of poetry and myth. The opening account of Mavis' escape, her magical adventures on the road, and her discovery of a feminist paradise is riveting as a story of fall and secular salvation on her own terms. And this high poetry is abetted by Morrison's myth of bourgeois constrictions and the freedom of the marginal. Yet as her authorial presence and narrative personae lose their moral sensitivity, her myths of "black experience" harden into poetic dogmas. In this process, Morrison herself displays an eroding sense of the complexity of her subjects.

This hardening of the imagination has become an increasing danger and tendency in Morrison's work. In her literary political mythology, all middle-class blacks become dead grotesques. The poor and socially unacceptable have, by contrast, a primitive sexual vitality, or at least its residue, which offers itself as a redemption for the middle class. Morrison's love triangle in *Paradise* turns on this myth. However, this book has insufficient complexity of moral and social perspective to make this psychology more than superficially vivid. Her characters' lack of inwardness, and its suggestion of moral inertness, perilously approach a commodified dehumanization unmitigated by the book's appeal to such varied tastes.

This is not a new problem in recent African-American literary tradition. James Baldwin, in considering Richard Wright's affirmative ending in *Native Son*, observed that Bigger Thomas remained—despite his existential discovery—a dehumanized character, choosing a theology that denied him life. The problem of fiction, as Baldwin put it, was the acceptance of the full burden of one's humanity. One way of criticizing the ending of *Paradise* is to ask what it might mean for Deacon and Mavis to do so. Among other things, such acceptance might require sober skepticism about human aspiration, a balanced understanding of tragedy, and a more complicated moral response to social conundrums. On this level of moral complexity, *Paradise*, like some other late Morrison fiction, is a failure. Horrific acts described melodramatically with a certain moral evasiveness have become Morrison's stock in trade. She displays an aesthetic impulse that, like the elder townsmen of Ruby, considers itself beyond the reach of serious ethical consideration. She allows the Way-Making tendencies of her style and fictional vision much of the freedom that she denies the elder townsmen. The more closely one examines the bare bones of *Paradise*, the more one suspects that Morrison provides a basically melodramatic response to our national tragedy. It suggests that the knotty dilemmas of the African-American experience are not subjects for Morrison's ethical intelligence, but sites for moral and intellectual escape, and ultimately undisciplined fantasy. She does not submit her wish-fulfilling images of human wholeness and freedom to a sufficiently rigorous test of ethical or psychological reality. She fashions her accounts with an appealing, but ultimately unsatisfying, license.

# Chapter Nine

# White Patrons, Black Clients, and Middle-Class Apocalypse

PART OF THE WIDE RECEPTION ACCORDED SIGNIFYING is the readiness of upper-class white academics to understand black bourgeois life as a self-contradictory proposition. This does not, I think, gain its wide credence from images of the French *évolué*, the British Wog, or the black bourgeoisie of Durham, North Carolina, depicted by E. Franklin Frazier.[1] The notion of mixed-up black middle-class life follows from a twentieth-century critique of America's inherited WASP culture. This critique has, over the past century, been made by the Lost Generation in France and such critics as H. L. Mencken and Sinclair Lewis. Assuming the black bourgeoisie to be engaged in an impossible task of Americanization, white intellectuals easily accept the black culture of rap as "authentically" and "naturally" black. The serious black intellectual becomes deeply problematic for white audiences who, in our present age of inequality, tend to assume that anything but a culturally or politically dysfunctional black person is impossible. The same may be said for the idea of a serious black social, political, and cultural self-consciousness—an impossible goal to which no realistic African American may be expected to aspire, in the eyes of American intellectual culture with its racial primitivism. These views provide a just basis for a white-dominated society's social knowledge. For a widespread black self-consciousness would complicate American life in unimaginable ways.

The apocalypticism which pervades the movie *Glory* owes its easy plausibility to the blithe white acceptance of black middle-class alienation and internal division as responses to the civilizing process. The deference with which the battle-weary Colonel Shaw accedes to the grim pessimism of Buck corresponds to the current white acceptance of the black sensibility embodied in signifying. Cynicism is a believable response to internal division. And white intellectuals often seem undisturbed by the prospect that nothing more than disingenuous exchange may result from their communication with blacks. Cynicism about communication rapidly infects both parties. In such an atmosphere of bad faith, apocalyptic anger easily passes for an authentic expression of a sincerely held point of view, anger being an emotion that cynics disdain. It is in this rhetorical context that signifying and its sensibility flourish.

The great power of *Glory* emerges as the film links this rhetoric of disingenuous communication to the American political ideal of consensus. Even this late in secular America, the ideal has a biblical ring: "Come now, and let us reason together, saith the LORD: though your sins be as scarlet, they shall be as white as snow; though they be red like crimson, they shall be as wool" (Isaiah 1:18).

The selection of a black battalion as the subject for this movie, what Sacvan Bercovitch has called a ritual of consensus, is deeply significant.[2] The Civil War is the American ur-struggle for such political community. In a democratic nation where the people are sovereign, the army—with its rituals of acculturation, its traditions of oratory, its ordered pattern of social action, and its collective aims—is perhaps our deepest image of the possibility of national unity. Black alienation is, it now seems, one more touchstone of the national consensus.

American national community has always been beset by the tragedy of race. Its symbolic representation now takes many highly commercialized and politicized forms. This would be evident alone from our careful monitoring of racial percentages in the armed services. But no one who now reads the Declaration of Independence can help but wonder whether the social contract, as Locke and the founding fathers understood it, is actually in force in certain neighborhoods in Brooklyn, the Bronx, and Upper Manhattan. In what sense does the American polity include the large numbers of black lumpen males who do not vote, and who routinely find themselves in prison? Even more to the point is the absence of powerful cultural symbols that convincingly cut across racial lines. The most pervasive such image of American political cohesion has been the Puritan notion of a covenanted America.

It is impossible not to regard Martin Luther King's "I Have a Dream," with its hopeful jeremiadic language, as a kind of anachronism. As the rate of murder and imprisonment among black males climbs, one finds more relevance in Baldwin's eschatological vision of the fire next time, in Stokely Carmichael's violent and dramatic despair in the late sixties, and in the imprisoned H. Rap Brown's threat to "burn America down if America don't come round." Although the black urban poor may not be in direct touch with the Protestant theological underpinnings of this discourse, they have nonetheless a revised standard version in the rap culture disseminated on MTV, a culture that routinely celebrates the marginality of the African-American world by converting it into prophecy or, more often, diverting play. If the black lumpen are caught in short-lived materialistic Babylon, then they can at least loose themselves in fantasy to the glitter of Mariah Carey, or thrive vicariously on the racist prophecies of Adidas-clad and -shod rap groups.

Despite its self-conscious claims to be political, the world of rap is curiously devoid of any politics by which people may be organized for coherent action.

Rap is far too improvisational and *ad hoc* to serve a powerful political purpose. Its techniques and social knowledge are stored in the archives of CD collections. But there are limits to how much such meager musical expression can hold, and how broad a range of information its audience seeks. The problem of creating a common American political culture traditionally comes to the fore, paradoxically, in periods of racial integration. What does it mean for blacks to internalize a system of religious and political values that pointedly do not work for them? This contradiction was the subject of several early twentieth-century considerations of black middle-class culture, the novels of Nella Larsen for example.

However, in the absence of a powerful critical realism in African-American fiction, this kind of scrutiny of present-day black middle-class life for the most part goes lacking. It is therefore not surprising that both blacks and whites experience their deepest anxieties as they approach the subjection of black Americanization. As African-American literary scholarship becomes more thorough and sophisticated in its historical coverage, it is emerging that in periods of ethnic rapprochement and the ensuing racial tensions, the impulse to Americanize is most furiously repressed: witness the Harlem Renaissance—the black leftist experience of the thirties and forties, as depicted in Wright, Ellison, and others—and present-day integrated America.

Mid-nineteenth-century abolitionist works—Douglass' *My Bondage and My Freedom*, Harriet Wilson's *Our Nig*, and Martin Delaney's *Blake*—are beginning to appear as anticipations of our contemporary predicament, the interaction of blacks and upper-class whites in the politically charged arenas of home, political organization, and church. As literary critics and historians examine these works more deeply, the tensions and behavior that have characterized life in the integrated campuses of the better universities since the sixties are thrown into sharp relief. The militant defiance of sympathetic white liberals, a deepening cynicism about the possibility of a truly integrated social order, and the emergence of various strains of black nationalism all shaped the 1850s and 1860s. There is a strangely contemporary ring to the phony black ex-slave who hustles the heroine in *Our Nig*; to Frederick Douglass' increasing sensitivity to abolitionists' slights of his diction; and, of course, to the fascination with folk culture that begins with figures like Charlotte Forten Grimke and finds its nineteenth-century apotheosis in Charles Chesnutt and Paul Lawrence Dunbar. In these works, the interaction between blacks and progressive white elites produced paradoxically a rich mosaic of intellectual and cultural variations within black society itself. Predictably, the various psychological patterns of interracial life—surely an important black literary subject—appear in these texts. However, while expressing the ultimate separation of black from white life, these books also dramatize what the two cultures most profoundly shared—the evangelically fueled expectation of apocalypse that was fulfilled in the Civil War and the racial conflicts of the early twentieth century. Read thus, these authors become, however strangely, our contemporaries.

The movie *Glory*—largely based, the credits tell us, on the papers of Robert Shaw—is significant because it attempts to dramatize *inter alia* the socialization of black soldiers in the increasingly problematic racial world of the 1860s, looking back to the apocalyptic vision of the 1850s and ahead to postbellum corruption. In its shrewd representation of the attempt to impose a traditional Protestant American consensus upon blacks, *Glory* strains to provide its viewers with a vision of common political destiny. Given the educative process of the army, the weight of New England liberal Protestantism, the influence of a genteel benevolence, what can blacks and whites come to share? This question is asked over and over again in works like Booker T. Washington's *Up from Slavery* and for that matter Du Bois' *The Souls of Black Folk*, as well as in the essays of James Baldwin—who appears, the more I read him, ever closer to the evangelical world of the late nineteenth century despite his clear intellectual and ethical propinquity to Henry James. A racial consensus that will not compromise African-American dignity in patronage relations is indeed not only a question, but a kind of challenge, that makes Du Bois (in *The Souls of Black Folk*) and James Weldon Johnson (in *Autobiography of an Ex-Coloured Man*) look back nostalgically to the intimate relationships between masters and privileged house slaves. This matter may be the most tragic American schism, a great national divide that divides blacks at least as much as it separates the two races from each other.

 Like one of the recently recovered mid-century African-American texts, *Glory* is tricked out in all of the ideological, generational, racial, social, and political trimmings of the 1830s, 40s, and 50s. The movie faithfully captures the apocalyptic character of the antislavery movement in the late fifties and early sixties, emphasizing Robert Shaw's duty-bound ethos that separates him from his genteel abolitionist parents, who stand in the crowd as he marches his black soldiers off to war. Frederick Douglass appears, as we increasingly know him, already the *éminence grise* suggested by his halo of grayish-white hair. Although Douglass states that his public goal is to give dignity to his race, his single-mindedness seems qualified: his ability to place himself in strategic symbolic spots, the upper-class white women fluttering in the outer rooms around the parlor where he holds forth, the deference shown him by upper-class abolitionists—all suggest a contemporary Douglass, the self-made man now on the make for political advantage. He has already become that most enigmatic of figures—a black leader—necessarily dependent upon white liberal patronage for his influence, drawing pointedly upon the most enlightened populace's perception of the masses' plight, and finally aloof from the most dangerous parts of the upcoming fray.

 Two figures stand out in the ranks. Buck is a runaway Tennessee slave, played by Denzel Washington. In the stereotypical guise of the nineteenth-century free black, he is nonetheless the image of the twentieth-century urban black lumpen, the essence of anomic resistance against all impositions of social and cultural order. Thomas is a young free black, son of free parents, who also serves as an enlisted man in Shaw's company. He, too, is a recognizable nineteenth-century type: a cultivated genteel black like the son of James Forten, or even the descendent of Frederick Douglass might have been. His decision to enlist in a black company is altogether typical of the black nineteenth-century bourgeois movement to participate in the uplift of the race. Thomas is motivated by the same genteel race-consciousness that we find in Charlotte Forten, Maria Stewart, and the many antebellum blacks who went south to help their fellows after the war.

*Glory* follows a cultivated, sensitive young man into war; in Shaw's case, however, this wholly typical story resounds with a different social significance. His attempt to create a regiment of fighting black men must counter a Northern antebellum culture that is deeply suspicious of black moral and intellectual ability, and the proposition that blacks can be citizens. At stake, then, is the larger question of whether black soldiers can be viable participants in the social order. Shaw accomplishes his goal with harsh discipline and deep human sympathy. He unrelentingly whips his raw black recruits into shape, all the while admiring the depth—indeed, the poetry—of the African-American folk, as a cultivated Northern liberal like Whittier might be expected to do. The regimen is imposed with especial harshness upon Shaw's friend Thomas, with whom he has grown up and shares a highbrow taste for Hawthorne and Emerson. At the same time, Shaw shows great compassion, carefully supervising the recovery of the deserter Buck after a fierce flogging; wisely choosing the oldest and most sensitive black soldier as his noncommissioned sergeant; and abandoning his horse to lead his men to battle on foot in the final apocalyptic scene.

Shaw symbolizes the civilizing force of abolitionist culture as encountered by blacks in the Civil War and afterwards in the late nineteenth and early twentieth centuries. In perhaps the only *mission civilatrice* that the United States has ever known, these New England missionaries brought an exemplary mixture of discipline and mercy as they imposed their civic order upon black Southern charges at Hampton Institute, Howard, Tuskegee, and Fisk. This tough-minded benevolence was blended with the Protestant humanity best known from figures like General Armstrong in *Up from Slavery*, and underpinning the Puritan Victorian values that blacks and whites would harmoniously share in these institutions. A nostalgia for this deferential civic order—still known to many black graduates and associates of the schools above—may be the deepest appeal of *Glory*. At bottom, the movie claims that the civic virtues of antebellum New England constitute the true ground of consensus between blacks and whites. These transplanted New England values are celebrated most explicitly in the contrast between Shaw's troops and the Jay Hawker-led band of black contrabands who pillage a rebel community inhabited only by women. Jay Hawker, who knows blacks only as dehumanized and thinks of them as children, represents a far more inhumane and immoral style of paternalism than does Shaw. And the symbolic torching of the community by Shaw's troops is a reflection of their commander's character, discipline, attitudes toward blacks, and, most significantly, the tragic meaning of war that has been communicated to the people whom Jay Hawker sees as not people at all.

As part of his initiation, Shaw predictably learns to engage and manipulate the most cynical—indeed, the most evil—aspects of the war department. He confronts the facts of military life that would come to the fore in the Grant administration. The erstwhile innocent young commander soon acquires the skill to intimidate incompetents who keep necessary supplies from his men and to bully immoral commanders to get his troop's first combat assignment. He relies on a racist Irish sergeant for the raw force with which to whip Thomas and the rest into shape. And as he matures in his command, making the necessary compromises with the world, Shaw acquires the world-weary sense of tragedy that makes plausible his acceptance of Buck's final cynical curse.

If Shaw's toughness, kindness, discipline, and tragic sense ally him with Booker T. Washington's Mrs. Ruffin and General Armstrong, his idealism still makes him a type of Mr. Norton in Ellison's *Invisible Man*. The severe yet paternal figures who govern Booker T. Washington and push him to high competence, an acute moral sense, and a benevolent spirit of institution building are also, of course, an innocent audience to be manipulated by crafty blacks, such as Washington himself. Furthermore, *Up from Slavery* and *Invisible Man* alert us to how New England paternalism can go sour in its tendency to project an ethnocentric destiny upon its objects, evade reality through its attempts at empathy, and create artificial and sometimes arbitrary patterns of authority. Significantly, the movie devotes significant time to the perspective of the runaway slave, Buck, who submits Shaw's ethos to the kind of scrutiny that it would be given by twentieth-century black authors. Although Buck is in some sense the street-wise urban tough we associate with Bed-Stuy and Watts, his cynicism and critical attitude toward Thomas' acceptance of the upper-class New England worldview give him a very contemporary legitimacy. Buck's vision represents the consistent deepening of an important insight that typically emerges in antebellum slave narratives, particularly the abolitionist narratives of the forties and fifties: the sense that the relationship between master and slave, and indeed that between white and black, is socially constructed, fictional. The slave narrators in works by Douglass, the Crafts, the Penningtons, and Delaney's novel *Blake* come to grasp what Peter Berger calls the "social knowledge" that supports racist white institutions and their constituent roles.

This realization, with all its sensitivity to anomie, appears as much in Buck as in the narratives of William and Ellen Craft, and more so than in Pennington and Douglass' first narrative. It makes what William Andrews has called the slave narrator's acceptance of marginality in the 1850s an intellectually and morally plausible stance. Much of recent African-American criticism celebrates the trickster, who often has the same sociological insight. As Denzel Washington's wonderful characterization of Buck shows, this perception comes not only with explanatory power but also tragic alienation. And the deepest cost of this slippery slope to cynicism is revealed in the blunt curse with which Buck otherwise inexplicably ends his moving confession that the black regiment has been his only family.

With Buck's help we come to see how Shaw's idealism is tempered by existence in a social world fraught with racism, class loyalties, and a paternalism that the young commander willy-nilly shares. Shaw, as we see him through Buck's eyes, is a creation of an oppressive system that, despite its mercies, still has much in common with its Southern adversary. The constraints of human nature and society had, by the 1850s, tempered the idealism of Shaw's hero, Emerson. And Buck's insight is not unlike the later wisdom of the sage of Concord. Predictably, then, the compromises revealed by Shaw's initiation into maturity lead Buck to reject the role of flag-bearer, symbolic carrier of the values of a society that will, despite his best efforts, continue to oppress him.

Paradoxically, however, much of the audience's sympathy for Buck comes from those characteristics that he shares with Shaw. The moral independence that fuels Shaw's idealism also appears in Buck's rejection of Thomas for accepting the white world in which he has been reared a genteel free black. We inevitably respect Buck for being free of the white fathers in ways that Thomas, Frederick Douglass, and perhaps Shaw himself are not. In its moral outrage, its utter insistence upon manly autonomy, and its impatience with merely social formalities, Buck's vision is not only a black consciousness that links him with Richard Wright and Malcolm X, but a deeply American individualism that has as many links with the earlier revolution of Shaw's "old fellows" as it does with the play revolts of Baraka.

Predictably Thomas, the black intellectual, is the film's most problematic character. In Boston today he might be mistaken for a tutor in American civilization at Winthrop House. At its beginning, *Glory* comes dangerously close to making him a buffoon, a supercilious free man who looks down upon the ignorance of his black brother. In the end, however, he has willingly submitted to the command of Shaw and embraced a purely idealistic patriotism (which is a little hard to take from a black man sophisticated enough to read Hawthorne). Not surprisingly, the film seems out of its depth in the treatment of what such a character's intellectual and psychological frames of reference might be. There is little mention of the colonization movements and the nationalism of figures like Martin Delaney, all issues that might have exercised a Thomas. What he would have thought of *Uncle Tom's Cabin* is really more to the point than any admiration he might have of Emerson. Thomas' tearful empathy with the black culture to which he earlier condescended is plausible; but given the ironic intelligence he has earlier revealed, we expect a richer, more critical perspective of his predicament. This is especially true because Thomas, unlike Buck, can read: we have it on the authority of Pennington and Douglass that literacy promoted a radical change of consciousness. It was this which stimulated Douglass' insight into the nature of slavery, but it also enabled him, as we see in *My Bondage and Freedom*, to explore his experience with white paternalism once a free man. Literacy was not seen by nineteenth-century blacks like Thomas as a means of assimilation—a notion that the film's makers seem to have gleaned from the more vulgar black nationalists of the 1960s. Rather, literacy was the vehicle for a far deeper understanding of the world than could be otherwise had. This was bound to be most traumatic for those who, like Douglass and Charlotte Forten, had the closest ties to white paternalists. It is precisely this tension that is lacking in Thomas. One now realizes how hard it is for any American artist to dramatize a kind of black intelligence that still does not fit into conventional definitions that are, after all, based on the fundamental—and quite typically American—assumption that whites are intellectually and morally superior to blacks.

The movie, of course, ends upon a note of consensus. Buck's black consciousness and Shaw's tragic vision lead to a final revelation of the utter ineradicability of racism in America. Buck has this realization first, sitting beside a body of water in a romantic nineteenth-century attitude which emphasizes the immensity of being that his new consciousness has given him. In the film's most profound reversal of its ethos of paternalism, Buck tells Shaw that, despite the company's best efforts, the blacks' plight will be the same, although Shaw himself will go back to Boston. Shaw, who has seen enough racism to agree, affirms the runaway slave's perception that the only means of resolving the national sin is to "ante up" and "kick in." Turning one's hand becomes a doomed, apocalyptic march against heavy fortifications, a foretaste and hastening of the Day of Judgment.

Within this vision, the fate of the nation has been forgotten; however, this too is another wholly traditional American appeal to the prophet Isaiah (40:21–23):

> Have ye not known? Have ye not heard? Hath it not been told you from the beginning? have ye not understood from the foundations of the earth?
> It is he that sitteth upon the circle of the earth, and the inhabitants thereof are as grasshoppers; that stretcheth out the heavens as a curtain, and spreadeth them out as a tent to dwell in:
> That bringeth the princes to nothing; he maketh the judges of the earth as vanity.

Thus, despite the clear appeal to the apocalyptic rhetoric of the "Battle Hymn of the Republic" (to which the title *Glory* clearly refers), this movie comes down on a very Hawthornian insight. An accepting knowledge of the sin of racism must be internalized, engaged, and endured by all Americans, black and white. Like the celebration of evil encountered by young Goodman Brown on his trip into the forest, one's reconciliation to the country's universal immersion in racism is, in the movie's view, the true American consensus on matters of race. Such shared wisdom to which lumpen black and Brahmin white all readily admit in our society should give us pause. If we believe that knowledge of the inevitability of racism is all that blacks and whites truly share, our plight is grim.

# Section Four

# Older Exemplars

The strengths and limitations of signifying as rhetoric, theory, and practice lead us directly to the virtues of the older generation of artists and critics. The best of them—Benjamin Mays, Robert Hayden, Charles Chesnutt, and Langston Hughes—saw themselves self-consciously engaged in the translation of a cosmopolitan Western culture into African-American intellectual life. They thought, quite correctly, that the various literary and rhetorical structures of the last two thousand years had acquired an institutional wisdom. Most impressive is not their acceptance of this belief, but their willingness to put it to the test in that segregated world where the folk could not be avoided—especially in the deeply traumatic movement from the rural South to the urban North, the Great Migration. Interracial contact, moreover, forced them into an intimacy with whites whereby, despite whatever racist feelings existed, they shared bonds of literature, politics, theology, and sociology. These bonds compelled a closeness that led to the intimacies with whites that Langston Hughes and Richard Wright clearly enjoyed. This intimacy, in turn, was the basis for a more convincing and powerful exploration of interracial race relations than we have seen since. This exploration, under such conditions, is perhaps their greatest achievement.

# Chapter Ten

# Theology and Black Literature
## The Early Work of Benjamin Mays

I FIRST ENCOUNTERED BENJAMIN MAYS' *The Negro's God as Reflected in His Literature* as a graduate student at the University of Chicago in the early and middle 1970s. Rambling through the stacks on late Friday and Saturday nights, I pursued my first and only course in African-American Studies in the library stacks. Deep in Regenstein Library, I encountered the dissertations or first editions of works by the sociologists E. Franklin Frazier and Charles Johnson, the historian Vincent Harding, the literary critic Benjamin Brawley, the psychologist Allison Davis, and the linguist Lorenzo Dow Turner. I had not thought before of Mays' life as a student at the University of Chicago, although I knew that he matriculated at the school.

I frequently wandered the streets of Woodlawn and Kenwood surrounding the University of Chicago's Hyde Park campus. It was slowly becoming a source of amazement to me that part of the modernist revolution in African-American literature and art had transpired in the sensibilities of black intellectuals walking through this very ghetto. I could still only vaguely conceive of the Great Migration, however, that extraordinary mass American movement that had brought my parents to Cleveland from Hampton, Virginia. I did not connect the flamboyant rituals I saw in the Sunday services of black churches—occasionally I would see the bent form of Leon Forrest taking notes in the back of the sanctuary—with the religions of the South. My parents had left this world behind them, and often expressed their horror at hearing those moans in the middle-class churches of the North. I myself had thought to escape this Southern world of black primitive religion, as my parents called it, and its Northern residue in New Haven. I could not have been more mistaken.

I was only slowly becoming aware of the route that an earlier generation of black education had taken to Harvard, Chicago, and Columbia from smaller schools in the South. These students had also been part of the Great Migration. They too had experienced the dislocations of the mass movement north. And their academic work and dissertations almost inevitably brought together and interpreted the authors' contact with white scholars in major centers of learning; with rural black Southern life in the teens, twenties, and thirties; with the small black Southern college; with the Great Migration north; with the ghetto; and with the black bourgeoisie of Washington, D.C. These texts told a complicated tale of Southern black intellectual acculturation to the Northern white academy.

More particularly, these texts applied the historical, literary, and sociological focus available at Chicago and Columbia to the lives of Georgia sharecroppers or Mississippi migrants in Detroit's inner city. It was perhaps inevitable that some of these scholars, so deeply aware of patterns of black migration and social trauma, should concentrate on an early African-American literature that emerged in the wake of black geographical, social, and cultural mobility during the revolutionary 1760s, 70s, and 80s. The pioneering work of Benjamin Brawley and Benjamin Mays quite naturally explored the deep traumas of the establishment of new social institutions.

Mays' work, like that of E. Franklin Frazier and Charles Johnson, was a product of the segregated academy and the larger world of the Great Migration. It grew from a intellectual journey that took the poor young man, born in 1908 in rural South Carolina, to college in Maine, at Bates, and then a Ph.D. at the University of Chicago in the mid-1940s. He became dean of the Howard School of Religion, and later president of Morehouse College. He wrote three major books: a study of African-American religion; a monograph on religion in African-American literature; and an underrated autobiography, *Born to Rebel*, which ponders many of the themes of his scholarship. Mays' interest in religion as an ideological vehicle of acculturation came naturally to him as an individual and as one of the many black intellectuals caught up in the Great Migration. In *The Negro's God*, this experience illuminates the literary canon shaped by Mays' conception of African-American religious culture—a canon grounded in the typically didactic, religious, and nationalistic early African-American writing.

Mays understood black literature through contemporary sociological accounts of the migration and its traumas. Unlike many more recent commentators, he did not romanticize the dislocation or intellectual disorientation that urban life created. Instead, he stressed that the ideological nature of early African-American literature responded to similar dislocations in the late eighteenth and early nineteenth centuries. One may respond to the trauma in a number of ways. Most striking about Mays' writing, in contrast to that of contemporaries like Frazier, is the rough-hewn quality of his research, his ability to deal with the bare-bones reality before him in all of its contradictory detail. Quite incongruously, Mays relies on surveys of early African-American church life and culture, enhanced by long and frequent quotations from the early African-American writers he interprets. Compared to the writing of Benjamin Brawley, a fellow Chicago alumnus and Howard colleague, Mays' work is much more grounded in the actual rhetoric and language of the early American writers. And his willingness to subordinate his own text to a hard-headed, homemade empiricism led to a literary history that often discussed such writers as Jesse Fauset and Walter White, who are only just being rediscovered today, as well as similarly neglected texts like Frederick Douglass' *My Bondage and My Freedom.*

Like Saunders Redding and Sterling Brown, Mays had worked his way through masses of black authors.[1] He had interpreted and understood them closely. He viewed the tradition not top-down from the vantage of broad paradigms, but up from the ground of innumerable particularities. All of this, in my eyes, gives Mays' work great authority and stature. I was deeply drawn to his rough-and-ready willingness to trace the central religious themes of African-American culture through the Harlem Renaissance and his own complicated present in the mid-1930s. He was clearly addressing the experience of the Great Migration as seen in his own day, but he was doing so through a rigorous parsing of past black culture. Moreover, I was attracted by what seemed missing in the current crop of signifying black commentators: a political, cultural, and social self-consciousness, the ability to place themselves and their intellectual work in a historical context. I was particularly aware of the earlier writers' lack of reticence in measuring themselves, as provincial blacks, against the often imposing intellectual presence of the colleges and universities they attended. They strove for that cosmopolitanism, aspiring to the charismatic center of the broader society's meanings, rather than the signifiers' sly skirting around it. This gave them a clear social understanding of the artistic, cultural, and political world they now inhabited. They accepted its structure as a definite reality into which, they confidently assumed, they and their people would eventually fit. In this they were asserting a black awareness far more authentic than that of my contemporaries. Their confidence was grounded in a tight grasp of their own histories, that of their peoples, and that of the larger world.

This knowledge and optimism allowed them to look beyond the limits of their origin in the black South and find meaningful historical analogies to their own experience. The resulting erudition only reinforced, in my mind, their powerful presence as intellectuals. As a student of early American history and culture, I found Mays' books and published dissertation instructive. I occasionally recurred to them for their shrewd literary and historical commentary. I still find in them the most important element the signifiers lack: the ability to articulate the elements of African-American Protestant culture that can speak to the ultimate traumas of death and social breakdown.

When I took a full-time job as an instructor in the Department of English at Howard University in the late 1970s, I necessarily encountered such elderly but still imposing figures as William Banner in philosophy and Carroll Miller in education—the Harvard- and Columbia-trained residue of the formidable segregation-age intellectuals I had known from the stacks of the Regenstein Library. Banner and Miller could be witheringly funny about their journeys through Cambridge or Morningside Park in the twenties or thirties, the segregated South, the trials of finishing a dissertation at Howard, and the great men and women—sometimes, one felt, the gods—they had seen: Alain Locke, the philosopher; Dorothy Porter, the bibliographer; Leo Hansberry, the historian of Africa; Rayford Logan, the great historian; and Charles Burch, the literary critic.

The style I met in this older generation was urbane, its members could be sometimes patronizing to those who had arrived to post-desegregation Howard. Among them was a nearly seventy-year-old Arthur Davis, still chipper and ironic, respected biographer of Isaac Watts, coeditor of a still important anthology of African-American literature, writer of important essays on black poetry, and author of *From the Dark Tower*, a vividly documented account of twentieth-century Black American literature. A Columbia student during the Harlem Renaissance, Davis had himself become a principal historical source for important recent work on black writers whom he knew personally. I suspect that he is best known to African-Americanists from the acknowledgments of a series of distinguished books on Langston Hughes, the Harlem Renaissance, Rayford Logan, and E. Franklin Frazier. A native of Hampton, Virginia, Davis was educated at Columbia College and in the English Department of Columbia University, becoming a professor at Virginia Union, from which he was fired, as he liked to joke (with Nathan A. Scott Jr., a colleague who later became a luminary at the University of Chicago). Although trained in eighteenth-century English literature, Davis wrote the first important new critical *explications de texte* of Langston Hughes and Gwendolyn Brooks. He came from a very distinguished academic family that included his cousin Charlie—Charles Davis, the distinguished textual scholar and critic who directed African-American Studies at Yale.

The casual outsider might mistake Arthur Davis' complicated ironic manner for provincial Southern folksiness. It was absolutely nothing of the sort. And the unwary who fell into this calculated trap—my colleague, the novelist Julian Mayfield, said that E. Franklin Frazier played the same games with newcomers to Howard—found themselves in a cultural abyss of meaning that in the late seventies had a contemporary, literary-critical ring. Academic irony, most of us learn, comes naturally to an American professorate that is relatively powerless to change its society. And this rhetorical posture had a special resonance for survivors of the segregated academies whose boundaries were defined and maintained in the early part of the twentieth century by the deep terror that American society could mobilize against blacks. Howard University, Davis lamented with elaborate weariness, had once been the home of the black elite. Young blacks like me, he would continue, his eyes twinkling, were now coming to Howard in search of their identities.

Davis' memories and critiques brought the thorny problems of segregated intellectual life in the thirties and forties to bear on texts and writers I had only known in the stacks. In particular, he had known Benjamin Mays (whom he liked to call Bennie) as a highly successful dean of the Howard School of Religion in the forties. He also knew him as a competitor—a fellow big fish in a very small academic pond—for the scarce resources and glories of segregated black Washington society. These facts illuminate Davis' harsh judgment on *The Negro's God as Reflected in His Literature*—that Mays' book was too sociological and insufficiently literary to do justice to the many religious themes in African-American literature.

This remark bears out the essential differences between these two scholars, whose work, learning, and lives mean much to me. Davis' understanding of religion was conditioned by his training as a formalist literary critic and a historian of ideas. He frequently ended our discussions of Isaac Watts with an account of the praise that Marjorie Nicholson, chair of his thesis defense, had bestowed upon the young black Ph.D. at the session's end. And one understands much about Davis by thinking of him side-by-side with Nicholson, the great historian of ideas, the author of *Newton Demands the Muse*.

On the other hand, Mays' rough-hewn, multifaceted work on the church and African-American literature had been shaped by his professional experience as a minister and close personal observation. His work on religion, in the coauthored *The Negro's Church*, as well as in *The Negro's God* and even the autobiographical *Born to Rebel*, is substantially sociological, based on evidence from surveys as well as his own quasi-ethnographic observations of numerous black churches. It is therefore not surprising that Davis noticed how Mays emphasized the broadly social and cultural function of religious conceptions for early black American writers—in contrast to the systematic formulation of ideas which preoccupied Davis in his study of Watts.

Although Arthur Davis, to my mind, was wrong about Mays, he identified the sociological grounds of his colleague's importance. That point cannot be overstated. Mays' reading of American Protestantism is a sensitive account of how early African-American writing relates to the late eighteenth- and early nineteenth-century literary and religious milieu, as well as to his contemporaries' studies of American political and evangelical culture in that period. His historical narratives, like those of Frazier, indicate a still largely ignored road to understanding the Protestant-romantic continuity that so profoundly informs African-American writing.

Mays' work was concerned with religion as ideology rather than theology. In *The Negro's God as Reflected in His Literature*, he effectively traces the social significance of "ideas" that permeated early African-American writing: God's vindictive justice, man's equality before God, and God's covenant status with his chosen people. Mays claims that these conceptions could be compensatory, helping their bearers endure the trials and tribulations of slavery; progressive, encouraging blacks to work for abolition; or affirmative, proclaiming black humanity in the face of racist social conditions. These ideas, as Mays sets them forth in the works of both cultivated "classic" writers and "uncultivated folk artists," as well as ministers addressing the folk, are not developed in the abstract, systematic manner of professional theologians like Jonathan Edwards Jr., William Taylor, or Horace Bushnell. They are literary and, more broadly, rhetorical adaptations of American Protestantism—what Sacvan Bercovitch, Gordon Wood, Nathan Hatch, and Ruth Bloch have recently defined as regional ideology, articulating the political, social, and cultural life of the revolutionary new nation.[2] Both the cultivated writers and uncultivated "folk" composers of spirituals reflect the political languages of Puritanism and evangelicalism, infusing their work with white and black discourse of the period from the Revolution to the Civil War. Indeed, the theologically influenced religious ideology that set the goals of national mobilization also defined and preserved civil order, explaining the traumas of social dislocation that accompanied revolution, nation building, modernization, and eventually internecine military conflict.

Apocalyptic divine punishment, millenarian fulfillment, the national satisfactions of God's chosen people—these sustained both the Protestant ideology which shaped early American political thought and its central discourses of providential rule, the jeremiad, and millennialism. The presence of popular ideological languages of religion in early African-American literature demonstrates the first black writers' participation in the powerful political-religious consensus of the new nation. This consensus clearly played a key role in shaping what Mays would call the progressive outlook of the rapidly growing and organizing black urban population. Significantly, Mays did not see such appropriations as subverting a black nationalist culture, judging instead its tendency to promote or retard black integration into the new society.

A plausible reading of early African-American literary tradition emerges from Mays' perspective. The political and religious ideologies formed in crisis demanded that black writers and preachers construct frameworks of meaning within which to address the persistent dislocation of black life. Such innovation by blacks was an appropriate intellectual response to the social and ideological instability of late eighteenth-century Revolutionary and post-Revolutionary American society. These early black writers formed their views in a new America that was politically, culturally, and socially fluid. These early crises of meaning foreshadowed the crises and trauma of the four periods into which Mays divided black writing from the eighteenth century to the Harlem Renaissance. In his historical narrative, black writers—drawing upon the Protestant-romantic continuity of African-American culture, periodically recover the social knowledge, cultural meanings, and ideological symbols that make black American society possible.

Mays' work appropriately explained the (now misinterpreted) early religious didactic literature studied in the early thirties by Dorothy Porter, who examined its social function in a comprehensive series of bibliographies and articles.[3] William Robinson, Mays' most important literary-historical descendent, takes the same scholarly point of departure.[4] For Robinson, Phillis Wheatley is a public ideological poet whose efforts stand at the beginning not of a folk tradition, but of a literary Americanization that appropriated Protestantism for the social purposes of black American life. Properly understood, the Protestant-romantic tradition of religious verse and prose allows greater comprehension of the sentimental, moralistic, and romance varieties of black women's fiction, from Harriet Wilson to Toni Morrison.

To see African-American literary history within this tradition clarifies the complex position of the Harlem Renaissance writers Countee Cullen, Georgia Douglass, Langston Hughes, and W. E. B. Du Bois—not to mention Walter

White and others whose names scholars have only recently revived. These figures must be examined in light of the earlier sentimental religious traditions which they had just abandoned or revolted against; while beginning to express themselves in secular, psychological terms, they continued to think and organize their views in religious categories. In Cullen's "Heritage," Mays pointed—in a deeply suggestive way—to the poet's disillusionment with earlier religious hopes, with the providential and millenarian worldview that promised a sense of humanity:

> Quaint, outlandish heathen gods
> Black men fashion out of rods,
> Clay, and brittle bits of stone,
> In a likeness like their own,
> My conversion came high-priced;
> I belong to Jesus Christ,
> Preacher of humility;
> Heathen gods are naught to me.
>
> . . . . . . . . . . .
>
> Wishing He I served were black
> Thinking then it would not lack
> Precedent of pain to guide it,
> Let who would or might deride it,
> Surely then this flesh would know
> Yours had borne a kindred woe.
> Lord, I fashion dark gods, too,
> Daring even to give you
> Dark despairing features where,
> Crowned with dark rebellious hair,
> Patience wavers just so much as
> Mortal grief compels, while touches
> Quick and hot, of anger, rise
> To smitten cheek and weary eyes.
> Lord, forgive me if my need
> Sometimes shapes a human creed.[5]

Despite his disillusionment with an earlier conservative Protestantism, Cullen persists in seeing his psychological crisis as one of religious faith. Mays, in stressing the black intellectual's continual need—and inclination—to find social explanations for the trauma of racism, falls upon a key insight into the will-to-power of the Way Maker. In its despair, Cullen's poetic persona creates a black Way-Making God with whom the African-American believer may sympathize as a man. In dramatizing this imaginative creation, however, Cullen shrewdly shows that this Way-Making idol can never provide wholly transcendent meanings of ultimate concerns. The Way Maker's creed—for all its attractiveness—continues to be human. Cullen's reading of his angry persona's idolatry represents a proleptic critique of today's academic black theology, its celebration of the African-American believer's will-to-power. These theologians have, in Cullen's view, implicitly co-opted God into the limitations of human desire. The Way-Making theologians' worship is not only idolatry but a displaced rebellion against whiteness—which has also become a mistaken stand-in for the deity. The signifiers, along with their black and white Gods, constitute a devil's party in rebellion against a truly omnipotent and perfectly virtuous deity. Despite their mock theological uprisings, they have not escaped the intellectual framework of traditional Protestant Christianity. However, their "black theology" is a spiritual and intellectual dead end.

Thus Cullen's "Heritage" powerfully and dramatically demonstrates the persistence of Protestant morality and belief even into the young intellectuals' revolution of the Harlem Renaissance. Mays further develops this insight by pointing suggestively to the religion-like role of radical politics for some "progressive" black intellectuals who turned away from traditional Protestantism. Mays admits that the rejection of piety may lead some to atheism and apparent nihilism. In this existential situation, however, Marxism may provide a secular faith, prophecy, and millennial utopia:

> The case of Langston Hughes is clear. The absolute repudiation of Christ, God, and religion, and the reliance upon Marx, Lenin, and Stalin is the extreme left to which the negation of God in the life of the Negro may lead. The negation stimulates the Negro to become Communistic and to resort to more violent means of attaining social, economic, and political justice.[6]

Reflecting on Hughes' Marxism, Mays insisted on the religious continuities of intellectual black American life, those continuities leading even twentieth-century blacks to look for sacred meanings in human existence. Such a continuity, Mays insisted, had led Hughes to apocalyptic, millenarian if secularized versions of history in Marx.

Present-day ideological criticism is concerned to show the links between the canon's cultural motifs and the literary structures of particular works. To read thus is to ask what is at stake, culturally speaking, in a given text. To interpret Frederick Douglass' first narrative as a jeremiad, as William Andrews does in *To Tell a Free Story*, is to consider how much the young abolitionist participates in the deeply consensual myths that define American national destiny and society.[7] Those who place early black printed preaching as well as the oratory of Maria Stewart and David Walker within the context of the black jeremiad are doing much the same thing. Ideological criticism—whether informed by Marx, Weber, Berger, or Geertz—examines the social function of the ideology or political languages that the early black writers absorbed. What have been the limits of an ideology's explanatory powers in particular historical situations? How have those limitations been inscribed in literary texts? What have been the consequences of a given ideological orientation at a particular moment?

The richness that I find in Mays' works comes from his willingness to ask these questions of early African-American writing. Not only did he explore the ideological dimension of black religious literature, but he also attempted to imagine the social world to which such an ideological worldview might give rise. He envisioned the black church as an embodiment of freedom existing within the larger context of modern (i.e., late eighteenth-century) society. Mays' speculation did not stop with his imagination of the church, but extended also to an analysis of how his conception of black religion had enabled him to understand and explain his own experience. In doing so, he sought not only the theological and ideological content of his belief, but also the texture of the life that he had chosen to lead. It is this search for the existential "feel" of black religion that marks Mays' great contribution to the subject.

Mays' historical work on the Negro church and, interestingly enough, his autobiography, *Born to Rebel*, both show blacks defining religious experience as a site for intellectually and spiritually liberated existence. Thus Mays and Nicholson note that

> [F]reedom in the Negro's religious and church life had an early historical beginning, and . . . this fact has served to give "freedom in Negro church life" precedence over that freedom which the Negro is allowed to experience in other phases of his life. Thus quite early the Negro preacher, highly restricted in other fields, achieved freedom in the church through his own initiative and sympathetic encouragement from white people and his own flock.[8]

And they go on to assert that this enhanced black experience had an important social payoff. Put simply, the black church endured largely because religion provided a freedom that made black life plausible, stimulating social reproduction:

> The freedom in his church, which the Negro merited and gained relatively early, while freedom in other realms was still denied him, has been one of the basic reasons for the rapid numerical growth of the Negro church in the United States.[9]

Later they extend this point to the assertion that the church characteristically provides free self-expression for blacks not found elsewhere in American society:

> Thus, not finding the opportunity that is given to members of other racial groups in civic and political life, in business enterprises and social agencies, the Negro through the years has turned to the Church for self-expression, recognition and leadership.[10]

From this beginning, Mays and Nicholson in *The Negro's Church* play out a rich institutional history that asks serious questions about the church's expressive function. At the core of compelling religious expression is the charisma of the speaker, his contact with sacred values. And part of the value of *The Negro's Church* is its rich meditation on the social implications of the black church's charismatic nature, particularly in the Jim Crow South and the twentieth-century Northern ghetto. The church itself, as it expanded between 1915 and 1930, faced a crisis of failed adaptation and social dislocation. As a locus for charismatic authority, the church could promote an authoritarian ministry that abused its power without the restraints of rationality, literacy, or a cosmopolitan worldview. Moreover, this ministry, and the tendency toward expressiveness, could resist the entrance of more cultivated elements into the church. The intense desire for personal fulfillment in the church could engender too many small, overweening congregations that sought to glorify themselves at the expense of the others. These conditions were politically and economically destructive, particularly in the Northern ghetto world created by the Great Migration.

In Mays and Nicholson's shrewd moral perspective, the Way-Making black drive for expressive freedom led not only to pragmatic political action, but also to a compensatory therapeutic impulse which could be as retrograde as the pragmatism was progressive. To take American Protestantism as an ideology for black social life and institutions could be the source of order or chaos. The cultural and social structure created by the black church was especially tenuous, and this in turn generated a correspondingly precarious psychology. As a literary critic, I cannot speak authoritatively upon the sociological perspective of Mays. However, the authors present a narrative that gives a complex ethical and psychological scope to the charismatic impulse—and its institutional consequences—that attracts so much attention in contemporary black cultural criticism. Their analysis of the black religious style has the social, political, and cultural richness which provides a far more plausible and useful account of the expressiveness that critics like Michael Dyson and Michael Awkward see in a Michael Jackson.

Such perspicacity equally informs the work of E. Franklin Frazier. In *The Negro Church in America*, Frazier also stresses the black church as a locus of institutionally approved black freedom and expression:

> The leadership of the preacher was recognized by his "congregation" as far as the white masters were willing to concede to him this role among the slaves. Although the masters were unwilling to tolerate any form of organized activities among the slaves, different members of the "congregations" played various roles according to their talents as singers or according to their ability to influence other slaves to get converted or attend religious services.[11]

And Frazier goes on to set forth the authoritarian, anti-intellectual abuses of this expressive behavior, chiefly on the part of ministers. He is far less even-handed than Mays in attributing constructive social responses to the black churches. In appropriating the dialectic of this narrative of the two-edged sword of black ecclesiastical life, he gives compelling descriptions of the displacement of numinous sacred impulses in the lives of secular twentieth-century black middle-class professionals:

> Some of them express contempt for religion and do not attend Church though they may pretend to have some church affiliation. Since they have neither an intellectual heritage nor a social philosophy except crude opportunism which enables them to get by in the white man's world, they may turn to all forms of superstition. This is because they are still haunted by the fears and beliefs which are a part of their folk heritage. They are often interested in "spiritual" and "psychic" phenomena. Very often the real religious feelings and faith of middle-class Negroes is expressed in their obsession with poker and other forms of gambling.[12]

In his autobiography, *Born to Rebel*, Mays goes beyond his psychological inquiry to examine the role of black religious impulses and vision within the freedom and limitations of his own experience. He describes Mount Zion, the church of his youth, as a refuge from the racist turn-of-the-century South, a compensatory other-worldly religion that sustained their day-to-day lives and moral judgment. This religion was deeply personal, providing him with the psychological support needed to make his ambitious way in the South. In approving this supportive piety, however, he affirms what elsewhere he attacks as politically and socially retrograde. Of his minister, Pastor Marshall—the very other-worldly, uneducated type he criticizes in an earlier book—Mays observes:

> I never heard him utter one word against lynching. If he had, he would probably have been run out of the community—or lynched. When a visiting minister attempted to condemn white people, Pastor Marshall stopped him. I was there. I saw it and I heard it. I am not necessarily condemning the use of religion as an opiate. Sometimes an opiate is good in medicine. Sometimes it may be good in religion. Certainly religious faith has helped me in my struggles.[13]

This opiate of religion signals the most important aspect of Mays' story. As an ambitious black in a racist, segregated society, his own attraction to opiates comes from a deep sensitivity to the pains of one seeking social, cultural, and geographical mobility. A deeply competitive youth, he is acutely aware of the slights that abound not only in the white world of the thirties, forties, and fifties, where he will flourish, but in the segregated world where even a black professor, goading him on to academic excellence, can hurt his pride. This sensitivity, cultivated in a home with a caring mother and a proud but violent and alcoholic father, inevitably made him aware of, and deeply pained by, the central contradiction of his existence: the same religious values that drove him to accomplishment also exposed him to the deepest threats that racism could bring to his fierce and precarious sense of self.

At such times Mays subjected to his own ironic scrutiny the appropriated middle-class cultural meanings which underlay his own professional and moral drive. Reflecting on his resignation from the Urban League in Tampa, where he had created deep controversy by his attacks on segregation, he wrote:

> The depth of the race problem was revealed throughout our two years in Tampa. Mr. Anderson of the School Board had no understanding of the Negro problem, and no sympathy whatsoever for a Negro who did not accept—and preferably lovingly embrace!—the insult, which man and custom placed upon him. What I had tried to say to Mr. Anderson was as difficult for him to understand as if I had spoken in Hebrew or Arabic. My article was equally unintelligible to Mr. Davis of the American Legion. Even Mrs. Atkinson, euphemistically called by some Negroes "our little white angel," had no empathy with our desire be given dignity and respect such as all people are entitled to by virtue of the fact that all are born in the image of God.[14]

With Mays' acceptance of the opiate of religion came a certain wryness about white "angels" and even, significantly, the "image of God." Further musing, he playfully suggested revising the final lines of Cullen's poem "Yet Does I Marvel" to "Yet do I marvel at this curious thing: / To make a man black, and bid him aspire." Mays significantly—like Cullen—is ironically distant about the imaginative and wish-fulfilling desires by which these breakdowns in meaning may be confronted. He is amused at his own capricious recreation of himself as a Way Maker rebelling against God's providential design. This sense of detachment from the impulse of desire contributes to the balanced judgment which Mays can elsewhere apply to complex moral questions about the ultimate social consequences of black expressive and charismatic impulses. It is this intellectual distance that I find lacking in the signifiers.

 I remember a long talk once with Arthur Davis, during which he described his fascination with Isaac Watts' eighteenth-century struggle with conversion. It was a wholly unwonted moment of self-revelation. And one thought not so much of the eighteenth-century hymnodist as the young black scholar up from a traditional church home in Hampton, Virginia, to study in Morningside Heights. He told this story laconically, but it was worth some consideration. My parents, raised in the middle-class South, had gone to school under the Davises at Hampton. There could have been no stricter representatives of the morally and academically demanding way of life than that family which dominated Hampton for years. Davis, as his ironic remarks about Howard revealed—"We at Hampton believe that some people should work with their hands"—was a product of that deeply traditional black middle-class academic sphere. What did the secularizing, newly modernist world of Columbia University mean to such an aspiring intellectual, raised in a strict Protestant home in the South? Although the urbane Davis might never directly discuss the tension and struggle within the meaningful categories of his worldview, it is hard to believe that it does not inform his affirmation of Phillis Wheatley's subtle literary construction of herself as a black poet, maintaining her African identity while formally addressing her white social betters. The segregated black intellectual's appropriation of the secular world was often not an easy one, and the striving for religious order must have been profound. To this is due that generation's acute perceptions of how earlier black writers had created ideological order in late eighteenth- and early nineteenth-century America, and their insight into the persistent Protestant-romantic complexities of African-American cultural life.

 Rather than confronting this tendency to charismatic style, numinous imagery, and world-explaining beliefs, today's generation of African-American critics have either romanticized or repressed it. They have neglected the difficult, self-contradictory processes of Americanization through which all blacks, and particularly intellectuals, must pass. This text-wrenching predictably appears most in current criticism of Phillis Wheatley, Ann Plato, and Harriet Jacobs, writers who embody the impulse in a deliberate and ineradicable way. We can only understand these writers if we read them against the grain of their historical meanings. Ignoring this important cultural continuity in black life inevitably represses present black anxieties over a similar and equally difficult process of Americanization in the complex era of modern integration.

# Chapter Eleven

## Robert Hayden
### The Poet as Cosmopolitan Historian

I MET ROBERT HAYDEN (1913–1980) in the midseventies at a poetry reading in a dark theater on the University of Chicago campus, somewhere on the South Side's Hyde Park. A few weeks earlier, I had discovered two of his books in Powell's, an old used bookstore near the corner of 57th and Lake Park. In the meantime I had read *Words in Mourning Time* and *Selected Poems* with great avidity. I eventually learned that Hayden was a black poet who had been born in 1913 and raised in Detroit. Educated at Detroit City College and the University of Michigan, he had taught for many years at Fisk. At the time, I was deeply disaffected with graduate school in English literature at the University of Chicago, but still spent most of my time reading and thinking about poetry and history in the small William Rainey Harper college library with its remarkable collection of modern verse. Hayden's poetry held me under a sustained spell.

Hayden was clearly a poet of the African-American historical experience. Here the ultimate problems of that history—the horrors of the Jim Crow South and the formation of the ghetto, the articulation of a meaningful worldview amidst trauma, the nature of prophets, the means of searching one's consciousness for a grounding in the past—seemed far better articulated than in my contemporary cohort of black literary writers. He had thought beyond the superficial solutions of their work. Moreover, he was unabashedly autobiographical in a way that consistently increased in psychological and moral depth as his career continued. He was ahead of his time. And his work still beckons me.

Hayden's coming to Hyde Park at that moment seemed the greatest of luck. A few English Department faculty attended his reading, some straggling graduate students, and a group of black elementary school students who after the performance asked the distinguished poet to autograph some scraps of brown paper. I was the only one there with an actual text, but Hayden paid no attention to this.

Nathan A. Scott Jr., by then the Shailer B. Mathews Professor in the university's divinity school, was also there. Scott had known Hayden in Ann Arbor as a fellow student at the University of Michigan. The poet did not seem to mind such a varied but undistinguished and less-than-awestruck assemblage. Amidst the restless schoolchildren, Scott's occasional raucous laughter at the poet's Michigan jokes, and a discomfited white academic audience, Hayden—dressed in a black velvet suit and red bow tie—seemed perfectly at home onstage. As a teacher and librarian at Fisk, Hayden had long been accustomed to a limited reputation among a few academics and people of letters. Indeed his oddly elaborate diction, and peculiarly formal postures amidst this motley audience, seemed to embody not only these contradictions but also his elegant acceptance of them.

He might have been a local or regional poet—say a Margaret Burroughs, Dudley Randall, or Carolyn Rivers—used to rough-and-ready gatherings, largely black, lightly sprinkled perhaps with white intellectuals or curious literary onlookers. He did not behave like the national figure he had become as recent Poet of the Library of Congress. As Hayden sadly admitted to George Kent, my mentor at Chicago, he had been an outsider so long that he did not know how to behave as an insider. His innocence extended to the matter of payment. At the end of the reading, Hayden refused the honorarium, asking that it be donated to some black student-association fund or scholarship for African Americans at the University of Chicago, or to monies set aside there for black cultural affairs. He was all right now, he told George before the reading, and did not need such money anymore. Exasperated, Kent finally ended what must have been a strained conversation with a frustrated response. In a voice and tone that might have come from the poet's own verse, he exhorted Hayden to "take this check while these people (i.e., the University of Chicago) still have their moneybags open."

Contemplating Hayden as a self-conscious provincial artist in the footlights of his sudden later fame is a sure—but not always comfortable—way into the poet's corpus and literary career, as well as important aspects of black intellectual life in the late twentieth century. The settings of Hayden's autobiographical work mark the central sites of his working-class Detroit childhood, his long career at Fisk, and his participation in the small black academic community of the South—a journey that finally brought him to the exalted worlds of Ann Arbor and New Haven.

Hayden began his career as a sensitive, bookish boy in tragic, often abusive Detroit. His life there is memorialized in many poems: "The Rabbi," "Witch Doctor," "Mourning Poem for the Queen of Sunday," "Summertime and the Living," "The Whipping," "Those Winter Sundays," "Smelt Fishing," and "Free Fantasia: Tiger Flowers." As recreated in these verses, the poet's childhood is a world of rites and ritual experienced in the teens and twenties by a young African-American boy in church, home, and even vicariously in synagogue. Hayden portrays his lower-class black environment as a scene of brutality, alluring female sexuality, and a hidden, insurgent masculinity. He creates an autobiographical persona of a restrained, shy youth in awe of threatening maternal figures that intimidate as they seduce, beset by the sexual forces of others as well as those deep within himself.

The violent, sexual ethos of his Detroit world is complicated by the emotional and intellectual life of the characters that emerge from anonymity in Hayden's later verse. I think here of the complicated figure of Floyd Collins in *Angle of Ascent* ("Beginning") and the women who people "Elegies for Paradise Valley" in *American Journal*.

> Of death. Of loving too:
> Oh sweet jellyroll:
> So the sinful hymned it while
> the church folk loured
>
> I scrounged for crumbs:
> I yearned to touch the chairlady's hair,
> I wanted Uncle Crip
>
> to kiss me, but he danced
> with me instead;
> we Balled the Jack
> to Jellyroll
>
> Morton's brimstone
> piano on the phonograph,
> laughing, shaking the gasolier
> a later stillness dimmed[1]

Mimicking the sly eroticism of Morton's performance of Jelly Roll, Hayden's run-on lines move with agility from the hiatus of desire to hopeful sexual contact and finally to that desire's sublimation in the dance. In his confrontation with this Detroit world in "Elegies for Paradise Valley" and "Free Fantasia: Tiger Flower" (Hayden's final poems in *Angle of Ascent* and *American Journal*), Hayden depicts what he himself describes as a homosexual orientation. An acute sense of vulnerability, marginality—even evil—both fueled his emergent poetic self and burdened it with traumatic memories.

The awkwardness of Hayden's position as a provincial intellectual signaled this self-consciousness in a striking way. His self-regarding postures and finery of dress were compensation—perhaps an apology—for a sense of marginality that only deepened as his fame increased. This was only exacerbated by his identification with the necessarily peripheral black intelligentsia at Fisk and the Southern black college world generally. The titles, acknowledgments, and dedications of Hayden's early poems place him within a network of black literary intellectuals of the fifties and sixties. Not only was he a friend and associate of Nathan Scott, who well may emerge as a central thinker in his cohort of black literati, but Hayden belonged to the period's larger literary scene, which included Ralph Ellison, Michael Harper, Charles Davis, and others. For years, moreover, he was a colleague of Arna Bontemps, teacher of Julius Lester and employee of Charles S. Johnson.

Hayden's acquaintances were the cream of the crop of the Southern black college world. And Hayden himself was a part of this brilliance. The trajectory of his career from Fisk to a distinguished professorate at the University of Michigan and his appointment as Poet of the Library of Congress paralleled the paths of John Hope Franklin, Nathan Scott, Allison Davis, George Kent, Kenneth Clark, Charles Nichols, Charles Nilon, and John Davis. From the world of the Southern black college, a distinguished group of black scholars and writers emerged to assume distinguished chairs at major American universities in the seventies and eighties. Theirs was the movement of a provincial black intellectual elite—often trained at the nation's best universities, which had opened their graduate schools in the thirties, forties, and fifties—to the faculties of those same institutions. This was the fulfillment of an earlier black academic world's commitment to cosmopolitan intellectual values. Hayden's poetry is an important document of the inner intellectual life of this class.

Theirs was a deep impulse to assimilate the best cosmopolitan values of Western culture. Like Ralph Ellison, they pursued intellectual mastery particularly of those great artists of the modernist movement. One sees this in Ellison's self-conscious urbanity, and that of other eminent black writers of the period like Richard Wright and the early Gwendolyn Brooks. Hayden reflects the same aspiration in the allusiveness of his poetry's moments of moral complexity, when the voices of his modernist and romantic predecessors may be heard. Thus Frost's meditative persona of "Stopping by Woods on a Snowy Evening" appears in Hayden's "The Diver"; the desert passage of Eliot's "The Wasteland" is invoked in his "Zeus over Redeye"; and Ariel's transformation in the "Tempest," quoted by Eliot, is echoed again in "Middle Passage."

Hayden's literary discourse moves between the matter-of-fact clarity and high-flown wordplay of intellectual tradition, a tendency that was perhaps the most conspicuous element of Nathan Scott's style, and perhaps less noticeably that of Ralph Ellison. When I arrived at Howard as a young instructor in the English Department in the late 1970s, I would hear William Banner, a Harvard-educated philosopher, give a brilliant speech on academic life. Banner's narrative account of his graduate school years deliquesced into a walk-through account of the differences between the separable German nouns *Lehrfreiheit* and *Lernenfreiheit*, both the playful elevated diction and his Cambridge experience a part of the message—his claim upon the breadth of intellectual experience to which he had aspired as a young Southerner in Harvard Yard.

Hayden's poems were ambitious acts of intellectual sport that explored historical, natural, and moral truths as pressed upon his attention in day-to-day experience or meditation. "The Diver" sees the historian as an deep-sea explorer, immersing himself in human experience. Can such an intellectual enter and comprehend the truth of history without loss of self-consciousness—a loss that significantly comes in a threateningly feminine embrace of death? And this death is itself seen as a yielding to the ravishment of powerful sexual attractions:

> . . . I yearned to
> find those hidden
> ones, to fling aside
> the mask and call to them,
> yield to rapturous
> whisperings, have
> done with self and
> every dinning
> vain complexity.
> Yet in languid frenzy strove,
> as one freezing fights off
> sleep desiring sleep;
> strove against
> the canceling arms that
> suddenly surrounded
> me, fled the numbing
> kisses that I craved.²

This is Hayden's habitual poetic world, alive with potentially destructive sexual seduction and loneliness, and darkened by moral complexities. All of these can, the scenario provides, be escaped by the easy way out: loss of consciousness and death. This submarine seascape offers the same temptation as Robert Frost's winter landscape in "Stopping by Woods on a Snowy Evening." Just as Frost's sleigh-rider returns to the world of social responsibility, the diver resurfaces to earthly existence and full self-consciousness. Yet even then the life-giving gases that permit his ascent may poison his blood with bubbles.

This poem might well be read as a modernist prophecy of the anomic social world of free-floating signs in which the signifiers have their being. What were the historical origins of the civilization that the diver and the signifiers seek? Can they engage a Western history that threatens to dissolve their identity, even as the persona's I is dissolved in his descent? Or can they, through memory, coalesce their scattered moments of consciousness into a saving personal unity? Here is the romantic return to origins of Du Bois, Hughes, and Morrison. But their return exacts a high intellectual and spiritual price, as it does not in Holloway or Gates. It involves a confrontation with the realities of life and death, not a continuous Way-Making affirmation of identity.

The diver arrives at a truth not associated with his original quest: that the critical question of his journey is the limits of inquiry itself. How far must he go before he loses the sense of consciousness and identity upon which human intellect and questioning itself depend? To what extent do his identity and history contain the sought-for answers? Can there be truth that is apprehended only by experience, and not also by intellect or moral will? Hayden's rejection of a union with nature puts the poet on the intellectual side of the conflict that Philip Rahv in the fifties described as the perpetual battle between Palefaces and Redskins—those American writers concerned with the intellectual apprehension of experience as opposed to those who sought immersion in experience in and of itself.³ The persona of "The Diver," unlike Hemingway's protagonist in *The Sun Also*

*Rises* or similar figures in the prose of Mailer, is unwilling to risk the dissolution of self-consciousness for truth.

Hayden's resistance to romantic self-dissolution stands in sharp contrast to Adrienne Rich's poem "Diving into the Wreck," in which an intellectual explorer also symbolically immerses herself into the dangerous depths of history. This diver throws off her mask to embrace the ebb and destructive flow of past experience. The measured rise of Hayden's diver seems a provincial gesture, out of touch with a contemporary experiential poetry exemplified best perhaps by Robert Lowell in *Near the Ocean* and *Imitations*—especially the verses that detail the white poet's own descent into insanity.

One also recalls here the influence of W. H. Auden, whose historical poems suggested that a writer's historical inquiries could be a way into the psychology of the literary intellectual or his society, so often embodied in the poetic persona. Hayden had won fellowships to the University of Michigan where he received an M.A. degree and studied under Auden, who visited the campus in Ann Arbor. It was Auden whose work often suggested that wisdom and moral stature are won through not only cultural observation but introspection into our deepest drives and aspirations. It was from Auden that Hayden took, besides a willingness to immerse himself in the psyche, his desire to maintain a balanced intellectual poise in the undertaking: the balance of wit, paradox, or irony. At the end of this journey lies an emblematic vision of nature, an understanding of an earlier perceived truth, now fully grasped and interpreted. The measured rise which the persona begins at the end of "The Diver" is such a comprehensive image of the journey.

This myth of fulfilled pilgrimage gives shape to Hayden's poetic corpus. And the poem that best illuminates this quest is "Electrical Storm." Here the poetic voice imagines responses to lightning storms that he has seen during childhood, youth, and middle-age. At the poem's end, the established academic grasps the wisdom of the elders of his youth. Here the correct perception appears in an image of self-consciousness that echoes the Old Testament's burning bush, as well as Robert Frost's poem "Design":

> Last night we drove
> Through suddenly warring weather.
> Wind and lightning havocked,
> beserked in wires, trees.
> Fallen lines we could not see at first
> lay in the yard when we reached home
> The hedge was burning in the rain.[4]

The image of the burning bush anticipates a reversal from the genre of autobiography to the apocalyptic vision of Frost's "Design." And Hayden concludes by expounding the providential pattern that—at least from one prophetic viewpoint—has ordered the persona's life:

>     Who knows but what
>     we might have crossed another sill,
>     had not our neighbors' warning
>     Kept us from our door?
>     Who knows if it was heavenly design
>     or chance.
>     (or knows if there's a difference, after all)
>     that brought us and our neighbors through—
>     Though others died—
>     the archetypal dangers of that night?
>
>     I know what those
>     cowering true believers would have said.[5]

At stake in this poem is more than the moment of religious epiphany that illuminates the world, both mysteriously and dangerously. What does this burning bush signify to the poet-persona for whom the old folks prophesied greatness? Is he himself a prophet? And can he measure up to the past? And what would he have seen, had he crossed the boundary, "the other sill" into the land of death inhabited by the "true believers"? Would he appear to be a prophet from this perspective? In the aftermath of this eerie light, the poet-persona's philosophical confusion becomes clarified by his surmise of the old folks' interpretation. However, he has only their understanding of a symbol based upon an oft-interpreted biblical text. The consequence of their conjecture is unclear—as is its significance for the reader.

Moments of spiritual illumination occur frequently in Hayden's poetry. They are marked by a calm poise that is neither wholly religious nor aesthetic, in a secular sense. They suggest the beauty of the sacred, in an Emersonian sense, which is for Hayden the spiritually enlightened self. On the other hand, these lights can take on the clarity of historical fulfillment or the transcendence of natural light. This calm beauty appears in the guise of the persona's aunt in "Full Moon"; in the liberating Allied soldiers of "Belsen, Day of Liberation"; and in "Monet's 'Waterlilies,'" where the great impressionist painter's play with light becomes an image of man's apprehension of truth. Hayden experiences in these moments an insight that seems not to be a displacement of Protestant Victorian inwardness into romantic meditation, but an extension of it. With self-conscious literary symbolism, Hayden discovers traces of an older middle-class Protestant piety and turns them into poetic vision. The spiritual illumination of Bahá'í plays a role in this imagery, which is nonetheless primarily constituted by more traditional conceptions of divine illumination.

Neither Hayden's aesthetic nor his tentative hold on imaginative vision was a popular doctrine in the sixties and seventies. At the heart of the Black Arts movement was the assumption that the folk language of urban and rural life was already a highly cultivated means of expression. Jazz and the blues, the argument went, provided modes of criticism and art, already there for the taking. An effective literary culture was not to be made but discovered in the language of folk and soul. And in the course of the movement, the conversational world of the folk and auditory sphere of musician and audience were reified into a timeless sphere of artistic tradition. In contrast, the enormous power of Hayden's poetic vision emerged from his insistence on drawing the wisdom of the folk through what Hurston herself called the spyglass of history: anthropology. In the process, black folk expression and feeling emerged into art empowered by the resources of tradition. And with his grasp of that literary-critical tradition came Hayden's deep awareness of the profoundly tragic dimension of the black experience. It was perhaps a human historical perspective that the Black Arts movement lost most quickly, just as the playful quality of Le Roi Jones' surreal poetry gave way to the sadomasochism of Imamu Baraka's *Black Magic*.[6] It is to the point that, in the long view of African-American poetic tradition, Hayden's symbolist poetry has proved more influential than the Black Arts movement. Hayden's verse has had an extended *Nachleben*, informing the work of writers like Jay Wright and Michael Harper. Black Arts literary theory has receded alongside the poetic careers of its most prominent versifiers: Baraka, Ted Jones, Nikki Giovanni, Haki Madhabuti, Carolyn Rodgers, Angela Jackson, Larry Neal, Ishmael Reed, and Stanley Crouch. Hayden, years after his death, remains our most influential black poet, and his followers the most productive and distinguished school of artist-intellectuals.

The collapse of Gwendolyn Brooks' poetic career represents the shortcomings of the Black Arts sensibility. Without the distanced perspective needed in the world of Chicago's South 47th Street, Gwendolyn Brooks' poetry changed in a way that illuminated the permanence of Hayden's achievement. In her career since the late seventies, Brooks' most interesting collection was *In the Mecca*, when she could parody the self-negating extremes of "Way Out Morgan." She could caricature the tension between her own cultivation of English literary tradition and the evolving culture of the black ghetto around her, while satirizing both the impulses toward the emulation of whiteness and its outright rejection. Brooks' strategies of introspection and indirection gave her poetry both its psychological depth and its distinctive force. As her range of response to the world of the South Side diminished, her art grew shallower, despite her new commitment to the urban black community.

Brooks' best known later poems are heroic celebrations of black figures or aspects of black life, such as "The Third Sermon on the Warplane," "Young Heroes," or "Young Afrikaans." These are nearly didactic accounts of the black ghetto community's values as expounded by the Black Arts movement. Missing here are the complication and ironies of black life that can only be appreciated from a point of view that is broader and deeper than Black Arts itself. Without that perspective, these poems remain flat, bombastic, unaware of their own potential ironies and complexities. And, ultimately, such a perspective must encompass a larger, more cosmopolitan world of values than Brooks evokes.

Hayden's "Free Fantasia: Tiger Flowers" and, much later, "Elegies for Paradise Valley" and "A Letter from Phillis Wheatley" show in their complexity of vision and cosmopolitan perspective a body of artistic strengths that Le Roi Jones and

Brooks herself could not sustain throughout their careers. Focusing on historical representatives of enlightenment, Hayden's poetry also admitted the possibility of false black prophets. His emphasis on truth necessarily admitted the presence of charlatans, grounded in the masses' need for the hastily improvised social and cultural vision that Black Arts intellectuals like Larry Neal (in the early seventies) and Imamu Baraka delivered. Hayden's central dramatization of the mind's movement toward the meaningful elaboration of the world gave pride of place to reflection as a central human activity. It is to the point that Hayden's vision not only dramatized his own quest for humane comprehension of his experience, but also drew upon the disruptive traumas of his early life, generalizing them to the African-American experience. Within this vision, black Americans emerge historically out of the great dislocations of historical experience, and come to intellectual consciousness with a profound need for explanation. It is precisely this disruption that makes the African American vulnerable to false prophecy and illegitimate explanation.

Hayden's "The Witch Doctor" and "A Ballad of Remembrance" represent powerful critiques of this explanation-nourishing aspect of African-American culture, which one suspects may have driven off a number of potential commentators. On the other hand, it is significant that the established black *littérateurs* Robert Stepto, Michael Harper, the late Michael Cooke, and the late Charles Davis have all been drawn to Hayden. Yet the most recent crop of critics, who exploit the vernacular for its semiotic and deconstructive potential, has paid little attention to the poet. They—like the Black Arts critics—celebrate a version of black culture that is not sufficiently informed by a larger moral, political, and social vision to appreciate the size of the canvas on which he paints. In their accounts of black literariness, they too are false prophets of folk culture, unable to exalt its art to a significant level of meaning. The witch doctor is another such deceiver, preaching a message that cannot lift the masses beyond the dreariness of their lives. As he exploits their need for explanation, the witch doctor represents the ultimate blasphemy in Hayden's view, the substitution of falsehood for the truth that men desire. The superficial glitter and illegitimate attractions of Hayden's Southern society in "A Ballad of Remembrance" represent a similar critique of the black folk world as a space of limited possible meaning and understanding. Within this African-American culture, Hayden's exemplary individuals are Nat Turner, Phillis Wheatley, and the black Southern soldiers of "The Dream," who carry on toward a better world. Not to mention Frederick Douglass, who embodies a dream that includes all of humanity.

To put this another way, Hayden squarely faced the issue of the role of the intellectual in black culture. Poetry was a site in which a poised, cultivated presence might create order in the world. As his poems often asserted, this need for intellectual order and poise was deepest in the "black community." However, the fruits of this world must undergo contact with that which remained beyond the black community. And this was a world whose complexities and otherness might test and define the African-American world, thus giving it knowledge of itself. This need brought deep meaning to Hayden's disciplined search to bring an edifying and illuminating vision to bear upon his experience. And it was this that gave Hayden's quest an almost sacred religious cast.

The superiority of Hayden's poetic vision and accomplishment is evidenced by his preeminent influence over the best of the later generation's black poets: Michael Harper, Jay Wright, Marilyn Waniek, and Ai (Florence Anthony). In their best poems, they are all historically informed searchers after the truth. Hayden has been influential because he developed such a suggestive model of the history poem, a poem that searches the personal or public past for a significant truth to present to the audience. Hayden's verses of this type acquired a stunning authority of voice, image, rhetoric, and metaphor, especially in the later poems of *Angle of Ascent* and the whole collection of *American Journal*. The promise of "Free Fantasia: Tiger Flowers" is fulfilled in the series of historical poems concerning Wheatley and Matthew Henson, figures who exemplified the poet's own quest for truth. Jay Wright's "The Homecoming Singer" is emblematic of the Haydenesque poem, reconnoitering personal history for a meaningful ritual. And the tradition of Hayden continues in the poetry of Harper, Wright, and Rita Dove.

Athwart the end of Hayden's mortal poetic road sat the collection of poems in *American Journal*. These essays represent encounters with historical events, persons, and elements from nature that engender a final self-consciousness. Continued re-readings show Hayden—despite the formality of his verse—to be like Whitman's poetic persona walking along the shore observing "electric," "self-seeking types." History and nature for Hayden ultimately represented imagery of the personal soul that corresponded to a deeper and greater world-spirit, for which the creed of the Bahá'í faith was only a foretaste. And in *American Journal* we see a record, a diary, of Hayden's visionary encounters with himself and his soul. It is a central work of twentieth-century American poetry in the Emersonian tradition; however, our parochial racial literary politics keeps us from recognizing it as such.

"Elegies for Paradise Valley" is an account of Hayden's stepfamily, his encounter with his homoerotic impulses in the form of Uncle Crip, and a recognition of the poet-persona's own moral disability. The poem ends with the insight that he encounters an image of himself, that he is "the devil's own rag baby doll." In "Astronauts," the poetic voice contemplates television images of the moon explorers only to realize that the questions whose answers they seek are the great human riddles pondered by us all. In the elegant verses on Phillis Wheatley, Hayden's authorial presence encounters a type of himself in Wheatley, who at the poem's end is asked by a Blakean chimney sweeper (the poet himself, perhaps, bound for heaven) whether her blackness allies her with his own human suffering. In the same vein, in "The Prisoners," Hayden—in high Emersonian fashion—describes the prisoner's recognition of the poet as a Christ-like figure who has worn the prisoner's (and, implicitly, all men's) woe for himself. The poet is someone who as "been there" too.

At the reading described earlier, Hayden joked about his fascination with flying saucers. In his flat Midwestern tones, he went on to read his one space travel poem, "Unidentified Flying Object," with an enthusiasm that fell flat. His remarks met what seemed to me a derisive response from the academics in the audience. At this moment Hayden seemed to be playing the role of the outsider to cosmopolitan life. Indeed in "American Journal" (the final poem and centerpiece of the collection by that name), a UFO from a superior extraterrestrial civilization became a fitting symbol for the cosmopolitan fulfillment he had sought all of his life. And yet ultimately in this poem Hayden also projects an idealized persona, the achievement of calm, superior enlightenment.

The poem's persona—a world-weary, hypercivilized alien—represents the central drive of Hayden's poetry: the projection of his own imagination and psychological insight across the whole realm of the human condition. Hayden's civilized alien's speech dramatizes the provincial character not only of himself (whom he often styles a rebel or alien in *American Journal*), but of all human life when seen from the perspective of a superior intelligence. The distance of the alien's bemusement suggests that all of us on Earth have come late into the universe, and perhaps at some distance from its centers of cosmopolitan knowledge, consciousness, and the world-spirit that the romantic ultimately recognizes in himself. The speaker's introspective report of his journey among the Americans not only is a symbolic catalogue of Hayden's life, but also dramatizes a humanist perspective in which the world is weighed in a balance of ultimate religious and moral truths.

At the heart of this poem is the poet's realization that this anticipation of vision, self-consciousness, and consciousness must be a wish—to be fulfilled in the future through spiritual striving, not immediately summoned on a whim. This quest must cover an inordinate territory, not just worlds but space. And Hayden signals his speaker's search for enlightenment with a sweep to a Whitmanian and Emersonian image of the terrestrial landscape. The American world becomes a metaphor for the possibility of self-transformation in its own national terms. The poem's Whitmanian catalogue embodies not only the intellectual reach of Emerson's "American Scholar," but also a Whitmanian assurance about America's status as a globally inclusive nation.

Hayden's poetry approached idealistic truth through a fierce engagement with the struggles of history. And as such, his verse represents an important time and place in the African-American and American literary traditions alike. In the mid and late seventies, my conversations with George Kent might start with a passage from Brooks' "Maud Martha" and work back through the Emerson-influenced regionalism of Robert Frost, only to arrive at Hayden's "The Diver." The discussion would move from an Eliotic concentration on the shards of human experience to a visionary concern with history and Emerson's high idealism. The glow of these talks enlightened many a gray Chicago day, even as an illuminating glow shines from the spiritual center of so many of Hayden's poems. Of course, not all Emersonians were friends of the blacks. Indeed, Kent read Frost and liked to talk about the black Boston critic William Braithwaite, who had promoted Frost's literary career early in the twentieth century. Kent liked to joke about a passage that Nathan Scott had showed him in Frost's letters: a racist attack by the young white poet on his older black colleague. Kent would slyly smile his toothy grin, pipe shaking in his hand.

Both Scott and Kent read T. S. Eliot's poetry with the avidity of their generation. The Eliotic parade of historical fragments had permanently impressed itself upon their imaginations. It was the necessary departure for hope and to be idealized. Indeed, their concentration on Eliot persisted long after his poetry's centrality had begun to wane in the mid-1970s. Both continued to teach Eliot through the seventies and eighties. It is hard to cite a black literary intellectual of their generation or the one after—Le Roi Jones, Charles Davis, or even Houston A. Baker—who did not share this point of departure. Robert Hayden, who joined the divergent streams of Eliot's modernism and American romanticism, was the most hopeful and visionary seer of this group. And in that awkward mid-seventies theatre at the University of Chicago, Hayden was for me—as he remains—the poet of my most hopeful moments.

# Chapter Twelve

## Earlier Integrated Worlds
### Langston Hughes and Charles Chesnutt

As a graduate student in Chicago, it was difficult not to recall that there had been earlier periods of apparently more successful efforts at integration. Many of these had occurred in Cleveland. As I read Langston Hughes and Charles Chesnutt, I remembered my father pointing out Central High School where Hughes had studied, and speaking of Chesnutt's life in Cleveland in the late nineteenth and early twentieth centuries. Hughes had gone to school with foreigners, many of them Jews. Chesnutt lived in Cleveland for much of his professional life, and many of his papers were housed in the downtown public library. He became part of upper-class society there, sending his daughter to Smith and his son to Yale. During the fifties and early sixties, my parents had gone to Karamu House, an interracial arts center where Hughes' plays had often been produced. They had done so in the company of the Jewish radicals who had hired my mother at Park Synagogue.

That world, which was nearly gone by the time I had entered the University of Chicago in the early seventies, has now wholly vanished. Its interracial bonding had its ultimate roots in the Protestant benevolence that had nurtured abolitionism and persisted after the Civil War in the founding and support of the black colleges. I am struck by this memory because the writing of both Hughes and Chesnutt is a literature of integration. Hughes writes from the perspective of a bohemian black intellectual who nevertheless participates in a highly integrated artistic world and a similarly mixed Left. The same may be said of Chesnutt, who ran a successful law practice and stenography business that inevitably brought him into contact with whites. As the ghetto began to form in Cleveland, he sometimes walked down to the East Side, his daughter Helen tells us, and observed the behavior of the newcomers. He did not, apparently, know what to make of them. Both Hughes and Chesnutt experienced close bonds with other white intellectuals, largely because of shared literary concerns, or business, or, in Hughes' case, a common feeling of bohemian fellowship.

Theirs was not, however, a literature of assimilation. Their sense of ethnic identity was linked to a deep political commitment and consciousness (Chesnutt would become an important figure in the NAACP and write significant political fiction). Moreover, their literature often turned upon the deeply American demand that those who dreamed of a new life, of success in America, must ultimately face the reality of the past. In Chesnutt, this was the past of the South and the deeply complicated relationships of slaves and masters. For Hughes, it was the urban world of the Northern ghetto. Both demanded confrontation with black history on the part of their most significant heroines, depicted in highly realistic and subtle terms. Indeed, their tales of encounters with blackness were opportunities for serious and profound reflections on the nature of race in America, and often on American culture itself.

It would have been impossible for Chesnutt to write at any other time than the late nineteenth century, with the increasing educational and professional opportunities for middle-class blacks in North Carolina and Ohio. Chesnutt was descended from the free blacks whose communities dotted the East by the 1850s and even the South. Born in Cleveland, Ohio, in 1858, he came from an enterprising mulatto family who had fled antebellum North Carolina only to return after the Civil War. Chesnutt's early career flourished during Reconstruction (1865–1877), an era that his novels would depict as one of educational, political, and social opportunity for Southern middle-class blacks. Driven by ambition, Chesnutt excelled academically and consequently rose through successively more responsible teaching and administrative posts in black North Carolina schools. Furthermore, he acquired an extensive literary education on his own. Intent on becoming a man of letters, he learned French and German from a local tutor, a Jew who was later ostracized for the instruction that he gave. He read nineteenth-century American and continental fiction, and sought instruction in the African-American folk practices that played such an important role in his first short stories.

Not surprisingly, given Chesnutt's ambition, in 1883 he went back to Cleveland after the post-Reconstruction backlash against black political progress. Here his successes multiplied. Learning stenography, he established a highly successful court reporting business, and studied law, earning his cohort's highest grade on the Ohio bar exam. He achieved no less in his literary calling. Deftly drawing upon black Southern traditions of magic, folk storytelling, and dialect, Chesnutt published a number of short stories in the *Atlantic Monthly* only a few years after settling in Cleveland. By 1899 he had published a collection of these, *The Conjure Woman*; a second volume, *The Wife of His Youth and Other Stories of the Color Line*, followed later that year.

To be sure, Chesnutt was a man of letters who wrote in the leisure provided by a successful profession. However, he pursued his literary avocation with the savvy and energy that had marked his legal career. He transformed his black middle-class Ohio and small town North Carolina experience into his distinctive fictional worlds. As he did so, Chesnutt astutely built upon the conventions of the then commercially successful regionalist fiction. The literary and marketing results of this experiment were remarkable. The early fictions collected in *The Conjure Woman*, which confront a black ex-slave with a Northerner come to the South to establish a profitable vineyard, not only establish a literary geography almost as fruitful as Faulkner's but also resonate with the economic, racial, and social energies of the Gilded Age, the aggressively entrepreneurial North, and a war-weary, racially torn South. The same might be said of the equally searching and often satirical *The Wife of His Youth*, which brings the same insight to black and mulatto figures striving with the contradictions of segregation in both the Northern world of a Cleveland-like city and a small Southern town like Fayetteville, North Carolina.

Chesnutt's early fiction reflects his deep desire to penetrate the heart of American literary life. He shrewdly drew and manipulated much of the characterization and plot structure available from his popular literary contemporaries, whose work was full of the plantation tradition, its paternalistic masters, faithful retainers, and generous black mammies. However, he added a new human complexity embodied in the folk tales of the ex-slave narrator, Uncle Julius. Within these wry animal fables, magical stories, and dream visions, Chesnutt deployed a more sophisticated version of the plantation myth, a world replete with intricate interracial understandings in which greedy masters might find their ruin, immoral slaves suffer unexpected justice, or wise bondsmen teach foolish overseers. Against this backdrop of a newly complicated antebellum world, Chesnutt created entertaining but morally serious encounters between the earnest Northerner of the tale's frame stories and the ex-slave Uncle Julius, teller of the folk narratives themselves.

At the heart of these stories, Chesnutt placed a critique not only of the longing for success, but of the American dream itself of unlimited fulfillment of unlimited desires. All desires have limitations; thus teach the many stories of *The Conjure Woman*. Neither the Northern planter's ambition for unlimited wealth and happiness, nor those of the black folk who use the trickery of the conjure myths, is without bounds in its fulfillment. These stories are—in a smirking, erotic Ovidian way—about the metamorphoses of self, career, and personal life available in the New World. In a Hawthornian mode, however, they are at pains to show the limits of this fulfillment.

These stories were therefore marked not only by the wit, human observation, and craft of a well-told tale, but also by Chesnutt's uncompromising and unembarrassed insistence on the tragic element in black folk culture. A sly Julius might outwit clumsy John for a fancy suit of clothes or even a sinecure, yet our attention is nevertheless drawn to the fact that even the conjure man's deepest satisfactions rarely exceed a physical, temporary, or cathartic level. Chesnutt ultimately insisted that his naive protagonists—white or black—confront, but never sentimentalize, the tragic limitations whereby the slaves seized meaning from their experience. These were the realities, cynical and ironic as they might be, that could threaten the ingenuous, optimistic plans of a Northerner businessman transplanted to the late nineteenth-century South.

Similar facts confronted the still raw, upwardly mobile black bourgeoisie in his *The Wife of His Youth and Other Stories of the Color Line*. These stories are not, at present, as fashionable as those of *The Conjure Woman*. They are, however, at least as rich. In "The Wife of His Youth" and "My Virginia Mammy," the main characters (who clearly live in a version of a late nineteenth-century Ohio town) are forced to face their antebellum, Jim Crow, and Reconstruction past before taking an important step in the life cycle. The central character must confront his slave wife before determining to take a new bride; the young mulatto schoolgirl must engage in a complicated struggle with her past. It was impossible, these stories argued, to create a new world in the South, just as the narrator of the frame stories of *The Conjure Woman* would not be able to find a brave new commercial world there. Told with moral subtlety, shaded with delicate detail, and complexly ironic, these tales were an important contribution to the short story tradition in American letters. It was this tough-mindedness that ultimately allied Chesnutt not only to Joel Chandler Harris, but also to the American tradition's most trenchant critiques of Emerson.

With the refocused energies of a mature, increasingly politicized artist, Chesnutt turned to the novel in *The Colonel's Dream* (1905), *The House Behind the Cedars* (1900), and, most importantly, *The Marrow of Tradition* (1901). Here he exercised an even tougher-minded vision of the postbellum past; this time, however, his results were equivocal. He aimed for a Balzac- or Zola-like portrait of American society. And in *The House Behind the Cedars* and *The Marrow of Tradition* he does capture both the middle-class black's memories of the promise of Reconstruction and the tragedy of Jim Crow, as well as the wealthy white Southerner's sense of lost social power. Among the especially trenchant portraits is the new man, the lower-class white Southerner wreaking his vengeance on the young Negro elite.

Chesnutt's intention to freight an increasingly sophisticated novelistic observation with political protest came at a high price. Although his social portraits were often incisive and powerfully drawn, his attempts to make a moral fable from the experience of the fallen black middle class lack the power of the metamorphoses of *The Conjure Woman*. There was something distinctive in the endless mythological evolutions of the conjure stories that set Chesnutt's imagination free to explore fully the sexual, psychological, and physical ethos of desire. This imaginative freedom constituted an unexpected victory over the Puritan-Victorian prudery of his time and released real creative power. This strength is lacking in *The House Behind the Cedars*, which otherwise provides a deft account of an interracial marriage contrived by an ambitious mulatto brother for his socially striving sister. Similar criticism might be made of *The Marrow of Tradition*'s otherwise expansive tale of an aristocratic family's encounter with the secret of its tragic racial past, the spiral into self-destruction by the clan's decadent scion, and the moral dilemma of a self-made black doctor. While Chesnutt clearly approached a new standard of literary technique in storytelling, point of view, and realism, he was nevertheless thwarted by his reliance on increasingly outdated black character types and an intrusive narrative commentary that often substituted political preaching for the literary solutions of character development and plot.

On the other hand, the themes and subject matter of these works were innovative and probably suggestive to later African-American writers. In *The House Behind the Cedars* and *The Marrow of Tradition*, Chesnutt engages in a degree of personal introspection and social observation that anticipated Du Bois' essays in *The Souls of Black Folk* and the novelist James Weldon Johnson's *Autobiography of an Ex-Coloured Man*. *The House Behind the Cedars* and *The Marrow of Tradition* provide a psychological account of the black middle class to which Chesnutt himself belonged: its memories of Reconstruction, the encounter with lower-class white resentment in the Jim Crow era in the 1890s, lower-class black rage, and the black intellectual's perception of political impotence. Most importantly, Chesnutt's writing suggested that this inner world was a perfectly adequate perspective for a broadly painted picture of the post–Civil War South with its declining Southern white aristocracy and a rising middle class of both races.

Chesnutt, as not only a distinguished practitioner of short fiction but an aspiring innovator, was already underway to the psychological insight we associate with nineteenth-century realist and psychological novelists and their twentieth-century descendents such as Faulkner and Ellison. However, what propelled him to the attention of the public was not merely his clever manipulation of the plantation myth, but a power to mine the psychological depths of a myth of success shared by whites and, increasingly, middle-class blacks. His sense of the weight of the past upon the present had a special significance in a nation still reeling from the tragedies of the Civil War, the white world turned upside down in Reconstruction, and the vicious backlash unleashed against blacks in the Jim Crow era. Chesnutt's stories were clearly written in an attempt to get inside the mainstream of American literature; but they were also an attempt to explain blacks like himself to a white middle-class audience. His powerfully realistic and psychologically shrewd explanation assumed the possibility of literary communication. This, in an important way, is denied in Gates' deconstructive view of signifying.

· · · · · · · · · · · · · · ·

Hughes belonged even more visibly to the integrated segment of Cleveland's pre–World War II world, even though he took part in the Great Migration, which settled in the city long after Chesnutt was part of a well-established black middle class. Hughes' immense charm carried him and his memory a long way. Even now one encounters Jewish graduates of Central High School who remember hearing of the famous black poet who had graduated before them. He was active in the Karamu House in its prosperous days of upper-class white patronage under the Jelliffes, and he remains a presence in Cleveland's historical life. Even more than Chesnutt, Hughes had his intellectual being in an integrated world. He kept close ties to Cleveland, where his book *Dreamkeeper*, a collection of some of the tamest poems from *The Weary Blues* and *Fine Clothes to the Jew*, was assembled in cooperation with the Cleveland Public Library. And in Harlem he associated with a group of black intellectuals who frequently gathered with similarly minded white bohemian writers. The publication and promotion of his work was made possible by a significant patron, Carl Van Vechten, with whom he had a long friendship.

To the degree that it shows changing varieties of white patronage in African-American literary culture, Hughes' friendship with Carl Van Vechten is of great importance. Little black intellectual life has ever emerged or been sustained without the patronage of some individual like Van Vechten or a group such as Garrison's abolitionists or the Communist Party. Certainly this was the case in the literary upsurge of black expression that occurred between the Harlem Renaissance and the mid-sixties. Hughes, Zora Neale Hurston, Countee Cullen, and Wallace Thurman were all promoted by older black intellectuals like W. E. B. Du Bois and James Weldon Johnson, with the aid of white cultural middlemen in publishing, the foundations, and education.

The forty-four-year-old Van Vechten, one of these middlemen, was already an established music critic, novelist, and literary journalist. His role in African-American letters, however, would extend far past the 1929 crash, which ended the Renaissance's heyday. In the next thirty-nine years, he would become patron, advocate, literary broker, photographer, and archivist for at least two generations of black writers and artists such as James Weldon Johnson and Imamu Baraka (then Le Roi Jones). Hughes' career reflected only one facet of Van Vechten's cultural interests, which included not only African-American letters but also literary high modernism. Persisting through the Depression, World War II, the booming fifties, and the sixties, Van Vechten and Hughes developed a sustained friendship. It survived a world of changing patronage relationships, shaping the careers of authors as different as Hughes and Ralph Ellison.

Early in the twenties, Van Vechten expressed his admiration of, and interest in becoming an editor for, Hughes and his work. Attracted to the blues, Harlem, and the black literary scene, Van Vechten, openly homosexual, was inevitably drawn to the handsome young poet who was creating literary art from spirituals, oral folk traditions, and jazzy uptown life. Van Vechten would send the writer's first manuscript, *The Weary Blues*, to Alfred Knopf and go on to submit samples of his verse to *Vanity Fair*, jumpstarting the fledgling career in a way that surprised even Hughes. By 1929, Hughes had, with Van Vechten's assistance, published two widely noticed books of poetry and a novel, *Not Without Laughter*. From this remarkable start, Hughes, one of the first African Americans to support himself with his own writing, went on to produce a steady stream of verse, plays, libretti, newspaper columns, fiction, and essays until his death in 1967, three years after Van Vechten's demise.

Although accused of being a decadent influence, Van Vechten had little to do with Hughes' actual literary innovation and creation. But the older writer exemplified shrewd literary enterprise to a clearly attentive pupil. Van Vechten always provided the often unwary Hughes with important business advice, encouragement, frank criticism, as well as help during a divisive conflict with Zora Neale Hurston over the play *Mule Bone*. From the beginning of their friendship, Van Vechten foresaw Hughes' lifelong autobiographical project, which produced two memoirs, *The Big Sea* and *I Wonder as I Wander*.

Hughes' later activities and success reflected Van Vechten's advice and example in important ways. As his published correspondence with Arna Bontemps shows, Hughes developed, albeit by necessity, into a perpetual literary entrepreneur who exploited all levels of the entertainment media, including theater and the children's book market (which became receptive to blacks in this period). Furthermore, he cultivated a network of African-American educators such as Bontemps, Charles S. Johnson, and Mary McCloud Bethune. Following his mentor's example, Hughes himself became a literary counselor and advocate for a younger generation of black writers, tirelessly reading their works and helping them with fellowships and support. Sharing Van Vechten's belief in the importance of the era's literary history, Hughes self-consciously acted as a personal contact between generations of black writers extending from the Harlem Renaissance through Ellison and Wright to Baraka and Alice Walker. In his personal contacts as well as in a host of anthologies and literary collections, Hughes became the living embodiment of the literary tradition whose papers Van Vechten collected in the James Weldon Johnson Memorial Collection at Yale.

Hughes reciprocated Van Vechten's attention with genuine affection and friendship. April Bernard's recent collection of their correspondence documents how the young Hughes often fed Van Vechten's avidity for the details of black life with accounts of his experience at Lincoln University, tales of knife fights, and fey comments on men he had observed. Not surprisingly, it has become a commonplace that Van Vechten—like so many white sojourners in Harlem during the twenties—was a voyeur of lower-class African-American life. Yet clearly he and Hughes often addressed each other as coracialists, sneering at the "ofays," saluting each other as "gate," and sharing understandings that educated blacks (Hughes was a college graduate) generally hid from whites. In their letters, this byplay seems not only genuinely good-natured but also affectionate. Their joking reflected a personal bond that allowed them to criticize each other directly. At its core was not Hughes' cynical deference to a patron but a shared value: a selfless commitment to art and rejection of inhibiting bourgeois standards, whether from the privileged Van Vechten's stance as a homosexual aesthete or Hughes' socially tenuous position as a struggling black poet. The two men's bohemianism and consequent marginality—albeit chosen by one while enforced upon the other—sustained the relationship despite differences that deepened with time.

Given their class and race, it is not surprising that the two were dissimilar. Van Vechten rejected Hughes' radical poetry and never understood or sympathized with the political implications of Hughes' decision to create a folk poetry accessible to the masses. A somewhat effete man, Van Vechten did not fall under the sway of the proletarian art that so influenced many writers and intellectuals (of both races) during the Depression. On his side, Hughes does not seem to have cared one way or the other whether he satisfied the aesthetic tastes of the cultural intelligentsia to which Van Vechten, who championed Gertrude Stein and her work, belonged. Other differences would divide the two as their reputations changed in the fifties and sixties. Hughes went on to enjoy eminence as a founding father of modern black literature in this new era, while Van Vechten dropped from view as other blacks, like Ralph Ellison, rejected him and his particular brand of white paternalism. In later years, Van Vechten often grew bitter toward the "new Negroes" who snubbed him and, worse, forgot him. Sometimes signing his letters as "the Patriarch," "Carlo" still clearly hoped that his relationship with Hughes and other black artists would remain the same, as the poet became increasingly occupied and new African-American literati emerged. Van Vechten's unhappy encounter with the brave new world of black art in the sixties contrasts vividly with the wry humor that Hughes could direct toward the black and white worlds in which he was gaining such acclaim. The changed situation of the two men appears vividly at the end of Bernard's collection, where Hughes offers Van Vechten the consolation that blacks not only neglected his own collection at Yale, but overlooked such enterprises in general.

It is significant that much of Hughes' most important writing was done in the thirties and forties: the remarkable collection of stories *The Ways of White Folks*, many of the "Simple" columns printed in the *Chicago Defender*, and work gathered in a number of collections. Hughes now carefully analyzed the social interaction between blacks and whites in many of the integrated worlds in which he had participated. He had written in his poetic manifesto, "The Negro Artist and the Racial Mountain," that such interaction could provide an inexhaustible source of literary subject matter.[1] And in these works, he vigorously mined that source.

Patronage—such as Hughes himself enjoyed from Van Vechten and Nancy Cunard—was for the most part the subject matter of *The Ways of White Folks*, which incisively drew upon the ways in which patrons might displace their erotic drives into parental impulses and their anger into authoritarian patience. Hughes' stories also made grim humor of how blacks manipulated, endured, and suffered under these projects. Some of the stories, such as "Poor Little Black Fellow" and "A Little White Dog," are especially notable for their examination of the psychological delusions in which whites mask or bury a sense of resentment or fear in supposedly benevolent relationships. *The Ways of White Folks* is a still unacknowledged masterpiece of the observation of American manners. And as we learn to read Hughes more acutely, we will find in this work important anticipations of Baldwin's remarks on the American fear of engagement in the risks of experience, a fear powerfully developed in *Giovanni's Room*—a text that owes much to Hughes as to Henry James. Baldwin's themes of the white American sexual hysteria inspired by blacks, and of revolt and displaced revolt against fathers (symbolic or otherwise), also have important precedents in Hughes. Here we see not only anticipations of "Alas Poor Richard" and "The Fire Next Time," but also the mock revolts of our latter-day academics against their white patrons in the universities—

the scholarly fathers (De Man, Bloom, and Richard Lanham *inter alios*) whom Gates mocks in *The Signifying Monkey*. Hughes powerfully examined such oedipal strife over forty-five years ago in such stories as "Poor Little Black Fellow."

When I returned to Hughes' first short story collection after nearly twenty years, most significant for me was its bittersweet depiction of black-white relations during a time of liberal hope for the future. There was still enough religious sentiment left in mid-twentieth-century American culture to make whites and blacks regret the separation that was on the horizon in the forties, fifties, and sixties. In "Poor Little Black Fellow," Arnie's eventual betrayal of his white family is a betrayal not just of a white past of patronage and loyal black servitude but of a growing black and white hope in an improved racial condition in the future. Why should, many of these stories ask, the alliance between blacks and whites, especially on a personal level, be broken when there are signs of a new day just over the horizon? However, Arnie's decision to leave his family and marry his young Rumanian pianist girlfriend is an assertion of autonomy, which is not the confident gesture of the Way Maker but a chance taken against high odds. It is only such assertions of the will, informed by historical perception—newly won by Arnie at this point in the story—that count in Hughes' fiction. All else is false hope. And an entente between blacks and whites cannot exist unless blacks may, with such independent calm, enjoy their cooperation with whites. This peace with himself may be the most impressive aspect of Hughes' letters in the Hughes-Van Vechten collection, and it contrasts vividly with Van Vechten's nervous, outraged sense of his own declining importance.

Much the same might be said of the *The Simple Takes a Wife* stories, which—although occasional pieces—also constitute a profound view of American social life, white and black. They examine the underside of black life—the dynamics of divorce and broken families, black male psychology, and in particular the signifying charades of power and arrogance adopted by the powerless. Here too are the vexed dramas of "love and trouble" between black women and men, analyzed by Hughes with the same acumen as Orlando Patterson. In "Simple Speaks His Mind," a series of short pieces ends with Simple's divorce from a demanding, materialistic wife and his preparation for marriage to his girlfriend of choice. Along the way, Hughes acutely depicts the internal conflicts of unhappy marriages, failed relationships, and the self-punishment they incur. Here, too, is the theme of revolt against those who impose the humiliating color line, as well as a celebration of the 1943 New York race riot (which plays an important role in *Invisible Man*, as well as in Baldwin's autobiographical account of his father). This horrifying event is depicted with a stern air of prophecy, uncannily foretelling the urban crises of the sixties. As usual, Hughes' work was not only prophetic, but right on time.

To speak of Hughes' sense of displaced longings, oedipal revolts, and sexual hysteria is, of course, to invoke Sigmund Freud—clearly an important influence for American writers of the twenties (not to mention Wright). In *The Ways of White Folks*, Freudianism is a newfangled school of thought, which Hughes slyly mocks in "Rejuvenation Through Joy" as a means of therapy. However, these stories make an impressive use of the Viennese thinker to explore interracial American life. There is, beyond plot structure and powerful psychological imagery—for example "Little Dog," in which a white woman eventually recognizes the symbolic significance of a black man's daily ascent up her backstairs with bones for her dog—an important similarity in the cultural criticism of the two writers. At the heart of Freud's method in *The Interpretation of Dreams* or *Totem and Taboo* was the reading of clinical experience against a broad background of ethnographic, autobiographical, biographical, or personal history, and at times against the still broader base of the romantic philosophical and literary traditions. Likewise, Hughes examines the white-black patronage-client artist relationships within a context not only of the paradigms of Freudian psychology but also of the broad romantic insight as opposed to a crude racial primitivism. Freud allows Hughes to take the Protestant-Victorian tradition seriously in a way that many of our current-day new black critics do not.

The title of Hughes' collection *The Ways of White Folks* suggests that he is providing an inside view of client-patron relations not only for naive whites but also for knowing "black folk." Like Freud, he intended to set both whites and blacks toward a healthy, honest relationship which neither had known before (at least not with each other). These relationships are based on a therapeutic understanding of the psychological forces at work in human relationships. In "Father and Son" this therapeutic intention comes though with a grim reminder of the apocalyptic consequences of not understanding emotional disorders of interracial relationships. His health-giving aim also suffuses "Slave on the Block" and "Cora Unashamed," in which not only whites are set straight but blacks are also caught in a questionable moral acquiescence with white misbehavior. Hughes could be disapproving, too, of the signifying that takes place by means of benign neglect, by the black's refusal to exert his own moral agency. Such instruction, however, was tempered; for he was more a genial humorist than a fierce master.

As Hughes and Chesnutt entered the white literary world, they explored the black-white relationships that had shaped not only their personal lives but also their artistic careers. The importance of this point cannot be overstated. Both writers were willing to delve deeply into the most personal aspects of their lives with whites, as well as to report and fearlessly interpret the evidence. In this way, they brought to the white reading public a vision of black life examined so acutely that it eventually sounded universal depths. Their portrait of the psychological, social and economic black underside of American race relations also provided them with an important vantage point on American life itself. From this perspective, they provided white middle-class readers with a political self-consciousness that they had never had before. They gave their white intimates something far more valuable than the privacy of which they had been deprived: truths that only friends contribute to their closest companions, the self-consciousness offered by an alter ego. And this, I suspect, was the basis of their continued and sustained intimacy with patrons whose power might otherwise intimidate them. This self-consciousness did not come, *pace* Gates, through a signifying irony, but through sympathy and an acute observation of the lives of patrons, the black masses, and themselves as writers and men. Their willingness to speak honestly about their people and themselves was the source of their literary power.

This insight is now being forced upon the reading public by newly published letters, papers, and social tracts of not only Hughes and Chesnutt, but also Ellison and Albert Murray. Our fascination with the bizarre black cocoons in which Hurston and now Toni Morrison wrap many of their fictional worlds—ostensibly to acquire a vision untainted by the white gaze—will eventually appear a matter of contemporary fashion as we examine this growing corpus. It will make possible a serious examination of black-white intimacies in such letters as those in the Ralph Ellison-Albert Murray collection, *Trading Twelves*—another word for the dozens, which is to say signifying as well as for a form of jazz improvisation. Although these letters are marked by the ironic indirection of signifying, we see enough of Ellison's discomfort with learned whites—at the American Academy of Arts in Rome, with his white students at Bard, and with the administrators of Fisk—to rid us of any simple generalizations about the meaning of an opened elite academic world to one of its most eminent black pioneers. He boasts, significantly, that he signifies on the white Bard students of the sixties, placing him on an ironic shared ground with those African-American youths who, driven by similar discomforts, would attack him on college campuses just a little while later. Ellison displays a remarkable mean-spiritedness about less talented, less learned, and less successful middle-class black men than himself; but, confronted with a possible tenured appointment at Brandeis, he wonders how he would live outside of the presence of other African American men. Nor could the competitive presence of his companion Albert Murray, with whom Ellison discusses the predatory world of the little magazines in the fifties, have been entirely a comfort for the rigors of the white world. His ambivalence may help to explain the terror with which he greeted black cultural nationalist impulses—implicit in characters such as Ras of *Invisible Man*—when he encountered them in his black student counterparts in the sixties and seventies. How did Ellison feel when Larry Neal, cultural nationalist, finally embraced him as a brother? He may, as Arna Bontemps told me during my senior year at college, have been most afraid of what he himself—and not the separatists—might do and say if left alone. The necessity of confronting this fear is a truth that black writers once held dear.

# Section Five

# A Marxist Humanism and Literacy

It is far too late in the day of Western civilization for black intellectuals to turn their backs upon the very intellectual languages and bodies of thought that have shaped them. Not surprisingly, the central figures of the latest, most successful phase of black writing have been those who—like Jean Toomer, Langston Hughes, Nella Larsen, Richard Wright, James Baldwin, Ralph Ellison, Robert Hayden, and Edward P. Jones—have been able to find themselves within Euro-American literary tradition. The power of black sociology has been, not surprisingly, in the willingness of African-American intellectuals to submit to the discipline's institutional wisdom that transcends the fashions of the moment. This focused depth has given us W. E. B. Du Bois, E. Franklin Frazier, William Julius Wilson, Kenneth Clark, Thomas Sowell, and Allison Davis in the social sciences, as well as Benjamin Brawley, John Hope Franklin, Benjamin Quarles, and Carter G. Woodson in history.

Indeed, as Arna Bontemps remarked, the movement of black intellectuals into a historically barren new critical formalism signaled an important breakdown in the black literary tradition. The remarkable criticism of Sterling Brown shows a deep debt to those folklorists at University of North Carolina at Chapel Hill with whom he corresponded, as well as to sociological principle in general. A similar understanding marked the historical narratives of Saunders Redding in *To Make a Poet Black* and George Kent in *Blackness and the Adventure of Western Culture*.

Not surprisingly, this generation's black intellectuals who have drawn upon the social sciences, the Marxist intellectual tradition, or both have proven the most durable. They display the benefits of humanism with an analytic power and traditional knowledge far superior to the current bag of rhetorical tricks toted by many black students of religion and literature. Despite their stance as engaged intellectuals, Angela Davis and Adolph Reed are writing for the future in the manner of Sterling Brown and Ralph Ellison. They deserve a wider audience.

What these writers gain from Marxism is not only a rich tradition of literary, political, cultural, and economic thought, but also an entry point into the broader civilization of the West. In particular, they find a coherent language for talking about the social world and psychology to which signifiers address themselves but cannot explain. This discourse, what I have called a political language, allows them to conceptualize past and utopian societies, as well as to describe the historical consciousness of blacks within present-day American culture. Very few black cultural commentators can avoid, it seems, the *ad hoc* combination of autobiographical history and literary criticism that now seems to make up a certain African-American cultural genre. What is most missing is a political language that can carry the distinctions needed to discriminate between the kinds of social, political, and philosophical knowledge that African-American literature might offer. And in this regard the brief—albeit sometimes journalistic—work of Davis and Reed is instructive.

# Chapter Thirteen

# Angela Davis as Cultural Critic

ON THE FACE OF IT, DAVIS IS A CELEBRITY intellectual whose eminence is partially bad. Little about her intellectual achievement is revealed by the fact that she is an ex-radical, fired (on account of her communist ties) from her UCLA philosophy post in 1970 and later charged with capital crimes in the wake of a courthouse insurrection that left four people dead. During the manhunt that followed her escape—chronicled in a book by her friend and comrade Bettina Aptheker—the FBI declared her one of the ten most wanted criminals. Similarly unrevealing are her early autobiographical writings, which lack the exploration of self and milieu central to serious memoir and also to self-understanding. Cultural criticism and scholarship reveal the self and mind in often embarrassing ways (a risk that the present writer has run at just about every step). The author of *The Angela Y. Davis Reader* is the academic social activist and radical polemicist who has established herself in the last quarter-century. Currently, she is a chaired professor in the prestigious Committee on the History of Consciousness at the University of California, Santa Cruz. Her media celebrity, notoriety, and intellectual accomplishments—taken together—are quite remarkable. There are times in her latest writing that she can appear bemused by her own reputation as a serious intellectual best-known for her Afro hairstyle. This humor is only the most superficial sign of her profound political and cultural self-consciousness as a black intellectual.

Davis' surface contradictions represent the ways in which she appears to be a product of her times. As a 1965 *magna cum laude* graduate of Brandeis, a graduate student at the Frankfort Institute and a professor at the University of California, Berkeley, she is an important part of the intellectual cohort that helped to integrate elite American universities in the seventies, eighties, and nineties. A glance through her scholarly treatments of Douglass narrative and Negro women's uplift shows the congruence of her concerns with those of many specialists in African-

American culture. Readers of this book who know her as a celebrity radical intellectual, an activist, and an acute cultural scholar will wonder what separates her from much of current African-American Studies. One might put the question thus: Would she have achieved intellectual authority without her earlier political celebrity, the integration of elite universities, the growth of the Black Studies movement, and the academic development of cultural studies?

Davis seems to have engaged in an ideological version of the literary endeavor described throughout this book. She has produced highly ideological accounts of her early life, her experiences in prison, and her political activities. This often mechanical writing is, however, offset by sensitive Marxist scholarship on the prison system, slave labor by inmates, and, most recently, the blues. Here the Marxist perspective, which appears to dehumanize her interpretation of her own experience, ironically provides rich and subtle accounts of the dehumanizing impact of racism. Her book on the blues, in particular, is exemplary for initiating the kind of inquiry to which Gates' scholarship once aspired. Indeed, in these cases, the Marxist ideological matrix has, as her footnotes and references indicate, given her a means of appropriating recent scholarship—one that is more sophisticated than that of the signifiers.

Marxism stands at the center of both the style and substance of Davis' best writing. In the essays that have come to make up her major collections, she has created a thoughtful persona, embodying deep human sympathy and a rigorous intellectual enquiry into the perquisites of black liberation. This humanity is visible, interestingly enough, on the level of style; the anthology gradually reveals her humanistic vision in both observation and wonderful literary gestures. She can say of a work by Feuerbach that it gives her joy. Her theoretical statements have the clarity of a serious writer wishing to share important reflection with a sympathetic audience. When her mind lays by its troubles and she speaks without ideology, this lucidity has the deep human warmth of the concerned teacher that she has become for her most serious African-American readers. At one point, Davis gently chides the younger generation for its secondhand acquaintance with essential Marxist texts through theory. Underlying the humor of this moment is a serious statement of value. For Davis, Marxism is a canon of fundamental texts, as well as a sense of theoretical issues that fall into central and peripheral categories. These divisions are grounded in a hierarchy of intellectual and moral worth.

Davis' work on the black presence in the new capitalist-industrial prison complex is, in light of this book's concerns, her most important achievement. These pieces frequently use Marxist ideology—particularly Enlightenment notions of human dignity as well as the romantic thought of the young Marx—as a framework for her excursions (here and elsewhere) on the imprisonment of blacks and the aesthetics of the blues. Within this Hegelian-Marxist view of human history, we encounter the central assumptions governing Davis' thinking about black culture and politics. The social and political domination imposed by Europeans upon Africans denied blacks their freedom in the eras of slavery and colonialism. In particular, European slavery in the New World systematically robbed blacks of the fullness of life that they experienced in precapitalist social relations, reducing them to the status of property and depriving the freedom fundamental to the human condition. Human liberty, she makes clear, goes beyond the existential choice to live or die. It is the power of choice within a social world characterized by the dignity of persons. It is thus within the modern era that Davis finds the radical dehumanization of blacks and their estrangement from the human condition.

Certain elements of the precapitalist world persisted in black life. At the same time, for Davis, the sense of blacks as nonpersons created possibilities for black politics, society, and culture in the post-slavery world. Female slaves, for example, were largely untouched, she argues, by the domestic sphere that cut modern white middle-class American women off from the possibility of meaningful work. Untainted by this historical innovation, African-American women have been able to protest oppression and racism without the restraints of a false, "natural" feminine order. On the other hand, this advantage has made African-American women victims of rape from white employers and social betters who animalize "unfeminine" black women for purposes of oppression. Finally, African-American culture, embodied first in spirituals and later in the twentieth-century blues art of Bessie Smith and Billie Holiday, articulated important forms of social, political, and sexual liberty.

Like many current avatars of black literary and artistic culture, Davis recognizes a will-to-power empowering a quest for liberty; however, she insists not only on the historical realities encountered by that will but also on the empowered will's own internal contradictions. Her political romanticism is like the cultural psychology of Freud (in *Civilization and Its Discontents* and *Totem and Taboo*) and the first of Marx' critiques (*The 1844 Political and Economic Manuscripts*), leavened by a reality principle, adequate notions of self-consciousness, historical process, and an account of human alienation. All of these factors serve to make the final utopianism of her advocacy of black art more plausible—and theoretically useful—than it would be otherwise. For this reader, she succeeds best in her account of Frederick Douglass' ambivalent attitude toward the leasing of inmate labor in a Jim Crow South where the "Black Codes" filled the jails with African-American men. This is, secondarily and implicitly, a subtle examination of Douglass' Victorian-Protestant ethic that led him to link prison labor with the criminal's "desert," but also to recognize the slippery slope to slavery inherent in the practice. Davis in this essay mainly concerns herself, however, with the particular racist twist of the American practice of criminal punishment. The devaluation of blacks to a subhuman level led directly in the late nineteenth century to a conception of the prison system as a profitable entity for the state. In the ruthlessly capitalistic era of the Gilded Age, labor-leasing inevitably became a money-making enterprise. Similarly, Davis incisively revises early twentieth-century notions of prison labor as a means of moral improvement, in the light of the debasement of black humanity. She endorses and develops Foucault's observation at Attica that the late twentieth-century prison system had become a means of dehumanizing an already dehumanized black populace, and of creating the conditions for their eventual return to prison. Davis' work on nineteenth-century black women exponents of African-American uplift is deeply beholden to the *Reader* essays, which expound the relation of black women to mainstream American feminism.

Davis' work on twentieth-century black blues women addresses, with exceptional thoughtfulness, the question of cultural response to black alienation and dehumanization—a phenomenon that she, like other commentators (some of them the subjects of this study), sees clearly in black music, particularly the blues. This book is the centerpiece of her intellectual project, and a high-water mark for cultural analysis written by a black American. It is no accident that this wholly exemplary book was written by a Marxist deeply enmeshed in the American tradition of communist, left-wing protest and Marxist social formation.

At the heart of the blues culture, as she understands it, is the early twentieth-century moment when female artists like Ma Rainey, Bessie Smith, and Billie Holliday came into prominence. Davis sees their jazz-art as an extension of the blues, expressing the black quest for freedom in erotic terms. This patently sexual, overtly antibourgeois conception of sexuality is a version of Hopkins' Way Maker. To a greater extent than Dwight Hopkins, however, Davis is able to locate this Way Maker historically, to identify the nature of its existence in society, and the means and consequences of its "sacred" legitimacy.

The erotic quest for freedom—like the nineteenth- and twentieth-century novel of female romance—sets forth sexual liberty and experience as a means of recovering a black humanity lost first in the oppression of slavery, then the Jim Crow South, and finally the Northern ghetto. Erotic choice was the exercise of the will that looked for utopian freedom in a satisfying sexuality. This was celebrated in the blues as a communal endeavor that was itself an important African cultural continuity. Within this community, the sexual travails of the individual were resolved by collective social wisdom. The blues were thus sacred as a cultural activity in which the group expressed the ultimate values and locus of its own humanity. In a still deeply religious American black culture, however, the sacred nature of the blues conflicted—as Davis incisively shows—with traditional spirituality in a struggle over how and where the community would express its ultimate value.

A second important insight comes from Davis' division of blues styles and genres by their function as social protest, cultural affirmation, individual identity, and historical analysis. The blues emerges as a cultural entity providing many of the existential explanations that a society in chaos makes. Although Davis is not explicitly concerned to denominate the blues tradition as an infinitely inventive, expansive, and numinous plenitude, she does establish it as an activity that creates the self-consciousness needed for meaningful human life in the spheres of politics, economics, and culture. This self-consciousness provides a context in which the Way Maker may be understood, directed, displaced, and even repressed, yielding for Davis a humanized vision of the African-American will-to-power—which otherwise denigrates the humanity of the black folk world that Hopkins, Cannon, and Coleman wish to celebrate.

This point is worth some reflection. The signifiers rarely come to an explicit statement of canonical purpose, although they often imitate the literary structures of such cultural historians as Curtius in *European Literature and the Latin Middle Ages* or M. H. Abrams in *Natural Supernaturalism*. These texts have the humanizing goal of translating either classical or biblical visions of society, culture, and personal life into the late twentieth century. The closest that Gates comes to this is an essay in *Loose Canons* in which he expresses hope that the cultural formulations achieved by the signifying method will lead to racial toleration in America. Whatever one may think of this goal and the means by which he seeks to achieve it, Gates' method is significant for the absence of a guiding historical moment of self-consciousness—Curtius' classical era, M. H. Abrams' Judeo-Christian biblical worldview, or even Davis' age of the black female blues singers.

Whatever self-consciousness is acquired in Gates' method comes from the manipulation and the demystification of semiotic mythologies or the codes that make them up. What we have is a play of differences, particularly what Gates calls the "black difference" (or Holloway's "gender difference"). However, the signifier's sense of the "black difference" is wholly amorphous without those social and economic contexts that emerge from inquiry into the history of prison labor or of the political consciousness borne by nineteenth-century black women activists. Without well-defined material, psychological, cultural, social, or even—in the case of Curtius, Huizinga, and Abrams—literary contexts, race itself is meaningless as a difference.

This meaninglessness characterizes the ultimately trivialized methods of gender and racial definition that run through the thinking of Baker, Awkward, and Holloway. In a world where "difference" becomes a mirrored "opposite," woman's literary traditions are characterized by "communal" relationships between texts, rather than the antagonistic revisions that link male-authored African-American texts. Whereas male texts are located in material human relationships, female texts are located in, and even generated by, a world of spirit. In Holloway, these opposites play on and on until the point of crisis is reached with her son Bem. Here the world of death becomes the sphere of male undertakers and funeral directors, like Holloway's grandfather and (for a time) her father. Death belongs largely to the realm of violence experienced by black men. And the recovery of a humanized conception of death means, in the context of her gendered mythology as a whole, recovering the male world of physical actuality so ruthlessly repressed in her feminized genealogy of black women's literary tradition.

One insight to be gleaned from a comparison of Holloway and Davis is the immediate Marxist recognition of the cultural and intellectual superiority of the black musical to the African-American literary tradition. It is, as Michael Dyson usefully notes, archived in recordings that may be studied, imitated, revised, parodied, or elaborated by future artists. And palimpsests, embodying a set of traditions, may be created by "sampling" these recordings, which are themselves palimpsests of an earlier state in the tradition—all validated by their material reality, in contrast to the metaphorical palimpsests described by Holloway in *Moorings and Metaphors*. Indeed, one of the consequences of the oral nature of black culture is that it cannot be usefully recovered in literary and literary-critical categories as the signifiers have tried to do.

Angela Davis' Marxism is similarly founded on a broader, richer, and deeper understanding of the romantic (i.e., early Marxist) political, philosophical, and literary tradition than that of the present generation of black intellectuals. They cannot fully grasp a tradition that they have not acknowledged, whose elaborations they have not explored, and whose categories they will not apply in an effort for self-consciousness. This refusal to acknowledge the Protestant-romantic sources of their tradition—sources that make them closer to Meyer Abrams and F. O. Mathiessen than to Derrida and de Man—represents yet another failure of self-consciousness and self-knowledge due to their self-imposed intellectual segregation. This isolation only deepens the highly racial inequality—economic, political, social, and cultural—that exists in America between blacks and their white and Asian fellow citizens.

Davis' self-consciousness gives her powers of political and cultural discrimination that let her identify the vulgarizing and dehumanizing effects of present-day consumer capitalism—perhaps the major contemporary American cultural form. Indeed, her sensitivity to the black variants of consumer-culture alienation makes her an attractive and authoritative presence. Angela Davis is at her most charming in those essays where she expresses her embarrassment at the posture of celebrity-radical which willy-nilly claims much public attention. She has become important not only for her political dicta, but for her personal suggestiveness for the fashion industry—an odd combination possible only in today's media. As she well knows, the image of revolutionary that she once embodied has long ago been co-opted by the liberal capitalist world that she attacks. Yet she calmly views this development from the wry perspective of an earlier cohort of the American Left.

In one of the *Reader*'s concluding interviews, she describes this leftist experience, appropriately enough in a characteristically self-conscious but moving autobiographical fragment:

> I grew up in a family which had numerous ties to individuals in the Communist Party. Although my mother never joined the Communist Party, she worked in organizations with black communists who were organizing in Birmingham, which, because of the steel mills, had become an industrial center in the '30s. She was an officer in the NAACP and in the Southern Negro Youth Congress, which had been established by communists. Because of my mother's connection with communists, we were often followed by the FBI during the McCarthy era. By the age of six, I was already aware of the extent to which the government would pursue people who had different ideas of what kind of social order should prevail in this country. While I was attending a progressive high school in New York, I read the *Communist Manifesto* for the first time. I was fortunate enough to have a history teacher who openly espoused Marxism and encouraged us to think critically about the class interests represented by dominant historiography. At the same time, I was active in a communist youth organization and for many months picketed Woolworth's every Saturday because of their policies of segregation in the South.[1]

Although we rarely think of her in this way, Angela Davis is a "red diaper" baby. Her hatred of gross materialism is the rebellion of an earlier left against a mid-century American culture. Her humanism is, at its heart, the product of an earlier interracial leftist self-consciousness, with its attendant nostalgias, social criticisms, and visionary hopes. This leftism was once the source of a profound humanism that recognized the obscene alienation of the capitalist marketplace and refused to accept it. Its hope was grounded not only in difficult adversary political action, but in exemplary cultural history of the sort displayed by Angela Davis in her marvelous book on the blues.

# Chapter Fourteen

# Adolph Reed
## Politics of Gesture

ADOLPH REED HAS ESTABLISHED HIMSELF as a distinguished political scientist in a number of books about black intellectual and social history. He is, moreover, a shrewd and articulate commentator on the current political and cultural scene. And it is with this aspect of his work that I chose to end this book, for it embodies the dialectical process of humanistic thought that I want to honor. The essays in *Class Notes* show that the decline in humanistic literacy has the direst consequences for the political life of African Americans.

Reed's analysis of ritualistic political symbols and gestures is a trenchant social commentary on a cultural style that extends beyond left-liberal politics. *Class Notes* examines this cultural style, and in doing so probes the nature of interracial communication and action in late twentieth-century America. Underlying Reed's account is a distinction between mere political gestures and a "real" politics that seeks consensus through an appeal to shared economic, social, and political issues. As he states forcefully:

> Cultural production can reflect and perhaps support a movement; it can never generate or substitute for one. There is no politics worthy of the name that does not work to shape the official institutions of public authority that govern and channel people's lives. Anything else is playacting.[1]

Driven by the romanticism, racial bad faith, and desperation of the left, the symbolic politics of "playacting" mystifies the realities of class and society, and understanding of which is vital to the construction of a "real" political movement. Exposing this divide between an authentic and an inauthentic politics, Reed seeks to call the left back from a world of gestures to the essential work of politics. By a real "political movement," Reed has a specific project in mind: the organization of working- and middle-class people into a broad-based Labor Party that will fight for a social democratic order in America. Paradoxically, however, this political program turns out to be far more utopian than the "playacting," particularly the racial variety that has entrenched itself in American cultural life. As his sometimes desperate tone suggests, even Reed himself is surprised at the ubiquity of gesture in the political life of the left.

Not surprisingly, *Class Notes* finds its most tangible examples of the rhetoric of gesture in the racial brokerage politics that Reed describes on the left. Here, a symbolic black voice speaks for a supposedly organized mass of the black population, presumably joined by premodern organic ties. This representative, who mediates between his race and powerful whites, gains his legitimacy from the putative identity of his view with that of the black masses. This figure is also legitimated indirectly by the attacks of white racists, whose opposition signals the authenticity of the victimized black. These premises of black political brokerage inform Reed's analysis of public intellectuals and the present middle-class nostalgia for the segregated black communities of the South, as well as the *modus operandi* of figures like Jesse Jackson and Louis Farrakhan. He shows the triumph of Farrakhan in deploying a demagogic political voice to create the impression of a mass movement from only a small constituency. The powerful symbolism of a black voice blurs important divisions in black society, mystifying the actual dynamics of its class politics. Lost are the nuances and tensions of African-American society, and serious political organization and interracial understanding within the left is discouraged.

In Reed's view, a disciplined analysis of class (hence the book's punning title) can reveal those mystified dynamics that lurk beneath the political icons. The current black middle-class nostalgia for the supposedly organic community of the Jim Crow era becomes, in Reed's view, a way of bolstering black bourgeois claims to privileged leadership roles in African-American society. Similarly, public intellectuals like Cornel West and Michael Dyson perform the task of explicating a supposedly homogeneous black world to a white audience which desires access to an otherwise opaque world of thought and feeling. In doing so, these public intellectuals assume the accomodationist role of their early twentieth-century predecessor Booker T. Washington.

Reed's voice often becomes shrill as he confronts the social myths, disingenuous racial attitudes, and cynicism that for him constitute an illegitimate politics of gesture and debased liberal left. Political and intellectual figures are caricatured, their views simplified. His is the partisan rage of an unreconstructed political radical, assessing those who have parlayed political symbols like the underclass into academic power or access to the very real power of the state. He is angered that this culture of symbolism is recognized as such by the elite of those public institutions that has the power to shape peoples' lives. Reed has an enemy-list of well-connected liberals like William Julius Wilson, David Ellwood, and Mary Jo Bane who, as influential political advisors and policymakers, have launched a betrayal of liberal values. He has, besides, a gallery of well-placed rogues like Charles Murray and Clarence Thomas, who have won the attention of an economically powerful conservative right that has dominated politics since the Reagan era and is deeply involved with powerful and influential corporate interests.

As the earlier excerpt shows, Reed tends to devalue the cultural dimension of politics. Yet political and economic transformations, such as the Civil Rights movement, have created cultural changes that inevitably influence the actions of the state. Reed's critique of the new class of black public intellectuals and academics is an implicit criticism of the culture of integration itself. As black professionals have won increased access to the mainstream of American society, they have ripened to an accommodation of its center and right values. What Reed takes to be Clinton's mystifying politics of tokenism is a historical phenomenon: the unexpected consequence of Civil Rights successes and the growing racial integration of American social institutions, particularly the elite academy.

Reed's disappointment in much present-day intellectual and political life leads, moreover, to his own nostalgia. Despite his attack on a romanticized Jim Crow era, Reed admires the segregated academy and its excellent social scientists, as well as its body of sophisticated social and literary commentary. In his own terms, the reasons for this excellence are not far to seek. The segregated intellectuals were informed by the politics of Depression-era radicalism and civil rights. They rarely found themselves mediating between the various audiences that Reed's public intellectuals address. Reed also quite clearly laments the passing of the sixties, when intellectuals had to confront the dose of political reality generated by the broad-based Civil Rights and antiwar movements. I suspect that this nostalgia forms a kind of historical vantage point for Reed's own activism as well. In many respects, his utopian Labor Party seeks to revive an earlier world in which intellectuals were more in tune with practical politics through experiences of radical organization.

Intellectuals are important for Reed. They are best placed to define the social worlds in which serious politics are forged. *Class Notes* makes the important point that intellectual life loses its cogency and force when cut off from the social, economic, and political realities of the public arena. And this point is deeply suggestive. Without a demystified understanding of their ideas, it is easy, as Reed continually argues, for public intellectuals to assume an all-purpose posture directed toward a variety of audiences. Without commitment to the secular and politically pragmatic orientations of the left, it is easy for radicals and liberals alike to give credence and legitimacy to black religious figures as the voice of the masses. Absent the demands of a political movement for equal rights, a black intelligentsia may become distracted by its own status anxieties.

Reed is probably right to argue that culture—even the culture of gesture—can never generate or substitute for serious politics. Yet the value of his book lies beyond his dismissal of the culture of symbolism. Reed's description of the black voice in politics shows only one site in which the culture of political symbolism can simplify the complexities of racial life, blur fundamental economic and political differences, and mystify social life. His account of the brokerage politics of race is applicable to a language of diversity and multiculturalism that pervades public and private politics. His shrewd political analyses suggest, moreover, the political functions of this language in the foundations of government and the schools.

Just as the inhabitants of this world of images have lost a certain textual literacy, so have they given up the demystifying political awareness that Reed describes. The cost of this loss is not only a decline of "real" liberal left politics but also an erosion of the self-consciousness that underlies serious political and intellectual life. The intellectuals in any ideal world—certainly in Reed's world of the thirties and forties—ought to be the bearers of this self-consciousness, a repository of knowledge about a society's tensions, its complexities, and its nuances of class. And the ubiquity of the politics of gesture (on both the left and the right) may reveal how the civic awareness critical to intellectual life has been lost in the nexus of racial integration, politics, and the media.

Ironically, the sleaziness of the language of diversity may be part of the popularizing and ultimately intellectually shoddy processes of a democratic society. Here it should be noted that this "language" is a conservative one that preserves current interests in the name of multiethnic consensus. The culture of symbolism is therefore quite congenial to an increasingly diverse society that seeks to keep its day-to-day balance—and a white-dominated society whose elite would maintain its mastery. Reed's real complaint may be that he lives in an age when social conditions do not drive intellectuals and organizers into political consciousness of themselves or others. One feels that Reed knows this and thus the scathing desperation of much of his book.

# Conclusion

## Part One: *Their Eyes Were Watching God* All Over Again

GATES, HOLLOWAY, DYSON, AND OTHER SIGNIFIERS rarely apply their deconstructive scrutiny to their own often thematic interpretations. There is a bait-and-switch in their intellectual style. They deck themselves out in demystifying semiotic modes, but then avoid a full decoding of the literary texts they study. The claim to have found an ironic black voice is never tested by a demystification or deconstruction of that voice to reveal the contradictory codes from which that identity is constructed. Much literary criticism takes the form of fictional projection; the critic elaborates a narrative or reality based upon his scanning of a text, what one critic has called an "allegory of reading." The demystification of a literary text demands a plenitude of sometimes contradictory, sometimes complementary readings. Only by mapping these interpretations can the reader find the fault lines in the text and discover the inevitably illusory quality of the writer's voice. The problem of African-American literary criticism is that it lacks a tradition of sufficiently varied, incisive readings to permit the effective identification of where, in any given text, meaning breaks down consistently, forms new codes, or persists in endless conflict. The signifiers do not work from a rich enough intellectual basis to evoke literature's dynamic forces or its messy human element of deception, contradiction, illusion, and misinterpretation. Because the new black critics often avoid the labor of identifying contradictory strands of meaning, they cannot produce adequately rich views of a text, the writer's authorial project, or the writer's voice in and of itself. The end result is an impoverished view of African-American literature.

The signifiers face a clear institutional problem which they seek to avoid by invoking, but rarely presenting, a plenitude of black oral and written texts. Yet demystifying and deconstructive reading demands, even more than canonical reading, an extensive literary tradition, itself produced by a well-established cultural enterprise. Such an enterprise has not yet established itself in African-American life, and it is difficult—given the history of African-American literature—to imagine such an enterprise apart from the mainstream American literary establishment. The humanizing act of demystification attempted by the new black critics may, ironically, be best carried out through the imaginative projection of African-American writers into the institutional world of American cultural tradition. Only this can provide the wealth of readings, texts, literary conventions, and institutional structures in which to locate black literary works and dissect their constituent threads of meaning.

At the core of the signifiers' dilemma, then, is an inadequate vision of the social, political, and cultural nexus in which African-American literature has been produced. They lack a full-fledged sense of the complicated institutional worlds from which literary critics and scholars draw possibilities for meanings. Not surprisingly, this failure of social vision reveals itself vividly in the new black critics' treatment of certain culturally volatile motifs, particularly that of the minstrel—the image with which this study began. I propose to conclude with another reading of Hurston's *Their Eyes Were Watching God*. In particular, I wish to show how Hurston's uncertain use of the minstrel—like a similar tentativeness in the signifiers—points to deeper uncertainties about the institutional nature of black community itself.

One aspect of *Their Eyes Were Watching God*—an early prophecy of the signifying critics' faulty social vision—was an image of minstrelsy that embarrassed the early twentieth-century black authors, but offered them a suggestive form of character treatment. Wright criticized Hurston's book for its minstrelsy and its lack of realistic motivation. Yet he himself experimented with the postures of minstrelsy in the depiction of Big Boy and his friends in the short story "Big Boy Leaves Home"; of Shorty in *Black Boy*; of the unemployed cook-hero in "A Man of all Work"; and of minor characters in *The Outsider*. Whether covert submission or resistance to white authority, a form of irony, or an interracially accepted genre of humor—minstrelsy is a commonplace in black writing. Although black intellectuals may attack the minstrel form explicitly, its persona offers numerous expressive possibilities. In their public appearances before interracial college audiences, Cornel West, Eugene Rivers, Henry Louis Gates, and Houston Baker all flaunt this style, as they often do in their written work.

Black writers' attitudes towards minstrelsy reflect the range and contradictory nature of their attitudes toward the masses. The minstrel image may seem to represent the folk's capacity for frank, unvarnished expression, but it also may reveal a lack of dignity, the psychological consequence of subordination to arbitrary white authority. Whereas Hurston's *Their Eyes Were Watching God* embodied the quests for identity, the celebration of black folk life, and the issues of literary style faced by the new black critics, it also portrayed hapless, silly, comical black figures engaged in mimicry of whites, aimless boasting, and sometimes self-destructive behavior. Moreover Hurston could, in her own self-presentation, easily slide into self-demeaning "darky" behavior before patrons or other influential whites. In this respect, her minstrelsy represented not a celebration of the folk, but real anxieties over her financial status, literary fame, personal dignity, and public image.

The early signifying readings necessarily repressed the vast investment that Zora Neale Hurston makes in the minstrel image as a vehicle for characterization, plot, and incident. However, her text is too rich to neglect the contradictory underside of her celebrations of the folk, complicating the book in engaging and provocative ways. Moreover, Hurston was too good an intellectual, social observer, and conscious artist not to realize that the carnivalesque play of her minstrel characters on the muck was a form of decadent riot, hardly distinguishable from the worst social disorder. Hurston risks the problems posed by these issues in order to provide a provocative commentary upon Janie's courtship, marriage, and escape from bourgeois values.

The intellectual complications presented by the riot of black folk life create a disturbing textual code in *Their Eyes Were Watching God*—as they do in *Jonah's Gourd Vine* and to a lesser extent in her succeeding book, *Moses, Man of the Mountain*. Within Hurston's much noticed, all-black social worlds, such self-destructive play reigns, and creates a disturbing tension between forces for the consolidation and dissolution of society. This tension stands at the center of *Eyes*. On the one hand, the embarrassing black waywardness is one more example of the currently approved way in which Hurston's characters seem to act without the pressures and constraints of an onlooking white world. And yet that white world *does* intrude in *Eyes*. It intrudes, significantly, just where social progress and order are promoted. Jody has earned his seed money for the town by working for white bosses in Georgia. Janie's privileged upbringing took place in the backyard of a generous white neighbor. Jody buys the property for the town from a white. And, significantly, the town's most important structures are painted a gleaming white, casting an aura of racial and ethnic superiority—or rather manipulating it symbolically. Related to these images is the diner run by Mrs. Turner and her husband on the muck. Like the buildings of Jody's town, this restaurant is connected to a black authority which legitimizes itself through its links to whiteness. All of these images of white-dependent order are essential for the social structure in which Janie grows up, becomes literate, achieves financial security, and ultimately enjoys the stability required for bohemian experiment.

This stable white society parallels a black mock realm, the crude community on the site of Jody's future town before the founder arrives. On the muck, Tea Cake, Motorboat and Bootany form a community of sorts during the hurricane. This is a world of play, food, and malingering. Significantly, this society is destroyed by imprudence. In the midst of thrill-deranged misjudgment, their house is thrown into the water and Tea Cake suffers a fatal bite from a rabid dog. The world-turned-upside-down of Tea Cake and his friends—involving Tea Cake's symbolic beating of Janie to prove his male dominance—is a world of disorder.

The interplay of these two codes gives their imagery an ironic ambiguity. On the one hand, black community celebrates itself through riot. On the other, the establishment of black community—like any other society—depends on rigidly enforced authority, like that of Jody and Mrs. Turner. A materialistic conception of society, marriage, and success are part of the cultural worldview that Jody imposes upon the town of Starkville. Yet this strictly governed community eventually allows Janie her freedom on the muck. Similarly, the riotous behavior of Hurston's clownlike characters on the muck gives plausibility and legitimacy to Mrs. Turner's stern demeanor and her insistence upon order in the diner. At the same time, her rigid snobbery makes us sympathize with the rioters. The self-destructive waywardness of Tea Cake ultimately justifies his shooting by Janie—an act necessary to maintain her right, as a civilized being, to life and liberty. But it is Janie's repressed character that makes Tea Cake charming and attractive at first.

Our current celebration of the theme of black community suppresses the text's coded expression of deep anxiety about folk blacks' ability to maintain community, and whether they can do so without the exercise of authority. The world of ironic disorder celebrated by the signifiers cannot yield a stable politics, society, or community. It lacks the terms to make the key distinctions of just and unjust authority, legitimate and illegitimate social order, good and bad social hierarchy, and citizenship as opposed to friendship. As such, it cannot pass a social structure through time. It cannot support what are generally assumed to be the world-defining cultural issues, beliefs, and images of any society. The signifying rhetorician's irony may represent blackness, but it can only represent a black institution or society by repressing some of the most virulent, disruptive qualities associated with the folk.

## Part Two: Home Again

During the late sixties and the seventies at Yale and the University of Chicago, I stayed aloof from the black literary movement. And throughout an extended graduate school and teaching career during most of the eighties, I was only in touch with it through the literary-critical journals that I continually read. Halfway through my graduate program career at the University of Chicago, it had become clear to me that I was expected to teach African-American literature. My advisor, looking at my record, was horrified to see no courses in Black Studies. I stubbornly resisted, an aging graduate student teaching composition while writing a dissertation on colonial American culture. When I finally became an assistant professor at Colgate University in the late eighties, I had been out of the loop for some time, and had missed the institutionalization of Black Studies and the performances of black literary critics and luminaries like Baker and Gates. In the early nineties, Baker had been a visitor at Colgate for a year, and as a matter of collegial courtesy later invited me to the 1991 Richard Wright lectures at the University of Pennsylvania when Henry Louis Gates was to lecture on Edmund Burke and post-colonial theory. I eagerly jumped at the opportunity as a chance to catch up on what I had missed in professional life, and knew only from *Critical Inquiry*, *New*

*Literary History*, and *PMLA*. But my shock at the performance I encountered there only deepened my sense of dislocation in the profession.

Arriving in Philadelphia, I went straight to the university after checking into my hotel and came early to the marvelously appointed venue; Baker had been in charge of Black Studies at Penn for some time and had secured not only an excellent lecture room, but also an extensive office facility. Before the event he introduced me to Gates, who was formally dressed in an elegant suit. Shortly afterwards, he and Baker ascended the stage where they sat with one of the deans, a tall, sixtyish, white-haired man, who apparently had been a professor of engineering or science. The dean introduced Baker and Gates as two of the country's most eminent speakers, a scholarly put-down referring to the black thinkers' popularity. He went on to discuss the copiousness of their writing and their excellence as "orators," noting that his own dissertation in the sciences had been no more than fifty pages.

Gates, clearly insulted, got up to speak—and lost the small microphone that was pinned to the lapel of his suit. Stooping to the floor to pick up the tiny device, Gates pinned it back on, now standing erect. "There," he said. And then breaking into the code of the street, he concluded, "and I didn't need no Ph.D. in physics to do this." As if in defiance, Gates unleashed his own flood of volubility, a wash of street talk and high deconstructive theory. Babbling from the podium, he became something other than the mild-mannered, elegantly suited man he had been before. He was now not so much a figure of scholarly dignity, but a comic parody of the well-dressed, professional type of fifteen minutes earlier.

Only later would I be struck by the most remarkable aspect of this event, the tall physicist's calm acquiescence to Gates' furious stream of theoretical discourse, an energetic flow clearly stimulated by the session's opening put-down. The dean, having said his piece, continued to sit onstage, politely gazing at Gates. Far from there being any bad will between the two, one sensed a kind of consensus, a shared understanding and realm of feeling that bonded Gates not only to the dean but also to some of the very distinguished white members of the audience. This bond, significantly, was not shared by a number of the equally distinguished black intellectuals in the crowd, particularly those who—after the lecture—tried to wedge their way into the intellectual structure of his hermetically complex presentation.

Thirteen years since this event, of course, I have learned to recognize the scene in Philadelphia as a generic phenomenon. The alternately jiving, intellectualizing black speaker addressing a calm, acquiescent white audience is—as the media performances of Michael Dyson and Cornel West attest—a commonplace, deeply entrenched not only in black intellectual tradition but in public American interracial communication. Cornel West pacing the floor as the jackleg folk minister (I had seen the real thing in Arkansas), Eugene Rivers doing a dance step out of West Philadelphia, Dyson freelancing on a talk show—such scenes are now not only accepted conventions, but a throwback to one of the most deeply established racial stereotypes in America, a figure of minstrel tradition. This style dramatizes the black's speaker deference to a white audience that considers him inferior, the speaker's knowledge of the black street culture inhabited by young black people, and thus the capacity to act not only as a go-between for the black masses, African-American elites, and his superiors in the foundations and academic world.

This figure, as commentators have often noted, informs the literary style of *Up from Slavery*, thus reflecting Washington's role as a shrewd collector of Northern and Southern white patrons, as well as a ruthless manager of black middle-class intellectuals. One of the most recently noticed features of *Up from Slavery* is Washington's use of "darky" jokes—the staple humor of the plantation myth. The dark side of this obscenely antisocial humor for his white patrons inhered in the rigorous authority that he exercised over his black charges. Washington could not duplicate the dignity of his white patrons because, as Ellison tellingly shows in his portrait of Bledsoe, the wizard of Tuskegee did not have the power, wealth, and social position to do so—whatever his boasts. The wizard, of course, knew this too. Indeed, some of the most acute moments in Washington's promotion-pamphlet-cum-autobiography are those in which the speaker places himself in the role of zip-coon trickster confronting his white patron in a quiet moment, when the submissive (if educated) "darky" sincerely listens to his white (if less educated) superior:

> In a jesting manner this man said: "Washington, you have spoken before the Northern white people, the Negroes in the South, and to us country white people in the South; but in Atlanta, tomorrow, you will have before you the Northern whites, the Southern whites, and the Negroes all together. I am afraid that you have got yourself into a tight place". This farmer diagnosed the situation correctly, but his frank words did not add anything to my comfort.[1]

This passage, of course, is one of the book's many moments of literary self-consciousness. For although *Up from Slavery* is not a great book, it is a shrewd one: full of insights into not only the advantages, but also the dangers, of the rhetorical-professional style that the author has chosen. At the heart of the book's narrative is the demonstration of a professional style that at once defers to white intellectual and moral superiority, while establishing authority over other blacks.

To a large extent, the persistence of the zip-coon persona among the most visible black media public intellectuals is—like Booker T. Washington's similar persona—a response to the task of engaging in a discourse directed to multiple audiences. When Michael Dyson breaks out into televised rap lyrics or begins his book on Malcolm X with an anecdote about interracial student sex, he is implicitly acquiescing to his place as a second-class intellectual citizen of a ruthlessly meritocratic American academic world in which lower-class Asian immigrants regularly outperform upper-class black students in English and math aptitude tests. Gates' sly and shallow mimicry of fashionable literary-theoretical modes in *The Signifying Monkey* is a similar accommodation. At the same time this admission of black inferiority advertises the need for social control and management—traditionally carried out by the black middle class from which the new arriviste intelligentsia springs.

To this end, the public intellectual's adaptation of street jive and intellectual demeanor signals his "knowledge" of those values which are embodied in the essential black character—which black vernacular now represents—as well as his capacity to communicate with the masses, particularly the youth. This last value is especially important, for two reasons. First, these intellectuals must participate in an academic world where their legitimacy is suspect. Moreover, they must vet and recommend the black scholars and intellectuals beneath them. For the academy, the foundations, the media and politicians, they are intellectual go-betweens who must speak the languages not only of the black *demi-monde* of the humanities in African-American Studies, but also of the academy. They must be able to move between the university, Senate committees and foundations, as well as the black-tilted or black-responsive political worlds of congressmen like Bill Bradley or street figures like Al Sharpton.

Second, and perhaps more importantly, communication with young black audiences at selective colleges like mine is a lucrative and significant task for these figures. They are paid often thousands of dollars to jet in and address crowds of young African Americans who, as an increasing number of statistics tells us, perform poorly in school and experience deep alienation. To these students—and to the nervous administrators who must control them—these writers provide the water-calming oil of black jive. On the face of it, one might easily mistake these figures and one of their facets—a high intellectual demeanor—with the formality of an older generation of black professors in the white university. One thinks in particular of the English accents, the exaggerated formal manner, the courtly dress of Nathan Scott at the University of Chicago, Martin Kilson at Harvard, and Charles Davis and Michael Cooke at Yale. At Howard, one saw this style in such highly respected figures as the philosopher William Banner and the eminent classicist Frank Snowden. Let me say that my most vivid memory of this period is the contempt these towering figures drew whenever their names were mentioned.

I particularly remember this in the case of Scott at Chicago. The mere mention of his name often caused knowing smirks and smiles among my white classmates and teachers, and would prompt one of them to take me aside to query my opinion of a black man who taught Jane Austen. (It is not clear to me that he was actually doing this at the time.) Michael Cooke or Charles Davis at Yale, Martin Kilson at Harvard—all could be a source of contempt not only for the high formality of their accents, but also their high academic standards. Of course, many of these heroic black figures had escaped the intellectual hells of the black colleges in the South—in particular Howard during its declining years—for the greener fields of the Northern integrated university (thereby offending different groups on many counts). In an age of black academic collapse, they stood for an excellence that offended both liberal whites and black students who held black intellectuals in contempt. Moreover, they did not kowtow to students in the manner of their younger black and white colleagues. Davis and Scott had been around the block a few times and understood the link between the intellectual and the dignity with which he restores order to a culture. They knew their obligation to the black constituency whose ultimate sacrifices of sweat, frustration, and blood had gained African Americans a place in the white academy. These scholars were more than ready to accept the contempt directed by both whites and blacks toward rigorous displays of black dignity. They were not afraid to put themselves, and their day-to-day comfort in public, on the line for what Martin Kilson now calls "the honor" of black people. Not surprisingly, the older generation of intellectuals refused to become lords of misrule for the African-American academic circus of the seventies and eighties.

It is to the point of this essay that the most damning thing that one can now say of a black academic is that he does not get along with black students—the very group that white colleagues see as the embodiment of intellectual weakness and poor performance. I have heard this said of some of the most eminent, older black intellectuals who come to the selective, almost wholly white college where I teach. This is never said of the minstrels—and with good reason. The most important aspect of the black minstrel intellectual is his consensual acceptance of the racism of the American academic world, in which black intellectual achievement and performance, as well as the exceptional abilities of black people, are so deeply, if invisibly, degraded.

I thought of all this as I watched an assemblage of graduate students, professors, and intellectuals—black and white—walk out of the room. Among them was a dark young teenager wearing a frilly pink dress clearly designed for a much younger girl. On further inspection, it was clear that she was a street person who had wandered in for some food. She ate a piece of cake topped with shiny white icing. I watched her as I left the hall. She, her dress, and her cake are the Kafkaesque reality—in all of its self-contradictory glitter, filth, trauma, and horror—romanticized in the discourse of recent African-American criticism in the academy. This young woman's life—like human life in Sierra Leone, Pacific Palisades, Zaire-Congo, Scarsdale, West Philadelphia, Bryn Mawr, West Memphis, the thirteenth arrondissement, Niamey, Shaker Heights, Glenville, and New Trier—is however complex in a way that only a deep and comprehensive acquaintance with literature can reveal. We need all of literary tradition to grasp her and ourselves.

# Notes

## Preface

1. Henry Louis Gates Jr., editor of both books, indicates that *Our Nig* was considered to be the work of whites by some earlier twentieth-century white scholars. See "Introduction—Henry Louis Gates, Jr.," in Harriet E. Wilson, *Our Nig: or, Sketches from the Life of a Free Black* (1859; repr., New York: Vintage Books, 1983), xxxiii; and "Introduction Henry Louis Gates, Jr.," in Hannah Crafts, *The Bondwoman's Narrative* (New York: Warner Books, 2002). Similarly, Harriet Jacobs' *Incidents in the Life of a Slave Girl* was similarly assumed to be heavily edited and rewritten by Lydia Maria Child, before the detective work of Jean Fagan Yellin discovered otherwise. See, in particular, Jean Fagan Yellin, "Introduction," in Harriet A. Jacobs, *Incidents in the Life of a Slave Girl, Written by Herself* (Cambridge, MA: Harvard University Press), xiii–xxxiv.
2. For a historically balanced and accurate account of Plato's literary importance, see Kenny J. Williams, "Introduction," in *Essays: Including Biographies and Miscellaneous Pieces, in Prose and Poetry* (New York: Oxford University Press, 1988), esp. xliii–liii. Note the contrast that Williams makes between the significance of Ann Plato and that of Maria Stewart. "Yet, at no point would she [Plato] be compared to Maria Stewart, who did so much for the essay in America prior to Ralph Waldo Emerson" (xlii). Williams' comparison of Stewart to Emerson is to my mind, however, an overstatement of Stewart's importance in American literature. On Bassard's reading of Plato's significance, see Katherine Bassard, *Spiritual Interrogations: Culture, Gender, and Community in Early African American Women's Writing* (Princeton, NJ: Princeton University Press, 1999), 77–86.
3. I do not wish to criticize the intention behind Levine's erudite and generous reading of Bassard's text and the suggestiveness of his discussion of Plato. Robert S. Levine, "Slavery, Race, and American Literary Genealogies," *Early American Literature* 36, no. 1 (2001): 110.
4. Farah Jasmine Griffith, "Review of *Spiritual Interrogations*" in *American Literature* 72, no. 1 (2000): 183–185.
5. Plato, *Essays*, 80–83.
6. The notion of a woman's canon that anticipates a community of women's readers begins with the work of Hortense Spillers. Spillers' essays look carefully and very suggestively

at the historical forms taken by the family in Africa, the Diasporean movements of the slave trade, and in slavery itself—drawing upon these forms as models for a semiotic encoding the matrifocal elements of African-American life. See, for instance, "Mama's Baby, Papa's Maybe: An American Grammar Book," pp. 203–229; "'The Permanent Obliquity of an In(pha)llibly Straight': In the Time of the Daughters and the Fathers," pp. 230–250, in *Black, White, and in Color: Essays on American Literature and Culture* (Chicago: University of Chicago Press, 2003). For Bassard's two claims, see first Katherine Bassard, *Spiritual Interrogations: Culture, Gender, and Community in Early African American Women's Writing* (Princeton, NJ: Princeton University Press, 1999), 83. For Wheatley's anticipation of black community, see Bassard's reading of "To a Lady on Her Coming to North-America": "If the poem began with the white lady's spoken desire for health in the '*Northern* milder climes,' it ends with the poet's (unspoken) desire for interconnection with family, kin, community, and land" (54). Notice that the "desire" is "unspoken" but discerned through Bassard's reading of a tradition in which black women writers wish for a future female audience such as the professional readership of black women professional literary critics today. This is as blatant a "narcissistic" wish-fulfilling dream as one might imagine. And the literary rhetoric of this desire forms much of the subject of this book.

7. See Neal's collected essays in Larry Neal, *Visions of a Liberated Future: Black Arts Movement Writings* (New York: Thunder's Mouth Press, 1989). For another severe critique of Neal at this stage of his Yale career, see Charles T. Davis' incisive criticisms of Neal and the Black Arts movement in "American Scholar, Black Arts, Black Power." in *Black is the Color of the Cosmos*, 45–46.

8. See, for instance, Ellison's important essays about American literary tradition, such as "Twentieth-Century Fiction and the Mask of Humanity," "Change the Joke and Slip the Yoke," "Stephen Crane and the Mainstream of American Fiction," "Richard Wright's Blues," and "Society, Morality and the Novel," in *The Collected Essays of Ralph Ellison*, ed. John F. Callahan (New York: Modern Library, 1995).

9. For an early example of an attempt to read all of black literature through a single rhetorical or semiotic element, see Houston A. Baker Jr., "Completely Well: One View of African American Culture," in *Long Black Song: Essays in Black American Literature and Culture* (Charlottesville, Virginia: The University Press of Virginia, 1972). Note the priority that Baker places upon folk tradition as the base of African-American culture, the "canonical" literature (which Baker refers to as "the classic works" and the "the existing monuments") as well as of the proper intepretation of Black American literature. "To understand the classic works of black literature, a knowledge of the existing monuments and of the group in which the writer had their genesis is a necessity. Black folklore stands at the base of the black literary tradition and black literary tradition as a whole" (41). The first two essays of this collection, "Completely Well: One View of Black American Culture" and "Black Folklore and the Black American Literary Tradition" both seek to create a literary plenitude—drawing from selected folk examples for the reading of black literature. Thus, Baker can affirm Ellison's *Invisible Man* for its embodiment of the "whole" of black tradition. Baker's quotation on Dryden's commentary on Chaucer only underlines the then young black critic's sense that he was enunciating a canonical strategy: "Dryden's comment on Chaucer—'Here is God's plenty'—offers a fitting characterization of *Invisible Man*. Ellison's protagonist is both a trickster and an urban, industrial seat hero, and his adventures carry him through almost every phase of the black folk experience" (40–41).

10. Henry Louis Gates Jr., "Songs of a Racial Self: On Sterling A. Brown," in *Figures in Black: Words, Signs, and the "Racial" Self* (New York: Oxford University Press, 1987), 233.

11. I draw here upon A. O. Lovejoy's concept of plenitude in Chapter VII, "The Principle of Plenitude and Eighteenth-Century Optimism," in *The Great Chain of Being: A Study*

*of the History of an Idea* (1965; repr., New York: Harper & Row), pp. 208–226. Writers of formalist histories often seek to convince their readers by evoking a seemingly infinite sphere of literary topoi, conventions, examples, and prooftexts. This sphere is a romantic displacement of earlier conceptions of an infinite divine plenitude. For Lovejoy's romantic conception of plenitude, see Chapter X, "Romanticism and the Principle of Plenitude," in *The Great Chain of Being*, 288–314.

12. For the work of the critics I cite and examples of the qualities I describe please see J. Saunders Redding, *To Make a Poet Black* (1939; repr., College Park, Maryland: McGrath PublishingCompany, 1968). Note Redding's extensive bibliography, documenting the broad erudition that informs his text (131–136). Sterling Brown, *Negro Poetry and Drama* and *The Negro in American Fiction*. Robert Bone, Introduction (1937; repr., New York: Atheneum, 1978). Note Brown's careful literary history of types of black characterization and representation in American fiction: a history drawing upon a rich and comprehensive examination of American fiction of a number of modes and genres; Arthur P. Davis, *From the Dark Tower: Afro-American Writers 1900–1960* (1974; repr., Washington, D.C.: Howard University Press, 1981). Davis' book includes not only thumbnail introductory sketches (rich with empirical observation) of major black writers from roughly the first half of the twentieth century, but also extensive bibliographical record of their publication. The work of Nathan Scott should also be considered in the context of Davis and Brown—both of whom were Scott's one-time colleagues at Howard. Nathan Scott's corpus, from which I name only a few major texts, is extensive. See in particular Nathan A. Scott, Jr., *The Broken Center: Studies in the Theological Horizon of Modern Literature* (New Haven, CT: Yale University Press, 1966); Nathan A. Scott, Jr., *Visions of Presence in Modern American Poetry* (Baltimore: Johns Hopkins University Press); *The Poetics of Belief: Studies in Coleridge, Arnold, Pater, Santayana, Stevens, and Heidegger* (Chapel Hill: University of North Carolina Press, 1985). Scott has consistently examined the theological and philosophical dimension of Anglo-European literature, ranging widely in English, American, French, and German fiction, poetry, theology, and philosophy. He too has given an encyclopedic account of the way in which many of the central issues of belief, existence, faith, language, communication, and interpretation, as well as all manner of cultural issues, may be read in the context of modern literature. His broad theological, philosophical, and literary project has proven an especially powerful context for his reading of African American literature, in particular the fiction of Richard Wright. See "A Search for Beliefs: The Fiction of Richard Wright," in *University of Kansas City Review*, XXIII (1956): 19–24, 130–138.
13. Crafts, *The Bondwoman's Narrative*, xxviii–xxxiv, lxiii–lxv.
14. Dickson Bruce, *Black American Writing from the Nadir: The Evolution of a Literary Tradition, 1877–1915* (Baton Rouge: Louisiana State Press, 1987); *The Origins of African-American Literature, 1680–1865* (Charlottesville: University Press of Virginia, 2001); Wilson Moses, *Black Messiahs and Uncle Toms: Social and Literary Manipulations of a Religious Myth* (University Park: Pennsylvania State University Press, 1982); *The Golden Age of Black Nationalism, 1820–1925* (New York: Oxford University Press, 1978); *Alexander Crummell: A Study of Civilization and Discontent* (New York: Oxford University Press, 1989); Carla Peterson, *Doers of the Word: African-American Women Speakers and Writers in the North (1830–1880)* (New York: Oxford University Press, 1995).
15. See, for example, Claudia Tate, *Domestic Allegories of Political Desire: The Black Heroine's Text of the Turn of the Century* (1992; repr., New York: Oxford University Press, 1996), 99–101.
16. Significantly, Tate's very thesis turns on the notion of "desire" as a "largely unnarrated" "implicitly" political force. "This is precisely my hypothesis—that post-Reconstruction domestic novels of black women are allegorical literary performances of political desire

that (re)tell a surface story about an exemplary marriage and a deeper story about the social climate that would promote such a marriage. Hence, the story about ideal family formation refers implicitly to another—a public discourse about an equitable political system that distributes rewards on the basis of personal integrity, commitment, and hard work. This external, largely unnarrated context makes the domestic story with its compatible and compassionate conjugal relationship possible by assuaging racial and/or other forms of social discrimination" (Tate, *Domestic Allegories*, 101). It is not clear to this writer how desire may be political without a material intervention in the political world, the world of the polis, politics, and society itself. That intervention for blacks would be a world of profound conflict unlike that of courtship.
17. Tate, *Domestic Allegories*, 12.
18. I refer to Daniel Hoffman's *Form and Fable in American Fiction* (1973; repr., New York: Oxford University Press, 1961) and to Richard Chase, *The American Novel and Its Tradition*, (1957; repr., Baltimore: Johns Hopkins University Press, 1983).
19. Private remarks made by Arna Bontemps to the author, spring 1972.
20. Charles Nichols, ed., *Arna Bontemps-Langston Hughes Letters, 1925–1967* (New York: Dodd, Mead, 1980), 472, 491.
21. The intrinsically "literary," "linguistic," and "semiotic" character of Henry Louis Gates' literary project emerged as one of the central themes in his criticism early in his career. See, for instance, "Criticism in the Jungle," in *Black Literature & Literary Theory*, ed. Henry Louis Gates Jr. (New York: Methuen, 1984). "And, because our life in the West has been one political struggle after another, our literature has been defined from without and rather often from within, as primarily just one more polemic in those struggles. The black literary tradition now demands, for sustenance and for growth, the sorts of reading which it is the especial province of the literary critic to render; and these sorts of reading all share a fundamental concern with the nature and functions of figurative language as manifested in concern with the nature and functions of figurative language as manifested in specific texts" (5).
22. I refer here to the work of John Pocock, *The Machiavellian Moment: Florentine Political Thought and the Atlantic Republican Tradition* (Princeton, NJ: Princeton University Press, 1975). The humanist phase of Yale romanticism is embodied in the work of Harold Bloom, *The Ringers in the Tower: Studies in Romantic Tradition* (Chicago: University of Chicago Press, 1971) and *Yeats* (New York: Oxford University Press, 1970); and Geoffrey Hartman, *Beyond Formalism: Literary Essays, 1958–1970* (New Haven, CT: Yale University Press, 1970).
23. The pioneering work in Du Bois and romanticism has been done by Shamoon Zamir in *Dark Voices: W. E. B. Du Bois and American Thought, 1888–1903* (Chicago: University of Chicago Press, 1995). Du Bois' links to pragmatism have been studied by Ross Posnock, *Color and Culture: Black Writers and the Making of the Modern Intellectual* (Cambridge, MA: Harvard University Press, 1998).
24. A list of visible recent works on African-centered psychology would include Lawrence N. Houston, *Psychological Principles and the Black Experience*, (Lanham, MD: University Press of America, 1990); Linda James Myers, *Understanding an Afrocentric World View: Introduction to an Optimal Psychology* (Dubuque, IA: Kendall/Hunt, 1993); Joseph L. White, *The Psychology of Blacks: An African-American Perspective* (Englewood Cliffs, NJ.: Prentice Hall, 1990).
25. Martin L. Kilson, "Anatomy of Black Intellectuals and Nationalism," in *Harold Cruse's The Crisis of the Negro Intellectual Reconsidered*, ed. Jerry Watts (New York: Routledge, 2004), 57. The white power elite's manipulation of blacks embodying this symbolic-cathartic style is a characteristic element of interracial patronage-client relationships —especially during unstable periods of institutional change. Kilson has been especially insightful on this dynamic. See, for example, Martin Kilson, "Political Change in the Negro Ghetto, 1900–1940s," in *Key Issues in the Afro-American Experience*, eds. Nathan

I. Huggins, Martin Kilson, Daniel Fox, vol. 2 (New York: Harcourt Brace Jovanovich, 1971), 44. ". . . perhaps no other factor has so marred and distorted Negro political adaptation to cities in this century as the way in which machine politics, by means of neoclientage ties, reinforced the structural pathologies of Lower-class urban life."

## Introduction

1. On the continuing academic influence of Gates and his work, see "A Citation Ranking of Black Scholars in the Humanities," in *Journal of Blacks in Higher Education*. No. 27 (Summer, 1998), 27–28.
2. J. G. A. Pocock, "Time, Institutions and Action: An Essay on Traditions and Their Understanding," in *Politics, Language and Time: Essays on Political Thought and History* (New York: Athenaeum, 1973), 233–272.
3. Ernst Robert Curtius, *European Literature and the Latin Middle Ages*. Trans. Willard R. Trask. Bollingen Series 36 (1953; pb repr., Princeton, NJ: Princeton University Press, 1963), 15.
4. "The Sense of an Approaching Looming End" appears in *Loose Canons* (New York: Oxford University Press, 1988), 124, 137; and Michael Awkward, *Negotiating Difference: Race, Gender, and the Politics of Positionality* (Chicago: University of Chicago Press, 1995).
5. Gates, *Loose Canons*, 79.
6. Gates, *Loose Canons*, 79.
7. Personal communication from Charles Long to the author.
8. Gates, *Loose Canons*, 57
9. David S. Reynolds, *Beneath the American Renaissance: The Subversive Imagination in the Age of Emerson and Melville* (pb repr.; Cambridge, MA: Harvard University Press, 1987), 75.
10. In the most important recent study of the slave narrative, William L. Andrews has provided a narrative of the slave narrative form which shows the development of the narrative form into fiction in the 1850s immediately before the genre's historical endpoint. See William L. Andrews, *To Tell a Free Story: The First Century of Afro-American Autobiography, 1760–1865* (Urbana : University of Illinois Press, 1986).
11. On irony, see Wayne Booth, *The Rhetoric of Irony* (Chicago: University of Chicago Press, 1974), 1–2.
12. My definition of "orality" and its indices relies primarily on the work of Fr. Walter J. Ong in particular, Walter J. Ong, *Orality & Literacy: The Technologizing of the Word*, (1991; repr., New York: Routledge, 1992), 30–77. Further debts to Ong are listed below in these notes.
13. Gates, *Loose Canons*, 32, 33.
14. This essay appears in the foreword of all the series' books. I have selected at random, Henry Louis Gates Jr., "Foreword," in *The Work of the Afro-American Woman* by Mrs. N. F. Mossell (1894; rprt., New York: Oxford University Press, 1988).
15. Booker T. Washington, "Up from Slavery," in *Three Negro Classics*, ed. John Hope Franklin (1927; repr., New York: Avon Books, 1965), 72.
16. Houston A. Baker Jr., *Blues, Ideology, and Afro-American Literature: A Vernacular Theory* (Chicago: University of Chicago Press, 1984), see chapter 1, 15–63.
17. Houston A. Baker has provided a suggestive reading of these jokes in *Modernism and the Harlem Renaissance* (Chicago: University of Chicago Press, 1987), 25–36.
18. For an account of this transition at Yale, see Nicholas Lemann, *The Big Test: The Secret History of the American Meritocracy* (New York: Farrar, Straus and Giroux, 1999), 149–154. On the contradiction between the assumptions of "meritocracy" and affirmative action, see Lemann, *The Big Test*, 164–165.
19. For a general statement of this problem and point of view, see Melvin L. Oliver and Thomas M. Shapiro, *Black Wealth/White Wealth: A New Perspective on Racial Inequality*

(London: Routledge, 1995), 3–10, 15–23, 127–170. On the patterns of ghetto formation, white flight to the suburbs, and resulting patterns of segregation in housing, see Douglass S. Massey and Nancy A. Denton, *American Apartheid: Segregation and the Making of the Underclass* (Cambridge, MA: Harvard University Press, 1993), 42–82, esp. "Shoring the Bulworks of Segregation, 1940–1970," 42–59. On the white reaction against court-ordered school desegregation, see among other works, Jennifer L. Hochschild, *The New American Dilemma: Liberal Democracy and School Desegregation* (New Haven, CT: Yale University Press, 1984), 28–34. Hochschild writing in 1984 describes the post-1960 reaction towards increased school segregation in the urban Northeastern United States.
20. On race and educational inequality, see, for example, Gary Orfield, Susan E. Eaton, and the Harvard Project on School Desegregation, *Dismantling Desegregation: The Quiet Reversal of Brown vs. Board of Education* (New York: New Press, 1996), 64–71.
21. Recent work by Hortense J. Spillers offers vivid accounts of the development of African-American literary studies during this period of interracial and generational conflict within the profession of English. See Hortense J. Spillers, "Preface," in *Black, White, and in Color: Essays on American Literature and Culture* (Chicago: University of Chicago Press, 2003), ix–xiii. See also, 7–9, 203.
22. Awkward, *Negotiating Difference*, 9.
23. Quoted in Henry Louis Gates Jr., *The Signifying Monkey: A Theory of African-American Literature* (New York: Oxford University Press, 1987), 72.
24. On the symbolic cathartic dimension of black student protest under conditions of inequality, see Thomas Sowell, *Education: Assumptions versus History*, Collected Papers (Stanford, CA: Hoover Institution Press, 1986), 131–134; 147–149.
25. For Awkward's remarks on Hemenway's claim, see *Negotiating Difference*, 69–70.
26. Gates, *The Signifying Monkey*, 72–74.
27. Gates, *The Signifying Monkey*, 65–66.

# Chapter One

1. For an account of the Davis family, see the family biography reprinted in Arthur P. Davis, "William Roscoe Davis and His Descendents," in *Black is the Color of the Cosmos: Essays on Afro-American Literature and Culture, 1942–1981*, ed. Henry Louis Gates Jr., with a foreword by A. Bartlett Giamatti (New York: Garland, 1982). 335–357.
2. For a biography of Charles T. Davis, see *Black is the Color of the Cosmos*, xiv–xviii.
3. Dexter Fisher, Robert Stepto, et al., *Minority Literature: The Reconstruction of Instruction* (New York: MLA, 1977).
4. See, for instance, Henry Louis Gates Jr., "Binary Oppositions in Chapter One of *Narrative of the Life of Frederick Douglass, an American Slave, Written by Himself*," in *Figures in Black*, 87–97.
5. I have through conjecture reconstructed the intellectual world of the Yale English Department in the late seventies. For Gates' stated connections to the intellectual world of English Studies at Cambridge, French theory, and to the work of black critics in particular, Sterling Brown, see Charles H. Rowell, "An Interview with Henry Louis Gates, Jr." *Callaloo*, Vol. 14, No. 2 (Spring, 1991), 445–449.
6. F. O. Mathiessen, *The American Renaissance: Art and Expression in the Age of Emerson and Whitman* (1941; pb repr., New York: Oxford University Press, 1968).
7. R. W. B. Lewis, *The American Adam: Innocence, Tragedy, and Tradition in the Nineteenth Century* (Chicago: University of Chicago Press, 1955); Leo Marx, *The Machine in the Garden: Technology and the Pastoral Ideal in America* (1972; pb repr., New York: Oxford University Press, 1964); Richard Poirier, *A World Elsewhere: The Place of Style in American Literature* (1968; pb repr., New York: Oxford University Press, 1966).

8. Harold Bloom, *The Ringers in the Tower: Studies in Romantic Tradition* (Chicago: University of Chicago Press, 1971).
9. Paul de Man, *Blindness and Insight: Essays in the Rhetoric of Contemporary Criticism*, ed. Wlad Godzich (Minneapolis: University of Minnesota Press, 1983); see especially "Form and Intent in the American New Criticism," 20–35.
10. Lionel Trilling, *The Liberal Imagination: Essays on Literature and Society*, (New York: Viking Press, 1950). See especially "Reality in America," 3–21; "Huckleberry Finn," 104–117; Philip Rahv, *Image and Idea: Twenty Essays on Literary Themes* (New York: New Directions Press, 1957). See especially "The Dark Lady of Salem," 27–50.
11. Geoffrey Hartman, *Beyond Formalism: The Fate of Reading and Other Essays* (Chicago: University of Chicago Press, 1975).
12. On Gates' academic biography from Yale to Cambridge and back to Yale, see Bruce Cole and Henry Louis Gates, Jr., "Thomas Jefferson Lectures: Interview." On-Line Interview, 2002 Posting, http://www.neh.gov/whoweare/gates/interview.html. On the impact of the Yale Experience on Gates, see inter alia "The Years of the Black Panthers at Yale University," *Journal of Blacks in Higher Education*, no 17 (Autumn 1997), 104; and more generally ____, "Joining the Black Overclass at Yale University," in *Journal of Blacks in Higher Education*, no 16 (Spring 1996), 95–100.
13. See, for instance, Gates on Jean Toomer in "Black Structures of Feeling," in *Figures in Black*, 206.
14. Jacqueline Fleming, *Blacks in College* (San Francisco: Jossey-Bass, 1976); Thomas Sowell, *Education: Assumptions versus History* (Stanford, CA: Hoover Institute Press, 1986); *Black Education: Myths and Tragedies* (New York: McKay, 1972). See also Joe R. Feagin, Hernan Vera, and Nikitah Imani, *The Agony of Education: Black Students at White Colleges and Universities* (London: Routledge, 1996).
15. Yale University, African-American Studies, *African-American Studies and Yale: Revisiting Origins, Imagining Futures* (n.p., n.d.), 14.
16. Yale University, *African-American Studies and Yale*, 14.
17. Gates, *The Signifying Monkey*, xi–xii.
18. Tom Wolfe, *Radical Chic and Mau-Mauing the Flak Catchers* (New York: Farrar, Straus and Giroux, 1970); Tom Wolfe, *The Bonfire of the Vanities* (New York: Farrar, Straus and Giroux, 1987).
19. James C. Scott, *Domination and the Arts of Resistance: Hidden Transcripts* (New Haven, CT: Yale University Press, 1990); Victor Turner, "Passages, Margins, and Poverty: Religious Symbols of Communitas" and "Metaphors of Anti-structure in Religious Culture," in *Dramas, Fields, and Metaphors: Symbolic Action in Human Society* (1974; repr., Ithaca: Cornell University Press, 1978).
20. For an excellent discussion of the powers of retention as well as of retrieval associated with written philology and literacy, see Walter Ong, "Typographic Rhapsody: Ravisisius Textor, Zwinger, and Shakespeare," in *Interfaces of the Word: Studies in the Evolution of Consciousness and Culture* (Ithaca, NY: Cornell University Press, 1977), 147–188.
21. Gates, *Loose Canons: Notes on the Culture Wars* (New York: Oxford University Press, 1992). See especially "Canon Confidential: A Sam Slade Caper" and "The Big Picture."
22. Gates, *Figures in Black*, 87–97.
23. Karla Holloway, *Codes of Conduct: Race, Ethics and the Color of Our Character* (New Brunswick, NJ: Rutgers University Press, 1995), 51–53.
24. Robert Stepto, *From Behind the Veil: A Study of Afro-American Narrative* (Urbana: University of Illinois Press, 1979).
25. Gates, *The Signifying Monkey*, 183–191, 193–196.
26. For a sampling of the essays that articulate the rhetorical strategies by which Hurston creates a coherent "voice" in *Eyes*, see Cheryl A. Wall, ed., *Zora Neale Hurston's Their Eyes Were Watching God: A Casebook* (New York: Oxford University Press, 2000). Besides

the Gates essay, excerpted from *Signifying Monkey*, see Barbara Johnson, "Metaphor, Metonymy and Voice in *Their Eyes Were Watching God*" (41–58) and Carla Kaplan, "The Erotics of Talk: 'That Oldest Human Longing' in *Their Eyes Were Watching God*." Within the essay of Shirley Anne Williams, Hurston's narrative voice comes to possess the "essence" or "presence" which so many Signifiers seek to give to black speech itself. "In the speech of her characters, black voices—whether rural or urban, northern, or southern—come alive. Her fidelity to diction, metaphor, and syntax— whether in direct quotations or in paraphrases of characters' thoughts—rings, even across forty years, with an aching familiarity that is a testament to Hurston's skill and to the durability of black speech"(21). My reading of *Eyes* and this brief look at the criticism intends in no way to be exhaustive. However, for a historical sampling of other essays on Hurston and *Eyes*, see *Zora Neale Hurston: Critical Perspectives: Past and Present*, eds. Henry Louis Gates Jr. and K. A. Appiah (New York: Amistad, 1993), 130–140.
27. For a biography of Hurston, consult Robert Hemenway, *Zora Neale Hurston: A Literary Biography*, with a foreword by Alice Walker (1977; repr., Urbana: University of Illinois Press, 1980).
28. Hurston, *Their Eyes Were Watching God*, 86.
29. Hurston, *Their Eyes Were Watching God*, 62.
30. Hurston, *Their Eyes Were Watching God*, 112.
31. Hurston, *Their Eyes Were Watching God*, 114.
32. See Hurston, *Their Eyes Were Watching God*, 76: "She didn't read books so she didn't know that she was the world and the heavens boiled down to a drop. Man attempting to climb to painless heights from his dung hill." See also Hurston, *Their Eyes Were Watching God*, 112: "Pheoby, these educated women got uh heap of things to sit down and consider. Somebody done tole 'em what to set down for. Nobody ain't told poor me, so sittin' still worries me. Ah wants tuh utilise mahself all over." In many ways, Hurston has a far deeper sense of retired leisure as a cultural convention than does Gates. Indeed, she distinctly makes important dramatic contrasts between upper-class retired leisure and the playful recreation of checkers or speechifying in which the lower-class people of Starkville of the muck engage. Hurston shows retired play as the site of courtship, the acting-out of social tensions, and the expression of important human emotions such as the fear of death. In the world of *Eyes*, retired play and leisure provide space for the folk to prepare themselves for significant tasks and experiences in adult life.
33. Hurston, *Their Eyes Were Watching God*, 112.
34. Hurston, *Their Eyes Were Watching God*, 86.
35. Hurston, *Their Eyes Were Watching God*, 87.
36. George E. Kent, *Blackness and the Adventure of Western Culture* (Chicago: Third World Press, 1972), 53–54.
37. See *Totem and Taboo: Resemblances between the Psychic Lives of Savages and Neurotics*, trans. A. A. Brill (1946; repr., New York: Vintage Books, 1961).
38. The commentary of Richard Wright and Alain Locke still provides us with a valuable point of entry into *Eyes* as a fictional work. See Gates and Appiah, eds., *Zora Neale Hurston: Critical Perspectives Past and Present* (New York: Amistad, 1993). Richard Wright, "Review of *Their Eyes Were Watching God*" (1937), 17; Alain Locke, "Review," 18.

# Chapter Two

1. My understanding of charisma, tradition, and institutions comes from Max Weber, *From Max Weber: Essays in Sociology*, ed. C. Wright Mills and Hans Gerth (1946; repr., New York: Oxford University Press, 1978); Edward Shils, *Center and Periphery: Essays in Macrosociology* (Chicago: University of Chicago Press, 1975); and Peter Berger

and Thomas Luckmann, *The Social Construction of Reality: A Treatise in the Sociology of Knowledge* (Garden City, NJ: Doubleday, 1966).
2. For a stimulating discussion of this problem, see Edward W. Said, *Beginnings: Intention and Method* (New York: Basic Books, 1975).
3. Vincent Leitch et al., *The Norton Anthology of Theory and Criticism* (New York: W. W. Norton, 2001), 2477.
4. Leitch, *Norton Anthology of Theory and Criticism*, 2482.
5. Houston A. Baker Jr., *Modernism and the Harlem Renaissance* (Chicago: University of Chicago Press, 1989), 33.
6. I have benefited a great deal from discussions with Beth Bennett concerning minstrelsy and its twentieth-century uses, as well as from her deeply suggestive dissertation chapter, treating Richard Wright's experimentation with minstrel forms. My understanding of minstrelsy has also been informed by Eric Lott, *Love & Theft: Blackface Minstrelsy and the American Working Class* (1995; pb. repr. New York: Oxford University Press, 1993).
7. Some sense of Sterling Brown's life and intellectual milieu in Washington, D.C. is given in Mark S. Sanders, "Forward," in Sanders, ed., *A Son's Return: Selected Essays of Sterling Brown* (Boston: Northeastern University Press, 1996), ix–xxi, and in Brown's autobiographical essay, "A Son's Return: 'Oh, Didn't He Ramble'" in Sanders, 1–21.
8. Brown, "Spirituals, Seculars, Ballads" in *A Son's Return: Selected Essays of Sterling Brown*, 263.
9. My understanding of the "constructed" nature of organic form draws upon the formulations of William K. Wimsatt, "Organic Form: Some Questions about a Metaphor," in *Romanticism: Vistas, Instances, Continuities*, eds. David Thorburn and Geoffrey Hartman, (Ithaca, New York: Cornell University Press, 1973). In "Preface to Lyrical Ballads, with Pastoral and Other Poems (1802)," Wordsworth is very explicit about the way in which the poet draws upon "meditation" in shaping the "purpose" of his poetic expression. "For all good poetry is the spontaneous overflow of powerful feelings: but though this be true, Poems to which any value can be attached, were never produced on any variety of subjects but by a man, who being possessed of more than usual organic sensibility, had also thought long and deeply. For our continued influxes of feeling are modified and directed by our thoughts, which are indeed the representatives of all our past feelings; and, as by contemplating the relation of these general representatives to each other we discover what is really important to me, so, by the repetition and continuance of this act, our feelings will be connected with important subjects, till at length, if we be originally possessed of much sensibility, such habits of mind will be produced, that, by obeying blindly and mechanically the impulses of those habits, we shall describe objects, and utter sentiments, of such a nature and in such connexion with each other, that the understanding of the being to whom we address ourselves, if he be in a healthful state of association, must necessarily be in some degree enlightened, and his affections ameliorated" (434–435). For Wordsworth, the poet's influx of feelings must be mediated by a wide range of thoughts flowing from a variety of sources. The overflow of sensation is worth nothing without this carefully cultivated sensibility. On the metaphors of organic and expressive literary form, see M. H. Abrams, *The Mirror and the Lamp: Romantic Theory and the Critical Tradition* (1953; repr., New York: W. W. Norton, 1958). See, in particular, Abrams' discussion of Coleridge, 167–177.
10. On realism, see Sterling Brown, *Negro Poetry and Drama and the Negro in American Fiction*, 115–130; "Our Literary Audience," *A Son's Return*, 138–139.
11. See Brown, *A Son's Return*, 277–280.
12. Brown, *A Son's Return*, 279–280.

13. Langston Hughes, "Cowards in the Colleges," in *Good Morning, Revolution: Uncollected Writings of Social Protest by Langston Hughes* (1973; repr., New York: Citadel Press, 1992).
14. Brown, *A Son's Return*, 147–148.
15. Gates, *The Signifying Monkey*, 75–76.
16. Gates, *The Signifying Monkey*, 106–107.

## Chapter Three

1. Henry Louis Gates Jr., "Writing, 'Race,' and the Difference It Makes," in *"Race," Writing, and Difference*, ed. Henry Louis Gates (Chicago: University of Chicago Press, 1989). The essay was reprinted in Gates, *Loose Canons*, ch. 3. This scene forms the substance of Gates' *The Trials of Phillis Wheatley: America's First Black Poet and Her Encounters with the Founding Fathers* (New York: Basic Books, 2003); and Nellie McKay, "Naming the Problem That Led to the Question 'Who Shall Teach African-American Literature?'; or, Are We Ready to Disband the Wheatley Court?" *PMLA* 113 (1998), 359–369.
2. McKay, "Naming the Problem," 360.
3. Bassard, *Spiritual Interrogations*.
4. Paula Bennett, "Phillis Wheatley's Vocation and the Paradox of the 'Afric Muse,'" *PMLA* 113(1998): 64–76.
5. Rosemary Fithian Guruswamy, "'Thou Hast the Holy Word': Jupiter Hammon's 'Regards' to Phillis Wheatley," in Philip Gould and William Andrews, *Genius in Bondage: Literature of the Early Black Atlantic*, ed. Vincent Carretta and Philip Gould (Lexington: University Press of Kentucky, 2001), 190, 192–193.
6. Kenny J. Williams suggests this connection in her introduction to Ann Plato's essays. "The latter part of the nineteenth century and the early years of the twentieth saw the exquisite lyrics of Henrietta Cordeliua Ray and the sonnets of Mrs. Alice Dunbar Nelson. And while it is perhaps too didactic and simplistic for modern readers, the poetry of Eva A. Jessye and Mrs. J. W. Hammond illustrates a type of homespun verse that became popular with some audiences. Hence by the time of the Harlem Renaissance and the work of that era's poets such as Georgia Douglas Johnson and Angelina Grimké of Washington, D.C., Anne Spencer of Lynchburg, Virginia and Jessie Fauset of Philadelphia, there had unwittingly developed a particular genre of verse from some black women. Devoid of great bitterness, much given to nature studies, occasionally devoted to racial issues, it was a poetry that by its very existence suggested that such abstract qualities as life, love, truth, beauty, or even death could transcend the mundane elements of everyday living." Plato, *Essays*, p. lii.
7. Gates et al., *Norton Anthology of African-American Literature*, 1–5.
8. Gates et al., *Norton Anthology of African-American Literature*, 1.
9. "For all good poetry is the spontaneous overflow of powerful feelings. . ." William Wordsworth, "Preface to Lyrical Ballads, with Pastoral and Other Poems (1802)" in *William Wordsworth: Selected Poems* (New York: Penguin, 1994), 434. Note that Gates overlooks Wordsworth's and Sterling Brown's influences on meditation, intellectual reflection, moral choice, and introspection as important elements in the refinement of these feelings into art.
10. Gates et al., *Norton Anthology of African-American Literature*, 5.
11. The writer is exceptionally close to both Wordsworth's conception of expressive poetry and his (and Emerson's) notion that the common language of rural men is closest to the emphatic expressions of poetry on which such poetry is based. "Low and rustic life was generally chosen, because in that condition of life our elementary feelings co-exist in a state of greater simplicity, and, consequently, may be more accurately contemplated. And more forcibly communicated; because the manners of rural life germinate from

those elementary feelings; and from the necessary character of rural occupations, are more easily comprehended; and are more durable; and lastly, because in that condition the passions of men are incorporated with the beautiful and permanent forms of nature." William Wordsworth, "Preface to Lyrical Ballads, with Pastoral and Other Poems (1802)," in *William Wordsworth*, 433
12. Crafts, *The Bondwoman's Narrative*, 5.
13. Langston Hughes, "The Negro Artist and the Racial Mountain," in *Voices from the Harlem Renaissance*, ed. Nathan Huggins (New York: Oxford University Press, 1976), 306–307.
14. Crafts, *The Bondwoman's Narrative*, 331–332.
15. Crafts, *The Bondwoman's Narrative*, ed. Henry Louis Gates Jr., lxxii.
16. E. Franklin Frazier, *The Black Bourgeoisie: The Rise of a New Middle Class in the United States* (1957; repr., New York: Collier Press, 1962), 129–145.

## Chapter Four

1. Bassard, *Spiritual Interrogations*; Margarite Fernández Olmos and Lizabeth Paravisini-Gebert, eds., *Healing Cultures: Art and Religion as Curative Practices in the Caribbean and Its Diaspora* (New York: Palgrave Macmillan, 2001); Will Coleman, *Tribal Talk: Black Theology, Hermeneutics, and African/American Ways of "Telling the Story"* (State College: Pennsylvania State University Press, 2001); Jon Cruz, *Culture on the Margins: The Black Spiritual and the Rise of American Cultural Interpretation* (Princeton, NJ: Princeton University Press, 2001).
2. This criticism is particularly strident in Peter J. Paris, *The Spirituality of African Peoples: The Search for a Common Moral Discourse* (Minneapolis: Fortress Press, 1984); Dwight Hopkins, *Shoes That Fit Our Feet: Sources for a Constructive Black Theology* (Maryknoll, NY: Orbis Books, 1993); and Katie Cannon, *Katie's Canon: Womanism and the Soul of the Black Community* (New York: Continuum, 1996), 58–59. See in particular Cannon's interpretation of Max Weber's notions of inner-worldly asceticism as the "dominant" Protestant ethical tradition in America.
3. Hopkins, *Shoes That Fit Our Feet*, 218.
4. Cornel West, *Keeping Faith: Philosophy and Race in America* (Routledge: New York 1993); see West's *ad hoc* variation of the theme of the organic intellectual in "Cultural Politics of Difference," 27.
5. Paris, *The Spirituality of African Peoples*; Neal, *Visions of a Liberated Future*, see especially "The Black Arts Movement," 63–65.
6. Stephen Reid Cross, "Endangered Reading: The African-American Scholar between Text and People," *Cross Currents* 44 (Winter 1994/1995): 476.
7. Hopkins, *Shoes That Fit Our Feet*, 14. See above for an example of the deconstructive rhetoric by which Hopkins finds incisive theological thinking in "chaos" or biblical hermeneutics in those too impoverished to master the interpretive traditions of their day.
8. Coleman, *Tribal Talk*, 194.
9. "And the poor people were so vexed with apparitors and pursuivants and the commissary courts, as truly their affliction was not small. Which, notwithstanding, they bore sundry years with much patience, till they were occasioned by the continuance and increase of these troubles, and other means which the Lord raised up in those days, to see further into things by the light of the Word of God. How not only these base and beggarly ceremonies were unlawful, but also that the lordly and tyrannous power of the prelates ought not to be submitted unto; which thus, contrary to the freedom of the gospel, would load and burden men's consciences and by their compulsive power make a profane mixture of persons and things in the worship of God. And that their offices and callings,

courts and canons, etc. were unlawful and antichristian: being such as have no warrant in the Word of God, but the same that were used in popery and still retained." William Bradford, *Of Plymouth Plantation*, in *The Norton Anthology of American Literature*, ed. Nina Baym et al. 6th ed., vol. A (New York: Norton, 2003), 157.

See also John Winthrop's frequently anthologized comments: "For the other point concerning liberty, I observe a great mistake in the country about that. There is a twofold liberty; natural (I mean as our nature is now corrupt), and civil or federal. The first is common to man with beasts and other creatures. By this, man as he stands in relation to man with beasts and other creatures. By this, man as he stands in relation to man simply hath liberty to do what he list. It is a liberty to evil as well as to do good. This liberty is incompatible and inconsistent with authority, and cannot endure the least restraint of the most just authority. The exercise and maintaining of this liberty makes men grow more evil, and in time to be worse than beast. The other kind of liberty I call covenant or federal or may also be termed moral, in reference to the covenant between God and man, in the moral law, and the politic covenants and constitutions amongst men themselves. This liberty is a liberty to that only which is good, just and honest. This liberty you are to stand for, with the hazard not only of your goods but of your lives if need be." *Norton Anthology of American Literature*, 157.

10. Cannon quite consistently makes black women's ethics a matter of "inversions" and "paradoxes" of bourgeois Protestant piety. "Black women writers authenticate, in an economy of expression, how Black people creatively strain against the external limits in their lives, how they affirm their humanity by inverting conventional middle-class moral assumptions (which she oddly identifies with what Max Weber described as the ethic of capitalism) and how they balance the continual struggle and interplay of paradoxes." It is not clear to me that present-day white middle-class Protestant churches preach an ethics based on what Weber described as a transformed Protestant piety. Cannon, *Katie's Canon*, 63.
11. Hopkins, *Shoes That Fit Our Feet*, 84, 85.
12. From an interview with Rias Body, "prepared by Ralph Jones" in Rawick, 1977, Supplement, Series 1, 3:74; quoted in Coleman, *Tribal Talk*, 115.
13. Coleman, *Tribal Talk*, 116.
14. W. E. B. Du Bois, *The Souls of Black Folk* in *Three Negro Classics*, John Hope Franklin, Introduction, (1903; repr., New York: Avon Books, 1999), 345–347.
15. Mechal Sobel, *Trabelin' On: The Slave Journey to an Afro-Baptist Faith* (Princeton, NJ: Princeton University Press, 1979), 31–32.
16. Benjamin Mays, *The Negro's God as Reflected in His Literature* (1938; repr., New York: Russell and Russell, 1968), 1–10.
17. Frazier, *Black Bourgeoisie*, 129–145.
18. Bassard, *Spiritual Interrogations*, 4–5.
19. On evangelical involvement in the late eighteenth-century New England antislavery movements, see *inter alios The Sacred Cause of Liberty: Republican Thought and the Millennium in Revolutionary New England* (New Haven, CT: Yale University Press, 1977).
20. See, for example, David Grimsted, "Anglo-American Racism and Phillis Wheatley's 'Sable Veil,' 'Length'ned Chain,' and 'Knitted Heart,'" in *Women in the Age of the American Revolution*, ed. Ronald Hoffman and Peter J. Albert (1989; repr., Charlottesville: University of Virginia Press, 1992), 338–444; Phillip M. Richards, "Phillis Wheatley and Literary Americanization," *American Quarterly* 44, no. 2 (1990):163–191.
21. For the obscure footnote in which Hopkins explains away the crucial exception to his interpretation, see Hopkins, *Shoes That Fit Our Feet*, n42, p. 225.
22. David Walker, *David Walker's Appeal in Four Articles; Together with a Preamble, to the Coloured Citizens of the World, But in particular, and very expressly, to those of the United States of America*, (1829; rpt,, New York: Hill and Wang, 2000), 31.

23. Charlotte Forten Grimke, *The Journals of Charlotte Forten Grimke*, ed. Brenda Stevenson (New York: Oxford University Press, 1988), *passim*.
24. Peterson, *Doers of the Word*, 191–192
25. Forten, *Journals*, 204, 239, 248, 259, 260, 307, 356, 501.
26. Forten, *Journals*, 397–399.

## Chapter Five

1. Michael Dyson on Martin Luther King Jr., *I May Not Get There with You: The True Martin Luther King, Jr.* (New York: Simon Schuster, 2000).
2. Walter J. Ong, *Orality and Literacy: The Technologizing of the Word* (London: Routledge, 1982), 6–15; Marshall McLuhan, *Understanding Media: The Extensions of Man* (New York: McGraw Hill, 1964), 316.
3. Michael Dyson, *Making Malcolm: The Myth and Meaning of Malcolm X* (New York: Oxford University Press, 1996), xix–xx; *Race Rules: Navigating the Color Line* (Reading, MA: Addison-Wesley, 1996), 95–100.
4. Dyson, *Why I Love Black Women* (New York: Basic Books, 2003), see esp. 214, 215, 242, 260–263, 273, 274, 275.
5. Hurston's work on the nature of African-American styles of self-presentation remains extremely suggestive, but not yet fully realized in the work of Dyson, who seems to come closest to following her. Hurston, "Characteristics of Negro Expression," in Leitch et al., *The Norton Anthology of Theory and Criticism*, 1146–1158.
6. Dyson, *Why I Love Black Women*, 18–25. This is the most imaginative and least developed part of the book.
7. Michael E. Dyson, *Between God and Gangsta Rap: Bearing Witness to Black Culture* (New York: Oxford University Press, 1996), 26.
8. Wolfe's fictional accounts of urban municipal courts in New York are nearly ethnographic in their richness of detail and analysis; see, in particular, *The Bonfire of the Vanities* (1987; repr., New York: Bantam Books, 1988), 113–114.
9. The behavior of black boys is another important area for empirical research on black self-presentation; see the very interesting work of Jawanza Kunjufu, *Conspiracy to Destroy Black Boys*, vol 1 (Chicago: African-American Images, 1986), "Female Teachers and Black Male Culture," 11–20. This chapter presents a fascinating account of face-to-face interaction between female teachers and young black males.
10. See reference to Frazier and the myth of black business, *Black Bourgeoisie*, 129–145.

## Chapter Six

1. Karla F. C. Holloway, *Passed On: African-American Mourning Stories* (Durham, NC: Duke University, Press, 2002).
2. Announcement, North Carolina Department of Corrections, June 30, 1999.
3. Karla Holloway, *Moorings and Metaphors: Figures of Culture and Gender in Black Women's Literature* (New Brunswick, NJ: Rutgers University Press, 1992), 24–25.
4. For an example of Holloway's mechanical, dehumanized account of the male literary sensibility see *Moorings and Metaphors*, 6–7. "The texts of black women are different from literature by black men. My argument is that the area of their distinctiveness lies between the spoken text and the expressive text—between voice and vision. Literature by black males does attest to the differences of race and gender and does inscribe this dialogic of difference and identity within the hermeneutic systems of their texts. However, where the place of complexity is extraterritorial for black women writers, texts by black males often isolate the word, circumscribe its territory, and subordinate its voice to expressive behaviors. The province of the word for black women commands

a perspective that does not isolate it from its community source. Black male writers' texts claim the power of creative authorship but do not seem to share the word with the reader, or among the characters, or within narrative structures of the text. Instead, the word is carefully controlled and its power is meagerly shared. Black women writers seem to concentrate on shared ways of saying, black males concentrate on individual ways of behaving."

5. Holloway, *Codes of Conduct*, 123–124. In a revealing statement, Holloway said that there was no "ritual" for her massaging her son's hair. This remark suggests the depth of the gender-centered theoretical framework that persisted in her "cultural criticism."
6. Philippe Aries et al., *Death in America*, ed. David E. Stannard (Philadelphia: University of Pennsylvania Press, 1975); David E. Stannard, *The Puritan Way of Death: A Study in Religion, Culture, and Social Change* (New York: Oxford University Press, 1977).
7. Holloway, *Passed On*, 2. Holloway makes this identification explicitly: "In that chapter [One], I carve out the landscape of black death and burial practices as experienced during the twentieth century, paying attention to both urban and rural histories—including specific narratives of southern undertakers who took up the business despite being subjected to white rage and violence" (2).
8. Holloway's failure to cite or significantly apply any of the rapidly expanding work on mourning in Anglo-American Studies is remarkable in itself. See, for instance, Mary Louise Kete, *Sentimental Collaborations: Mourning and Middle-Class Identity in Nineteenth-Century America* (Durham, NC: Duke University Press, 2000); Pamela A. Boker, *The Grief Taboo in American Literature: Loss and Prolonged Adolescence in Twain, Melville, and Hemingway* (New York: New York University Press, 1998); Jahan Ramazini, *Poetry of Mourning: The Modern Elegy from Hardy to Heaney* (Chicago: University of Chicago Press, 1994); Neal L. Tolchin, *Mourning, Gender, and Creativity in the Art of Herman Melville* (New Haven, CT: Yale University Press, 1988).
9. Holloway, *Passed On*, 2.
10. Arnold Rampersad, *The Art and Imagination of W. E. B. Du Bois* (Cambridge, MA: Harvard University Press, 1976), 72–73.
11. Du Bois, *The Souls of Black Folk*, 353.
12. Du Bois, *The Souls of Black Folk*, 353–354.
13. Arthur P. Davis, "Langston Hughes: The Cool Poet," *CLA Journal* 11, no. 4 (June 1968): 280–296.

## Chapter Eight

1. George E. Kent, *Blackness and the Adventure of Western Culture* (Chicago: Third World Press, 1972), 76–77.
2. Ambivalence about Sula inhabits a long line of criticism that evaluates some of the more outrageous cultivated/folk pairings in African-American literary tradition. See, for instance, George Kent's comments on the marriages and relations between the cultivated and the folk in *Their Eyes Were Watching God* and *Banana Bottom* in George Kent, "Substance George Kent," in *Sturdy Black Bridges: Visions of Black Women in Literature*, ed. Roseanne P. Bell (New York: Anchor Books, 1979), 244; George Kent, *Blackness and the Adventure of Western Culture*, 50; Hortense Spillers, "'The Permanent Obliquity of an In(pha)llibly Straight': In the Time of the Daughters and the Fathers" in *Changing Our Own Words: Essays on Criticism, Theory, and Writing by Black Women*, ed. Cheryl Wall (New Brunswick, NJ: Rutgers University Press, 1989).
3. Toni Morrison, *Sula* (1973; repr., New York: Plume, 1984), 29.
4. Morrison, *Sula*, 122–123.
5. Ralph Waldo Emerson, "Circles," in *Emerson's Essays* (1926; repr., New York: Harper & Row, 1951), 216. See, for example, "Our moods do not believe in each other. To-day I am full of thoughts and can write what I please. I see no reason why I should not have the same thought, the same power of expression, to-morrow. What I write, whilst I

write it, seems the most natural thing in the world: but yesterday I saw a dreary vacuity in this direction in which now I see so much; and a month hence, I doubt not, I shall wonder who he was that wrote so many continuous pages. Alas for this infirm faith, this will not strenuous, this vast ebb of a vast! I am God in nature; I am a weed by the wall."
6. Morrison, *Sula*, 149.
7. E. Franklin Frazier, "In the City of Destruction," in *The Negro Family in the United States*, abridged, rev. ed. (1939; repr., Chicago: University of Chicago Press, 1948), 209–291.

## Chapter Nine

1. E. Franklin Frazier, *The Black Bourgeoisie*, 107–108
2. Sacvan Bercovitch, "The Rituals of Consensus," in *The Rites of Assent: Transformations in the Symbolic Construction of America* (New York: Routledge, 1993), 47. I take the phrase from Bercovitch's essay of that name.

## Chapter Ten

1. Mays, *The Negro's God as Reflected in His Literature*; Saunders Redding, *To Make a Poet Black* (1939; repr., College Park, MD: McGrath, 1968); Sterling Brown, *Negro Poetry and Drama and the Negro in American Fiction* (1937; repr., New York: Atheneum, 1968), 1–209.
2. Sacvan Bercovitch, *The American Jeremiad* (Madison: University of Wisconsin Press, 1978); Gordon Wood, *The Creation of the American Republic, 1776–1787* (Chapel Hill: University of North Carolina Press, 1969); Hatch, *The Sacred Cause of Liberty*; Ruth Bloch, *Visionary Republic: Millennial Themes in American Thought, 1756–1800* (Cambridge: Cambridge University Press, 1985).
3. See, for example, Dorothy Porter, *Early Negro Writing 1760–1837* (Boston: Beacon Press, 1971).
4. William Robinson, *Black New England Letters: The Uses of Writings in Black New England* (Boston: Trustees of the Public Library of the City of Boston, 1977).
5. Countee Cullen, "Heritage," in Huggins, *Voices from the Harlem Renaissance*, 144.
6. Mays, *The Negro's God as Reflected in His Literature*, 243.
7. William Andrews, *To Tell a Free Story: The First Century of Afro-American Autobiography, 1760–1865* (Urbana: University of Illinois Press, 1986).
8. Benjamin Elijah Mays and Joseph William Nicholson, *The Negro's Church* (1933; repr., New York: Arno Press, 1969), 5.
9. Mays and Nicholson, *The Negro's Church*, 5.
10. Mays and Nicholson, *The Negro's Church*, 9–10.
11. Frazier, *The Negro Church*, 84–85.
12. Frazier, *The Negro Church*, 106–107.
13. Mays, *Born to Rebel: An Autobiography* (Athens: University of Georgia Press, 1987), 15–16.
14. Mays, *Born to Rebel*, 122–123.

## Chapter Eleven

1. Robert Hayden, "Elegies for Paradise Valley," in *American Journal: Poems by Robert Hayden* (New York: Liveright, 1978), 25–32.
2. Robert Hayden, "The Diver," in *The Angle of Ascent: New and Selected Poems* (New York: Liveright, 1975), 75.

3. See Philip Rahv, "Paleface and Redskin," in *Literature and the Sixth Sense* (Boston: Houghton Mifflin, 1969), 1–6; "The Cult of Experience in American Writing" in *Literature and the Sixth Sense*, 21–37.
4. Robert Hayden, "Electrical Storm," in *Angle of Ascent*, 77–78.
5. Robert Hayden, "Electrical Storm," in *Angle of Ascent*, 77–78.
6. Imamu Baraka, *Black Magic: Sabotage, Target Study, Black Art; Collected Poetry, 1961–1967* (Indianapolis: Bobbs-Merrill, 1969).

## Chapter Twelve

1. Langston Hughes, "The Negro Artist and the Mountain," in Huggins, *Voices from the Harlem Renaissance*, 305–309.

## Chapter Thirteen

1. Angela Davis, *The Angela Davis Reader*, ed. Joy James (New York: Blackwell Publishers, 1998), 315.

## Chapter Fourteen

1. Adolph Reed, Jr., *Class Notes: Posing as Politics and Other Thoughts on the American Scene* (New York: New Press, 2000), 170.

## Conclusion

1. Booker T. Washington, *Up from Slavery*, in *Three Negro Classics*, 143–144.

# Bibliography

Andrews, William L. *To Tell a Free Story: The First Century of Afro-American Autobiography, 1760–1865*. Urbana: University of Illinois Press, 1986.
Aries, Philippe, et al. *Death in America*. Edited by David E. Stannard. Philadelphia: University of Pennsylvania Press, 1975.
Auerbach, Erich. *Mimesis: The Representation of Reality in Western Literature*. Trans. Willard R. Trask. Princeton, NJ: Princeton University Press, 1953.
Awkward, Michael. *Negotiating Difference: Race, Gender, and the Politics of Positionality*. Chicago: University of Chicago Press, 1995.
Baker, Houston A., Jr. *Long Black Song: Essays in Black American Literature and Culture*. Charlottesville, VA: University Press of Virginia, 1972.
———. *Blues, Ideology, and Afro-American Literature: A Vernacular Theory*. Chicago: University of Chicago Press, 1984.
———. *Modernism and the Harlem Renaissance*. Chicago: University of Chicago Press, 1987.
Baraka, Imamu. *Black Magic: Sabotage, Target Study, Black Art; Collected Poetry, 1961–1967*. Indianapolis: Bobbs-Merrill, 1969.
Bassard, Katherine. *Spiritual Interrogations: Culture, Gender, and Community in Early African American Women's Writing*. Princeton, NJ: Princeton University Press, 1999.
Baym, Nina, et al. *The Norton Anthology of American Literature, Sixth Edition*. Volume A. New York: Norton, 2003.
Bell, Roseanne P. *Sturdy Black Bridges: Visions of Black Women in Literature*. New York: Anchor Books, 1979.
Bellow, Saul. *Herzog*. New York: Viking Press, 1964.
———. *Mr. Sammler's Planet*. New York: Viking Press, 1970.
———. *Ravelstein*. New York: Viking, 2000.

Bennett, Paula. "Phillis Wheatley's Vocation and the Paradox of the 'Afric Muse,'" *PMLA* 113(1998), 64–76.
Bercovitch, Sacvan. *The American Jeremiad*. Madison: University of Wisconsin Press, 1978.
———. *The Rites of Assent: Transformations in the Symbolic Construction of America*. New York: Routledge, 1993.
Berger, Peter, and Thomas Luckmann. *The Social Construction of Reality: A Treatise in the Sociology of Knowledge*. Garden City, NY: Doubleday, 1966.
Bloch, Ruth. *Visionary Republic: Millennial Themes in American Thought, 1756–1837*. Boston: Beacon Press, 1971.
Bloom, Harold. *Yeats*. New York: Oxford University Press, 1970.
———. *The Ringers in the Tower: Studies in Romantic Tradition*. Chicago: University of Chicago Press, 1971.
———. *The Anxiety of Influence: A Theory of Poetry*. New York: Oxford University Press, 1973.
Boker, Pamela A. *The Grief Taboo in American Literature: Loss and Prolonged Adolescence in Twain, Melville, and Hemingway*. New York: New York University Press, 1998.
Booth, Wayne. *The Rhetoric of Irony*. Chicago: University of Chicago Press, 1974.
Brown, Sterling. *Negro Poetry and Drama, and The Negro in American Fiction*. Introduction by Robert Bone. (1937) New York: Atheneum, 1978.
———. *The Collected Poems of Sterling A. Brown*. Edited by Michael S. Harper. Chicago: TriQuarterly Books, 1989.
———. *A Son's Return: Selected Essays of Sterling Brown*. Edited by Mark S. Sanders. Boston: Northeastern University Press, 1996.
Bruce, Dickson. *Black American Writing from the Nadir: The Evolution of a Literary Tradition, 1877–1915*. Baton Rouge: Louisiana State Press, 1987.
———. *The Origins of African Amerian Literature, 1680–1865*. Charlottesville: University Press of Virginia, 2001.
Cannon, Katie. *Katie's Canon: Womanism and the Soul of the Black Community*. New York: Continuum 1996.
Carby, Hazel. *Reconstructing Womanhood*. New York: Oxford University Press, 1987.
Carretta, Vincent, and Philip Gould. Eds. *Genius in Bondage: Literature of the Early Black Atlantic*. Lexington: University of Kentucky Press, 2001.
Chase, Richard. *The American Novel and Its Tradition*. (1957) Baltimore, MD: Johns Hopkins University Press, 1983.
Chesnutt, Charles W. *The Wife of His Youth and Other Stories of the Color Line*. (1899) Ann Arbor: University of Michigan Press, 1968.
———. *The Conjure Woman*. (1899) Ridgewood, NJ: Gregg Press, 1968.
———. *The House Behind the Cedars*. (1900) New York: Collier Books, 1971.
———. *The Marrow of Tradition*. (1901) New York: Arno Press, 1969.
———. *Stories, Novels, and Essays*. New York: Library of America, 2002.

Coleman, Will. *Tribal Talk: Black Theology, Hermeneutics, and African/American Ways of "Telling the Story."* State College: Pennsylvania State University Press, 2001.
Crafts, Hannah A. *The Bondwoman's Narrative*. Edited by Henry Louis Gates. New York: Warner Books, 2002.
Cross, Stephen Reid. "Endangered Reading: The African-American Scholar between Text and People," *Cross Currents* 44 (Winter 1994/1995).
Cruz, Jon. *Culture on the Margins: The Black Spiritual and the Rise of American Cultural Interpretation*. Princeton NJ: Princeton University Press, 2001.
Curtius, Ernst Robert. *European Literature and the Latin Middle Ages*. Trans. Willard R. Trask. (1953) Princeton, NJ: Princeton University Press, 1963.
Davis, Angela. *If They Come in the Morning: Voices of Resistance*. New York: Third Press, 1971.
———. *Angela Davis: An Autobiography*. New York: Random House, 1974.
———. *Women, Culture, & Politics*. New York: Random House, 1989.
———. *Blues Legacies and Black Feminism: Gertrude "Ma" Rainey, Bessie Smith, and Billie Holiday*. New York: Pantheon Books, 1998.
———. *The Angela Davis Reader*. Edited by Joy James. New York: Blackwell Publishers, 1998.
Davis, Arthur P. "Langston Hughes: The Cool Poet," *CLA Journal* 11, no. 4 (June 1968), 280–296.
———. *From the Dark Tower: Afro-American Writers 1900–1960*. (1974) Washington, DC: Howard University Press, 1981.
de Man, Paul. *Blindness and Insight: Essays in the Rhetoric of Contemporary Criticism*. Edited by Wlad Godzich. Minneapolis: University of Minnesota Press, 1983.
Dyson, Michael. *Race Rules: Navigating the Color Line*. Reading, MA: Addison-Wesley, 1996.
———. *Making Malcolm: The Myth and Meaning of Malcolm X*. New York: Oxford University Press, 1996.
———. *Between God and Gangsta Rap: Bearing Witness to Black Culture*. New York: Oxford University Press, 1997.
———. *I May Not Get There With You: The True Martin Luther King, Jr*. New York: Simon and Schuster, 2001.
———. *Why I Love Black Women*. New York: Basic Books, 2003.
Ellison, Ralph. *Invisible Man*. New York: New American Library, 1952.
———. *Shadow and Act*. New York: Random House, 1964.
———. *Going to the Territory*. New York: Random House, 1986.
———. *The Collected Essays of Ralph Ellison*. Edited by John F. Callahan. New York: Modern Library, 1995.
———. *Trading Twelves: The Selected Letters of Ralph Ellison and Albert Murray*. Edited by Albert Murray and John F. Callahan. New York: Modern Library, 2000.

Emerson, Ralph Waldo. *Emerson's Essays*. (1926) New York: Harper and Row, 1951.

Feagin, Joe R., Herman Vera, and Nikitah Imani. *The Agony of Education: Black Students in White Colleges and Universities*. London: Routledge, 1996.

Fisher, Dexter, et al. *Minority Literature: The Reconstruction of Instruction*. New York: MLA, 1977.

Fleming, Jacqueline. *Blacks in College*. San Francisco: Jossey-Bass, 1976.

Frady, Marshall. *Martin Luther King, Jr.* New York: Penguin, 2002.

Franklin, John Hope. Ed. *Three Negro Classics*. (1927) New York: Avon Books 1965.

Frazier, E. Franklin. *The Negro Family in the United States*. (1939) Chicago: University of Chicago Press, 1948.

———. *The Black Bourgeoisie: The Rise of a New Middle Class in the United States*. (1957) New York: Collier Press, 1962.

———, and C. Eric Lincoln. *The Negro Church in America; The Black Church Since Frazier*. (1963) New York: Schocken Books, 1974.

Freud, Sigmund, *The Interpretation of Dreams*. Trans. A. A. Brill. New York: Macmillan Company, 1923.

———. *Civilization and Its Discontents*. Trans. Joan Riviere. (1930) London: Hogarth Press, 1955.

———. *Totem and Taboo: Resemblances between the Psychic Lives of Savages and Neurotics*. Trans. A. A. Brill. (1946) New York: Vintage Books, 1961.

———. *The Freud Reader*. Edited by Peter Gay. (1989) New York: W.W. Norton, 1995.

Garrow, David J. *The FBI and Martin Luther King, Jr.* (1981) New York: Penguin, 1983.

Gates, Henry Louis, Jr. Ed. *Black is the Color of the Cosmos: Essays on Afro-American Literature and Culture, 1942–1981*. New York: Garland, 1982.

———. *Black Literature and Literary Theory*. New York: Methuen, 1984.

———. *Figures in Black: Words, Signs, and the "Racial" Self*. New York: Oxford University Press, 1987.

———. "Forward." In *The Work of the Afro-American Woman*. By Mrs. N. E. Mossell. (1894) New York: Oxford University Press, 1988.

———. *The Signifying Monkey: A Theory of African-American Literature*. New York: Oxford University Press, 1989.

———, and K. A. Appiah. Eds. *"Race," Writing, and Difference*. Chicago: University of Chicago Press, 1989.

———. *Loose Canons: Notes on the Culture Wars*. New York: Oxford University Press, 1992.

———, and K. A. Appiah. *Zora Neale Hurston: Critical Perspectives: Past and Present*. New York: Amistad, 1993.

———. *Colored People: A Memoir*. New York: Knopf, 1994.

———. *The Trials of Phillis Wheatley: America's First Black Poet and Her Encounters with the Founding Fathers*. New York: Basic Books, 2003.

Gayle, Addison. *The Black Aesthetic*. Garden City, NY: Doubleday, 1971.

Griffin, Farah Jasmine. "Review of Spiritual Interrogations: Culture, Gender, and Community in Early African American Women's Writing by Katherine Clay Bassard," *African American Review* 34, no. 4 (2000), 709–710.

Grimke, Charlotte Forten. *The Journals of Charlotte Forten Grimke*. Edited by Brenda Stevenson. New York: Oxford University Press, 1988.

Grimsted, David. "Anglo-American Racism and Phillis Wheatley's 'Sable Veil,' 'Length'ned Chain,' and 'Knitted Heart,'" in *Women in the Age of the American Revolution*, edited by Ronald Hoffman and Peter J. Albert. (1989) Charlottesville: University of Virginia Press, 1992.

Hartman, Geoffrey. *Beyond Formalism: Literary Essays: 1958–1970*. New Haven, CT: Yale University Press, 1970

———. *The Fate of Reading and Other Essays*. Chicago: University of Chicago Press, 1975.

Hatch, Nathan. *The Sacred Cause of Liberty: Republican Thought and the Millennium in Revolutionary New England*. New Haven, CT: Yale University Press, 1977.

Hayden, Robert. *Selected Poems*. New York: October House, 1966.

———. *Words in the Mourning Time*. London: October House, 1970.

———. *Angle of Ascent: New and Selected Poems*. New York: Liveright, 1975.

———. *American Journal: Poems by Robert Hayden*. New York: Liveright, 1978.

Hemenway, Robert. *Zora Neale Hurston: A Literary Biography*. (1972) Urbana: University of Illinois Press, 1980.

Hochschild, Jennifer L. *The New American Dilemma: Liberal Democracy and School Desegregation*. New Haven, CT: Yale University Press, 1984.

Hoffman, Daniel. *Form and Fable in American Fiction*. (1961) New York: Oxford University Press, 1973.

Holloway, Karla F. C. *Moorings and Metaphors*. New Brunswick, NJ: Rutgers University Press, 1992.

———. *Codes of Conduct: Race, Ethics and the Color of Our Character*. New Brunswick, NJ: Rutgers University Press, 1995.

———. *Passed On: African-American Mourning Stories*. Durham, NC: Duke University Press, 2002.

Hopkins, Dwight. *Shoes That Fit Our Feet: Sources for a Constructive Black Theology*. Maryknoll, NY: Orbis Books, 1993.

Huggins, Nathan, et al. Eds. *Key Issues in the Afro-American Experience*. New York: Harcourt Brace Jovanovich, 1971.

———. Ed. *Voices from the Harlem Renaissance*. New York: Oxford University Press, 1976.

Hughes, Langston, *The Weary Blues*. New York: Knopf, 1926.

———. *Not Without Laughter*. New York: Knopf, 1930.

———. *The Ways of White Folks*. New York: Knopf, 1934.

———. *The Big Sea, An Autobiography*. New York: Hill and Wang, 1940.

———. *Simple Takes a Wife*. New York: Simon and Schuster, 1953.

———. *I Wonder as I Wander: An Autobiographical Journey.* New York: Rinehart, 1956.

———. *Good Morning, Revolution: Uncollected Writings of Social Protest.* Edited by Faith Berry. (1973) New York: Citadel Press, 1992.

———. *The Collected Works of Langston Hughes.* Edited by Arnold Rampersad. Columbia, MO: University of Missouri Press, 2001.

———. *Remember Me to Harlem: The Letters of Langston Hughes and Carl Van Vechten, 1925–1964.* Edited by Emily Bernard. New York: Knopf, 2001.

Huizinga, Johan. *Homo Ludens: A Study of the Play-Element in Culture.* Trans. R. F. C. Hull. London: Routledge and K. Paul, 1949.

Hurston, Zora Neale. *Jonah's Gourd Vine: A Novel.* New York: Perennial Library, 1934.

———. *Their Eyes Were Watching God.* (1937) New York: Perennial Library, 1990.

———. *Moses, Man of the Mountain.* (1939) Urbana: University of Illinois Press, 1984.

———. *Novels and Stories.* New York: Library of America, 1995.

Jacobs, Harriet. *Incidents in the Life of a Slave Girl, Written by Herself.* Introduction by Jean Fagin. (1861) Cambridge, MA: Harvard University Press, 1987.

Jones, Leroi, and Larry Neal. *Black Fire: An Anthology of Afro-American Writing.* New York: Morrow, 1968.

Kent, George E. *Blackness and the Adventure of Western Culture.* Chicago: Third World Press, 1972.

Kete, Mary Louise. *Sentimental Collaborations: Mourning and Middle-Class Identity in Nineteenth-Century America.* Durham, NC: Duke University Press, 2000.

Kunjufu, Jawanza. *Conspiracy to Destroy Black Boys.* Chicago: African-American Images, 1986.

Leitch, Vincent, et al. *The Norton Anthology of Theory and Criticism.* New York: W. W. Norton, 2001.

Lemann, Nicholas. *The Big Test: The Secret History of the American Meritocracy.* New York: Farrar, Strauss and Giroux, 1999.

Levine, S. Robert. "Slavery, Race, and American Genealogies," *Early American Literature* 36 no. 1 (2001), 89–113.

Lewis, R. W. B. *An American Adam: Innocence, Tragedy and Tradition in the Nineteenth Century.* Chicago: University of Chicago Press, 1955.

Lott, Eric. *Love and Theft: Blackface Minstrelsy and the American Working Class.* New York: Oxford University Press, 1993.

Lovejoy, A. O. *The Great Chain of Being: A Study of the History of an Idea.* (1936) New York: Harper and Row, 1965.

Marx, Leo. *The Machine in the Garden: Technology and the Pastoral Ideal in America.* (1967) New York: Oxford University Press, 1999.

Massey, Douglass S., and Nancy A. Denton. *American Apartheid: Segregation and the Making of the Underclass.* Cambridge, MA: Harvard University Press, 1993.

Mathiessen, F. O. *The American Renaissance: Art and Expression in the Age of Emerson and Whitman*. (1941) New York: Oxford University Press, 1968.

Mays, Benjamin. *The Negro's God as Reflected in His Literature*. (1938) New York: Russell and Russell, 1968.

———, and Joseph William Nicholson. *The Negro's Church*. (1933) New York: Arno Press, 1969.

———. *Born to Rebel: An Autobiography*. Athens, GA : University of Georgia Press, 1987.

McKay, Claude. *Banana Bottom*. (1933) Chatham, NJ: Chatham Bookseller, 1970.

McKay, Nellie. "Naming the Problem that Led to the Question 'Who Shall Teach African-American Literature'; or Are We Ready to Disband the Wheatley Court?" *PMLA* 113 (1998), 359–369.

McLuhan, Marshall. *Understanding Media: The Extensions of Man*. New York: McGraw Hill, 1964.

Miller, J. Hillis. *The Linguistic Moment: From Wordsworth to Stevens*. Princeton, NJ: Princeton University Press, 1985.

Morrison, Toni. *The Bluest Eye*. New York: Pocket Books, 1970.

———. *Song of Solomon*. New York: Knopf, 1977.

———. *Sula*. (1973) New York: Plume, 1984.

———. *Beloved*. New York: Knopf, 1987.

———. *Paradise*. New York: A. A. Knopf, 1998.

Moses, Wilson. *Black Messiahs and Uncle Toms: Social and Literary Manipulations of a Religious Myth*. University Park: Pennsylvania State University Press, 1978.

———. *Alexander Crummell: A Study of Civilization and Discontent*. New York: Oxford University Press, 1989.

Neal, Larry. *Visions of a Liberated Future: Black Arts Movement Writings*. New York: Thunder's Mouth Press, 1989.

Nichols, Charles. Ed. *Arna Bontemps-Langston Hughes Letters, 1925–1967*. New York: Dodd Mead, 1980.

Oliver, Melvin L., and Thomas M. Shapiro. *Black Wealth/White Wealth: A New Perspective on Racial Inequality*. London: Routledge, 1995.

Olmos, Margarite Fernandez, and Lizabeth Paravisini-Gebert. Eds. *Healing Cultures: Art and Religion as Curative Practices in the Caribbean and Its Diaspora*. New York: Palgrave/Macmillan, 2001.

Ong, Walter J. *Orality and Literacy: The Technologizing of the Word*. (1991) New York: Routledge, 1992.

———. *Interfaces of the Word: Studies in the Evolution of Consciousness and Culture*. Ithaca, NY: Cornell University Press, 1978.

Orfield, Gary, et al. *Dismantling Desegregation: The Quiet Reversal of Brown vs. Board of Education*. New York: New Press, 1996.

Paris, Peter J. *The Spirituality of African Peoples: The Search for a Common Moral Discourse*. Minneapolis: Fortress Press, 1984.

Peterson, Carla. *Doers of the Word: African-American Women Speakers and Writers in the North (1830–1880)*. New York: Oxford University Press, 1996.

Plato, Ann. *Essays; Including Biographies and Miscellaneous Pieces, in Prose and Poetry*. New York: Oxford University Press, 1988.

Pocock, J. G. A. *Politics, Language, and Time: Essays on Political Thought and History*. New York: Athanaeum, 1973.

———. *The Machiavellian Moment: Florentine Political Thought and the Atlantic Republican Tradition*. Princeton, NJ: Princeton University Press, 1975.

Poirier, Richard. *A World Elsewhere: The Place of Style in American Literature*. (1968) New York: Oxford University Press, 1966.

Porter, Dorothy. *Early Negro Writing, 1760–1837*. Boston: Beacon Press, 1971.

Posnock, Ross. *Color and Culture: Black Writers and the Making of the Modern Intellectual*. Cambridge, MA: Harvard University Press, 1998.

Rahv, Philip. *Image and Idea: Twenty Essays on Literary Themes*. New York: New Directons Press, 1957.

———. *Literature and the Sixth Sense*. Boston: Houghton Mifflin, 1969.

Ramazini, Jahan. *Poetry of Mourning: The Modern Elegy from Hardy to Heaney*. Chicago: University of Chicago, 1994.

Rampersad, Arnold. *The Art and Imagination of W. E. B. Du Bois*. Cambridge, MA: Harvard University Press, 1976.

———. *The Life of Langston Hughes*. New York: Oxford University Press, 1986.

Redding, Saunders. *To Make A Poet Black*. (1939) College Park, MD: McGrath Publishing Company, 1968.

Reed, Adolph, Jr. *Class Notes: Posing as Politics and Other Thoughts on the American Scene*. New York: New Press, 2001.

Reynolds, David S. *Beneath the American Renaissance: The Subversive Imagination in the Age of Emerson and Melville*. Cambridge, MA: Harvard University Press, 1987.

Richards, Phillip M. "Phillis Wheatley and Literary Americanization," *American Quarterly* 44, no. 2 (1990), 163–191.

Robinson, William. *Black New England Letters: The Uses of Writing in Black New England*. Boston: Trustees of the Public Library of the City of Boston, 1977.

Rowley, Hazel. *Richard Wright: The Life and Times*. New York: Henry Holt, 2001.

Scott, James C. *Domination and the Art of Resistance: Hidden Transcripts*. New Haven, CT: Yale University Press, 1990.

Scott, Nathan A. "A Search for Beliefs: The Fiction of Richard Wright," *University of Kansas City Review* XXIII (1956), 19–24, 130–138.

———. *The Broken Center: Studies in the Theological Horizon of Modern Literature*. New Haven, CT: Yale University Press, 1966.

———. *The Poetics of Belief: Studies in Coleridge, Arnold, Pater, Santayana, Stevens, and Heidegger*. Chapel Hill: University of North Carolina Press, 1985.

———. *Visions of Presence in Modern American Poetry*. Baltimore, MD: Johns Hopkins University Press, 1993.

Shils, Edward. *Center and Periphery: Essays in Macrosociology*. Chicago: University of Chicago Press, 1975.
Sobel, Mechal. *Trabelin' On: The Slave Journey to an Afro-Baptist Faith*. Princeton, NJ: Princeton University Press, 1979.
Sowell, Thomas. *Black Education: Myths and Tragedies*. New York: McKay, 1972.
———. *Education: Assumptions versus History, Collected Papers*. Stanford, CA: Hoover Institution Press, 1986.
Spillers, Hortense J. *Black, White, and in Color: Essays on American Literature and Culture*. Chicago: University of Chicago Press, 2003.
Stannard, David E. *The Puritan Way of Death: A Study in Religion, Culture, and Social Change*. New York: Oxford University Press, 1977.
Staples, Brent A. *Parallel Time: Growing Up in Black and White*. New York: Pantheon Books, 1994.
Stepto, Robert. *From Behind the Veil: A Study of Afro-American Narrative*. Urbana: University of Illinois Press, 1979.
Tate, Claudia. *Domestic Allegories of Political Desire: The Black Heroine's Text of the Turn of the Century*. (l992) New York: Oxford University Press, 1996.
Thorburn, David, and Geoffrey Hartman. *Romanticism: Vistas, Instances, Continuities*. Ithaca: Cornell University Press, 1973.
Tolchin, Neal. L. *Mourning, Gender, and Creativity in the Art of Herman Melville*. New Haven, CT: Yale University Press, 1988.
Trilling, Lionel. *The Liberal Imagination: Essays on Literature and Society*. New York: Viking Press, 1950.
———. *Beyond Culture*. New York: Viking Press, 1965.
Turner, Victor. *Dramas, Fields, and Metaphors: Symbolic Action in Human Society*. (1974) Ithaca: Cornell University Press, 1978.
Walker, David. *David Walker's Appeal in Four Articles; Together with a Preamble, to the Coloured Citizens of the World, But in Particular, and Very Expressly, to Those of the United States of America*. (1829) New York: Hill and Wang, 2001.
Wall, Cheryl A. Ed. *Zora Neale Hurston's* Their Eyes Were Watching God*: A Casebook*. New York: Oxford University Press, 2000.
Watts, Jerry. Ed. *Harold Cruse's The Crisis of the Negro Intellectual Reconsidered*. New York: Routledge, 2004.
Weber, Max. *From Max Weber: Essays in Sociology*. Edited by C. Wright Mills and Hans Gerth. (1946) New York: Oxford University Press, 1978.
West, Cornel. *Keeping Faith: Philosophy and Race in America*. Routledge: New York, 1993.
Wideman, John Edgar. *Brothers and Keepers*. New York: Holt, Rinehart and Winston, 1984.
Wilson, Harriet E. *Our Nig: Or Sketches from the Life of a Free Black*. Introduction by Henry Louis Gates Jr. New York: Vintage Books, 1983.
Wolfe, Tom. *Radical Chic & Mau-Mauing the Flak Catchers*. New York: Farrar, Straus and Giroux, 1970.
———. *The Bonfire of the Vanities*. New York: Bantam Books, 1987.

Wood, Gordon. *The Creation of the American Republic 1776–1787*. Chapel Hill: University of North Carolina Press, 1969.
Wordsworth, William. *William Wordsworth: Selected Poems*. New York: Penguin, 1994.
Wright, Richard. *Eight Men*. (1961) New York: Pyramid Books, 1969.
———. *Native Son*. (1940) New York: Harper and Row, 1969.
———. *Twelve Million Black Voices*. (1941) New York: Thunder's Mouth Press, 1988.
———. *Black Boy: A Record of Childhood and Youth*. (1945) New York: Harper and Row, 1969.
Zamir, Shamoon. *Dark Voices: W. E. B. Du Bois and American Thought, 1888–1903*. Chicago: University of Chicago Press, 1995.

# Index

*Characters in major works are indexed by first name (if given) followed by the title of the work in which they appear.*

## - A -

Abraham, Karl, 123
Abrams, M.H., 5, 6, 9, 27, 29, 201
academic black-white competition, 14–16
African-American literary tradition, 11–12
　*See also* Gates, Henry Louis, Jr.
African-American studies
　African-Hispanic culture and, 96–97
　author and, ix–x, xvi, 212
　black theology and, 87
　Elizabeth Alexander on, 34–35
　failures of, x, xxiv, xxviii, 2, 5–6, 102–3
　strategies of, xxx
　*See also* folk culture
African-American woman's canon. *See* women
*Afro-American Literature* (Baker), 4, 6
"Alas, Poor Richard" (Baldwin), 190
Alexander, Elizabeth, 34–35
*The American Adam* (Lewis), 31, 32
*American Journal* (Hayden), 180, 181
*American Renaissance* (Mathiessen), 6
*The American Renaissance* (Mathiessen), 30–31
Andrews, William, 164
*The Angela Y. Davis Reader* (Davis), 197, 200, 202–3

*Angle of Ascent* (Hayden), 173, 180
*The Anxiety of Influence* (Bloom), 57
*Appeal in Four Articles* (D. Walker), 99–100
Aptheker, Bettina, 197
Aries, Phillippe, 122
"As I Ebbed with the Ocean of Life" (Whitman), 139
"Astronauts" (Hayden), 180
Auden, W.H., 176
Auerbach, Erich, 4, 9
Aunt Tempy (*Not Without Laughter*), 64–65
*Autobiography of an Ex-Coloured Man* (Johnson), 59, 74, 98, 136–37, 187
Awkward, Michael, xx, 2, 16–17, 20, 41

## - B -

Baker, Ella, 111
Baker, Houston, x, xix, 13–14, 60, 218n9
Baker, Houston (works)
　*Afro-American Literature*, 4, 6
　*Blues, Ideology, and Afro-American Literature*, 4, 6, 13–14, 46, 221n15
　*The Journey Back* , 4
　*Long Black Song*, xix
Baldwin, James, xix, 145, 190
"A Ballad of Remembrance" (Hayden), 179
*Banana Bottom* (C. McKay), 136, 137
*The Bandwoman's Narrative* (Crafts), xxi, 75–79, 81, 82
Bane, Mary Jo, 206
Baraka, Imamu, 178

## INDEX

Bassard, Katherine, xiv, 85–86, 89, 93–95, 98, 99
"Battle Hymn of the Republic," 154
Beatty, John, 121
Beckham, Barry, xvii, xxv
Bellow, Saul, 37
"Belsen, Day of Liberation" (Hayden), 177
*Beneath the American Renaissance* (Reynolds), 7
Bernard, April, 189
Berryman, John, xxvii
*Between God and Gangsta Rap* (Dyson), 108
*Beyond the Pleasure Principle* (Freud), 133
"Big Boy Leaves Home" (Wright), 65–66, 210
*The Big Sea* (Hughes), 189
Black Arts movement, xxv–xxvi, 177–79
*The Black Bourgeoisie* (Frazier), 108
*Black Boy* (Wright), 69, 210
black education, crisis in, 22, 98–99, 205
*Black Is the Color of the Cosmos* (Davis), 26
black literary movement, xxvi, 212
*Black Magic* (Baraka), 178
*Blackness and the Adventure of Western Culture* (Kent), 196
Black studies. *See* African-American studies
black theology, 87–89, 102–3, 163–64
black-white competition, academic, 14–16
*Blake's Apocalypse* (Bloom), 31
Blassingame, John, x
"Blood and Fire" (Wright), 65–66
Bloom, Harold, 27, 31–32, 34
*Blues, Ideology, and Afro-American Literature* (Baker), 4, 6, 13–14, 46, 221n15
*The Bluest Eye* (Morrison), 144
*The Bonfire of the Vanities* (Wolfe), 37, 107, 229n8
Bontemps, Arna, xxv, 173
*Born to Rebel* (Mays), 167
Bowlby, John, 123
Bradford, William, 90, 227–28n9
Bradley, Bill, 215
Brent, Linda (pseud). *See* Jacobs, Harriet
Brett (*The Sun Also Rises*), 53–54
Brooks, Gwendolyn, xix, 121, 178–79
*Brothers and Keepers* (Wideman), xiii, 121, 188
Brown, Charles Brockden, 58
Brown, H. Rap, 17–18, 21, 148
Brown, Nelson, 66
Brown, Sterling
  black humanism and, 66–67, 99
  black literary movement and, 218–19n11

folk culture and, xix, 61
on Great Migration, 61–62
on Hughes, 64–65
organic black spirit and, 62–63, 225n9
as scholar-author, 26, 66–67
style of, 63–64
works of, xix, xx, 28
on Wright, 65–66
Broyard, Anatole, 39, 40
Bryce-La Porte, Roy, x
Buck (*Glory*), 150–54

- C -

Campbell, Bebe Moore, 76, 127, 130–34
*Cane* (Toomer), xix, xx, 74, 121
Cannon, Katie, 87, 90, 228n10
Caravera, Ray, 122
Carby, Hazel, xxii–xxiii, 3
Carmichael, Stokely, 148
Cayton, Horace, xxv
*The Character of the Word* (Hurston), 118
Charlie Rose show, 106, 108
Chesnutt, Charles
  analysis of, 185–87
  background of, 184–85
  as cultural observer, xi, xxii, 149
  folk double and, 135–36
  interracial bonding and, 183–84, 192–93
Chesnutt, Charles (works)
  *The Colonel's Dream*, 186
  *The Conjure Woman Tale*, 14, 21, 96, 184–86
  *The House Behind the Cedars*, 186–87
  *The Marrow of Tradition*, 186–87
  *The Wife of His Youth*, 135, 184, 186
Chomsky, Noam, 116–17
"Circles" (Emerson), 139, 230n5
*Civilization and Its Discontents* (Freud), 199
Civil Rights movement, 207
Civil War, 148, 187
*Class Notes* (Reed), 205–8
Clinton, Bill, 207
Cochran, Johnnie, 107–8
*Codes of Conduct* (Holloway), 41, 118–19, 130, 230n5
Coleman, Will, 85, 89–93, 98, 99
Coleridge, Samuel Taylor, 85
*The Colonel's Dream* (Chesnutt), 186
*Colored People* (Gates), xiii, 35, 38, 40, 58
*The Color Purple* (Walker), 46, 121
conduct books, 130
"Conduct of Life" (Emerson), 32

# INDEX

Cone, James, xxv, 85, 88
*The Conjure Woman Tale* (Chesnutt), 14, 21, 96, 184–86
*Contending Forces* (Hopkins), 63
*Coquette (Foster)*, 130
"Cora Unashamed" (Hughes), 192
"Cowards in the Colleges" (Hughes), 65
Crafts, Hannah, xi, 75–79, 81, 82
Cruz, Jon, 85
Cullen, Countee, 163–64
culture of symbolism, 205–8
*Culture on the Margins* (Cruz), 85, 98
Curtius, Ernst, 4, 6, 9, 201

### - D -

Davis, Angela
   black blues women and, 200–201
   as celebrity-radical, 197–98, 202
   Holloway and, 201–2
   Marxist humanism of, 198–203
   political romanticism of, 199, 202
   prison reform and, 199–200
   *the Reader* (autobiography), 197, 202–3
Davis, Arthur P., 26, 126, 160–61, 168
Davis, Charles, xvi, 25–27, 160, 215, 222nn1-2
Davis, Thulani, 26
"Dead in There" (Hughes), 126
De Chabert, Glen, x
Declaration of Independence, 148
deconstruction of African-American literature
*See also* Gates, Henry Louis, Jr.
deconstruction of African-American literature, 4, 88, 106, 209–10
Defoe, Daniel, 132
de Man, Paul, 32, 57
"Design" (Frost), 176
"The Diver" (Hayden), 174–76
"Diving into the Wreck" (Rich), 176
*Doers of the Word* (Peterson), 101
Douglass, Frederick, 80, 99, 150, 153, 164, 199
   *See also* Frederick Douglass (*Glory*)
Douglass, Frederick (works)
   *My Bondage and My Freedom*, 86, 149, 159
   *Narrative of the Life of Frederick Douglass*, 27, 74, 80, 99
   "Down by the Riverside" (Wright), 65–66
dozens, playing the, 67, 193
Drake, St. Clair, xxv

Du Bois, W.E.B., xii, xxv, 74, 92–93, 220n23
DuToit, Brian, 97
Dyson, Michael Eric
   alienation of, 41
   on black culture, 107–8
   Hurston and, 107, 229n5
   as literary critic, 2, 129, 206
   as rapper-scholar, xxvi, 105–6
   televised antics of, xxix, 106, 214
Dyson, Michael Eric (works)
   *Between God and Gangsta Rap*, 108
   *I May Not Get There with You*, 108, 109
   *Making Malcolm*, 106
   *Race Rules*, 108

### - E -

*Ebony*, 76
*Economic Philosophical Manuscripts (1844)*, 85
education institutions, competition in, 105–6
Edwards, Jonathan, xv
"Electrical Storm" (Hayden), 176–77
"Elegies for Paradise Valley" (Hayden), 178, 180
Eliot, T.S., 182
Ellis, Trey, 69
Ellison, Ralph, xviii, 68–70, 121, 137, 174, 193
Ellwood, David, 206
Emerson, Ralph Waldo, 32, 58, 85, 139
English departments, 19, 21
"Epistles" (Pope), 129
*Essence*, 76, 131
*European Literature and the Latin Middle Ages* (Curtius), 4, 6, 201
Eva Peace (*Sula*), 137, 141
exemplars, older (overview), 155
Exeter, Phillips, 38–39

### - F -

Farrakhan, Louis, 206
"Fate" (Emerson), 32
"Father and Son" (Hughes), 192
*The FBI and Martin Luther King, Jr.* (Garrow), 109
feminist writing. *See* women
*Figures in Black* (Gates)
   analysis of, 4, 38
   essays of, xix, xx, 35, 44, 46
   on Wheatley, 72–73, 225–26n1

*Fine Clothes to the Jew* (Hughes), 188
"The Fire Next Time" (Baldwin), 190
Floyd Collins (*Angle of Ascent*), 173
*Flying Home* (Ellison), 121
folk culture
    cultivated/folk pairings and, 135–37, 142, 230n2
    earliest appearance of, 73
    Gates and, 7, 9–11, 59, 223n17
    Hurston and, 98, 212
    orality and, xxvii, 9–10, 36–38
    rap culture and, 147–48
    Sterling Brown and, xix, 61
    symbolism and, 151, 205–8
    tradition and, 7–10, 107–8
    *See also* signifying, culture of
Forten, James, 99
Foster, Hannah Webster, 130
Foucault, Michael, 199–200
Frady, Marshall, 109
Frazier, E. Franklin, xxv, 82, 93, 108, 166
Frederick Douglass (*Glory*), 150–51
"Free Fantasia: Tiger Flowers" (Hayden), 172, 178, 180
Freud, Sigmund, 101, 133, 191–92
*From Behind the Veil* (Stepto), 44
*From the Dark Tower* (A. Davis), 160
Frost, Robert, 174, 175, 176
"Full Moon" (Hayden), 177

### - G -

Garrow, David, 109
Gates, Henry Louis, Jr.
    antihumanist style of, 58–59, 66, 70
    biographical data on, 23, 38–39
    black literary tradition and, 7, 9–11, 35, 59, 67–68, 223n17
    canon-formation and, xix, 33, 34, 71, 218n9
    Davis as mentor, 25–27
    deconstruction and, 43–45, 57–58
    Ellison and, 69–70
    influence of, 3–4, 11, 29–30, 83–84
    as literary entrepreneur, xxvi, 2–4, 25, 58, 220n23
    mask of theory and, 59–60
    models of, 27–30
    persona of, 17, 33–34, 40–41, 213
    on "playful father," 35–38
    professional politics of, 30
    as signifier founder, xii, xxv–xxvii, 3
Gates, Henry Louis, Jr. (works)

*Colored People*, xiii, 35, 38, 40, 58
*Loose Canons*, 7, 39, 201
*Norton Anthology of African-American Literature*, 73–75
*Thirteen Ways of Looking at a Black Man*, 3, 39–41
    *See also Figures in Black*; *The Signifying Monkey*
Gaye, Marvin, 21
Genovese, Eugene, 86
G.I. Bill, 15
Giddings, Paula, 72
*Giovanni's Room* (Baldwin), 190
Girffiith, Farah Jasmine, xiv
*Glory* (film), 127, 149–54
Gramsci, Antonio, 88
Grandmother (*Their Eyes Were Watching God*), 47, 49, 52
Great Migration
    Hughes and, 64, 187
    Northern black ghetto and, 64, 155, 157–58, 166
    Sterling Brown on, 61–62
Grimke, Charlotte Forten, 86, 98, 99, 100–102, 149
guidebooks, popular, 130

### - H -

Harlem Renaissance, xxi, 72, 86, 137, 159, 162, 188
Harper, Frances, xxii–xxiii, 63
Harris, E. Lynn, 130
Hawthorne, Nathaniel, 53, 135
Hayden, Robert
    analysis of, 173–77, 181–82
    background of, 171–72, 176
    influence of, 178
    influences on, 174–76, 180
    style of, 172–73
Hayden, Robert (works)
    *American Journal*, 180, 181
    *Angle of Ascent*, 173, 180
    "Astronauts," 180
    "A Ballad of Remembrance," 179
    "Belsen, Day of Liberation," 177
    "The Diver," 174–76
    "Electrical Storm," 176–77
    "Elegies for Paradise Valley," 178, 180
    "Free Fantasia: Tiger Flowers," 172, 178, 180
    "Full Moon," 177
    "A Letter from Phillis Wheatley," 178

# INDEX                                                     247

"Monet's 'Waterlilies'," 177
"Mourning Poem for the Queen of Sunday," 172
"The Prisoners," 180
"The Rabbi," 172
"Smelt Fishing," 172
"Summertime and the Living," 172
"Those Winter Sundays," 172
"Unidentified Flying Object," 179
"The Whipping," 172
"The Witch Doctor," 179
*Healing Cultures* (Olmos and Paravisini-Gebert), 85, 96–98
Helene (*Sula*), 136–38, 140–44
Hemenway, Robert, 20
Hemingway, Ernest, 53–55, 175–76
"Heritage" (Cullen), 163–64
Hester Prynne (*Scarlet Letter*), 53
Higgenson, Thomas Wentworth, xxii, 98
Holloway, Bem Karin, 115, 118–19, 120, 121, 125
Holloway, Karla, 132, 198
  alienation of, 41–42
  Angela Davis and, 201–2
  contributions of, 4
  feminine/masculine discourse by, 117–18, 229n4
  as literary critic, 115, 120
  orality and, 117
  romantic myth and, xx, 12, 116–18
  style of, 117, 129
Holloway, Karla (works)
  *Codes of Conduct*, 41, 118–19, 130
  *Hurston: The Character of the Word*, 46
  *Moorings and Metaphors*, 6, 8, 115, 116, 118, 202
  *See also Passed On*
*Homo Ludens* (Huizinga), 4–5, 38
Hopkins, Dwight, xii, xxiii, 87–88, 91–93, 200
  *See also Shoes That Fit Our Feet*
Hopkins, Pauline, 63
*The House Behind the Cedars* (Chesnutt), 186–87
Howard School of Religion, 160
Howard University, 160
Hughes, Langston
  background of, 187
  death and, 121, 125–26
  influence of, 189
  influences on, 137
  interracial bonding and, 155, 183–84, 187–88, 192–93

Marxism and, xxi, 164
Van Vechten and, 188–90
Hughes, Langston (works)
  *The Big Sea*, 189
  "Cora Unashamed," 192
  "Cowards in the Colleges," 65
  "Dead in There," 126
  "Father and Son," 192
  *Fine Clothes to the Jew*, 188
  *I Wonder as I Wander*, 189
  "Little Dog," 192
  "A Little White Dog," 190
  "The Negro Artist and the Racial Mountain," 65, 190
  *Not Without Laughter*, 63–65, 188
  "Poor Little Black Fellow," 190, 191
  "Rejuvenation Through Joy," 192
  *Simple Takes a Wife*, 66, 191
  "Slave on the Block," 192
  *The Ways of White Folks*, 121, 190, 191, 192
  *The Weary Blues*, 188
Huizinga, Johan, 4, 38
Hurston, Zora Neale
  background of, 48, 53
  as foremother in female tradition, 46
  as literary radical, xxi, 45
  style of, xix, xxvii, 107, 229n5
  as woman of letters, 45
Hurston, Zora Neale (works)
  *The Character of the Word*, 118
  *Jonah's Gourd Vine*, 45, 54, 211
  *Moses, Man of the Mountain*, 211
  *Mules and Men*, 50
  "Spunk," 45
  "Sweat," 45
  *See also Their Eyes Were Watching God* (Hurston)
*Hurston: The Character of the Word* (Holloway), 46

- I -

*I May Not Get There with You* (Dyson), 108, 109
*Incidents in the Life of a Slave Girl* (Jacobs), 76, 79–80, 81–82, 130
integration, culture of, 207
*The Interpretation of Dreams* (Freud), 192
interracial bonding, 155, 183–84, 187–88, 192–93
*Invisible Man* (Ellison), xix, 68–70, 191
*Iola Leroy* (Harper), xxii, 53, 63
irony, 9–10, 16, 221n11

*I Wonder as I Wander* (Hughes), 189

- **J** -

Jackson, Jesse, 206
Jackson, Michael, 21, 108
Jacobs, Harriet, 76, 79–80, 130, 168–69
Jacoby, Tamar, 110
Jake Barnes *(The Sun Also Rises)*, 53–54
James, Henry, 58, 135
James, William, 58
Janie *(Their Eyes Were Watching God)*
   ambivalence of quest for, 46–47, 49–51, 52
   analysis of, 47
   educational background of, 47, 224n32
   marriages of, 46, 211
   racial attitudes in, 51
   rejection of "high chair," 47–48
   releasing of hair and, 50–51
   shooting of Tea Cake by, 136
   *See also* Tea Cake *(Their Eyes Were Watching God)*
Jim Crow oppression, 15
Jody (Joe Starks) *(Their Eyes Were Watching God)*, 47, 49–50, 52, 211–12
Johnson, Barbara, 45, 223n26
Johnson, Fenton, 137
Johnson, James Weldon, 58, 74, 85, 98
*Jonah's Gourd Vine* (Hurston), 45, 54, 211
Jordan, Jane, 35
*Journals* (Grimke), 86, 99
*The Journey Back* (Baker), 4
Jude Green *(Sula)*, 138, 140, 141

- **K** -

Karamu House, 183, 187
*Katie's Canon* (Cannon), 87
Kelly, Emma, xxii–xxiii
Kennedy, Edward, xvi–xviii
Kent, George, xx, 50, 136, 181–82, 196
Killocks *(Their Eyes Were Watching God)*, 47, 49, 52
Kilson, Martin L., xxix, 215–16, 220–21n26
King, Coretta Scott, 111
King, Martin Luther, Jr., 108–13, 148
Klein, Melanie, 123

- **L** -

*Lady Chatterley's Lover* (Lawrence), 53
Larsen, Nella, 149

Lawrence, D.H., 53
"Letter from a Birmingham Jail" (King), 112
"A Letter from Phillis Wheatley" (Hayden), 178
Levine, Lawrence, 86, 96
Levine, Robert S., xiv, 217n4
Lewis, R.W.B., 31, 85
*Liberal Imagination and Beyond Culture* (Trilling), 33
Lindy *(Singing in the Comeback Choir)*, 131
*The Linguistic Moment* (Miller), 5
literacy, 22, 98–99, 205
literary criticism
   Dyson and, 2, 129, 206
   forms of, 1–3
   Gates and, 3–5, 57–59
   Holloway and, 110, 115
   value of, xxvii–xxx
   *See also* deconstruction of African-American literature
"Little Dog" (Hughes), 192
"A Little White Dog" (Hughes), 190
*Long Black Song* (Baker), xix
*Loose Canons* (Gates), 7, 39, 201

- **M** -

*The Machine and the Garden* (Marx), 31
*To Make a Poet Black* (Redding), xxi, 26, 196
*Making It* (Podhoretz), 39
*Making Malcolm* (Dyson), 106
males, urban black, 107, 115, 119–20, 229n9
"A Man of All Work" (Wright), 210
"Man the Reformer," 85
*The Marrow of Tradition* (Chesnutt), 186–87
Marshall, Paule, 46
*Martin Luther King, Jr.* (Frady), 109
Marx, Karl, 86
Marx, Leo, 31
Marxism, 164, 195–96, 198–203
Mather, Cotton, xv
Mathiessen, F.O., xiii, xxiii, 30, 30–32
Maxine *(Singing in the Comeback Choir)*, 131–34
Mayfield, Julian, xii
Mays, Benjamin
   background of, 158
   on Cullen's "Heritage," 163
   ideological worldview of, 164–65
   influences on, 159
   on Langston Hughes, 164
   on Negro church, 165, 167

perspective of black religious style by, 165–66
regional ideology of, 161–62
on segregation in Tampa, 167–68
style of, 158–60
Mays, Benjamin (works)
  *Born to Rebel*, 167
  *The Negro's Church, The Negro's God*, 161, 165–66
  *The Negro's God as Reflected in His Literature*, 93, 157, 161, 165–66
McCarthy, Karen, 97
McClane, Kenneth, 121
McKay, Claude, 136, 137
McKay, Nellie, 72
"The Meaning of Progress" (Du Bois), 137
*In the Mecca* (Brooks), 178
Miller, J. Hillis, 5
*Mimisis* (Auerbach), 4–5
minstrelsy, mask of, 59–60, 99, 210–11, 216, 224–25n6
*The Mirror and The Lamp* (Abrams), 27
*Moll Flanders* (Defoe), 132
"Monet's 'Waterlilies'" (Hayden), 177
*Moorings and Metaphors: Figures of Culture and Gender in Black Women's Literature* (Holloway), 6, 8, 115, 116, 118, 202
Morrison, Toni, xii, 76, 94–95, 145
Morrison, Toni (works)
  *The Bluest Eye*, 144
  *Paradise*, 142–45
  *The Song of Solomon*, 144
  See also *Sula*
*Moses, Man of the Mountain* (Hurston), 211
Moses, Wilson, xxi
"Mourning and Melancholia" (Freud), 123
"Mourning Poem for the Queen of Sunday" (Hayden), 172
*Mr. Sammler's Planet* (Bellow), 37
*Mule Bone (Hurston and Hughes)*, 189
*Mules and Men* (Hurston), 50
Murray, Albert, 193
Murray, Charles, 206
music, religious, 101
*My Bondage and My Freedom* (Douglass), 86, 149, 159
*My Main Mother* (Beckham), xvii, xxv

- N -

NAACP (National Association of Colored People), 22, 184
*On Narcissism: An Introduction* (Freud), 101

*Narrative* (Equiano), 14
*Narrative of the Life of Frederick Douglass* (Douglass), 27, 74, 80, 99
National Endowment for the Humanities, xvii
National Humanities Center, 72
*Native Son* (Wright), 4, 55, 144, 145
*Natural Supernaturalism* (Abrams), 5, 6, 27, 29, 201
"Nature" (Emerson), 32, 117
Neal, Larry, xvi–xix, 85
*Negotiating Differences* (Awkward), 16
"The Negro Artist and the Racial Mountain" (Hughes), 65, 190
*The Negro Church in America* (Frazier), 166
*The Negro in American Fiction* (Brown), 28
*The Negro's Church (Mays)*, 161, 165–66
*The Negro's God* (Mays), 93, 157, 161, 165–66
Nel (*Sula*), 136–41
New Criticism, xxvi, 32
*Newton Demands the Muse* (Nicholson), 161
New Yorker, 39
Nicholson, Joseph, 161, 165, 166
Nicholson, Marjorie, 161
*Norton Anthology of African-American Literature* (Gates et al.), 73–75
*Not Without Laughter* (Hughes), 63–65, 188

- O -

*O* (Oprah's Magazine), 76
Olmos, Margarite Fernández, 85, 89, 97
"On Being Brought to America" (Wheatley), 94–95
oral tradition, commentary on, 35–38
*Our Nig* (Wilson), xi, 75, 76, 149, 217n1
*The Outsider* (Wright), 210

- P -

*Pamela* (Richardson), 130, 133
*Paradise* (Morrison), 142–45
paradox, black modernist, xxix, 220–21n26
*Parallel Lives* (Staples), xiii, 121
Paravisini-Gebert, Lizabeth, 85, 89
Paris, Peter, 87
*Passed On* (Holloway)
  Du Bois contrasted with, 124–25
  Hughes contrasted with, 125–26
  literary approaches and, 121–23, 230n8
  as study of black death, 118, 120, 122, 201, 230n7

style of, 123–24, 129
patronage, 187–88, 190
Peace Family (*Sula*), 137, 138, 141
Pell, Julia Ann, xiv–xv
persona of, 158, 165
Peterson, Carla, xxi, 101
Pheoby (*Their Eyes Were Watching God*), 46, 47, 49
Plato, Ann, xi, xiii–xv, 168–69, 217n4
playing the dozens, 67, 193
"play" of folk culture, 35–38, 58, 68–69
Plum (*Sula*), 141
*Of Plymouth Plantation* (Bradford), 90
PMLA (Modern Language Association of America), 72, 212–13
Pocock, J.G.A., xxvii, 5
Podhoretz, Norman, 39
Poirier, Richard, 31
"Poor Little Black Fellow" (Hughes), 190, 191
Pope, Alexander, 129
popular culture and Gates, 58
Porter, Dorothy, 75, 162
post–World War II policies, 15–16, 221–22n19
Pound, Ezra, xxvii
Powell, Colin, 39, 40
*Praisesong for the Widow* (Marshall), 46
"The Prisoners" (Hayden), 180
*The Protestant Ethic and the Spirit of Capitalism* (Weber), 58
Protestant-romantic literary tradition, xxiv
women writers and, xxii–xxiv

- Q -

*Quality Book Review*, 76

- R -

"The Rabbi" (Hayden), 172
race relations. *See* interacial bonding
*Race Rules* (Dyson), 108
racism
*Glory* (film) and, 152, 154
King and, 110
signifying and, 13, 18, 20
of white academy, 87–88, 227n2
*Radical Chic* (Wolfe), 37
Rahv, Philip, xiii
Rampersad, Arnold, 124
Ransom, Reverdy S., 110
rap, culture of, 147, 148–49

"Reading Black; Reading Feminist," 76
*Realpolitik* leverage, x, xxiv, 21, 103
Redding, Saunders, xx, xxi, 26
Reed, Adolph, 205–8
Reed, Ishmael, 21, 68–69
Regenstein Library, University of Chicago's, x, xi, 157
"Rejuvenation Through Joy" (Hughes), 192
religion as opiate, 167
representation, rhetoric of, 9–10
*See also* signifying, culture of; *The Signifying Monkey*
*Revelstein* (Bellow), 37
Reynolds, David, 7
Rich, Adrienne, 176
Richards, Phillip M., xii
Richardson, Samuel, 130
Rinehart (*Invisible Man*), 69–70
*The Ringers in the Tower* (Bloom), 29, 31
Robert Shaw (*Glory*), 150–53
Robinson, William, 162
romances, black, 130–31
romanticism, 98, 135

- S -

Sandy (*Not Without Laughter*), 64
Satchel (*Singing in the Comeback Choir*), 131–32
Saussure, Ferdinand de, 57
Scarborough, George, 26
*Schonburg Library Collection of Black Woman Writers*, 11, 221n14
SCLC (Southern Christian Leadership Conference), 111
Scott, Nathan, Jr., xx, 4, 58, 172, 173, 215
"Self Reliance" (Emerson), 32, 139
Shakur, Tupac, 21
Sharpton, Al, 215
*Shelley's Mythmaking* (Bloom), 31
Shepard, Thomas, xv
*Shoes That Fit Our Feet* (Hopkins), 87–88, 91–92, 96
signifying, culture of
acceptance of, 147–49
the American university and, 21–22
criticisms of, 7–9, 10, 11–13
as cultural explanation, 127
definition of, 9–10, 221n12
in historical context, xxiv
as illusory source of freedom, 19–22
overview of, 23

racism and, 20
rhetorical strategies and, 18–19
tragedy of, 58
women writers and, 127
See also Gates, Henry Louis, Jr.; *The Signifying Monkey*
*The Signifying Monkey* (Gates)
  analysis of, 6, 8, 46, 129, 214
  anecdote from, 22
  founding work of signifiers, 3–4
  as guide to African American culture, 58
  pedagogical purpose of, 27–29
  "playful father" anecdote from, 35–38
  publication of, 18
*Simple Takes a Wife* (Hughes), 66, 191
*Singing in the Comeback Choir* (Campbell), 131–34
slave narrative, 7, 221n10
"Slave on the Block" (Hughes), 192
"Smelt Fishing" (Hayden), 172
Sobel, Michal, 93
*The Song of Solomon* (Morrison), 144
*The Souls of Black Folk* (Du Bois), 45, 74, 124–25, 187
*Southern Road* (Brown), xix, xx
Spillers, Hortense, 16, 115, 222n23
*Spiritual Interrogations* (Bassard), 85, 89, 93–95, 115
*The Spirituality of African Peoples* (Paris), 87
"Spunk" (Hurston), 45
Stannard, David, 122
Staples, Brent, xiii, 121
Stepto, Robert, x, xvi, 44, 85
Stewart, Maria, 52, 151, 164
Stone, Chuck, 26
"Stopping by Woods on a Snowy Evening" (Frost), 174, 175
Stowe, Harriet Beecher, 78–81, 142
*The Street Flypaper* (Caravera), 122
street jive, the black intellectual and, 215–16
*Successful Women, Angry Men* (Campbell), 132
*Sula* (Morrison)
  analysis of, 137–41
  cultivated/folk pairing and, 137, 230n2
  as feminist romance, 46, 76
  mourning and, 121
  publication of, 135
  signifying and, 127
  theme of, 137
  See also names of characters
Sula (*Sula*), 136–40

"Summertime and the Living" (Hayden), 172
*The Sun Also Rises* (Hemingway), 53–55, 175–76
Sundquist, Eric, 85
"Sweat" (Hurston), 45
Swift, Jonathan, 129
symbolism, culture of, 205–8

- T -

*A Tale of the Tub* (Swift), 129
tapoi, 221n13
Tate, Alan, xxvi
Tate, Claudia, xxii–xxiii, 219–20n16
Tea Cake (*Their Eyes Were Watching God*), 46, 48, 50–51, 136, 211–12
*To Tell a Free Story* (Andrews), 164
*Their Eyes Were Watching God* (Hurston)
  analysis of, 46–55
  economic themes in, xix
  folk culture and, 98, 212
  Gates's readings on, 4, 43, 44–46, 223n26
  imperfections of, 47–48, 51, 53, 54–55, 224n38
  marriage as theme, 52–53
  minstrelsy and, 210–11
  *The Sun Also Rises* and, 53–55
  as wish-fulfilling fantasy, 55
  See also Janie (*Their Eyes Were Watching God*)
"The Third Sermon on the Warplane" (Brooks), 178
*Thirteen Ways of Looking at a Black Man* (Gates), 3, 39–41
Thomas (*Glory*), 150–51, 153
Thomas, Clarence, 207
Thoreau, Henry David, 85, 133
"Those Winter Sundays" (Hayden), 172
Thurman, Wallace, xxi
"To a Deist" (Wheatley), 71
"To An Atheist" (Wheatley), 71
Tomasky, Michael, 110
Toomer, Jean, xxvi, 137
Toomer, Jeffrey, xix
*Totem and Taboo* (Freud), xxiii, 192, 199
*Trading Twelves* (Ellison-Murray collection), 67, 193
*Tribal Talk* (Coleman), 85, 89
Trilling, Lionel, xiii, 9, 33
*Tuff* (Beatty), 121
Turner, Henry McNeal, 110

*Twelve Million Black Voices* (Wright), 98, 122

### - U -

Uncle Julius (*The Conjure Woman*), 96, 185
Uncle Rias (*Shoes That Fit Our Feet*), 91–92
*Uncle Tom's Cabin* (Stowe), 78–81
*Uncle Tom's Children* (Wright), 46, 63, 65, 121
"Unidentified Flying Object" (Hayden), 179
*Up from Slavery* (Washington), xix, 13, 60, 136–37, 214

### - V -

*Vanity Fair* (magazine), 188
Van Vechten, Carl, 188–90
*The Visionary Company* (Bloom), 29, 31

### - W -

*Walden* (Thoreau), 85, 133
Walker, Alice, 46
Walker, David, 99–100, 164
*Walls (McClane)*, 121
Warren, Robert Penn, xxvi
Washington, Booker T., xix, 13–14, 60, 206, 214, 221n17
  See also *Up from Slavery*
Washington, Denzel, 150, 152
Watts, Isaac, 168
Way Maker
  Campbell and, 133–34
  definition of, 91
  Hopkins and, 91–93, 200
  theologians and, 91, 163–64
"Way Out Morgan" (Brooks), 178
*The Ways of White Folks* (Hughes), 121, 190, 191, 192
*The Weary Blues* (Hughes), 188
Weber, Max, 58
West, Cornel, x, xxvi, xxix, 206
Wexler, Anna, 97
Wheatley, Phillis
  as adversarial voice, xxvii
  African-American women's canon and, xv, 217n6
  deconstruction by Bassard, 94–95
  as evangelical poet, 71–73, 162, 168–69
  Gates on, 72–73, 225–26n1
  Hayden and, 180

Wheatley, Phillis (works)
  "On Being Brought to America," 94–95
  "To a Deist," 71
  "To An Atheist," 71
  "The Whipping" (Hayden), 172
Whitman, Walt, 27, 85, 139
*Why I Love Black Women* (Dyson), 106, 108
Wideman, John, xiii, 121
*The Wife of His Youth* (Chesnutt), 135, 184, 186
Wilson, Harriet, xi, 76, 217n1
Wilson, William Julius, xxv, 206
Wily Wright (*Sula*), 138, 140
Wimsatt, William, xxv
Winthrop, John, 90, 227–28n9
Wirth, Louis, xxv
"The Witch Doctor" (Hayden), 179
Wolfe, Tom, 37, 107, 229n8
women
  black feminist writing of, xiii–xvi, 74–76, 127
  blues and, 200–201
  canon of, xv, 71–72, 115–16, 217n6
  post-WW II fiction of, 130
  Protestant-romantic literary tradition and, xxii–xxiv
  See also *names of women writers*
Wordsworth, William Wadsworth, 84, 85
Wordsworthian terminology, Gates' use of, 75, 226n9-11
*A World Elsewhere* (Poirier), 31
Wright, Richard, 155, 210
Wright, Richard (works)
  "Big Boy Leaves Home," 210
  *Black Boy*, 210
  "A Man of All Work," 210
  *Native Son*, 4, 55, 145
  *The Outsider*, 210
  *Twelve Million Black Voices*, 98, 122
  *Uncle Tom's Children*, 46, 63, 65, 121

### - Y -

Yale University, ix–x, xvii–xviii, xxiv, xxv
*Yeats (Bloom)*, 29
"Young Afrikaans" (Brooks), 178
"Young Heroes" (Brooks), 178

### - Z -

Zamir, Shamoon, 85

# Intersections in Communications and Culture
Global Approaches and Transdisciplinary Perspectives

***General Editors: Cameron McCarthy & Angharad N. Valdivia***

*An Institute of Communications Research, University of Illinois Commemorative Series*

This series aims to publish a range of new critical scholarship that seeks to engage and transcend the disciplinary isolationism and genre confinement that now characterizes so much of contemporary research in communication studies and related fields. The editors are particularly interested in manuscripts that address the broad intersections, movement, and hybrid trajectories that currently define the encounters between human groups in modern institutions and societies and the way these dynamic intersections are coded and represented in contemporary popular cultural forms and in the organization of knowledge. Works that emphasize methodological nuance, texture and dialogue across traditions and disciplines (communications, feminist studies, area and ethnic studies, arts, humanities, sciences, education, philosophy, etc.) and that engage the dynamics of variation, diversity and discontinuity in the local and international settings are strongly encouraged.

### LIST OF TOPICS

- Multidisciplinary Media Studies
- Cultural Studies
- Gender, Race, & Class
- Postcolonialism
- Globalization
- Diaspora Studies
- Border Studies
- Popular Culture
- Art & Representation
- Body Politics
- Governing Practices
- Histories of the Present
- Health (Policy) Studies
- Space and Identity
- (Im)migration
- Global Ethnographies
- Public Intellectuals
- World Music
- Virtual Identity Studies
- Queer Theory
- Critical Multiculturalism

Manuscripts should be sent to:
**Cameron McCarthy OR Angharad N. Valdivia**
Institute of Communications Research
University of Illinois at Urbana-Champaign
222B Armory Bldg., 555 E. Armory Avenue
Champaign, IL 61820

To order other books in this series, please contact our Customer Service Department:
(800) 770-LANG (within the U.S.)
(212) 647-7706 (outside the U.S.)
(212) 647-7707 FAX

Or browse online by series:
www.peterlangusa.com